Sons of Union Veterans of the Civil War

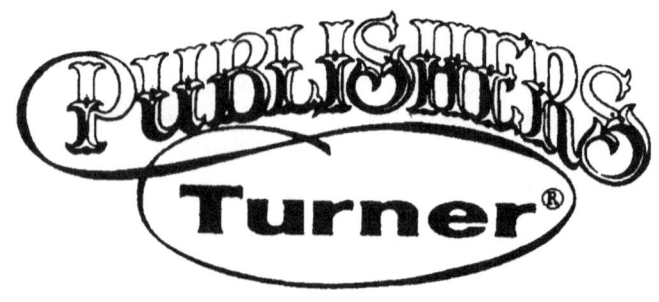

Turner Publishing Company
Publishers of America's History
P.O. Box 3101
Paducah, Kentucky 42002-3101

Co-published by Turner Publishing Company
and Mark A. Thompson, Associate Publisher

Copyright © 1996
Sons of Union Veterans of the Civil War

This book or any part thereof may not be reproduced without the written consent of the SUVCW and Publishers.

The materials were compiled and produced using available information; Turner Publishing Company, Mark A. Thompson and the Sons of Union Veterans of the Civil War regret they cannot assume liability for errors or omissions.

Members of the Sons of Union Veterans of the Civil War were invited to write and submit biographies for inclusion in this publication. Those found within the member chapter are those who chose to participate. The biographies were printed as received, with only minor editing. The publishers regret they cannot accept responsibility for omissions or inaccuracies in this section.

Author: Barbara Stahura
Compiler & Editor: Gary L. Gibson
Graphic Designer: Elizabeth A. Dennis

Library of Congress Catalog
Card No. 96-60400

ISBN 978-1-63026-957-9

Limited Edition

Contents

	Page
Acknowledgments	4
Introduction	5
History of SUVCW	
Founder of Our Order	8
History of the Years 1881 - 1883	9
National Encampments 1883 - 1995	13
The Auxiliary to the SUVCW	23
The Sons of Veterans Reserve	25
Sons' Memorial University	29
SUVCW Act of Incorporation	30
Roster of Departments	32
Badges of SUVCW	32
The Grand Army of the Republic	33
Memorial Day	38
Memories of the Great Civil War	42
Members of SUVCW	45
SUVCW Roster	108

ACKNOWLEDGEMENTS

The Commandery-in-Chief is a great legislative body. It always has, and always will, find plenty upon which to legislate.
  Marvin E. Hall
  Commander-in-Chief, 1892

Dear Brothers;

A project such as the writing of the history of any organization is a major undertaking, especially 114 years worth. This work is based on a history that was published and distributed to the delegates of the 1939 National Encampment by Davis * Camp of Pittsburgh.

I would like to thank the brothers who have helped compile the information. PC-in-C Richard C. Schlenker of Maryland had just completed a personal project of reading all the printed proceedings and making notes on each, when this book was begun. His notes on events and accomplishments of the Order are the basis of the section on the National Encampments. Jerry Orton, PDC of New York and Past National Historian, was generous with his help and loan of photos from his personal collection, and notes from his extensive research. Jerry's dedication to preserving the history of our Order is something we are all grateful for.

The several photographs and illustrations found in this volume are from the following collections, and are noted as such: Jerry L. Orton (JLO), Gary L. Gibson (GLG), National Organization SUVCW (NO-SUV), and Michigan Department, SUVCW (MI-SUV).

The credit for the idea of putting together a history book belongs to James T. Lyons, PDC of Michigan and Past National Secretary. It was also Jim's idea to saddle me with/give me the opportunity to compile this volume. Thanks, Jim.

I must also thank my wife, Beth, for her patience and understanding while I have worked on this project for the last two years. She has been very supportive of my involvement in the Sons of Union Veterans. Thank you, Beth.

Sincerely in F., C., and L.,

Gary L. Gibson, PDC Michigan
Past National Historian
February 1996

INTRODUCTION

This book represents the third (and most complete) history of the Sons of Union Veterans of the Civil War. It provides an insight into three basic aspects of the Order's existence. The first deals with the Order's parent organization, the Grand Army of the Republic (GAR), and its relationship to the Order through a series of historical treatises on the GAR, the GAR's establishment of May 30th as Memorial Day, the Order's founder, A. P. Davis, and the creation and early years of the Order. The second provides a synopsis of the Order's various accomplishments during its almost 115 years of existence with summaries of its 114 National Encampments, and histories of its Auxiliary and military component, the Sons of Veterans Reserve. The last presents biographies of a representative cross-section of the over 4,500 members who currently make up the Sons of Union Veterans of the Civil War and, more importantly, of their Union soldier ancestors who sacrificed so much to preserve the unity of this country during our American Civil War.

As an organization, the Sons of Union Veterans of the Civil War is unique among other hereditary/patriotic/ educational organizations in that it was:

1. Created by a parent organization (the GAR) to ensure that the contributions and accomplishments of that organization and those of the individuals that it represented (the Union Veterans) would be forever remembered by this country;
2. Created to be a perpetual organization forever living on as successive generations of sons are born;
3. Created in the image of the parent organization to be more of a service rather than just another social organization;
4. Granted a Congressional Charter; and
5. Recognized as the legal heir and representative of the interests of its parent organization.

As this history will demonstrate, the Sons of Union Veterans of the Civil War has had numerous accomplishments and has experience many milestones during its existence. Similarly, it has also had a few set backs. Probably, the most significant was its decline in membership from a high of almost 60,000 members in 1917 to a low of less than 2,000 members in the 1970s and early 1980s. Along with this loss in membership also came a considerable reduction in the Order's ability to adequately fulfill all the responsibilities given to it by the GAR.

During the last five to six years, the Order has purposefully and significantly modified and modernized its basic ways of recruiting and doing business which, in turn, has resulted in more than doubling of the membership, lowering the average age of the membership and greatly improving member retention. As a direct consequence of these and other changes, the Order has been able to achieve in a relatively short period of time a much greater presence throughout the country and a resurgence of activity at the Camp, Department and National levels. This, in turn, has resulted in the Order being better able to fulfill its obligations to the memory of the GAR.

This trend is expected to persist well into the next Century. With the continued increase in members and creation of more Camps and Departments, the Sons of Union Veterans of the Civil War will again lead the way to help ensure that the accomplishments, sacrifices and memory of the Union Veteran remains continually before the eyes and in the hearts of the American public.

Keith G. Harrison, PC-in-C
(Commander-in-Chief 1994-1995)
Sons of Union Veterans of the Civil War
March 1996

PUBLISHER'S NOTE

It is with great pleasure that we introduce this publication on the Sons of Union Veterans of the Civil War.

We especially want to thank Gary Gibson, PDC Michigan, Past National Historian, for researching and compiling the material used in the writing of the manuscript and for overseeing the project through to its completion.

We are indebted to the many individuals who submitted photographs, biographies and additional historical material from which information was ascertained.

Turner Publishing Company leads the way in association history book publishing, and we hope that all will enjoy our newest title that chronicles the history of the Sons of Union Veterans of the Civil War

                    Dave Turner, President
                    Mark A. Thompson, Associate Publisher

HISTORY OF

Sons of Union Veterans of the Civil War

Founder Of Our Order

I had an idea there ought to be some such an Order of the Sons of Veterans for some time before its organization. A number of others shared the opinion with me, but when I would bring the matter before the Grand Army Encampment, a majority would be found opposing it and the matter would be set aside. In the year 1880, I organized a "Junior Marching Club", composed of small boys, and it was so much of a success, Mrs. Davis and my son suggested to organize a permanent organization. The matter came before us strikingly by the event of Memorial Day. Who would strew the flowers on the graves of heroes when the shallow fragment of the GAR was no more? I went to work on the prospectus, mapped out the constitution and endevored throughout the summer unsuccessfully with my project.

On November 12, 1881, I got together 8 boys and the first camp of the Sons of Veterans was organized. The first two weeks afterwards we met again and exemplified the ritual, and it was adopted.

Major Augustus Plummer Davis
Interview, St. Joseph (MO) Ballot
August 25, 1891

Augustus Plummer Davis
By Jerome L. Orton

Augustus Plummer Davis was born in Gardiner, Maine, on May 10, 1835. As a youngster he loved the sea. This may be the reason why at age 14 he sailed to California during the gold rush. Later he joined the U. S. Navy and was discharged in 1855 after five years of service at the age of 20. He later served as a volunteer subordinate officer of the French Navy during the Crimean War. As of this date, French Naval Archives have not found records of his service.

On November 12, 1861, he was mustered as captain of Co. F, 11th Maine Infantry for three years. On February 4, 1863, he tendered his resignation after receiving a surgeon's certificate that read as follows:

> *Headquarters, Suffolk, VA. Medical Director's Office, February 4, 1863. I have carefully examined Capt. A. P. Davis, Provost Marshall of the Post and find that he has tubercular deposits in the right lung with plursitic adhesions on that side. In consequence, I believe the exposures incedent to field service will very soon assuredly break down his health. D.W. Hand, Surg. and Med. Director, Peck's Division.*

Davis was breveted a major for faithful service, effective March 13, 1865.

After his resignation, he returned to Maine. However, illness acquired during the war compelled him to move to a more suitable climate — Pittsburgh, Penn. He was engaged in the insurance business for many years. Davis married Nancy E. Fulton of Derry, Penn., on June 22, 1876.

On November 12, 1881, the twentieth anniversary of his enlistment in the Union Army, he formed a camp of Sons of Veterans. This was Davis Camp #1 of Pittsburgh. Later, the camp was designated Davis * Camp, as it was the first camp of the Order. Davis Camp still holds its meetings in Soldier's and Sailor's Memorial Hall and owns the original charter, leather flag, seal and meeting book. The seal is quite unusual, as it has a lion in the center.

At the second national encampment, Davis was invested with the rank of Past Commander-in-Chief and received $200 for expenses. He was instrumental in the adoption of our badges and ribbons. At the fifth national encampment he was appointed ordnance officer. He was to keep regalia within regulations, supply ribbons at cost, and badges at $6 per dozen. In 1907, Mrs. Davis sold all the remaining ribbon to the Order for $100.

A. P. Davis died May 21, 1899 at 6:00 AM at his home at 6335 Howe St. in Pittsburgh. The Pittsburgh *Commercial Gazette* read:

> *Major Augustus P. Davis, age 64, a prominent member of the Grand Army of the Republic and the originator of the 'Sons of Veterans' died at his home yesterday morning after a short illness. For many years Mr. Davis was engaged in the insurance business. He was a member of the Loyal Legion, Union Veterans Legion, Knights of Pythias and Masonic Order.*

The same day, the *Pittsburgh Press* ran the following:

> *A mass meeting of the Sons of Veterans of Pittsburgh, Allegheny and vicinity is called to meet tonight at 7:30 PM in the Armory of Co. A, 14th Regiment, in old City Hall to take suitable action regarding the death of Major A. P. Davis."*

John Seiferth, Past Colonel of Pennsylvania and oldest member of Davis Camp issued the call.

Davis was buried in Pittsburgh's Allegheny Cemetery, 4734 Butler St., Section 28, Lot 35. His mausoleum has been marked with a bronze tablet honoring him as the founder of the Sons of Union Veterans of the Civil War. His wife, Nancy, died June 13, 1912, and was laid to rest in the tomb with her husband.

History of the Years 1881 - 1883

"It is only through such membership I can best show to the world my pride in being a descendent of one who served his country in the darkest period of its history, thus helping to preserve it, and my own gratitude for such service."

This excerpt from a 1930 essay titled "Why I am a Member of the Sons of Union Veterans of the Civil War" most succinctly explains why this organization was formed. Even in 1995, 130 years after the end of this war, this brief paragraph explains why its membership is still active. First organized in 1881, Sons of Union Veterans of the Civil War perpetuates the memory of that horrible conflict and honors the soldiers and sailors of the Union Army who fought in it. They want the country to remember the sacrifices their ancestors made to keep the United States a whole and undivided nation.

After the War of the Rebellion, later to be called the Civil War, various army societies sprang up among the Union veterans, based in the feeling of fraternity that originates when men have faced battle together. Two of the most prominent were the Military Order of the Loyal Legion of the United States, which embraced a provision of transferring membership from father to son, and the Grand Army of the Republic (GAR), which had no such provision. Because of this omission and the natural dwindling of its numbers as the years passed, many members of the GAR were dissatisfied despite their dedication to their organization. Yet they could find no satisfactory solution.

The organization that eventually came to be known as the Sons of Union Veterans of the Civil War had its origins as several independent groups affiliated with the GAR. While no one person can be given credit for originating these Sons of Veterans groups, the first true organizing effort took place in Philadelphia in 1878. Several posts of the GAR there had been allowing the sons of Union soldiers to join in the Memorial Day parade with members of the posts. Posts in other Eastern cities such as Boston followed this practice, where even boys not yet in their teens were permitted to join in the parade. It was a logical progression to create an official organization for these boys aged 12 to 16.

Therefore, James A. Holt, at a meeting of Anna M. Ross Post No. 94, Department of Pennsylvania, Grand Army of the Republic, Philadelphia, Pa., made a motion on August 27, 1878 to form a GAR Cadet Corps. The idea on which this and subsequent Cadet Corps rested was that they would perpetuate the principles, objects, and work of the GAR. The committee appointed to investigate the means by which this could be done was composed of Holt, Levi W. Shengle, Carl Frederic, Charles Weiss, and William H. Morgan.

The committee submitted a report on the plan at the Post meeting on September 15, 1878, which was adopted. They presented a constitution at the next month's meeting, which was also adopted. The committee was then instructed to take applications for membership in the Cadet Corps. Only the sons of deceased or honorably discharged soldiers, sailors, or marines who had served in the Union Army or Navy during the Civil War were permitted to join.

The first Captain or Commander of the Cadet Corps attached to the Anna M. Ross Post No. 94 was Lewis E. Vandergrift, who lived until 1910.

Other posts followed in the organization of Cadet Corps. Not surprisingly, the second one was also in Philadelphia, the Capt. P. R. Schuyler Post No. 51, Department of Pennsylvania, GAR.

These original Cadet Corps were designated as the Philadelphia or Eastern Pennsylvania Sons of Veterans. The word soon spread to other states, and new groups of sons of Union soldiers and sailors were formed. In New England, the cadets became known as the Earp Sons of Veterans because of the activity of Edwin M. Earp of Lynn, Mass., and were allied with the Philadelphia Sons of Veterans.

In Albany, N. Y., the Sons of Veterans were known as the Post System of Sons of Veterans because the titles of their officers and the form of the organization closely matched that of the GAR.

The organization in Pittsburgh, Pa., called the Sons of Veterans U. S. A., soon became the best known and most active of all the Sons of Veterans groups, thanks to the efforts of Maj. A. P. Davis, a member of the GAR. He believed the only right course of action for the sons of veterans was to create a distinct, separate order from the Loyal Legion and the GAR. *The History of the Sons of Union Veterans of the Civil War 1881-1939* describes Maj. Davis as "a good organizer with a large circle of acquaintances in the Loyal Legion and the G. A. R. whom he induced to take active part in the work for the young men." After working

Badges of the different Sons of Veterans factions (l. to r.) Philadelphia, Albany, and Pittsburgh. (GLG)

for several years to reach this goal, he organized the first Camp (Davis Camp) in November 1881 with less than a dozen members.

From his association with the GAR, Maj. Davis knew about the concern regarding the group's ceasing to exist with the death of its last members, whenever that might occur. Therefore, he proposed the idea that the Sons of Veterans be a permanent and perpetual organization, with membership passing from fathers to their eldest sons. The national mission of the Sons of Veterans, U. S. A. was to be "Friendship, Charity, and Loyalty."

Other Camps were soon organized in the area of Pittsburgh and elsewhere.

In December 1881, the group received a charter from the Commonwealth of Pennsylvania, which was valid not only throughout that state but, under United States statute law, also throughout the country.

During 1882, the Sons of Veterans, U. S. A. expanded even further. In the Pittsburgh vicinity, the growth was large enough to form a Division Organization. As its senior officer, Harry T. Rowley was its Commander. Second in command was Henry W. Orth, Commander of Lt. James M. Lysle Camp No. 2 in Allegheny City, while third in command was John A. Woods, Commander of Garfield Camp No. 3 in McKeesport, Allegheny County.

While the Order continued to grow, it did not do so without challenges or problems, according to a 1884 book about the Sons of Veterans, which pointed out:

> *...it must not be gathered that the course of the organization has been wholly one that has not been beset by obstacles, for such has not been the case. As the Order spread out from its central point, it soon developed and met with opposing elements and influences, who were both anxious and determined that their peculiar views and wishes should prevail. Fortunately, by prudent and judicious treatment and management, these and many other minor obstacles and difficulties have been most happily overcome, and harmony and unity of action to all practical intents is now substantially secured.*

One of the earliest dissensions came from East Pennsylvania, which was growing with Camps being mustered without charters and other features, mainly for financial reasons. In Western Pennsylvania, the Sons of Veterans, U. S. A. and the Philadelphia Sons of Veterans were growing as separate organizations. Therefore, a special Division Convention was held at Harrisburg, Pa., in 1883, during which 33 Camps in the Philadelphia Sons of Veterans decided to unite with the Sons of Veterans, U. S. A. Three camps remained loyal to the Philadelphia organization.

Maj. Davis continued to make plans to expand the Order both west and east. Adjoining states soon had their own permanently established and separate Divisions. However, Maj. Davis, who suffered from several disabilities, found he no longer had the energy to carry on this work alone. He needed more support and the expertise of other men as equally committed to the project. Therefore, he divided the country into five Grand Divisions and solicited the assistance of prominent members of the GAR. This recruiting campaign proved very successful.

At the GAR's 15th Encampment, a resolution was issued, which said, "The Sons of Veterans are all that their name implies; that they are of the best blood of the land, and as such should be encouraged in following the footsteps of their illustrious predecessors."

Paul Vandevoort, Commander-in-Chief of the GAR, became interested in the movement and gave his encouragement. At the 1883 Encampment held in July in Denver, Colo., he made an address regarding his support of the Sons of Veterans, and the Encampment issued the following resolution: "Resolved, That we hail with pleasure all organizations having for their object the perpetuity of the principles which are dear to us, and we recognize in the Sons of Veterans of the U. S. A. one that is entitled to the support of all comrades of the Grand Army of the Republic."

Thanks to Maj. Davis's continued encouragement, along with the GAR support, GAR members agreed to assist in the growth of the Sons of Veterans. William E. W. Ross of Baltimore, Md., the GAR Senior Vice Commander-in-Chief, accepted the post of Commander of the Second and Fifth Grand Divisions, and thus to organize them. Isaac S. Bangs, of Waterville, Me., the GAR Junior Vice Commander-in-Chief, did the same for the First Division. William J. Maskell of Chicago, Ill., who was widely known as a tireless worker in the cause of the GAR, agreed to assume command of and organize the Third Grand Division. A. V. Bohn of Leadville, Colo., took charge of the Fourth Grand Division.

Prior to these events, it was decided that the Order was large and advanced enough to organize on a national basis and to have a nominal head. In July 1882 at a meeting attended by Division representatives from 13 states, Harry T. Rowley, Senior Camp and Division Commander, was declared Provisional Commander-in-Chief. The first national meeting was called on the same day, to be held in Pittsburgh on October 18, 1882.

Representatives effected a permanent national organization, and various laws, ritual, insignia, having been prepared by Maj. Davis, were unanimously approved and adopted. The following officers were elected: Commander-in-Chief — Harry T. Rowley, Pittsburgh, Pa.; Lieutenant Commander-in-Chief — Charles M. Durfee, Decatur, Ill.; and Vice-Lieutenant Commander-in-Chief — Wheeler C. Wikoff, Columbus, Ohio.

In the few years since its beginning in 1881, the Order had grown to include a membership of over 17,000 in 25 states and territories. With its growth, the question within the GAR regarding how "children and descendants could be best and permanently made to fully understand and properly sustain the principles he fought for, and sacrificed so much to maintain" was answered.

A major activity of the GAR was the observance of Memorial Day, May 30, a day for remembrance of their dead comrades. They wondered who would continue this observance in the coming years. In 1931, at their 65th Annual Encampment, the GAR issued the following resolution: "Resolved, That the Grand Army of the Republic establish and have given proper observance, on Memorial Day

Sons of Veterans Decoration Day postcard postmarked 1910. (GLG)

Byington Camp #55 of Battle Creek, Michigan circa 1890. (MI-SUV)

since 1868, we in National Encampment now assembled grant whatever right we have to maintain our memories and see that our graves are properly decorated on Memorial Day to the Sons of Union Veterans of the Civil War, and protest against any other Organization usurping that right in any place where a Camp of the Sons of Union Veterans exists. Unanimous vote of the Committee."

The Order continued its growth and moved into many new localities. At the second Encampment, held in Columbus, Ohio in August 1883, twenty-one states or Divisions were represented. They decided to make no revisions to the organic laws or ritual of the Order. The delegates scheduled their next national meeting for August 1884 in Philadelphia, Pa.

Some of the main principles an objects of the Sons of Veterans of the United States of America, as reported in 1884, are:

Principles

SECTION 1. A firm belief and trust in Almighty God, and a realization that under His beneficent guidance the free institutions of our land — consecrated by the services and blood of our Fathers — have been preserved, and the integrity and life of the nation maintained.

SECTION 2. True allegiance to the Government of the United States of America, based upon a respect for and devotion and fidelity to its Constitution and Laws, manifested by the discountenancing of anything that may tend to weaken Loyalty, to incite Insurrection, Treason or Rebellion, or in any manner impair the efficiency and permanency of our National Union.

Objects

SECTION 1. To keep green the memory of our Fathers, and their sacrifices for the maintenance of the Union.

SECTION 2. To aid the members of the Grand Army of the Republic in the caring for their helpless and disabled Veterans; to extend aid and protection to their widows and orphans; to perpetuate the memory and history of their heroic deeds, and the proper observance of Memorial Day.

SECTION 3. To aid and assist worthy and needy members of our Order.

SECTION 4. To inculcate patriotism and love of country, not only among our membership, but among all the people of our land, and to spread and sustain the doctrine of equal rights, universal liberty, and justice to all.

Maj. Davis was widely credited with building this organization. Regarding this achievement, someone identified only as "one standard authority" in an 1884 book on the Sons of Veterans wrote,

"Major A. P. Davis has builded wiser than he knew. The Sons of Veterans is destined to become the great military organization of this country, while at the same time its devotees, the American youth, will be permeated with that love of our country, that glory in its supremacy, that thrilling of the senses when its National hymns are sung, that none others not thus reared can know or feel. Through this organization the declining days of the Union veteran will be made pleasant, his record of service to his country preserved, his memory honored, patriotism promoted, while, if the dire necessity of the Nation should demand, the Sons of Veterans, uniformed, drilled, and equipped, would come at once to her defense with the glory of their fathers surrounding them, each heart pulsating in unison with the rising and falling of the Nation's emblem; and who would be powerful to prevail against such a host!"

National Encampments 1883 - 1995

The Second National Encampment of the Commandery-in-Chief was held at Columbus, Ohio, August 6, 1883. Frank P. Merrill of Maine was elected Commander-in-Chief. The business included reports of all Grand Divisions, exemplification of the unwritten work, and a per capita fee fixed. The GAR recognized and endorsed the Order at their 17th National Encampment at Denver, Colorado.

Third
Philadelphia, Pennsylvania — August 27-30, 1884
This meeting was held at Independence Hall and was said to be the first body or society of the kind to have the honor and distinction of meeting there. Harry W. Arnold of Pennsylvania was elected. There was support for the Ladies' Aid Society. The Eastern Pennsylvania Sons of Veterans affiliated with A. P. Davis' organization. Davis Camp of Pittsburgh was allowed to carry a gold camp flag, symbolizing their status as the first camp of the Order.

Fourth
Grand Rapids, Michigan — September 17, 1885
Walter S. Payne of Ohio was elected on the ninth ballot. Membership of the Order was reported at 6,903. Grand Divisions were abolished. The first report from the Ladies' Aid Society was received. It was reported that most of the Massachusetts Sons of Veterans under Edwin Earp had affiliated, and the New York "Post System" Sons of Veterans under George T. Brown were doing the same. The "Sons of Veterans Advocate" of Bloomington, Illinois, was declared the official organ. The Constitution and Regulations of 1882 were updated.

Fifth
Buffalo, New York — August 31-September 2, 1886
Walter S. Payne was re-elected. During the year, many new Divisions were formed. Davis Camp was authorized to drop "#1" and use "*."

Sixth
Des Moines, Iowa — August 17-19, 1887
George B. Abbott of Chicago, Illinois was elected. At this Encampment, the death of Gen. John A. Logan was reported. There was also a call for military preparedness of the Order to serve in the Armed Forces of the United States, if need be.

Seventh
Wheeling, West Virginia — August 15-17, 1888
George B. Abbott was re-elected. During the year, 678 camp charters had been approved by the Commander-in-Chief, with the aggregate of 12, 105 new members. The membership of the Order stood at 56, 472. The Commandery-in-Chief was incorporated in the State of Illinois. The death of Gen. Phillip Sheridan was reported.

Eighth
Paterson, New Jersey — September 10-13, 1889
Charles L. Griffin of Indiana elected. The "National Reveille" of Chicago, Illinois, was declared the official organ. February 12 was designated as Union Defenders' Day. A circular was sent out to GAR comrades with the origins and aims of the Sons of Veterans. A contract was entered into with A. P. Davis for membership medals and other badges.

Ninth
St. Joseph, Missouri — August 26-29, 1890
Leland J. Webb of Kansas elected. The proceedings of the previous encampments were published in one volume. There was a complaint that there was an over-use of decorations on uniforms. The Ladies' Aid Society was reported organized in 16 states. A committee was appointed to draft regulations for military rank.

Tenth
Minneapolis, Minnesota — August 24-29, 1891
Bartow S. Weeks of New York elected on the twentieth ballot. At this Encampment, major changes were made to the Constitution and Regulations, civilian titles were adopted for National and Division officers, and the Sons of Veterans Guard was established. The deaths of Gen. Wm. T. Sherman and Admiral David D. Porter were reported. Past Commander-in-Chief status was voted for George T. Brown of the "Post System" Sons, and Edwin Earp of the "Earp" Sons of Veterans.

Eleventh
Helena, Montana — August 8-12, 1892
Marvin E. Hall of Michigan elected. The Sons of Veterans Guard was organized during the year with many successes reported. A new stand of colors for the Commandery-in-Chief was authorized.

A Michigan Division Officer of A. T. Mc Reynolds Camp #14, Grand Rapids, MI ca. 1890. (GLG)

Twelfth
Cincinnati, Ohio — August 15-18, 1893
Joseph B. Maccabe of Massachusetts elected. The "Sons of Veterans Waltz" was introduced. The largest camp mustered in, Ottowa, Kansas, #116, with 126 charter members. The eligibility age was changed from 18 to 21. The Sons of Veterans Guard was voted independent of the Sons of Veterans. A committee was appointed to draft a three-degree ritual.

Thirteenth
Davenport, Iowa — August 20-23, 1894
William E. Bundy of Ohio elected. The eligibility age was returned to 18. The three-degree ritual was approved. It was also voted that each Division would have control of its own military, the Sons of Veterans Guard.

Fourteenth
Knoxville, Tennessee — September 16-18, 1895
William H. Russell of Kansas elected. The Sons of Veterans National Hymn, "The Banner of Beauty and Glory," was adopted.

Fifteenth
Louisville, Kentucky — September 8-10, 1896
James L. Rake of Pennsylvania elected. House Resolution #5562 was introduced in Congress authorizing the Secretary of War to recognize Sons of Veterans Guard units as Reserve. The Encampment voted that the membership badge was to appear on stationery, not the Coat of Arms.

Sixteenth
Indianapolis, Indiana — September 9-11, 1897
Charles K. Darling of Massachusetts elected. It was reported that Congress took no action on H. R. #5562.

Seventeenth
Omaha, Nebraska — September 12-14, 1898
The Commander-in-Chief, Charles K. Darling, was at the head of his Regiment, the 6th Mass. Inf., in Puerto Rico (Spanish-American War). Many of the members of the Order were in the U. S. service in the war with Spain. In the absence of the C-in-C, George E. Cogshall of Grand Rapids, Michigan, the Sr. Vice, presided. The Encampment was saddened and very little enthusiasm was manifested by reason of the war and so many of the Brothers "gone to the front." The War Service Medal was approved at this time. Frank L. Sheppard of Illinois was elected.

Eighteenth
Detroit, Michigan — September 7-9, 1899
Asa W. Jones of Ohio elected. The death of Major A. P. Davis on May 21, 1899 was reported. The "Banner" of Illinois was declared the official organ. Congress voted to donate captured Spanish cannon to the Order, to be used to produce the Bronze War Service Cross. A proposal was brought before the Encampment to sponsor a military college.

Charles C. Lawrence, New Jersey Division Commander in 1906. (GLG)

Nineteenth
Syracuse, New York — September 11-13, 1900
Edgar W. Alexander of Pennsylvania elected. Mason City, Iowa, was approved as the site of "Sons Memorial University." The Board of Regents was elected. A new buttonhole decoration, a tri-colored bar, was approved.

Twentieth
Providence, Rhode Island — September 17-18, 1901
Edward R. Campbell of Washington, D. C., elected. The members were greatly depressed by the death of President McKinley. A. P. Davis' bequest to the Order was released. It was voted that the "Banner" was to be mailed to all members. The cornerstone for Sons Memorial University was laid June 26, 1901. There was an apparent lack of interest in the Sons of Veterans Guards.

Twenty-first
Washington, D. C. — October 7-9, 1902
Frank Martin of Indiana was elected. The Order began simultaneous Encampments with the GAR. Viva voce voting was established throughout the Order.

Twenty-second
Atlantic City, New Jersey — September 15-17, 1903
Arthur B. Spink of Rhode Island elected. The titles of camp officers was changed from military to civilian (i.e., Camp Captain to Camp Commander). A National Military Department was created. The Sons of Veterans Reserve was approved by the Encampment and a SVR Commanding Officer was appointed.

Twenty-third
Boston, Massachusetts — August 17-19, 1904
William G. Dustin of Illinois elected. During the year, the SVR was formed and organized. By-laws, Rules, and Regulations were approved at Encampment. A new edition of the C&R was published.

Twenty-fourth
Gettysburg, Pennsylvania — September 18-20, 1905
Harley V. Speelman of Ohio elected. A five-year term was instituted for the National Secretary.

Twenty-fifth
Peoria, Illinois — August 20-23, 1906
Edwin M. Amies of Pennsylvania elected. The office of Patriotic Instructor was created. Aid was encouraged and voted for the San Francisco fire victims.

Twenty-sixth
Dayton, Ohio — August 20-21, 1907
Ralph Sheldon of New York elected. The badges of the Order were listed in the Constitution and By-Laws. The Military Affairs Committee was established. The Order's 1888 incorporation had lapsed and was subsequently reinstated by the State of Illinois.

Twenty-seventh
Niagara Falls, New York — August 25-27, 1908
Edgar Allen, Jr., of Virginia elected. The Past Commander-in-Chief's badge had always been paid for by donations

from members. It was voted that the National Organization should pay for it. A new, revised ritual was approved. The word "Fraternity" was substituted for "Friendship" (Fraternity, Charity & Loyalty).

Twenty-eighth
Washington, D. C. — August 24-26, 1909
George W. Pollit of New Jersey elected. The Rules & Regulations for the SVR were approved.

Twenty-ninth
Atlantic City, New Jersey — September 20-22, 1910
Fred E. Bolton of Massachusetts elected. There was an attempt to change the name of the Order to "Sons of the GAR." The idea was that the Order would be more readily identified with the GAR. It was defeated. During the year, a camp was organized in Buenos Aires, Argentina. Support was voted for House Resolution #12390 pension for Civil War veterans.

Thirtieth
Rochester, New York — August 20-25, 1911
Newton J. McGuire of Indiana elected. It was voted to withdraw support for Sons Memorial University in Mason City, Iowa, due to lack of funds. A new buttonhole decoration was approved — the rosette. Members that were dropped by their camp were also considered as dropped by the SVR. The tradition of appointing National Aides and presenting National Ribbons for membership recruitment was begun.

Thirty-first
St. Louis, Missouri — August 27-29, 1912
Ralph M. Grant of Connecticut elected. A committee to write the history of the Order was approved.

Thirty-second
Chattanooga, Tennessee — September 16-18, 1913
John E. Sautter of Pennsylvania elected. A membership certificate was approved. On the topic of dual membership, one must be declared principle, another must be associate or honorary.

Thirty-third
Detroit, Michigan — September 1-3, 1914
Charles F. Sherman of New York elected. An historical sketch of the Order appeared in the "Banner." It was voted that ladies in good standing with the Auxiliary may be admitted to camp meetings.

Thirty-fourth
Washington, D. C. — September 28-30, 1915
A. E. B. Stephens of Ohio elected. A new camp was established at the Iroquois Reservation in New York. A Junior Order was authorized for 12-18 year-olds. A new recognition buttonhole decoration was adopted — miniature of the badge.

Thirty-fifth
Kansas City, Missouri — August 30-31, 1916
William T. Church of Illinois elected. A change in the eligibility age to 16 years was defeated. The history of the Order written in 1914 was entered into the proceedings.

Thirty-sixth
Boston, Massachusetts — August 22-23, 1917
Fred F. T. Johnson of Maryland elected. World War I. Many members enlist in the Armed Forces of the United States. A letter was sent to President Woodrow Wilson pledging war support. A statement on National Preparedness was issued. The khaki uniform was approved for Sons of Veterans Reserve.

Thirty-seventh
Niagara Falls, New York — August 20-21, 1918
Francis Callahan of Pennsylvania elected. $26,426.65 was raised for the War Ambulance Fund with assistance of Auxiliary. Fourteen ambulances were purchased. An appeal was made for field glasses for the U.S. Navy. November 19 was designated a Sons of Veterans holiday – Veterans' Night. The first listing of Past Commanders-in-Chief and National Encampments was printed in the proceedings.

Thirty-eighth
Columbus, Ohio — September 9-11, 1919
Harry D. Sisson of Massachusetts elected. World War I ends. A new application form #3 allows obligation outside of camp meeting.

Thirty-ninth
Indianapolis, Indiana — September 22-23, 1920
Pelham A. Barrows of Nebraska elected. The "Banner" was cut from twelve to nine issues per year. A "mini" history of the Order was printed. An attempt was made to change the name of the Order to Sons of the GAR — defeated. The War Service Medal was reinstated.

Fortieth
Indianapolis, Indiana — September 27-29, 1921
Clifford Ireland of Illinois elected. It was voted to let the individual Divisions govern its own Sons of Veterans Reserve Units.

Forty-first
Des Moines, Iowa — September 26-28, 1922
Frank Shelhouse of Indiana elected. The first school of instruction at Encampment was held. The U.S. Flag Code was recommended to Congress. The ribbons of the badges of the Order were in the public domain. A proposal to change the name of the Order was referred to committee.

Forty-second
Milwaukee, Wisconsin — September 4-6, 1923
Samuel S. Horn of Pennsylvania elected. Commander-in-Chief Shelhouse recommended a name change to "Sons of Union Veterans of the Civil War." This was referred to a conference with the GAR.

Forty-third
Boston, Massachusetts — August 12-14, 1924
William M. Coffin of Ohio elected. The placing of ceremonial swords on the Altar was discontinued. The Junior Order begun in 1915 was disbanded. The eligibility age was changed from 18 to 16.

Forty-fourth
Grand Rapids, Michigan — September 1-3, 1925
Edwin C. Irelan of Maryland elected. A resolution was presented to change the name of the Order from Sons of Veterans, United States of America, to Sons of Union Veterans of the Civil War, subject to approval of the Grand Army of the Republic.

Forty-fifth
Des Moines, Iowa — September 21-23, 1926
Ernest W. Homan of Massachusetts elected. Change of name ratified by 20 of 24 Divisions. It was voted to discontinue the issuing of the War Service Medal when supply is depleted. It was reported that there was a complete set of National Encampment Proceedings in the Library of Congress.

Forty-sixth
Grand Rapids, Michigan — September 13-15, 1927
Walter C. Mabie of Pennsylvania elected. Division was changed to "Department" (i.e. Department of Michigan).

Forty-seventh
Denver, Colorado — September 18-20, 1928
Delevan Bates Bowley of California and Pacific elected. Support was voted to make the "Star Spangled Banner" the National Anthem.

Forty-eighth
Portland, Maine — September 10-12, 1929
Theodore C. Cazeau of New York elected. The Order, being incorporated in Illinois under the name Sons of Veterans, U. S. A., changed incorporation papers to reflect new name.

Forty-ninth
Cincinnati, Ohio — August 26-28, 1930
Allen S. Holbrook of Illinois elected. The Great Depression. The peak membership of the Order was reported as 57,824 in 1917. The greatest number of camps was 1,225, in 1915.

Fiftieth
Des Moines, Iowa — September 14-17, 1931
Frank C. Huston of Indiana elected. The Encampment concerned itself with the problem of mass unemployment due to the Depression. Some camps reported 50-60 percent of members unable to pay dues. By resolution, those Brothers unable to pay dues were not dropped but encouraged to pay back dues when able.

Fifty-first
Springfield, Illinois — September 19-22, 1932
Titus M. Ruch of Pennsylvania elected. An anti-Communist and anti-Russian resolution was passed.

Fifty-second
St. Paul, Minnesota — September 19-21, 1933
Park F. Yengling of Ohio elected. The Bank of Reading, Pennsylvania closed, freezing $4,400 of SUVCW funds. The song "SVR March" was introduced. Words written by C. Leroy Stoudt, music by Fred Cardin.

Fifty-third
Rochester, New York — August 14-16, 1934
Frank L. Kirchgassner of Massachusetts elected. The U.S. Supreme Court decides that the war of 1861-1865 was a "Civil War" not a "War Between the States." The Order receives recognition by the Internal Revenue Service. First Program and Policy Committee reports to Encampment. It was voted that national officers may wear membership badge on a national ribbon and the Commander-in-Chief to participate each February 12 at Lincoln Memorial in Washington, D. C.

Fifty-Fourth
Grand Rapids, Michigan — September 9-12, 1935
Richard F. Locke of Illinois elected. Opposition was voted by Encampment for a statue of Robert E. Lee at Arlington National Cemetery and commemorative medals for Lee and Jefferson Davis. Establishment of geographic regions — New England Region, Eastern Region, Central Region, Western Region.

Fifty-fifth
Washington, D. C. — September 22-24, 1936
William Allen Dyer of New York elected. A bronze tablet inscribed with Lincoln's Gettysburg Address was presented to Ford's Theatre. The Rhode Island Department proposed naming U.S. 6 as GAR Memorial Highway. The 50 year badge was approved.

Fifty-sixth
Madison, Wisconsin — September 6-9, 1937
Wm. A. Dyer re-elected. The National Organization published and distributed the pamphlet "A Civil War" not a "War Between the States."

Fifty-seventh
Des Moines, Iowa — September 5-8, 1938
William L. Anderson of Massachusetts elected. The C&R Committee was directed to formulate rules and regulations for the Sons of Veterans Reserve. The Americanization Committee was created.

Fifty-eighth
Pittsburgh, Pennsylvania — August 29-30, 1939
Ralph R. Barrett of California elected. The rank of Past Commander-in-Chief was voted by Encampment to Horace H. Hammer of Reading, Pennsylvania. He served as National Secretary for 35 years. The War Service Medal was re-instituted and the Miniature Membership Badge was approved. The Grant Cup Award was instituted. September 2, 1939 was SUVCW Day at New York Worlds Fair.

Fifty-ninth
Springfield, Illinois — September 10-12, 1940
J. Kirkwood Craig of Minnesota elected. U. S. Congress passed a bill authorizing the War Department to give or lend condemned ordnance or weapons to SVR units.

Sixtieth
Columbus, Ohio — September 15-18, 1941
Albert C. Lambert of New Jersey elected. SVR regulations adopted. A war victory fund was established.

Sixty-first
Indianapolis, Indiana — September 15-17, 1942
Henry Towle of Maine elected. World War II. Most members of the Order were serving in the Armed Forces or engaged in war work.

Sixty-second
Milwaukee, Wisconsin — September 20-23, 1943
C. Leroy Stoudt of Pennsylvania elected. A "Special Executive Committee" for emergency action was created. This committee was to act in the absence of a National Encampment if one could not be called due to the war. The words "Sovereign States" in the American's Creed were questioned.

Sixty-third
Des Moines, Iowa — September 12-14, 1944
Urion W. Mackey of Michigan elected. Funds frozen by Reading Bank in 1933 are restored. Badge production is halted due to metal shortage for war effort.

Sixty-fourth
Columbus, Ohio — October 1-4, 1945
H. Harding Hale of Massachusetts elected. The Grand Army of the Republic adopts U. S. Highway 6 as their memorial. The Commander-in-Chief's badge is approved.

Sixty-fifth
Indianapolis, Indiana — August 25-29, 1946
Neil D. Cranmer of New York elected. Badge production halted in 1944 is resumed. November 19, 1946 is declared Dedication Day by Congress. Kathrine Flood, Executive Secretary of the GAR, died. Cora Gillis is appointed replacement. GAR requests Allied Orders to continue joint encampments.

Sixty-sixth
Cleveland, Ohio — August 10-14, 1947
Charles H. E. Moran of Massachusetts elected. The Department Commander's Badge was approved.

Sixty-seventh
Grand Rapids, Michigan — September 26-30, 1948
Perle L. Fouch of Michigan elected. The Encampment voted to approve the granting of Past Camp Commander rank to Camp Secretary or Treasurer after ten consecutive years of holding office.

Sixty-eighth
Indianapolis, Indiana — August 28-31, 1949
John H. Runkle of Pennsylvania elected. Last National Encampment of the Grand Army of the Republic (83rd). Colors and standards of the GAR are turned over to the Smithsonian Institution in Washington, D. C. This Encampment voted to begin registration fee at 1950 National Encampment. Resolution passed on disposition of Camp property upon disbandment.

Sixty-ninth
Boston, Massachusetts — August 20-24, 1950
Cleon E. Heald of New Hampshire elected. The Commandery-in-Chief applies for the Congressional Charter.

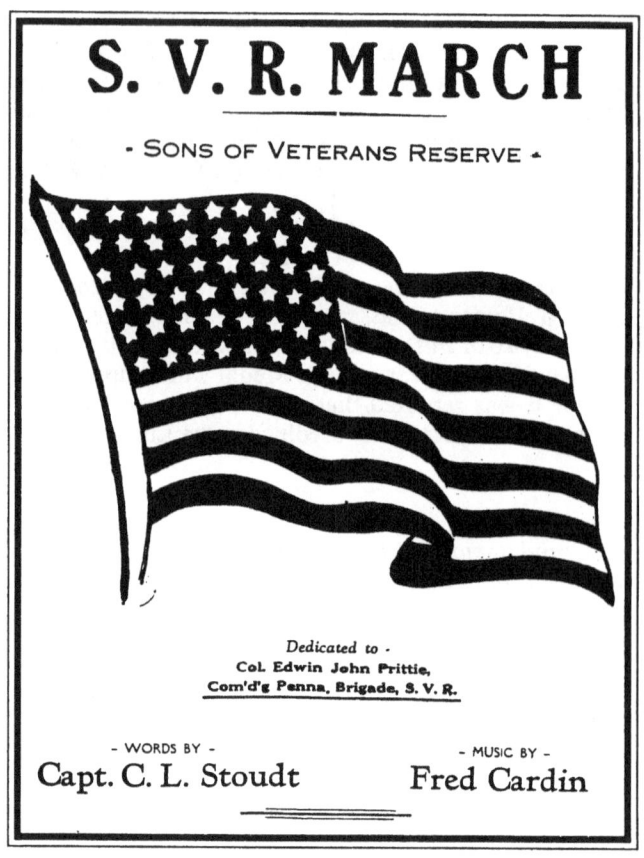

Seventieth
Columbus, Ohio — August 19-23, 1951
Roy J. Bennett of Iowa elected. The Membership Card is adopted. The GAR Memorial Fund is created.

Seventy-first
Atlantic City, New Jersey — August 24-28, 1952
Fredrick K. Davis of Oregon elected. Council of Administration replaces Council-in-Chief. Iowa Department Auxiliary presents National Organization with U. S. flag. Duties specified for Senior Vice Commander-in-Chief and Junior Vice Commander-in-Chief.

Seventy-second
Buffalo, New York — August 23-27, 1953
Maj. Gen. U. S. Grant III of Maryland elected. The rank of Past Commander-in-Chief voted to Albert Woolson, last survivor of the GAR and last Union veteran. Associates approved. A new Commandery-in-Chief flag presented.

Seventy-third
Duluth, Minnesota — August 8-13, 1954
Gen. Grant re-elected. Congressional Charter/Act of Incorporation approved by U. S. Congress August 20. Auxiliary commissions Woolson statue to be placed at Gettysburg. Associate Badge approved. Annual audit by CPA begins. Permanent Fund and Associates ratified by departments. Ceremony honoring Albert Woolson held at Encampment.

Seventy-fourth
Cincinnati, Ohio — August 21-25, 1955
Col. Fredric G. Bauer of Massachusetts elected. Illinois Charter superseded by Congressional Charter. Transfer of GAR property to SUVCW effected. GAR campfire program revived.

Seventy-fifth
Harrisburg, Pennsylvania — September 1-5, 1956
Fred E. Howe of New York elected. Albert Woolson dies August 2 at age 109. Woolson statue dedicated in Ziegler's Grove at Gettysburg September 2. U.S. District Court in District of Columbia expedites transfer of GAR property. The Lincoln Tomb Ceremony in Springfield, Illinois is established. The Daughters of Union Veterans and Women's Relief Corps meet in separate encampments. A 75-year mini history is included in the Commander-in-Chief's report.

Seventy-sixth
Detroit, Michigan — August 18-22, 1957
Albert B. DeHaven of Maine elected. Tax exempt notice received from Treasury Department. The Civil War Centennial Committee established. Support was voted for first Remembrance Day in November.

Seventy-seventh
Boston, Massachusetts — August 17-21, 1958
Earl F. Riggs of California elected. Graves Registration Officer established. GAR medallion presented to Cathedral of the Pines in New Hampshire. Life Member Bar for badge approved.

Seventy-eighth
Long Beach, California — August 16-20, 1959
Harold E. Arnold of Rhode Island elected. Grant's Tomb in New York City is transferred to National Park Service. It is enacted that "SUVCW" is the proper designation. "Encampment" remains the name of our annual meeting as "Convention" is voted down.

Seventy-ninth
Springfield, Illinois — August 21-25, 1960
Thomas A. Chadwick of Vermont elected. The Military Affairs committee is established for Civil War centennial activities. A two-year term for the Commander-in-Chief is rejected.

Eightieth
Indianapolis, Indiana — August 21-24, 1961
Charles L. Messer of New York elected, but dies in office. Sr. Vice C-in-C Chester S. Shriver elected by Council of

P-C-in-C Chester Shriver (left) and P-C-in-C U.S. Grant III (right). (NO-SUV)

Administration to complete term. GAR scholarship changed from Lincoln University in Kentucky to Gettysburg College.

Eighty-first
Washington, D. C. — August 19-23, 1962
Chester S. Shriver of Pennsylvania elected. Appropriation made for benches to be installed at the Woolson Monument in Gettysburg.

Eighty-second
Miami Beach, Florida — August 18-23, 1963
Joseph S. Rippey of New York elected. U.S. flag on altar replaced by colored cloth; National - gold; Department - red; Camp - blue. A clarification of "Blood Relative" was made.

Eighty-third
Providence, Rhode Island — August 16-20, 1964
Joseph S. Rippey re-elected. History of GAR is project of Civil War Centennial Committee. SVR reorganized into six military districts. National Historian starts collection of state Civil War veteran registers.

Eighty-forth
Richmond, Virginia — August 15-19, 1965
W. Earl Corbin of Ohio elected. The Centennial of Appomattox is observed.

Eighty-fifth
Grand Rapids, Michigan — August 14-18, 1966
Frank Woerner of California elected. Benches at Woolson Monument dedicated. Employer Identification Number (EIN) assigned by IRS. A contribution was made to the National Cathedral for the Lincoln nave.

Eighty-sixth
Chicago, Illinois — August 6-10, 1967
William W. Haskell of Massachusetts elected. Past C-in-C Riggs opens Civil War museum in California. Gold Altar Cloth presented to Commandery-in-Chief in memory of Past C-in-C Lambert. Effort to name US 20 the U. S. Grant Highway started.

Eighty-seventh
Wilmington, Delaware — August 18-22, 1968
Frank M. Heacock, Sr., of Pennsylvania elected. New SVR regulations established.

Eighty-eighth
St. Louis, Missouri — August 17-21, 1969
Fred H. Combs, Jr., of New Jersey elected. A bequest was received from the estate of Maj. Gen. U. S. Grant III. Daughters of Union Veterans National Headquarters dedicated April of 1969. The Arnold Award for largest department membership increase begun. Encampment voted that Associates are not to hold national elected office.

Eighty-ninth
Miami Beach, Florida — August 23-27, 1970
George L. Cashman of Illinois elected. Contents of printed proceedings of National Encampments to be limited. A flag disposal ceremony pamphlet was developed.

Nicholas Scholl, Camp 2nd Lt. (Jr. Vice Commander), Camp #77, Chillicothe, Ohio circa 1890. (GLG)

Ninetieth
Boston, Massachusetts — August 15-19, 1971
Norman R. Furman of New York elected. A resolution condemning the erection of the Gettysburg Tower passed. The 100th anniversary fund was established.

Ninety-first
Philadelphia, Pennsylvania — August 13-17, 1972
John C. Yocum of Pennsylvania elected. The eligibility age was changed to 14 years.

Ninety-second
Palm Springs, California — August 5-9, 1973
Allen B. Howland of Massachusetts elected. Flag stands presented to Commandery-in-Chief by camp in California. It was voted the SVR members must be SUVCW members. The SVR uniform was changed to the 1870-1880 style.

Ninety-third
Bretton Woods, New Hampshire — August 18-22, 1974
John H. Stark of Pennsylvania elected. The first membership-at-large coordinator, Past C-in-C Fred H. Combs, Jr., was appointed.

Ninety-fourth
Rochester, New York — August 10-14, 1975
Clarence J. Riddell of Pennsylvania elected. The regulations were amended to provide that to qualify for the office of Department Commander, one must first be a Past Camp Commander. A ribbon for the SVR Distinguished Service Medal was approved.

Ninety-fifth
Columbus, Ohio — August 15-19, 1976
Kenneth T. Wheeler of New Hampshire elected. The nation celebrates the Bicentennial. A Bible, gavel, and gavel block are presented to the Commandery-in-Chief as a memorial to Past C-in-C Albert C. Lambert.

Ninety-sixth
Des Moines, Iowa — August 14-18, 1977
Harold T. Beilby of New York elected. Certain omissions are restored to the Ritual. It is affirmed that the SVR is a male organization. A proposal to hold the next National Encampment outside of the U. S. is rejected, as it would be in violation of our Congressional Charter.

Ninety-seventh
Grand Rapids, Michigan — August 13-17, 1978
Richard L. Greenwalt of Ohio elected. A new seal and seal press is purchased for the Commandery-in-Chief.

Ninety-eighth
Hartford, Connecticut — August 12-15, 1979
Elton P. Koch of Pennsylvania elected. All paperwork forms of the Order are made a part of the Regulations.

Ninety-ninth
Richmond, Virginia — August 10-14, 1980
Richard E. Wyman of New Hampshire elected. The United States Military History Institute at Carlisle Barracks, Pennsylvania, is designated as the official repository of SUVCW and GAR records. A description of department and camp flags was reinserted into the regulations. Lapel rosettes were made available again. The chartering of provisional camps is approved.

One-hundredth
Philadelphia, Pennsylvania — August 9-13, 1981
Harry E. Gibbons of New York elected. Our Centennial Encampment: SUVCW neckties introduced by National Patriotic Instructor. New membership certificates were approved. The Arnold Award for department membership increase is retired to the Rhode Island Department (1969-1981); the Howland Award takes its place.

One-hundred-first
Providence, Rhode Island — August 14-18, 1982
Richard C. Schlenker of Maryland elected. The National Organization affiliates with the Lincoln Birthday National Commemorative Committee in Washington, D. C. The chartering of Provisional Departments is approved. The Training and Education committee is established.

One-hundred-second
Portland, Maine — August 15-19, 1983
William J. Simpson of Pennsylvania elected. A new supplier of medals and insignia was sought. Membership inquiries were to be sent on to Jr. Vice C-in-C. Gold sash for formal wear approved for Past CinC and national officers. The editor of the Banner to be appointed for calendar year.

Delegates to the 100th National Encampment. (JLO)

One-hundred-third
Akron, Ohio — August 12-16, 1984
Eugene E. Russell of Massachusetts elected. A bronze plaque was obtained by Davis Camp for the tomb of Maj. A. P. Davis, identifying him as the founder of the SUVCW. The History Book Committee was created and department histories were sought.

One-hundred-fourth
Wilmington, Delaware — August 11-13, 1985
Donald L. Roberts of New York elected. Life membership for infant sons approved. Life memberships may be granted to brothers with 75 years of service to the Order. A request was made for location and inventory of GAR property. The bronze bar for the War Medal was approved.

One-hundred-fifth
Lexington, Kentucky — August 10-14, 1986
Gordon R. Bury II of Ohio elected. The purchase of new station banners for the Commandery-in-Chief was approved. It was voted that the Sr. Vice C-in-C and Jr. Vice C-in-C require the same eligibility as the Commander-in-Chief. Dual memberships were approved. A liaison is to be maintained with the Sons of Confederate Veterans.

One-hundred-sixth
Buffalo, New York — August 9-12, 1987
Rev. Richard O. Partington of Pennsylvania elected. A bequest was received from Past C-in-C Clean Heald's estate. Publicity for the GAR Memorial Highway (US 6) was voted. It was voted to produce a national membership list.

One-hundred-seventh
Lansing, Michigan — August 14-17, 1988
Clark W. Mellor of Massachusetts elected. Authorization was granted for the wearing of Past Department Commander's badge and membership badge suspended from a neck ribbon to Past Department Commanders and Life members, respectively.

One-hundred-eighth
Stamford, Connecticut — August 13-16, 1989
Charles W. Corfman of Ohio elected. A committee was appointed to close the office of the late national secretary/treasurer, Chester S. Shriver. In-house advertising in the Banner was approved. It was voted that a membership badge may be silver-dipped to identify Camp Commander, and that Past Camp Commanders may wear their badge on neck

Wreath bearers at Lincoln Tomb Ceremony on April 15, 1989. (Used by permission of Marlin Roos, photographer, Lincoln, IL)

ribbon. James T. Lyons, PDC of Michigan, succeeded Shriver as national secretary. Richard D. Orr, PDC of Pennsylvania national treasurer.

One-hundred-ninth
Des Moines, Iowa — August 12-15, 1990
George W. Long of Pennsylvania elected. The Encampment voted to shorten the length of National Encampments to three days: Friday, Saturday and Sunday – to take advantage of hotel rates and more delegates able to attend weekend meetings. This is to begin in 1992. An assistant treasurer for supplies is appointed. The National Organization affiliated with the National Congress of Patriotic Organizations.

One-hundred-tenth
Indianapolis, Indiana — August 11-14, 1991
Lowell V. Hammer of Maryland elected. The Commandery-in-Chief flag is replaced — old flag turned over to GAR museum in Philadelphia. The C.R.&R. is reprinted for the first time since 1954 in loose leaf format. The Publications Committee is approved.

One-hundred-eleventh
Pittsburgh, Pennsylvania — August 14-16, 1992
Elmer F. "Bud" Atkinson of Pennsylvania elected. Revisions are made in the information brochure and application form. It was recommended that a GAR highway officer be appointed in each department in which US 6 passes through.

One-hundred-twelfth
Portland, Maine — August 13-15, 1993
Allen W. Moore of Indiana elected. Major changes are made in the C.R.&R. to bring it in line with the Congressional Charter. Other changes include membership-at-large shall have same delegate ratio to National Encampment as departments. The Council of Administration is to have three elected members with three-year staggered terms. Provisional camps must have 15 members to attain full camp status. Commander-in-Chief, Sr. Vice C-in-C, and Jr. Vice C-in-C must hold PDC rank. A second scholarship was authorized, and both dollar amounts are set at $1,000.

One-hundred-thirteenth
Lansing, Michigan — August 12 -14, 1994
Keith G. Harrison of Michigan elected. Departments ratify changes to C.R.&R. A policy is established on the use of badges, emblems, seals and symbols of the SUVCW. The "junior" category is approved for 8 through 13-year-olds. Honorary Life Membership is granted for Real Sons. Honorary SUVCW Membership is granted for Real Daughters.

One-hundred-fourteenth
Columbus, Ohio — August 11 -13, 1995
David R. Medert of Ohio elected. The title of "National Personal Aide" was changed to "National Aide de Camp'. The National Patriotic Instructor was relieved of fund raising responsibility for the GAR fund. The position of National Quartermaster was made a voting member of the Council of Administration. A "Home Page" was established on the Internet. The wearing of a sash of ribbon colors on formal occasions for officers was discontinued due to cost. A committee was to find a new storage facility for records held at Carlisle Barracks, and an inventory made of same.

The Auxiliary to the Sons of Union Veterans of the Civil War

The women's organization formed to assist and support the Sons of the Union Veterans of the Civil War was also begun by Maj. A. P. Davis. Largely through his efforts was the first Ladies' Aid Society organized as an Auxiliary to the Order in Philadelphia in 1883. The women's organization was officially recognized at the Sons of Veterans fourth Encampment of the Commandery-in-Chief on August 28, 1884, held in Independence Hall. The resolution read: "Resolved, That the efforts of the Ladies' Aid Society are truly appreciated by this Commandery-in-Chief, and that their work be heartily endorsed, and recommended to the various Camps under this jurisdiction."

As the Philadelphia chapter flourished, the Ladies' Aid Society spread to other states. The formation of a national organization was begun in 1886, and Laura Martin of Lancaster, Penn., was elected as National President. The formation was completed in 1887 at the Society's first National Encampment, held in Akron, Ohio. Eighteen delegates were present. Soon, nearly all Divisions of the Sons of Veterans had Auxiliaries.

Within several year, the name Ladies' Aid Society was found to be not distinctive enough for the organization's true purpose and working ideals. At the National Encampment held in Boston in 1894, the name was changed to Sons of Veterans Auxiliary, with the consent of the Sons of Veterans. Finally, the name was changed once more, in 1925, to Auxiliary to Sons of Union Veterans of the Civil War.

The Auxiliary has always held its Annual Encampments at the same time and place as that of the Sons of Union Veterans of the Civil War. According to History of the Sons of Union Veterans of the Civil War 1881-1939, the first principle of the Auxiliary is "to assist the Sons of Union Veterans of the Civil War in all its principles and objects." The account continues: "To this end, the Auxiliary has continuously and consistently worked and has been of real value to the Sons of Union Veterans of the Civil War, in performing distinctively patriotic work that can best be done by women."

Past National Presidents
Auxiliary to the Sons of Union Veterans of the Civil War

1887	Mrs. Laura Miller, Pennsylvania
1887-88	Mrs. W. D. A. O'Brien, Ohio
1889-90	Mrs. Ella L. Jones, Pennsylvania
1891	Mrs. J. S. Mason, Ohio
1892-93	Mrs. Belle Gray Rice, Iowa
1894-96	Mrs. Margaret Howey Coe, Illinois
1897	Mrs. Kate G. Raynor, Ohio
1898	Mrs. Elizabeth H. R. Davis, D. C.
1899	Mrs. Mary L. Warren, Massachusetts
1900-02	Mrs. Lida Tomer-Miller, New York
1903-04	Mrs. Addie M. Wallace, Indiana
1905-06	Mrs. Kate E. Hardcastle Carr, New Jersey
1907	Mrs. Julia A. Moynihan, New York
1908	Miss Mam E. Herbst Ohio
1909-10	Mrs. Molly Donaldson Hammer, Pennsylvania (NJ Dept.)
1911	Mrs. Pauline Creighton, Illinois
1912	Mrs. Flora A. S. Whitney, Massachusetts
1913	Mrs. Frances Fox Moynihan, New York
1914	Miss Edna Bergwitz, Ohio
1915	Mrs. Bessie B. Bowser, Indiana
1916	Mrs. Libbie Meis, Pennsylvania
1917	Mrs. Mae E. Clothier, Illinois
1918	Mrs. Mayme E. Dyer, New York
1919	Mrs. Margaret Carney, Massachusetts
1920	Miss Mary L. Tredo, New Jersey
1921	Mrs. Blanche L. Beverstock, New Hampshire
1922	Mrs. Margaret Patterson Stephens, Ohio
1923	Mrs. Minnie E. Groth, Wisconsin
1924	Mrs. Emma Stuart Finch, Indiana
1925	Mrs. Ida Rokes Klein, New York (ME Dept.)
1926	Mrs. Mamie M. Deems, California
1927	Mrs. Anna F. Keene, Pennsylvania
1928	Mrs. Margaret L. Waters, Massachusetts
1929	Mrs. Elizabeth C. Hansen, New Jersey
1930	Mrs. Ida B. Lange, New Jersey (NY Dept.)
1931	Mrs. Celeste C. Gentieu, Delaware (MD-DE Dept.)
1932	Mrs. Wilma L. Combs, Iowa
1933	Mrs. Jean B. Thompson, Florida (OH Dept.)
1934	Mrs. Margaret F. Anderson, Washington (MA Dept.)
1935	Mrs. Gertrude M. Sautter, Florida (PA Dept.)
1936	Mrs. Stella B. Owen, New Jersey
1937	Mrs. Ida L. Lewis, Wisconsin
1938	Mrs. Margaret C. Brady, New York
1939	Mrs. Anne E. Lockyer, Ohio
1940	Mrs. Eva B. Blackman, Illinois
1941	Mrs. Clara M. Gallagher, Pennsylvania
1942	Mrs. Margaret D. Schroeder, Florida (NJ Dept.)
1943	Mrs. Mary E. Stapleton, New York
1944	Mrs. Maude B. Warren, Massachusetts
1945	Mrs. Edith B. Nile, Ohio
1946	Mrs. Gladys B. Sallman, Indiana (IL Dept.)
1947	Mrs. Edna S. Lambert, Georgia (NJ Dept.)
1948	Mrs. Katherine L. Joyce, Pennsylvania
1949	Mrs. Lena G. Barrett, California
1950	Mrs. Ethelyn C. Tucker, California (NH Dept.)
1951	Mrs. Lela B. Shugart, Indiana
1952	Mrs. Phyllis Dean, Massachusetts
1953	Mrs. Lila A. Macey, New York
1954	Mrs. Mildred R. Webster, Maine
1955	Mrs. Ellinore K. Johnson, Wisconsin
1956	Mrs. Lenore D. Glass, California
1957	Mrs. Margaret McKinney, New Jersey (PA Dept.)
1958	Miss Anne O. Clayton, New Jersey
1959	Mrs. Ursula W. Shepardson, Massachusetts
1960	Mrs. Beatrice Riggs, California (Pacific Dept.)
1961	Miss Edith M. Paulding, New Jersey
1962	Mrs. Dorothy Hilyard, Delaware
1963	Mrs. Anna I. Stoudt, Pennsylvania
1964	Mrs. Anita Selby, Ohio
1965	Mrs. Emma Wheeler, New Hampshire
1966	Mrs. Edith Snyder, Florida (NY Dept.)
1967	Miss Flora D. Bates, Massachusetts
1968	Mrs. Hazel L. Moushey, Missouri
1969	Mrs. Irene Stoudt, Pennsylvania
1970	Mrs. Florence M. Jansson, Texas (NJ Dept.)
1971	Mrs. Eileen Coombs, Rhode Island (ME Dept.)
1972	Mrs. Agnes D. Davis, Delaware
1973	Miss Viola L. Bremme, Pennsylvania
1974-75	Mrs. Jessie G. Wells, Massachusetts
1976	Mrs. Caroline E. Riddell, Pennsylvania
1977	Mrs. Minnie E. Madeiros, Maine
1978	Mrs. Marion E. Combs, Florida (NJ Dept.)
1979	Mrs. Florence H. Forbey, Arizona (IL Dept.)
1980	Mrs. Nellie H. Hawley, Iowa
1981	Mrs. Lelia M. Turner, Massachusetts
1982	Miss Ann E. Willeke, Connecticut
1983	Mrs. Dorris W. Schlenker, Maryland
1984	Mrs. Mary Jane Simpson, Pennsylvania
1985	Mrs. Jennie Russell, Massachusetts
1986	Mrs. Isabelle Roberts, New York
1987	Mrs. Esther Peiper, Ohio (PA Dept.)
1988	Mrs. Betty Woerner, California
1989	Mrs. Catherine Zapatka, Connecticut
1990	Mrs. Beatrice Greenwalt, Ohio
1991	Mrs. Ora Moitoso, Rhode Island
1992	Mrs. Ethel Carver, Delaware
1993	Mrs. Frances Murray, Maine
1994-95	Mrs. Margaret Atkinson, Pennsylvania

Honor conferred by national organization:
- 1941 Mrs. Lillian S. Ball, Indiana
- 1975 Mrs. Catherine McCoy, California

The Sons of Veterans Reserve

The Sons of Veterans was formed as a military organization. Its Commander-in-Chief held the rank of General, and all members down to Camp officers had military titles. Dress uniforms for the officers and regulation army uniform of the Civil War period were compulsory for membership. The Order could also grant warrants for the formation of Companies. This led to many Camps forming "Firing Squads" or "Camp Guards," principally for the purpose of providing military rites at the funerals of members of the Grand Army of the Republic and other veterans of the Civil War.

By 1891, the military structure was abandoned because of the embarrassment caused by the presence of the pseudo-officers among many veterans, Sons of Veterans, and GAR officers. At this time, the Sons of Veterans Guard was created for those who wished to participate in uniform. They were guided by strict regulations.

During the Spanish-American War in 1898, two companies of Sons of Veterans were raised for Michigan Militia Regiments, Co. L, 33rd MVI, and Co. B, 35th MVI. The Indiana Sons of Veterans offered a full regiment, and six of the 21 companies were accepted for militia service. Many individual members also volunteered.

The Guard was disbanded after the war when nationally-sponsored military organizations fell into disfavor.

Sons of Veterans Reserve insignia.

Yet some Sons of Veterans still favored a military organization within the Order, so in 1903 the Sons of Veterans Reserve (SVR) was created. Since encampments were held in conjunction with the GAR, the SVR was often asked to furnish a military escort for the Grand Parade. The Chief of Staff for the occasion was the SVR's highest ranking officer present.

In World War I, trained SVR units volunteered for service, although no Camps or SVR units were federalized.

Mounted Pennsylvania Sons of Veterans Reserve unit circa 1910. (JLO)

Following is the text of the documents that formally created the Sons of Veterans Reserve in 1903.

Creation of Sons of Veterans Reserve

HEADQUARTERS
COMMANDERY-IN-CHIEF

Providence, R. I., October 5, 1903.

General Order No. 5, Series 1903

I. As directed by the Commandery-in-Chief at the Encampment held at Atlantic City, September 14 to 17, 1903, I hereby promulgate such amendments to the constitution and laws of the order as were made at said Encampment, together with such important resolutions effecting the laws as were passed.

Military Department, Sons of Veterans, U. S. A.

I. That the incoming Commander-in-Chief shall at once appoint and Commission a Chief of Staff to command the Military Department, with the rank of Brigadier-General.

II. The Chief of Staff, by and through the advice and consent of the Commander-in-Chief shall formulate proper Laws and Rules for the Government of the Military Department; said laws to be promulgated in general orders by the Commander-in-Chief; and when adopted, said Laws and Rules shall become a part of the rules and regulations of the Constitution.

III. Military companies or guards of all Camps through the Order, shall become attached to Battalions, Battalions shall be organized into Regiments, and Regiments to Brigades.

Companies shall consist of not less than twenty-three Non commissioned Officers and privates, with the proper number of Commissioned officers. Battalions shall consist of from two to four companies. Regiments shall consist of two or more Battalions. Two or more Regiments shall constitute a Brigade.

IV. Camps shall be permitted to maintain a firing squad, to be composed of not more than ten men; and said firing squad shall not be compelled to become attached to a company, battalion or regiment.

V. Officers of companies shall be elected by the men composing the company.

Officers of a battalion shall be elected by the commissioned officers of the companies constituting the battalion.

Officers of a regiment shall be elected by the commissioned officers of the companies and battalions constituting the regiment.

VI. All officers above the rank of Colonel shall be appointed by the Commander-in-Chief.

VII. No unattached or independent companies, battalions or regiments shall be permitted in any Division of this Order, where the Military Department exists, except the firing squad, provided for in Sec. 4.

VIII. The Chief of Staff commanding the Military Department shall at once appoint the required number of staff officers, said officers to hold the rank specified in the army regulations.

IX. The Chief of Staff commanding the Military Department shall make an annual report to the Commander-in-Chief of the condition and requirements of his department.

X. The Military Department shall at times be subject to the orders of the Commander-in-Chief, said orders to be promulgated through the proper intermediate official channels.

XI. The Military Department shall be known and styled "Sons of Veterans Reserves."

The uniform shall consist of dark blue blouse, light blue pantaloons, fatigue or dress cap of the U. S. Army and campaign hat, laced leggings, woven web belt and such arms as desired or adopted by the companies constituting the Sons of Veterans Reserves. Insignia of rank and pantaloon stripes shall conform to U. S. Army regulations. The Commissioned Officers may have the Division mark of their Division appear on the breast of the Eagle, which is embroidered on the cap.

XII. On and after the adoption of these amendments to the Constitution, rules and regulations of the Sons of Veterans U. S. A., it shall not be lawful for any member of the Order, not connected with the Military Department of the Sons of Veterans Reserves, to wear any insignia or rank or sidearm, except the miniature rank straps and chevrons now in use by the officers of a Camp.

XIII. All officers and members of the Sons of Veterans Reserves, shall be subject to the orders of their superior officers; and for refusal to obey such orders, or for conduct unbecoming a member of the Sons of Veterans, prejudicial to good order and discipline, or to the Order of Sons of Veterans, shall be reprimanded, fined, suspended or expelled; as may be determined after due trial. Any members of the Sons of Veterans Reserves guilty of any of the above offences, shall be reported by his commanding officer, or a superior officer to the Commander of the Camp to which he belongs. The Commander of this Camp shall order a trial by a Committee of five members of said Camp, two of whom shall be members of the Sons of Veterans Reserves. Ten days notice of the meeting of said Trial Committee shall be given accused and accuser.

The findings of the trial committee shall be in writing and submitted to the Camp. The Commander of the Camp shall forward the said finding of the Trial Committee together with the action of he Camp, to the Division Commander whose approval or disapproval shall be final, unless appealed from to the Commander-in-Chief.

XIV. Immediately after the adoption of these additions to the Constitution and Laws or as soon thereafter as possible, the Commander-in-Chief, his Adjutant-General and the Chief of Staff commanding the Military Department shall meet and formulate proper rules governing the Military Department in accordance with the provisions of these amendments.

Official:
WILLIAM R. CONGDON,
Adjutant-General

By order of
ARTHUR B. SPINK,
Commander-in-Chief

Original Structure of Sons of Veterans Reserve

COMMANDERY-IN-CHIEF, S. OF V., U.S.A.

MILITARY DEPARTMENT

HEADQUARTERS, S. OF V. RESERVE
PHILADELPHIA, PA., NOV. 19, 1903

General Orders No. 1, C. S.

I. Having been appointed Chief of Staff in command of the "Sons of Veterans Reserves" by the Commander-in-Chief, I hereby assume command with headquarters at 2510 West Lehigh Ave., Philadelphia, Pa.

II. The following appointments are hereby announced:

Theodore A. Reed, Philadelphia, Pa., Assistant Adjutant General

John H. Leonard, Rumford, Rhode Island, Assistant Quartermaster General

E. R. Campbell, Washington, D. C., Assistant Inspector General

All of the above officers to hold the rank of Lieutenant Colonel.

Edwin J. Prittie, of Philadelphia, Pa., Aide-de-Camp, assigned to duty in office of the Assistant Adjutant General.

W. Harry Moore, Washington, D. C., Aide-de-Camp, assigned to duty in office of Assistant Inspector General.

The aforesaid officers to rank as Captain.

III. Division Commanders are respectfully requested to promulgate these orders and lend their valuable assistance in encouraging the formation of military companies. The commanding officers of all companies, battalions and regiments will report a full roster of their command to the assistant Inspector General, Lieut. Colonel E. R. Campbell, Washington, D. C.

A copy of these rosters will also be forwarded to assistant Adjt. General, Lieut. Colonel Theodore A. Reed at these headquarters, 2510 West Lehigh Ave., Philadelphia, Pa.

IV. Companies, battalions and regiments will be organized in accordance with United States Army regulations.

V. The uniform as adopted by the Commandery-in-Chief is as follows:

Officers — Dark blue sack coat, single breasted, standing collar, with regulation S. V. Reserve insignia on points of collar. Concealed fastenings, slit at side for hooking up sabre. Coat trimmed with $1^{1}/_{4}$ inch lustrous flat black mohair braid.

Trousers of light blue cloth with $1^{1}/_{2}$ inch stripe, color of stripe to correspond to arm of service.

Cap. U. S. Army regulation (latest pattern). The several States may have a miniature division mark on the breast of the eagle in place of the shield.

Sabre and Belt. Latest U. S. Army regulation.

Non-Commissioned Officers and Privates — Single breasted sack coat, rolling collar. Light blue pantaloons. Cap. U. S. Army pattern, trimmed with metal cross guns, sabre or cannon, according to the arm of service, with number of regiment in the upper angle and letter of troop, battery or company in lower angle.

Laced canvas leggins, dark blue woven webb, concealed hook fastening.

Chevrons and trouser stripes to correspond with the arm of the service.

A full company will be entitled to the following non-commissioned officers:

One First Sergeant.
One Quartermaster Sergeant.
Three Duty Sergeant.
Six Corporals.

VI. All communications, reports and requests for information will be addressed to the Assistant Adjutant General, Lieut. Colonel Theodore A. Reed.

VII. As this department is largely experimental and wholly in the interests of the Order of Sons of Veterans, and believing from years of experience that it will prove one of the most potent factors in building up the Order and increasing its numerical strength, we earnestly solicit the hearty support and co-operation of every member of the Order.

The Assistant Adjutant General will cheerfully respond to any request for information.

By order of
R. M. J. Reed,
Brig. Gen'l and Chief of Staff

Attest:

Theodore A. Reed,
Assistant Adj. Gen'l.

Headquarters Commandery-in-Chief,
Sons of Veterans, U. S. A.,
Room 535, Banigan Building,
Providence, R. I., November 20, 1903.

"Approved." Division Commanders will promulgate to all camps in their respective Divisions.

ARTHUR B. SPINK,
Commander-in-Chief

Attest:

Wm. R. Congdon
Adjutant General

Sons of Union Veterans at Bristol, Pennsylvania on November 1, 1929. Several are wearing NJ belt buckles. (JLO)

Jacob Ten Eck Camp #154, Albany, NY circa 1920. (JLO)

Sons' Memorial University

By Gary L. Gibson

The year 1901 was a year of change and progress. At the 20th National Encampment held at Providence, Rhode Island, more changes were made in the Sons of Veterans than any previous encampment.

The encampment was presided over by Commander-in-Chief Edgar W. Alexander, of Reading, PA. It is recorded that the membership was greatly depressed by the death of President William McKinley. Edward R. Campbell, of Washington, D.C., was elected Commander-in-Chief. Bro. Campbell, interestingly, was a Civil War veteran, and a member of the Grand Army of the Republic.

At the encampment, The Constitution and Regulations were thoroughly revised, being cut to about two-thirds in content. The *Banner* was formally adopted as the official publication of the Order, and replaced the *National Reveille*, which was printed in Chicago, IL. An increase in the per capita tax of 5¢ was to cover printing and mailing costs. Another increase in fees and dues was the Muster Fee, or as we now call it, the application fee. The fee was raised to $3.00. Fifty cents of this was earmarked for Sons' Memorial University.

Sons' Memorial University was the dream of Captain Alexander Lewis Sorter, Jr., of Minneapolis, MN. Brother Sorter was the son of A.L. Sorter, 20th Ohio Battery. For several years, Brother Sorter talked of his dream at the National Encampments to all who would listen, and all told him that it couldn't be done. Finally, at the 1900 National Encampment in Syracuse, New York, it was voted to establish Memorial University, as "the greatest memorial to the men and women of the Civil War". SMU was to be the "Harvard of the West".

The campus was placed on "Patriot Hill", just south of the Mason City, Iowa limits. Mason City was chosen for several reasons. Foremost, its central location. Also, with accessibility by five trunklines of railway, modern water works, gas, electricity, paved streets, and streetcars, Mason City was the ideal location for a great seat of learning. Another factor was that Mason City had no saloons. It was felt that with all the young men coming to the area, a "dry city" would be a great asset.

The campus was comprised of forty acres. The only collegiate building built was the Liberal Arts building, a three story limestone structure. It contained over thirty large classrooms, a chapel with seating for 400, and the library of 4,500 volumes. In the basement were the gymnasium and the armory. The building was built at a cost of $75,000, the money given by the citizens of Mason City.

Also on campus were the dormitories; Lincoln Hall for men, and Barton Hall for women. (Named for Clara Barton). The cost for accommodations was $1.00 per week.

The college also had its own electric railway station. Other buildings that were planned, but never built, were the Administration building, a library building, a Civil War Museum, and a National Headquarters building for the Sons of Veterans.

The cornerstone for the Liberal Arts building was laid June 26, 1901. The *Mason City Globe-Gazette* carried the Headline MEMORIAL UNIVERSITY CORNERSTONE LAID, and THE DAY OF JUBILEE IS HERE. The entire front page of the paper was devoted to the event. There was a parade consisting of members of the Grand Army of the Republic, Sons of Veterans, Women's Relief Corps, Daughters of Veterans, and many other civic organizations. At the formal ceremonies, several prominent citizens and officers of the GAR and Sons spoke to the immense crowd. The exercises were held in a big circus tent formerly owned by the Ringling Bros. Circus. The tent seated five thousand people, and was not able to hold everyone.

On Wednesday, September 10th, 1902, the building was formally opened to students. A dedication ceremony was postponed until arrangements could be made. The guest of honor was to be President Theodore Roosevelt. No record has been found as of this writing to tell if a dedication took place or not.

The college offered the usual courses of study: the Normal (Teachers) College, Commercial College, School of Oratory, and College of Music. Memorial University also offered two "unique" courses of study. The School of Military Science and Tactics, which may be comparable with today's ROTC, and the School of Applied Patriotism.

The June, 1908 college catalog states that "Applied Patriotism was a year long course and begins with the origin and development of government, followed by a brief study of constitutional liberty in England, leading up to the adoption of the Constitution of the United States. Throughout the course, special stress is laid upon the duties and applications of citizenship and the necessity of early and thorough preparation for them."

The first graduating class was the class of 1903, with seven students receiving diplomas. The biggest class was 1908, with ten graduates. The University was not a large school, as was originally planned.

Overall, only forty-six students graduated from SMU. The college was closed in 1910, presumably from lack of enrollment, and perhaps, support. The evidence for this is that no other buildings were ever built.

The building was used for many years as a school building by the Mason City school system. Sometime in the 1980s, the old Liberal Arts building was torn down.

Sons of Union Veterans of the Civil War Act of Incorporation By The Congress of The United States

SONS OF UNION VETERANS OF THE CIVIL WAR
INCORPORATION
Chapter 774 — Public Law 605

(H. R. 8034)

August 20, 1954

An Act for the Incorporation of the Sons of Union Veterans of the Civil War.

Be it enacted by the Senate and House of Representatives of the United States of America in Congress assembled, That:

The following named persons to wit: General of the Army Douglas MacArthur, New York; Major General Amos A. Fries, retired, and Major General Ulysses S. Grant, 3d, retired, Washington, District of Columbia; Charles Boynton, Long Beach, California; Frank Worner, Inglewood, California; Wilbur Corsey, Fresno, California; Roy A. Davis, Colorado Springs, Colorado; Argus Ogborn, Richmond, Indiana; Thomas M. Horn, Lafayette, Indiana; Alonzo R. Standfield, Indianapolis, Indiana; Roy J. Bennett, Des Moines, Iowa; Homer L. Young, Waterloo, Iowa; Dr. L. L. Shoppe, Des Moines, Iowa; E. S. Spangler, Newton, Kansas; A. P. Phillips, Newton, Kansas; William Dix, Newton, Kansas; F. Harold Dubord, Waterville, Maine; Hon. Burleigh Martin, Augusta, Maine; General William E. Southard, Bangor, Maine; George W. Kimball, Chelsea, Massachusetts; Brigadier General Otis M. Whitney, Concord, Massachusetts; Charles H. E. Moran, Holyoke, Massachusetts; Governor Alvan Tufts Fuller, Boston, Massachusetts; Charles R. Cowdin, Detroit, Michigan; Birt Hammond, Jackson, Michigan; Charles F. Dexter, Detroit, Michigan; Donald F. Peacock, Detroit, Michigan; Dewey B. Mead, Minneapolis, Minnesota; Donald C. Bennyhof, Hennepin County, Minnesota; William A. Anderson, Minneapolis, Minnesota; Laurence J. Parker, Bennington, New Hampshire; Wallace L. Mason, Keene, New Hampshire; Cleon E. Heald, Keene, New Hampshire; Colonel Edward Black, retired, Bennington, New Hampshire; Albert C. Lambert, Trenton, New Jersey; Colonel Frederic G. Bauer, Ridgewood, New Jersey; Charles A. Otto, Elizabeth, New Jersey; C. Wesley Armstrong, Trenton, New Jersey; Doctor Karl Rothschild, New Brunswick; Rev. Hermon L. Brockway, Ithaca, New York; William M. Coffin, Cincinnati, Ohio; Homer A. Ramey, Toledo, Ohio; Miles S. Kuhn, Dayton, Ohio; S. Anselm Skelton, Portsmouth, Ohio; Frederick K. Davis, Eugene, Oregon; Doctor W. E. Buchanan, Eugene, Oregon; Austin D. McReynolds, Eugene, Oregon; Glenn L. Adams, Salem, Oregon; John H. Runkle, Harrisburg, Pennsylvania; C. Leroy Stoudt, Reading, Pennsylvania; Walter C. Mabie, Philadelphia, Pennsylvania; Edgar L. Gale, Seattle, Washington; Edward T. Fairchild, Madison, Wisconsin; Roland J. Steinie, Milwaukee, Wisconsin; Lyall T. Beggs, Madison, Wisconsin; and Doctor William Martin Lamera, Wauwatosa, Wisconsin; and their successors, are hereby created and declared to be a body corporate of the District of Columbia, where its legal domicile shall be, by the name of the Sons of Union Veterans of the Civil War (hereinafter referred to as the corporation), and by such name shall be known and have perpetual succession and the powers, limitations, and restrictions herein contained.

Sec. 2. A majority of the persons named in the first section of this Act, acting in person or by written proxy, are authorized to complete the organization of the corporation by the selection of officers and employees, the adoption of a constitution and bylaws not inconsistent with this Act, and the doing of such other acts as may be necessary for this purpose.

Sec. 3. The purposes of the corporation shall be: To perpetuate the memory of the Grand Army of the Republic and of the men who saved the Union in 1861 to 1865; to assist in every practicable way in the preservation and making a available for research of documents and records pertaining to the Grand Army of the Republic and its members; to cooperate in doing honor to all those who have patriotically served our country in any war; to teach patriotism and the duties of citizenship, the true history of our country, and the love and honor of our flag; to oppose every tendency or movement that would weaken loyalty to, or make for the destruction or impairment of, our constitutional Union; and to inculcate and broadly sustain the American principles of representative government, of equal rights, and of impartial justice for all.

Sec. 4. The corporation shall have power —

(1) to have succession by its corporate name;

(2) to sue and be sued, complain or defend in any court of competent jurisdiction;

(3) to adopt, use, and alter a corporate seal;

(4) to choose such officers, managers, agents, and employees as the activities of the corporation may require;

(5) to adopt, amend, and alter a constitution and bylaws; not inconsistent with the laws of the United States or any State in which the corporation is to operate, for the management of its property and the regulation of its affairs;

(6) to contract and be contracted with;

(7) to take by lease, gift, purchase, grant, devise, or bequest from any public body or agency or any private corporation, association, partnership, firm, or individual and to hold absolutely or in trust for any of the purposes of the corporation any property, real, personal, or mixed, necessary or convenient for attaining the objects and carrying into effect the purposes of the corporation, subject, however, to applicable provisions of law of any State (A) governing the amount or kind of property which may be held by, or (B) otherwise limiting or controlling the ownership of property by, a corporation operating in such a State;

(8) to transfer, convey, lease, sublease, encumber and otherwise alienate real, personal, or mixed property; and

(9) to borrow money for the purposes of the corporation, issue bonds therefor, and secure the same by mortgage, deed of trust, pledge or otherwise, subject in every case to all applicable provisions of Federal and State laws; and

(10) to do any and all acts and things necessary and proper to carry out the objects and purposes of the corporation.

Sec. 5. Eligibility for membership in the corporation and the rights, privileges, and designation of classes of members shall, except as provided in this Act, be determined as the constitution and bylaws of the corporation may provide. Eligibility for membership in the corporation shall be limited to male blood relatives of persons who served between April 12, 1861, and April 9, 1865, as soldiers or sailors of the United States Army, Navy, Marine Corps or Revenue-Cutter Service, and of such State regiments as were called into active service and were subject to orders of United States general officers between the dates above mentioned and were honorably discharged therefrom at the close of such service or who died in such service.

Sec. 6. The supreme governing authority of the corporation shall be the national encampment thereof, composed of such officers and elected representatives from the several States and other local subdivisions of the corporate organization as shall be provided by the constitution and bylaws: *Provided*, That the form of the government of the corporation shall always be representative of the membership at large and shall not permit the concentration of the control thereof in the hands of a limited number of members or in a self-perpetuating group not so representative. The meetings of the national encampment may be held in any State or Territory or in the District of Columbia.

Sec. 7. (a) During the intervals between the national encampments, the council of administration shall be the governing board of the corporation and shall be responsible for the general policies, program, and activities of the corporation.

(b) Upon the enactment of this Act the membership of the initial council of administration of the corporation shall consist of the present members of the council of administration of the Sons of Union Veterans of the Civil War, the corporation described in section 18 of this Act, or such of them as may then be living and are qualified members of said council of administration, to wit: Major General Ulysses S. Grant 3d, retired; Dewey B. Mead; Reverend Hermon L. Brockway; Laurence J. Parker; George W. Kimball; Frederick K. Davis; and Albert C. Lambert.

(c) Thereafter, the council of administration of the corporation shall consist of not less than seven members elected in the manner and for the term prescribed in the constitution and bylaws of the corporation.

Sec. 8. The officers of the corporation shall be a commander in chief, a senior vice commander in chief, a junior vice commander in chief, a secretary and a treasurer (which latter two offices may be held by one person), and such other officers as may be prescribed in the constitution and bylaws. The officers of the corporation shall be selected in such manner and for such terms and with such duties and titles as may be prescribed in the constitution and bylaws of the corporation.

Sec. 9. (a) The principal office of the corporation shall be located in Trenton, New Jersey, or in such other place as may be determined by the council of administration; but the activities of the corporation shall not be confined to that place, but may be conducted throughout the United States, the District of Columbia, and Territories and possessions of the United States.

(b) The corporation shall have in the District of Columbia at all times a designated agent authorized to accept service of process for the corporation; and notice to or service upon such agent, or mailed to the business address of such agent, shall be deemed notice to or service upon the corporation.

Sec. 10. (a) No part of the income or assets of the corporation shall inure to any of its members or officers as such, or be distributable to any of them during the life of the corporation or upon its dissolution or final liquidation. Nothing in this subsection, however, shall be construed to prevent the payment of compensation to officers of the corporation or reimbursement for actual necessary expenses in amounts approved by the council of administration of the corporation.

(b) The corporation shall not make loans to its officers or employees. Any member of the council of administration who votes for or assents to the making of a loan or advance to an officer or employee of the corporation, and any officer who participates in the making of such a loan or advance, shall be jointly and severally liable to the corporation for the amount of such loan until the repayment thereof.

Sec. 11. The corporation and its officers and agents as such shall not contribute to or otherwise support or assist any political party or candidate for public office.

Sec. 12. The corporation shall be liable for the acts of its officers and agents when acting within the scope of their authority.

Sec. 13. The corporation shall have no power to issue any shares of stock or to declare or pay any dividends.

Sec. 14. The corporation shall keep correct and complete books and records of account and shall keep minutes of the proceedings of its national encampments and council of administration. All books and records of the corporation may be inspected by any member, or his agent or attorney, for any proper purpose, at any reasonable time.

Sec. 15. (a) The financial transactions of the corporation shall be audited annually by an independent certified public accountant in accordance with the principles and procedures applicable to commercial corporate transactions. The audit shall be conducted at the place or places where the accounts of the corporation are normally kept. All books, accounts, financial records, reports, files, and all other papers, things, or property belonging to or in use by the corporation and necessary to facilitate the audit shall be made available to the person or persons conducting the audit; and full facilities for verifying transactions with the balances or securities held by depositories, fiscal agents, and custodians shall be afforded to such person or persons.

(b) A report of such audit shall be made by the corporation to the Congress not later than March 1 of each year. The report shall set forth the scope of the audit and shall include a verification by the person or persons conducting the audit of statements of (1) assets and liabilities, (2) capital and surplus and deficit, (3) surplus or deficit analysis, (4) income and expense, and (5) sources and application of funds. Such report shall not be printed as a public document.

Sec. 16. On or before March 1 of each year the corporation shall report to the Congress on its activities during the preceding fiscal year. Such report may consist of a report on the proceedings of the National Encampment covering such fiscal year. Such report shall not be printed as a public document.

Sec. 17. The corporation and its subordinate divisions shall have the sole and exclusive right to use the name, the Sons of Union Veterans of the Civil War. The corporation shall have the exclusive and sole right to use, or to allow or refuse the use of, such emblems, seals, and badges as have heretofore been used by the Illinois corporation described in section 18 and the right to which may be lawfully transferred to the corporation.

Sec. 18. The corporation may acquire the assets of the Sons of Union Veterans of the Civil War, a corporation organized under the laws of the State of Illinois, upon discharging or satisfactorily providing for the payment and discharge of all the liability of such corporation and upon complying with all laws of the State of Illinois applicable thereto.

Sec. 19. Upon dissolution or final liquidation of the corporation, after discharge or satisfaction of all outstanding obligations and liabilities, the remaining assets, if any, of the corporation shall be distributed in accordance with the determination of the council of administration and in compliance with the constitution and bylaws of the corporation and all Federal and State laws applicable thereto.

Sec. 20. The right to alter, amend, or repeal this Act is expressly reserved.

Roster of Departments (Divisions) Past and Present

	Chartered	Disbanded
Alabama & Tennessee	March 12, 1889	1945
Arkansas	May 1889	1894
California & Pacific	July 1, 1886	*
Colorado & Wyoming	March 22, 1929	*
Connecticut	May 15, 1883	*
Dakota	1885	1905
Florida	1886	1893
Gulf	1895	1900
Idaho	June 26, 1911	1915
Illinois	July 1883	*
Indiana	June 12, 1885	*
Iowa	June 2, 1883	*
Kansas	June 1883	1971
Kentucky	1887	1919
Maine	April 10, 1883	*
Maryland	June 15, 1887	*
Massachusetts	July 17, 1882	*
Michigan	June 24, 1884	*
Minnesota	January 1, 1885	1975
Missouri	June 2, 1883	1955
Montana	1887	1895
Montana & Idaho	1915	1919
Nebraska & Oklahoma	September 2, 1884	1985
New Hampshire	August 1883	*
New Jersey	June 14, 1883	*
New York	November 6, 1883	*
North Dakota	July 23, 1889	1891
Ohio	August 1, 1883	*
Oklahoma	July 25, 1891	1892
Oregon [1]		
Pennsylvania [2]	July 4, 1882	*
Rhode Island	February 14, 1884	*
Southwest (Texas & Oklahoma)	May 13, 1995	*
Vermont	October 1883	*
Washington [1]	January 1, 1890	
Washington & Oregon [1]		
West Virginia	1886	1905
Wisconsin	September 1887	*

* Currently active departments

[1] The states of Washington and Oregon were seperate departments and joint departments so many times, (at least three), that it would be too confusing to try to list them all here.

[2] From 1882 to 1887, Pennsylvania was divided into two divisions (departments), Eastern PA, and Western PA. This was due to the fact that the west was of A.P. Davis' organization, and the east was of the Earp Sons of Veterans. By 1887, most all the Earp camps had joined with Davis or disbanded.

Badges of the Sons of Union Veterans of the Civil War

Membership Badge

War Medal

Fifty Years Membership Badge

Past Camp Commander's Badge

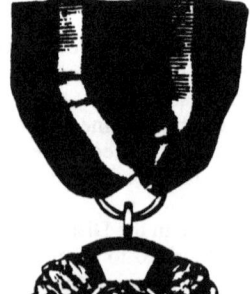

Past Department Commander's Badge

Past Commander-in-Chief's Badge

The Grand Army of the Republic

About a decade before the Sons of Union Veterans of the Civil War was formed, another organization of veterans was created to preserve "those kind and fraternal feelings, which have bound together the comrades in arms of many battles, sieges, and marches." The name of this organization was the Grand Army of the Republic.

The GAR really began in 1864, in the tent of Major Benjamin F. Stephenson and Chaplain W. J. Rutledge. They became close friends and often spoke of a time when they might be able to come together in the comforts of their homes, rather than at the site of battle. Chaplain Rutledge suggested that many of the Union soldiers might wish to form some sort of organization by which to preserve friendships and memories. Major Stephenson and the chaplain therefore agreed: They would help each other to form such an organization if they both survived the war.

After the war ended, the two men kept in close contact via correspondence, and many of the letters that flew back and forth concerned this organization they wished to form. They met again in Springfield, Illinois, in March 1866 to compile the ritual for their new order.

Their plans were grand: to gather together in one organization former soldiers from all divisions, Army and Navy, that had served in the War of the Rebellion, so that they might be able to renew friendships and reexamine the days of strife they had passed through.

They had much assistance in their endeavor. Among their helpers were Richard J. Oglesby, governor of Illinois, who had been a soldier, and Mayor A. A. North, Col. John M. Snyder, Mayor Robert M. Woods. They held their organizational meetings at the office of Drs. Allen and Hamilton, and also in the office of John M. Snyder, then secretary to Gov. Oglesby.

The men searched for a name for their organization, finally deciding upon "The Grand Army of the Republic." During the dedication of the Bronze Tablet marking the building where the organization was founded, Robert Mann Woods told how the name was decided upon:

> *The selection of the name of the order, 'The Grand Army of the Republic' was an inspiration of genius in Dr. Stephenson. The name was suggested by Napoleon's 'Grand Army of France,' which was changed to adapt it to this republic, adding, it has not only given great strength to the order from the beginning, but like the uniform of a soldier, it has enveloped us in a halo of glory in the eyes of the people in this and every other land.*

Two former soldiers, I. N. Coltrin and Joseph Prior, owned a printing business in Decatur, Illinois. Dr. Stephenson instructed Capt. John S. Phelps of Springfield to go to Decatur, have the ritual printed at their place of business, and swear the two men into the organization. Other soldiers in the area became interested, including Col. I. C. Pugh, Col. J. H. Nale, Major George R. Steele, Capt. M. F. Kanan, Capt. George H. Dunning, and Capt. Chris Riebsame. Their enthusiasm was so great that they were named Post 1 on April 6, 1866 by Commander-in-Chief Stephenson.

But before this naming, on April 1, Dr. Stephenson first instituted the department of Illinois in order to charter posts and districts. This is the first order ever issued within the GAR:

**Headquarters Department of Illinois,
Grand Army of the Republic,
Adjutant-General's Office,
Springfield, Illinois, April 1st, 1866.**

GENERAL ORDERS
  No. 1
  The following named officers are hereby announced on duty at these headquarters:
  Colonel Jules C. Webber, Aid-de-Camp and Chief of Staff.
  Major Robert M. Woods, Adjutant-General.
  Colonel John M. Snyder, Quartermaster-General.
  Lieutenant John S. Phelps, Aid-de-Camp.
  Captain John A. Lightfoot, Assistant Adjutant-General.

By order of
B. F. STEPHENSON,
Commanding Department

ROBERT M. WOODS,
  Adjutant-General.

One of the organizers of Post 1, Capt. M. F. Kanan, told the following story about the formation of the organization, as related by his comrade W. F. Calhoun:

> *On the eve of Friday, April 6, 1866, twelve veterans of the Civil War, with their teacher, B. F. Stephenson, might have been seen quietly turning the corner, walking with the serious tread of veterans going into battle. They passed up a stairway to a second floor room in a building and there under the direction of their leader, Major Stephenson, formed the first Post of the Grand Army of the Republic, the greatest patriotic, the most comradely and unselfish organization that was ever known up to that time since the lowly Nazarene with his twelve apostles traversed the hills and valley of Galilee.*

> *They carried with them posters, some triangular, some square, bearing the letters G. A. R. printed in large bold type. These were posted all over the town that night and when the residents arose the next morning they were amazed at the sight of the cabalistic letters. Gathered in groups they discussed the strange sight but could not decide what they meant. Today the letters G. A. R. are familiar to people everywhere. Thus the Grand Army of the Republic was started.*

The charter of Post 1 reads as follows:

**GRAND ARMY OF THE REPUBLIC
DEPARTMENT OF ILLINOIS**

To all whom it may concern, greeting:

Know ye, that the Commander of the Department of Illinois, reposing special trust and confidence in the patriotism and fidelity of M. F. Kanan, G. R. Steele, George H. Dunning, I. C. Pugh, J. H. Nale, J. T. Bishop, C. Riebsame, J. W. Routh, B. F. Sibley, I. N. Coltrin, Joseph Prior, and A. Toland, does, by the authority in him vested, empower and constitute them Charter members of an encampment of the Grand Army of the Republic, to be known as Post 1, of Decatur, District of Macon, Department of Illinois, and they are hereby constituted as said Post, and authorized to make Bylaws for the government of said Post and to do and perform all acts necessary to conduct and carry on said organizations in accordance with the Constitution of the Grand Army of the Republic.

Done at Springfield, Illinois, this 6th day of April, 1866.

B.F. STEPHENSON,
Commander of Department.

ROBERT M. WOODS,
Adjutant-General

Article I, of the GAR Constitution, provided the "Declaration of Principles":

"SECTION 1. The soldiers of the volunteer army of the United States during the rebellion of 1861-1865, actuated by the impulses and convictions of patriotism and of eternal right, and combined in the strong hands of fellowship and unity by the toils, the dangers and the victories of a long and victoriously waged war, feel themselves called upon to declare, in definite form of words and in determined co-operative action, those principles and rules which should guide the honest patriot, the enlightened freeman and the consistent citizen in his course of action, and to agree upon those plans and laws which should govern them in a united and systematic working method, with which, in some manner, shall be effected the preservation of the grand results of the war, the fruits of their labor and toil, so as to benefit the deserving and the worthy."

The GAR met in its first convention in Indianapolis, Indiana, on November 20, 1866. Representatives were present from Illinois, Missouri, Kansas, Ohio, Iowa, Wisconsin, New York, Pennsylvania, Kentucky, Indiana, and the District of Columbia.

The organization's objectives as originally set down were:

1. The preservation of those kind and fraternal feelings, which have bound together the comrades in arms of many battles, sieges and marches;

2. To make these ties available in works and results of kindness, of favor and material aid to those in need of assistance;

3. To make provision, where it is not already done, for the support, care and education of soldiers' orphans, and for the maintenance of the widows of deceased soldiers;

4. For the protection and assistance of disabled soldiers, whether disabled by wounds, sickness, old age or misfortune;

Membership Badge
of the Grand Army of the Republic

5. For the establishment and defense of the late soldiery of the United States, morally, socially, and politically, with a view to inculcate a proper appreciation of their services to the country, and to a recognition of such services and claims by the American people.

Membership in the GAR was open to "all soldiers, sailors of the United States Army, Navy, or Marine Corps, who served between April 12, 1861 and April 9, 1865, having been honorably discharged therefrom after such service, and of such State regiments as were called to active service and subject to the orders of the U. S. General Officers, between the dates mentioned.

"No person shall be eligible for membership who has, at any time, borne arms against the United States."

In 1868, the GAR made clear its position on political tendencies within the membership. At the National Encampment in January in Philadelphia, Pennsylvania, they added the following clause to the fifth section of their Declaration of Principles:

"This organization does not design to make nominations for office, or to use its influence as a secret organization for partisan purposes."

And in 1869, the following was added to the Rules and Regulations:

"No officer or comrade of the Grand Army of the Republic shall in any manner, use this organization for partisan purposes, and no discussion of partisan questions shall be permitted at any of its meetings; nor shall any nominations for political office be made."

President Taft escorted by the GAR, Middletown, Connecticut on November 12, 1909. (GLG)

Unidentified GAR Post. (GLG)

The Influence of the GAR

Despite the prohibitions against political activity within the GAR, the organization wielded a strong arm in politics. It is said that the "GAR vote" put the following Civil War commanders into the office of the presidency of the United States: Grant, Hayes, Garfield, Arthur, Harrison, and McKinley. The "Bloody Shirt" was waved many times in Congress by veterans looking for increased benefits and pensions.

Besides establishing Memorial Day and veterans pensions, the GAR's influence is still felt today. The flying of the U. S. flag in front of schools and public buildings is a tradition established by the old soldiers. Many veterans' hospitals and facilities are the result of the GAR's clout. The creation of national military parks, such as Gettysburg and Chickamagua were fostered by the GAR.

The Grand Army supported the war efforts from the Spanish American War in 1898 through the Korean War. Today's veterans owe a debt of gratitude to the Civil War veterans for help in establishing their organizations, such as the Veterans of Foreign Wars and the American Legion.

National GAR Encampments

The national encampments of the Grand Army of the Republic were massive affairs. Major U. S. cities would vie for consideration as host. Thousands of veterans, the Women's Relief Corps, the Sons of Union Veterans, Daughters of Union Veterans, the Ladies of the Grand Army of the Republic, and the Auxiliary to the Sons of the Union Veterans, would all crowd into the chosen city for the week-long affair.

In fact, so many people attended from across the country that railroads re-organized their schedules, rerouted trains, and gave special rates to accommodate the crowds. In the cities themselves, there was often not enough hotel space, so special tent cities were set up.

The national encampments were held in various cities in almost every Union state, but some cities were more popular than others. Indianapolis, Indiana, hosted nine encampments, while Boston, Massachusetts, and Grand Rapids, Michigan, tied at five each. Washington, D. C., and Des Moines, Iowa hosted four each. Three states — Vermont, New Hampshire, and Delaware — never hosted a national encampment.

The highlight of the encampments was the Grand Parade. The veterans would line up by state and march down the main street with their flags flying and the fifes and drums playing. The Sons of Union Veterans would supply an "escort" of not less than 100 members. The parade was reviewed by the Commander-in-Chief of the GAR, the President of the United States, the Cabinet, senators, congressmen, governors, and other dignitaries.

The End of the GAR

As time passed, the "thin blue line," as the Union veterans were known, withered and faded away. No longer would the "river of blue" pass through the cities and villages of America. The GAR no longer wielded the power they once had, but they still commanded the respect of all.

Little Brown Button

The Little Brown Button,
   The sacred bronze button;
The Grand Army Button
   He wears on his coat.
"How much did it cost?"
   Said a man to the soldier,
"That flat little button
   You wear on your coat?"
"Ten cents in good money,"
   He answered the stranger,
"And four years of marching
   And fighting to boot."
The wealth of the world
   Cannot purchase this emblem
Except that the buyer
   Once wore the brave blue;
And it shows to mankind
   The full marks of a hero:
A man, who to honor
   And Country, was true.

It was common for local newspapers to run stories on the last remaining veteran(s) at nearby GAR posts in the late 1920s and 1930s.

The last Union veteran, and also the last veteran of the Civil War, was Albert Woolson of Duluth, Minnesota. Mr. Woolson was a drummer with the 1st Minnesota Heavy Artillery. He died on August 2, 1956 at age 109.

The Grand Army Button

The Grand Army Button is a bronze, star-rimmed circle made from cannon captured in decisive battles of the Civil War and donated by Congress for this purpose. In the center of the circle is the Goddess of Liberty representing Loyalty, the rallying word of the Grand Army of the Republic and its Auxiliary, the Women's Relief Corps. On one side of the Goddess stands a Union soldier and on the other side a Union sailor. These two are clasping hands to represent Fraternity, which would bind in closer ties the men who followed the Flag upon the land and those who fought beneath the folds upon the sea.

Two little children kneeling before the Goddess are receiving benediction and assurance of protection from the comrades who offered all they possessed upon the altar of their country. This represents Charity — the Charity which would protect and care for the needy ones among the Nation's defenders — their widows, wives and little ones.

On each side of the central group is the National Flag. Under one Flag is an eagle to represent Freedom; under the other is an axe and bundle of rods to represent Union. The stars in the rim represent the states of the Union and the Departments comprising the Grand Army of the Republic.

Published bi-monthly by the Commandery-in-Chief, Sons of Union Veterans of the Civil War
Organized 1881—the only male organization recognized by the Grand Army of the Republic
Chartered by Act of Congress

Volume 60   265 Erie Street, Owego, N. Y., July- August, 1956   No. 4

CONFIRMATORY DEED OF CONVEYANCE

On February 25, 1956. Albert Woolson, acting Commander-in-Chief and sole surviving member of the Grand Army of the Republic, executed a Confirmatory Deed of Conveyance which ratified and confirmed the original deed dated February 13, 1954 which "grants, bargains, sells and conveys to the Sons of Union Veterans of the Civil War. a corporation created by Act of Congress of August 20, 1954, all the property, real and personal, tangible and intangible, conveyed by said deed of February 13, 1954 . . ."

The following are photostatic copies of the Judgment and certificate recently issued by the United States District Court for the District of Columbia.

IN THE UNITED STATES DISTRICT COURT FOR THE DISTRICT OF COLUMBIA

In re
GRAND ARMY OF THE REPUBLIC
    Petitioner

No. 3966-54

Filed June 15, 1956
Harry M. Hull, Clerk

JUDGMENT

Upon consideration of the motion filed herein by Sons of Union Veterans of the Civil War, a corporation created by Act of Congress, representing that it is the successor of Commandery-in-Chief, Sons of Union Veterans of the Civil War, the grantee in a certain deed from the Grand Army of the Republic dated February 13, 1954, and confirmed by this Court on December 22, 1954, and praying for confirmation of a certain confirmatory deed to it from the Grand Army of the Republic dated February 25, 1956, made for the purpose of correcting a clerical error in said deed of February 13, 1954, a copy of said confirmatory deed being filed in this Court and the original being submitted to the Court for inspection, and it appearing to the Court that the allegations of said motion are true and that the purpose of said confirmatory deed is to carry out the true intent and purpose of the original deed of February 13, 1954, it is this fifteenth day of June, A.D. 1956, by the Court,

ORDERED, Adjudged and decreed that the title and ownership of the property covered by said deeds of February 13, 1954 and February 25, 1956, be and hereby is vested in Sons of Union Veterans of the Civil War, a corporation created by Act of Congress approved August 20, 1954.

/s/ Alexander Holtzoff
    JUDGE.

A TRUE COPY
TEST:
HARRY M. HULL, Clerk
By Doris L. Fisher
    Deputy Clerk

A. O. Form 105   Exemplification Certificate

United States District Court
for the
DISTRICT OF COLUMBIA

I, HARRY M. HULL, Clerk of the United States District Court for the District of Columbia, and keeper of the records and seal thereof, hereby certify that the document attached hereto is a true and correct copy of the Judgment No. 3966-54 and filed June 15, 1956. (and further according to the record no appeal has been perfected to date)

In testimony whereof I hereunto sign my name and affix the seal of said Court, in said District, at Washington, D. C., this 11th day of July 1956.
HARRY M. HULL, CLERK
By: Doris L. Fisher
    Deputy Clerk.

I, RICHMOND B. KEECH, United States District Judge for the District of Columbia, do hereby certify that HARRY M. HULL whose name is above written and subscribed, is and was at the date thereof, Clerk of said Court, duly appointed and sworn, and keeper of the records and seal thereof, and that the above certificate by him made, and his attestation or record thereof, is in due form of law.

July 11th, 1956

    United States District Judge.

I, HARRY M. HULL, Clerk of the United States District Court for the District of Columbia, and keeper of the seal thereof, hereby certify that the Honorable RICHMOND B. KEECH whose name is within written and subscribed, was on the 11th day of July 1956, and now is Judge of said court, duly appointed, confirmed, sworn, and qualified; and that I am well acquainted with his handwriting and official signature and know and hereby certify the same within written to be his.

In testimony whereof I hereunto sign my name, and affix the seal of said Court at the city of Washington, in said District, on this 11th day of July 1956.
HARRY M. HULL, CLERK
By: Doris L. Fisher
    Deputy Clerk.

Grand Army of the Republic Recognition

From the official proceedings of the Grand Army of the Republic the following Resolutions are quoted, showing the official recognition of our Order, by the Parent Order, from our earliest history to the recent past.

From resolution adopted at the 15th Annual Encampment, Grand Army of the Republic, June, 1881, we quote: "The Sons of Veterans are all that their name implies; that they are of the best blood of the land, and as such should be encouraged in following the footsteps of their illustrious predecessors."

From the report of the committee on the address of Commander-in-Chief Van Dervoort, at the 17th Annual Encampment, July, 1883: "Resolved, That we hail with pleasure all organizations having for their object the perpetuity of the principles which are dear to us, and we recognize in the Sons of Veterans of the U.S.A. one that is entitled to the support of all comrades of the Grand Army of the Republic."

Resolution adopted at the 22nd Annual Encampment, September, 1888: "Resolved, That this encampment endorse the objects and purposes of the Order of the Sons of Veterans, U.S.A., and hereby give to that Order official recognition of the Grand Amry of the Republic and recommend that Comrades aid and encourage the institution of Camps of Sons of Veterans, U.S.A.

At the 23rd Annual Encampment, Milwaukee, Wis., August 26-28, 1889: "Resolved, By the 23rd National Encampment of the Grand Army of the Republic that the Order of the Sons of Veterans, U.S.A., be, and it is hereby recognized as the Order of Sons of Veterans, and we bid them "Godspeed" in their noble and patriotic work, and recommend to all sons of ex-Union soldiers and sailors over the age of eighteen years that they unite with that Order, so as to be prepared to take up and carry on the work of Fraternity, Charity and Loyalty and the maintenance of the Federal Union, saved and preserved by their fathers."

At the 35th Annual Encampment, Cleveland, Ohio, 1901: "Resolved, That the Sons of Veterans U.S.A., be invited to hold the Annual Encampment of their Commandery-in-Chief at the same time and place fixed for the National Encampment of the Grand Amry of the Republic."

At the 54th Annual Encampment, 1920: "Resolved, That the column of parade at such future Encampments include, First, an escort of uniformed Sons of Veterans not exceeding one hundred (100) in number."

At the 57th Annual Encampment, Milwaukee, Wis., 1923, the Committee on Rules and Regulations presented the following: "That so much of the Rules and Regulations as is necessary be amended to provide for the members of the organization of the Sons of Veterans meeting with the Post in regular session, without vote."

At the 61st Annual Encampment, Grand Rapids, Mich., August 29-September 4, 1927: "That in order that the Status of the Sons of Union Veterans of the Civil War may be more clearly indicated and determined in its relation with the Grand Army of the Republic, we have agreed upon and report for the consideration of this Encampment the following resolution, to wit:

"Resolved, That We, the Representatives of the 61st Annual Encampment of the Grand Army of the Republic, in session in Grand Rapids, Michigan, this third day of September, A. D. 1927, do hereby recognize the noble, generous and patriotic objects, aims and purposes of the Sons of Union Veterans of the Civil War, and believe that Organization to be worthy of the support and encouragement of all loyal people; and be it

"Resolved, That we cheerfully extend to the said Sons of Union Veterans of the Civil War a cordial welcome as an allied society of the Grand Army of the Republic and we bid this Organization of our Sons Godspeed in the noble work to which it is consecrated, and recommend all Departments, Posts and Comrades of the Grand Army of the Republic to accept their services on all occasions when it is proper so to do, to the end that it may increase and prosper and teach to future generations of our Nation the principles of Fraternity, Charity, and Loyalty.

At the 65th Annual Encampment, Des Moines, Iowa, September 14-17, 1931: "Resolved, That the Grand Army of the Republic establish and have given proper observance, in Memorial Day since 1868, we in National Encampment now assembled grant whatever right we have to maintain our memories and see that our graves are properly decorated on Memorial Day to the Sons of Union Veterans of the Civil War, and protest against any other Organization usurping that right in any place where a Camp of the Sons of Union Veterans exists. Unanimous vote of the Committee."

Memorial Day
Instituted May 30, 1868 — Its Origins and Purpose

The frequent inquiries from various parts of the country with regard to the origin and purpose of Memorial Day, and the erroneous statements made concerning some of the facts which have been called to my attention, impel me to put in printed form the true history of the observance.

The organization known as the Grand Army of the Republic is composed of the veteran soldiers, sailors and marines who carried the flag of the republic to victory during the great rebellion of 1861-1865. This unique and patriotic association of the loyal soldiers of the nation came into being in 1866. It spread rapidly throughout the northern states and by 1868 it had achieved a nation-wide body with national headquarters at the national capital, having department organizations embracing posts in cities and towns and a membership of several hundred thousand. Its fundamental object was expressed in the three words: "Fraternity, Charity, Loyalty."

Memorial Day Parade float in Reading, Pennsylvania circa 1930s. (GLG)

In 1868 Gen. John A. Logan, who typified the highest example of the volunteer soldier, was commander-in-chief and I was adjutant general of this splendid organization. I will not now trace its growth and influence upon the national life during the half century it has been in the nation's great school of patriotism. Its membership is rapidly yielding to the ravages of time and old age, and will in a few years cease to exist. But its spirit survives and will in the uncharted future of our beloved country continue to shed its inspiring influence so long as the sentiment of liberty and free government is the guiding motive of our people.

Early in May, 1868, I received a letter from a comrade residing in Cincinnati, O., suggesting that in some of the countries of Europe it was the custom to strew with flowers in the springtime the graves of heroes who had fallen in defense of their country, and asked if such custom would not be appropriate to commemorate the services of our comrades who had given their lives that the nation might not perish. Upon reading this letter there seemed to me to open up a great opportunity through our organization to institute observances which might grow into a custom that would help to advance its great objects, and at the same time be a fitting means of perpetuating memories of our departed comrades.

Moved by the thought which had thus been inspired. I made a rough draft on May 5, 1868, of General Orders No. 11, and took it to General Logan at the House of Representatives, who promptly approved of its issuing, and after having inserted a paragraph directed me to issue the order at once.

My object was to have the ceremonies come in a Spring month, but to postpone it to a date which would give opportunity for flowers to mature. The 31st of May that year fell upon Sunday, and so I named May 30. This is the true and only reason for having named May 30 as the date to be observed.

The order was given to The Associated Press, and was sent to all parts of the country as rapidly as telegraph and mail could convey it.

The day was observed by comrades of the Grand Army of the Republic, aided by citizens, in twenty-seven states of the Union, very imposing ceremonies were observed at the Arlington Cemetery in the District of Columbia, at which Gen. James A. Garfield, afterward President of the United States, delivered the principal address.

Annually on each succeeding 30th day of May this tribute to the loyal heroes of the Civil War has been observed.

The purpose of instituting Memorial Day very clearly appears in the General Orders, as follows:

**Headquarters Grand Army of the Republic,
Washington, D. C., May 5, 1868.**

General Orders, No. 11.

1. The 30th day of May, 1868, is designated for the purpose of strewing with flowers or otherwise decorating the graves of comrades who died in defense of their country during the late rebellion, and whose bodies now lie in almost every city, village and hamlet churchyard in the land. In this observance no form of ceremony is prescribed, but posts and comrades will in their own way arrange such fitting services and testimonials of respect as circumstances may permit.

We are organized, comrades, as our regulations tell us, for the purpose, among other things, of preserving and strengthening those kind and fraternal feelings which have bound together the soldiers, sailors and marines who united to suppress the late rebellion. What can aid more to assure this result than by cherishing tenderly the memory of our heroic dead, who made their breasts a barricade between our country and its foes? Their soldier lives were the reveille of freedom to a race in chains and their death a tattoo of rebellious tyranny in arms. We should guard their graves with sacred vigilance. All that the consecrated wealth and taste of the nation can add to their adornment and security is but a fitting tribute to the memory of her slain defenders. Let no wanton foot tread rudely on such hallowed ground. Let pleasant paths invite the coming and going to reverent visitors and fond mourners. Let no vandalism of avarice or neglect, no ravages of time, testify to the present or the coming generations that we have forgotten as a people the cost of a free and undivided republic.

If other eyes grow dull and other hands slack and other hearts cold in the solemn trust, ours shall keep it well as long as the light and warmth of life remain to us.

Let us then, at the appointed time, gather around their sacred remains and garland the passionless mounds above them with the choicest flowers of springtime. Let us raise above them the dear old flag they saved from dishonor. Let us in this solemn presence renew our pledges to aid and assist those whom they have left among us a sacred charge upon the nation's gratitude — the soldier's and sailor's widow and orphan.

2. It is the purpose of the commander-in-chief to inaugurate this observance with the hope that it will be kept up from year to year while a survivor of the war remains to honor the memory of his departed comrades. He earnestly desires the public press to call attention to this order, and lend its friendly aid in bringing it to the notice of comrades in all parts of the country in time for simultaneous compliance therewith.

3. Department commanders will use every effort to make this order effective.

> By order of
> JOHN A. LOGAN, Commander-in-Chief.
> N. P. CHIPMAN, Adjutant-General.

It seemed to me that this ceremonial was of sufficient importance to justify its recognition in some manner by the nation, and so believing, I suggested to General Logan that he secure the passage of a resolution by the House of Representatives authorizing the publication of the proceedings on Memorial Day, which I thought could be obtained by communicating with the various posts and department headquarters. General Logan thereupon offered and there was passed the following resolution:

**CONGRESS OF THE UNITED STATES.
In the House of Representatives,**
June 22, 1868.

On motion of Mr. Logan,
RESOLVED, That the proceedings of the different cities, towns, etc., recently held in commemoration of the gallant heroes who have sacrificed their lives in defense of the Republic and the record of the ceremonial of the decoration of the honored tombs of the departed, shall be collected and bound under the direction of such person as the Speaker shall designate, for the use of Congress.

ATTEST: EDWARD McPHERSON, Clerk."

Unidentified member of Sons of Veterans Reserves in 1911. (GLG)

HOUSE OF REPRESENTATIVES, WASHINGTON
June 22, 1868.

Frank Moore, Esq., Editor of the 'Rebellion Record,' is hereby appointed under this resolution.

SCHUYLER COLFAX,
Speaker House of Representatives.

To carry out the object of resolution I prepared and General Logan directed to be issued the following:

Headquarters Grand Army of the Republic, Washington, D. C., June 25, 1868.

General Orders NO. 14.

The Commander-in-Chief calls attention to the Congressional action with regard to the Memorial Ceremonies on the 30th ultimo.

In order to make successful this effort to perpetuate the record of a just tribute to our patriotic dead, departments, posts and comrades will forward to these headquarters everything pertaining to the ceremonies alluded to which can aid to complete the work proposed, — newspaper paragraphs, editorials, and reporters' accounts, and also manuscript copies of addresses and observances, which may not have been printed. It is hoped that material may be collected out of which a book of value to the country may be edited.

By order of
JOHN A. LOGAN,
Commander-in-Chief.
N. P. CHIPMAN,
Adjutant-General.

In response to this order there came to headquarters prompt and quite complete proceedings by the various posts upon Memorial Day, which I placed in the hands of Mr. Frank Moore, pursuant to the action of the House of Representatives.

The book was gotten out in 1869 and the usual number of 250 copies printed by order of Congress. Later the stereotype plates were used by Mr. Moore in publishing the book for general circulation.

On April 12, 1869, I issued General Orders No. 21, by direction of General Logan, calling attention of departments and posts to the approaching Memorial Day, and as the 30th of May occurred on Sunday posts were at liberty to observe either that day or Saturday, the 29th.

The ceremonies for 1869 were very much more general than in the preceding year, and were held in thirty-one states.

Reports of the proceedings throughout the country were sent to the headquarters and were edited and published in book form as a private enterprise. No similar publication of Memorial day proceedings has since been issued.

Ted Barnea (left), son of Monroe Barnea, 1st Michigan Light Artillery, and Gary L. Gibson, both of Benjamin Pritchard Camp #20, Kalamazoo, MI in 1987. (GLG)

The foregoing is the simple story of the origin and purpose of Memorial Day.

For more than half a century the sacred and beautiful ceremonies in honor of the nation's heroic dead have been observed, and by the legislatures of many states of the Union May 30th has been declared a legal holiday. Thus have been realized the hopes of the Grand Army of the Republic expressed in General Orders No. 11.

N. P. CHIPMAN
Sacramento, California.
March 28, 1921

Memories of the Great Civil War

Autobiographical excerpts from the journal of William S. Baird

William Sidney Baird, an 18-year-old from a farm in Watson (Allegan County), Michigan, enlisted in the 28th Michigan Infantry in the fall of 1864. Assigned to Co. E, he traveled with the 28th to Kentucky and Tennessee that fall. In January 1865, the unit was ordered to Alexandria, Virginia.

The following passages are excerpts from his journal, *Memories of the Great Civil War,* which he dictated to his second wife Hannah S. Picket Baird in 1897. These excerpts were provided by Daniel H. Grable.

My Early Experiences With The Convalescent Corps

At night we again boarded the boat and started for Cincinnati. Our quarters on the boat was the hurricane deck where we had the full benefit of the wind and storm, which was no small matter for it was very cold and we had no fire or protection of any kind. By the time we reached Cincinnati several of our number were so overcome by the cold and exposure that they had to be taken to the hospital. My brother (John) was so sick that he had to be carried to the cars. He would have been taken to the hospital but he begged so hard to go with us that they finally consented to his doing so.

(Upon reaching Alexandria, Virginia,) my brother was taken to the hospital. The next day I went to see him. He was feeling some better. I stayed with him two or three hours and then as it was nearly noon, I started for camp to get my dinner. As I was going along the street I began to feel sick and sat down on some steps to rest. After a little I became completely bewildered and if some of my comrades had not come along and taken me to camp I do not know what would have become of me. After I got there I began to vomit blood and kept growing worse until morning when they took me to the hospital. I was very sick for a few days and then began to get better. One day as I lay there sick and lonesome, a man came through the hospital visiting the sick soldiers.

He had a pleasant word for everyone as he passed along. When he came to me he took me by the hand, put his other hand on my head and said, "Well, my boy, you look pretty young to be here. Where are you from?" I answered, "Michigan." "Well," he said, "you have been pretty sick, haven't you? I hope you will get well, go home and make a useful man. Goodbye and God bless you" and he passed on. When I looked into that homely face, yet beautiful with the love which beamed from it, I needed no one to tell me that he was Abraham Lincoln. May his memory ever be green in the hearts of loyal Americans for the love and consideration he bestowed on his soldier boys, if for no other reason.

I gained rapidly from that time and was soon able to be outdoors. Soon after, an order came for men and we were sent to headquarters for examination. The doctor said he would give me my choice to go into the convalescent corps or to take a furlough and go home. I told him I would rather stay at the hospital awhile longer and then go to my regiment. He let me stay but I wonder now that I had not taken the furlough but it seemed almost like being dismissed from the service. My comrades were going to the front and I wanted to be there with them.

A short time afterward there was a call for the convalescent men who were assigned duty at the front, and took position at the front of the hospital. Just before they were to start I saw one fellow leave the ranks and steal back into the hospital. The desire took possession of me to take his place for it was very evident that he had no wish to go. I quietly stepped into his place and the mistake was not noticed. So I was once more on the way to the front but without blanket, overcoat, or knapsack. They took us first to the place where the equipment of the sick soldiers had been stored. They offered the other man's knapsack, haversack, canteen and gun but I told them they were not mine and left them there.

As we were marching along toward the transport, a boat which was to take us down the river, I saw a couple of soldiers ahead of me who were pretty laden. Before we reached the wharf one of them threw away his overcoat and the other his blanket. When I came to them, I picked them up an took them along with me. They were very acceptable indeed as I had nothing but my blouse to wrap up in and the sea breezes were very damp and chilly. We boarded the boat, and were steaming down the river toward old fortress Monroe. It was lamplight before we got onto the boat and then we had supper. I was plenty tired enough by that time to enjoy it hugely. After supper I put the overcoat on, wrapped up in the blanket and cuddled down among some bales of hay for a nap. I slept a short time and when I awoke I saw a soldier standing not far away with nothing but a dress coat to keep off the damp cold wind. I called to him and asked if he was cold. He answered yes and I told him to come and share my bed and blanket with me. He did so gladly — he was very cold. We talked a long time, like old friends, but finally went to sleep. A short time before day we reached fortress Monroe. There we were put into barracks with other convalescents. After breakfast, we, or quite a few of us, went out along the beach to pick up clams as the tide went out. I picked up about half a bushel; and got back in time for dinner for which I was more than ready. After dinner we were all drawn up in line and formed into a regiment. When they formed the companies I was made orderly Sargeant of Co. E and I found out then that my bunk mate on the ship was a doctor ranking as Major.

I found an empty knapsack and took it to put my belongings in. So in every time of need I seemed to be provided for. I did not know where my knapsack was or my descriptive list either. So I did not know what I could do when I got to the front but I went on just the same.

After serving a time with the convalescents and his doctor friend after the unit was disbanded, William located the 28th Michigan Infantry at Wise Forks, North Carolina, and joined them and his brother John in time to fight the Battle of Wise Forks. By the spring, the 28th Michigan Infantry was in North Carolina assisting General Sherman in his march to the sea. Following the end of hostilities later in the spring, the 28th was assigned to hunting guerrillas. The following passage is the story of one of Baird's most memorable pursuit.

Hunting Guerrillas

At another time we started west (from Lincolnton) and rode about forty miles. We were out in quest of a large band of desperadoes. We reached our destination about four o'clock in the afternoon having ridden since very early morning. I was one of those left with the horses so could not help surround the house where the Guerrillas were hidden away. Captain Kenyon and one of the men started right up the stairs to the chamber where they were. The Guerrillas fired at them and the Captain was severely wounded and the soldier instantly killed. Our men picked them up and retreated with them to the woods. The officers made up their minds that a large force was necessary to capture them. As the Colonel's orderly or courier, I was the one who had to go back for reinforcements. I lay down and slept until dark and the rest kept a good watch over the house. After eating my Supper, I started on that lonely ride of forty miles through a country infested by Guerrillas. I traveled along without any interruption until within ten miles of Lincolnton. I was passing over a gently rolling country at that time and the road led through a thick growth of blackjack. As I came up on top of a rise of ground I could look ahead quite a distance. About a mile ahead I saw men in the road coming toward me. They were on another rise of ground so I could not tell whether they had seen me or not. I could hear their voices plainly, laughing and calling to each other. As quickly as possible I turned my horse into the brush. It was so thick that we could scarcely penetrate it but I succeeded in getting ten or twelve feet, far enough so I could not be seen from the road. It was the best I could do but I did not feel very safe for they had had as good a chance to see me as I had them, if they had been equally watchful.

As I sat there waiting I leaned forward and put my arms around her neck and patted her nose to keep her quiet for the least noise would have betrayed me. I could not describe my feelings as I sat there waiting; hearing them come nearer and nearer each moment and knowing well that if they discovered me they would show me no mercy whatever. They made the night hideous with their drunken laughter, coarse jests and profanity. As they passed where I was concealed, they did not seem to have the least suspicion of my being there. There was ten or fifteen of the gang, I should think. My horse though spirited and nervous was as quiet as though graven out of stone. I waited until they were out of sight and then made my way back to the road again. I had not gone far when I saw a light ahead and as I drew near the next little town I saw that several of the buildings were burning. I found out afterwards that the village had been visited by Guerrillas, probably the band who had put in their Satanic work of pillaging, burning and murder. The grass did not grow under Kittie's feet the rest of the way to Lincolnton. She fairly flew along the road and in about five hours from the time I left my comrades were there. I went direct to headquarters, delivered my dispatches to the Col. and then went home and to bed. As soon as they could get the necessary arrangements made to go, the doctor came in and said he was sorry to wake me so soon but did not know how they could get there if I did not go with them as guide. That was before daylight, and as it was about two o'clock when I reached there I had not slept very long. I went with the doctor to headquarters where they had a nice breakfast ready. We ate it and then started as soon as possible. The men had started on before for they knew the way until it branched off from the "Big Road" as they called it there. It was about seven o'clock when we came up with those who were in advance. They had marched about fifteen miles I should think; we reached our comrades at the log house before sundown and they were glad that help had come. The Col. ordered the men to go around to strengthen the different bands who were guarding the house and then called for volunteers to take kindlings and build a fire under the stairway. The house was a double log, with a space between, roofed over but not enclosed. The stairway was under the roof and they called the space the dining room. Two men, one named Lee Collins and the other Earl Bristol, volunteered to do this dangerous work. They started on the run from the woods, kindled the fire and were soon back again. They fired at them from the chambers but they (our men) escaped uninjured. Some of the Guerrillas showed themselves on the stairway and were shot. The rest waited until the heat was unbearable and then put out the white flag. Then by leaving their arms they were allowed to come down. This they could do on the opposite side of the building from where the fire was kindled as the stairway was double, and went up from each way. Fifty men gave themselves up and quite a number, I do not know how many must have perished in the building. The prisoners were put under guard and then we had supper. We were tired and hungry enough to enjoy it, surely. We encamped there that night and the next morning started on our return march to Lincolnton. We staid at Lincolnton one night and then started in pursuit of the band that I came so near meeting. We could easily follow the trail of fire and rapine which they left behind them. We finally overtook them in South Carolina. In chasing them it happened we ran them into a squad of Indiana Cavalry who were hunting still another band. As they were much nearer their camp than we were ours, they took charge of them and we came back.

The 28th Michigan Infantry continued its service until it was mustered out at Raleigh, North Carolina on June 6, 1866.

Tomb of Major A.P. Davis, Allegheny Cemetery Pittsburgh, PA (GLG)

Bronze plaque on tomb honoring A.P. Davis as the founder of the Sons of Union Veterans of the Civil War (GLG).

MEMBERS OF

Sons of Union Veterans of the Civil War

Edward P. Alff

EDWARD P. ALFF, joined the Order in 1987 as a member of Anna M. Ross #1.

Alff based his right to membership on his great-great-grandfather Pvt. John Alff. John Alff served in the 114th PA Vols. from May 15, 1861 to August 15, 1964. He served in a number of major campaigns and was wounded during the war. He was married and produced two sons. John Alff is buried in Military Hospital Cemetery, Dayton, Ohio.

GREGORY L. ALLEN, is an architect and family man who lives in Bountiful, UT. He joined the Sons on July 16, 1994 and is a charter member of Lot Smith Camp No. 1, Department of Utah. He is also a member of the Veterans Reserve. When he was a young man, his grandmother told him many stories about her grandfather, Malachi McCoy Jr.

Gregory L. Allen   *Malachi McCoy, Jr.*

Malachi McCoy Jr. was born in Salem, IN on September 16, 1829. His father was a veteran of the Revolutionary War, and died five days before Malachi Jr. was born. Malachi Jr. served during the War with Mexico, and mustered out as a corporal. Malachi Jr. was equal to the tough life on the Indiana frontier, as he stood six feet four inches tall. On September 15, 1861, he enlisted in the 50th Indiana Infantry and received a commission as a second lieutenant in Company A. On September 8, 1862, he was injured when the train in which he was riding derailed near Munfordsville, KY. On September 17, he was captured by Confederates at Munfordsville. He was paroled, but before long, he was back in the fight. On April 4, 1863, he was promoted to captain. He served in the Western theater until he was honorably discharged with his company on January 5, 1865. At his death in Vernal, UT on July 11, 1923, he was the oldest veteran of the War with Mexico, and one of the oldest of the Civil War, within the State of Utah.

ROBERT JOSEPH AMSLER, JR., joined the Sons in February, 1994 when he went to a meeting of the William T. Sherman Camp No. 65 in St. Louis, MO. He is an assistant attorney general for the state of Missouri. Two of his ancestors fought for the Union and possibly some more. His great-great-grandfather, Casimer Amsler, enlisted as a private in the 2nd U.S. Reserve Corps, Missouri Infantry (U.S.), Co. D on April 6, 1861 and was mustered in on May 7, 1861. This unit was attached to Nathaniel Lyon's Army of the West and participated in the capture of Camp Jackson in St. Louis on May 10, 1861. Afterwards, he guarded various strategic points in Missouri before he was honorably mustered out on August 16, 1861.

Robert J. Amsler, Jr.

He is currently researching information that he may have reenlisted for an additional three years. Robert's great-great-great uncle Joseph Amsler was Casimer's brother. He enlisted as a private in the 2nd Regt., Missouri Volunteer Infantry (U.S.), Co. C on April 22, 1861 and was mustered in on May 1, 1861. His unit was attached to the 3rd Brigade, Lyon's Army of the West. Joseph participated in the capture of Camp Jackson also. He then participated in the capture of Jefferson City, MO, on June 14, 1861 and the capture of Mexico, MO on July 15, 1861. Joseph took part in the battle of Wilson's Creek, MO on August 10, 1861 and afterwards returned to St. Louis where he was honorably mustered out on August 31, 1861. He is also researching information that Joseph reenlisted for three additional years and died in battle in 1863.

DR. MAURICE E. ANKROM, was born June 30, 1928, at New Castle, IN. A graduate of Christian Theological Seminary in Indianapolis. Pastor for 45 years in Christian Churches (Disciples of Christ). Became a Member-At-Large October 30, 1992 in SUVCW. Great-grandson of Sampson Ulysses Ankrom, who with his brothers Thomas and Joseph, enlisted as privates in Co. C of the 178th Ohio Volunteer Infantry on August 15, 1864.

Dr. Maurice E. Ankrom   *Sampson Ulysses Ankrom*

They saw action in Tennessee, and then at the battle of Wyse Fork, NC, in March, 1865. Joseph, at age 18, died of inflammation of the lungs on March 8, and is buried in the National Cemetery at New Bern, NC. The three brothers served in the 3rd Brigade, 1st Div. of the 23rd Army Corps. Thomas and Sampson were mustered out June 29, 1865, at Charlotte, NC.

DOUGLAS R. ARMSTRONG, joined the George W. Anderson Camp No. 58 - Dept. of Michigan on July 17, 1995. He has served as Camp GUIDE and is a Charter Member.

Douglas R. Armstrong

Douglas bases his right to membership on his great-great-great-grandfather John Tait, Sergeant, Co. G, 24th Mich. Vol. Infantry (Iron Brigade). Tait was mustered into service August 13, 1862, and was wounded in the shoulder at the Battle of Fredericksburg in December 1862. Tait was killed-in-action by a single cannonball at Fitzhugh Crossing, leaving a wife and five children. Sgt. Tait is buried in grave number 2162, Fredericksburg National Military Cemetery.

KENT L. ARMSTRONG, joined the Sons March 9, 1992. He is the Commander and Charter Member of the George W. Anderson Camp No. 58 - Dept. of Michigan.

Kent L. Armstrong

He bases his membership on his great-great-grandfather, John Tait, Sergeant, Co. G, 24th Mich. Vol. Infantry (Iron Brigade). Tait was mustered into service August 13, 1862, and was wounded in the shoulder at the Battle of Fredericksburg in December 1862. Tait was killed-in-action by a single cannonball at Fitzhugh Crossing, leaving a wife and five children. Sgt. Tait is buried in grave number 2162, Fredericksburg National Military Cemetery.

KEITH DREW ASHLEY, joined February 21, 1984, as Life Member At-Large No. 147. In 1988 he became a charter member of Gov. William Dennison Camp No. 125 of Albany, OH, he transferred serving as senior vice-commander and secretary-treasurer. He organized Brooks-Grant Camp No. 7 of Middleport, OH, with 34 new members and 16 transfers. He is currently serving the Ohio Department as historian, Constitution & By-laws Committee chairman, member of the Membership Committee, and camp organizer. He is serving nationally as member of the Program & Policies Committee for his third year previously serving on the G.A.R. Records Committee. He is a member of the 1st Ohio Light Artillery, Battery I, of the Sons of Veterans Reserve.

Keith D. Ashley

His second great-grandfather was Cpl. William Ashley of Co. I, 36th Ohio Volunteer Infantry and is buried at Letart Falls, OH. Keith lives in Pomeroy, OH.

ROBERT DREW ASHLEY, joined Gov. William Dennison Camp No. 125 of Albany, OH in July, 1988, as a charter member. He transferred to Brooks-Grant Camp No. 7 of Middleport, OH, being a charter member there. His son, Keith Drew Ashley, formed Brooks-Grant Camp. He is a descendant of the Lincoln family. He is a life member.

His great-grandfather was Cpl. William Ashley of Co. I, 36th Ohio Volunteer Infantry enlisting August 13, 1861. He was discharged January 19, 1864, due to illness after having been in the Invalid Corps. He is buried Letart Falls Cemetery, Meigs County, OH (101).

Robert resides in Racine, OH.

ELMER "BUD" F. ATKINSON, Past C-in-C, joined the Anna M. Ross Camp #1 in Philadelphia, PA in 1938. He became Camp Commander in 1946 after his discharge from service in World War II. Camp #1 was later disbanded and the members transferred. In 1978, Bud reorganized Camp #1, serving as treasurer and secretary/treasurer until 1992. He served several offices on the state level, then two terms as department commander, 1985 to 1987. Nationally, he served as Patriotic Instructor, Council, Jr. and Sr. Vice Commander, and Commander-in-Chief 1992-1993. He is now the National Quartermaster.

Elmer F. Atkinson

Organizer of the 28th PA Vol. Infantry, Sons of Veterans Reserve, he served as company commander, then rose in rank to colonel commanding the 2nd Military District.

His ancestors are Pvt. Balthasar Moeckel, Co. G, 75th Regt. PA. Volunteers and Pvt. William Brown, U.S. Marine Corps.

Brother Atkinson is married to Margaret, National President of the Auxiliary, 1994-1995. Two sons and a daughter are members as are three of eight grandchildren. He resides in Philadelphia, PA.

HERBERT J. ATKINSON, joined the SUVCW Oliver Tilden Camp #26, New York, NY on June 23, 1992 after learning about the organization while doing a genealogical study of his family tree. Being a member of the largest camp in New York State has provided him with many opportunities to participate in various activities honoring the memories of great-grandfather and great uncle and their service in the Civil War. He is presently researching the history of the Hart Island New York's use as a hospital-prisoner of war camp - separation center during the Civil War and welcomes any information anyone may have on the subject.

Pvt. Michael Ryan - Civil War veteran ancestor. Mike Ryan is the citizen-soldier's tradition of his family, laid down his mason's trowel and picked up his gun in answer to President Lincoln's call for volunteer in April 26 of 1861. As a member of the 10th NY, VI, the National Zouaves, he first saw action at Bull Run, the whole of the Peninsula Campaign, Antietam, and Fredericksburg, among others. The exploits of the 10th New York volunteers were carefully chronicled by Chas. W. Cowtan and were published in a book by him after the war.

He was mustered out at Hart's Island, NY, May 7, 1863 and it was reported in the *New York Times* that only half of his regiment had returned from the war. He died October 13, 1898, and was buried at Calvary Cemetery, New York, NY.

LaVERNE L. AVES, joined Curentius Camp #17 - Lansing/Sunfield October 14, 1989. She is a member of the Color Guard, Camp Council, and was a delegate to the 1994 State/National encampment, member 30th Mich Infantry Co. A - survivor.

LaVerne L. Aves

She bases her claim to membership on ancestor Pvt. Thomas Dysinger, 3rd Mich Co. E Reg. He enlisted on October 15, 1864. Pvt. Dysinger took ill with Typhoid fever in fall of 1864 in Decatur, Alabama. His regiment was ordered on, and when the hospital moved, he was put on a train for Nashville. Since there is no record of his arrival there, it is assumed he died and was taken off the train. Where, or if, he was buried, is not known.

PAUL BACHMANN, joined the Gov. Crapo #145 (Michigan) in November of 1992.

He bases his right to membership on his great granduncle, Jacob H. "Jake" Perine, 1840-1942. Jake, who belonged to GAR Post E.W. Hollingsworth #210, Albion, Mich., joined August 15, 1862 and was discharged June 15, 1865. He served in both Co. E 4th MI Infantry and Co. K 1st MI Infantry Jake was wounded at Gettysburg during the battle of July 1-3, 1863. He lived to be 102 and 1/2 years old and was the last surviving veteran in his GAR Post.

MICHAEL BACKAUSKAS, joined Phil Sheridan Camp #4 in October 1994. He bases his right to membership on his great-great grandfather, John J. Harrison. Michael Backauskas is one of Sgt. John Harrison's many great-great-grandsons, descended from the soldier's youngest child, Everett. He has no photograph of his ancestor but hopes another descendant may one day read this and share John J. Harrison's likeness. Michael has been active in the motion picture visual effects field since 1976 and holds two Emmy Awards for his work on *Star Trek, the Next Generation* and *Star Trek, Voyager*. He lives in Los Angeles with his wife Alysia Vanitzian.

John, who was born in 1824 near the town of White Oak in Fayette County, OH, was a farmer, the son of Ohio state legislator Batteal Harrison, who had served as a junior officer in William Henry Harrison's old northwest campaign in the War of 1812, and grandson of Kentucky state representative Benjamin Harrison, who had been a Captain of Virginia Continental Line and a militia Colonel for Westnoreland County, PA in the Revolutionary War.

Michael Backauskas

John married Cynthia M. Shuffleberger on September 15, 1850. They had five children, Scott, Mary Elizabeth, Benjamin, Floyd and Everett. On August 13, 1862, when John was 37 years old, he enlisted in Co. D of the 114th Regt. of Ohio Infantry Volunteers. He was mustered into service as a corporal on September 9 to serve three years and paid a bounty of $25. His brother, Capt. Scott Harrison commanded Co. D.

From December 20, the 114th Ohio participated in Sherman's expedition from Memphis, TN to the Yazoo River and the campaign against Vicksburg, MS, seeing action at Chickasaw Bayou and assaulting Chickasaw Bluffs. On January 3, 1863 the 114th continued to Arkansas Post, AR, assaulting and capturing Fort Hindeman, moving on to Young's Point, LA. John was promoted to fourth sergeant on February 28, seeing operations about Milliken's Bend and New Carthage. 33,000 Union soldiers traversed downstream on the Louisiana side of

47

the Mississippi River. The terrain was swampy, with a tangle of bayous and lakes in the way. John contracted chronic camp diarrhea while in service. He was sick in hospital at Perkins Plantation, LA, April 25, then left behind at Raymond, MS on May 16 while the company marched away. He had one knapsack, one haversack and one canteen with him. The place was taken by the enemy May 22 and John was captured in poor health.

John died a prisoner of war at Atlanta, GA on June 11, 1863, of disease unknown. He rests in the Marietta National Cemetery, Marietta, GA, section E, grave number 6523. His widow Cynthia was paid a pension of $8 per month and an additional sum of $2 per month for each child until 16 years of age. The pension was raised to $12 per month March 19, 1886. Cynthia died June 7, 1910.

MARK S. BACKUS, joined Lone Star Camp No. 1, Arlington, TX, SUVCW in 1994, on the service of his great-great-grandfather Benjamin Boydston Condray. Brothers Ben and John Condray, sons of Elnathan and Elizabeth Condray of Lauderdale County, TN, joined Co. E, 14th (often referred to as the 13th) Tennessee Cavalry in 1864. Ben was present at Ft. Pillow during the Confederate assault. After the battle and subsequent disbandment of the unit Ben accepted his discharge while John remained in service until his death on January 9, 1865, at U.S. Army Hospital, Jeffersonville, IN.

Mark S. Backus

In 1872, Ben Condray moved his family to Faulkner County, AR where he lived the remainder of his life. He died on December 20, 1921 and is buried at Oak Grove Cemetery, Conway. Mark Backus was raised in Arkansas; graduated from the University of Arkansas; served in the U.S. Army; and resides in Irving, TX with his wife Teresa and daughter Jennifer.

GILBERT B. BAGLEY, joined Order 1992. Organized Camp 83 Thomas H. Mann in 1993 elected commander. 1993 elected senior vice commander. Department of Massachusetts, Member Sons of Veterans Reserve.

Gilbert B. Bagley   *Norman G. Baxter*

Great-grandfather Norman G. Baxter member of Co. E, 16th New York, Cavalry enlisted at Plattsburg, NY March 14, 1865 served in, Defenses of Washington. A member of one of the Detachments in the pursuit of John Wilkes Booth.

Three of Co. E members at Garretts Farm when Booth was shot.

Transferred to 3rd Provisional Cav. discharged September 21, 1865 at Camp Barry Washington, DC.

Norman a member of George H. Maintien Post 133 Department of Massachusetts in Plainville holding several offices.

Gil also has five other Civil War relations in U.S. Navy 118th New York Infantry and 31st of Maine Infantry

Bro. Bagley lives with his wife Cha in Plainville, MA.

GARY ALMONY BAGNALL, joined the Joshua Lawrence Chamberlain Camp #20 SUVCW of Roanoke, VA on July 18, 1994. He is descended from George W. Almony who enlisted August 31, 1861 in York, PA with the 87th Pennsylvania Infantry, Co. D as a musician. He was honorably discharged on February 21, 1864 and re-enlisted as a Veteran volunteer on February 22, 1864. He was again honorably discharged on June 29, 1865. He was described as being five feet seven inches tall, with hazel eyes, brown hair and a fair complexion.

Gary A. Bagnall

George W. Almony was born November 3, 1846 in York County, PA, and married Lavinia Miller on October 3, 1867. To this marriage were born Maria Alto, Estella Elizabeth, and Edmund Alexander. Gary A. Bagnall is a descendant of Edmund Alexander Almony. After the death of Lavinia, on September 10, 1904, George married Ellen Roth. George died September 27, 1910 and is buried in the Mt. Zion Cemetery, Baltimore County, MD.

Gary Almony Bagnall is a graduate of the University of Virginia and is the office manager of Hutton Electric Company. He married Robin Hope Wall on September 19, 1987, and they have one daughter Carter Grace Bagnall.

HARRISON SCOTT BAKER II, initiated into the General James B. McPherson Camp Number 66 on May 15, 1994 at Fort Meigs in Toledo, OH. Member of Co. E, 72nd O.V.I. of the Sons of Veterans Reserve.

Memberships include the John Hancock Chapter of the Sons of the American Revolution, the Ohio Society of the General society of the War of 1812 and the Descendants of Mexican War Veterans.

Harrison S. Baker II   *William Baker*

William Baker was his Civil War ancestor, who enlisted at Camp Chase in Columbus, OH on September 29, 1864 into Co. I of the 175th O.V.I. He was promoted to corporal on April 1, 1865 and mustered out with the company on June 27, 1865 at Nashville, TN. He took part in the Battle of Franklin, TN on November 30, 1864. He was commander of the Wilkerson Post Number 264, GAR, in Wharton, Wyandot County, OH.

THOMAS E. BALL, joined Camp Gov. William Dennison #125 from Albany, OH in February 1992. In January, 1994 a new camp was formed in Middleport, OH, Brooks-Grant Camp #7, of which he is a charter member.

Tom Basis his right of membership on his great-great-great uncle, Pvt. Henry Genheimer Co. M 1st West Virginia Vol. Cavalry. He enlisted on September 8, 1861 in Mason City, VA just across the Ohio River from the Southeastern Ohio town of Pomeroy. At this time Mason City was still a part of Virginia because the western part of the state had not yet broken away to form the state of West Virginia.

He was discharged on November 17, 1864 and was a member of Abe Lincoln Post #29 G.A.R. Council Bluffs, IA. He died February 9, 1894 in Clarinda, IA.

Tom and his wife Debbie have two children, Chris and Sarah and reside in Syracuse, OH.

TED L. BARNES, joined the Gov. William Dennison Camp 125 S.U.V.C.W. January 11, 1994. Twenty days later some members held an organizational meeting for a new camp at Middleport, Oh. This camp became a reality on March 14, 1994 when 19 members met for election of officers. He was elected secretary. The camp was named Brooks Grant Camp No. 7 after two of the highest ranking officers from Meigs County, OH during the Civil War. Their membership has grown to 54 by November 1994.

His Civil War ancestor is his great-great grandfather Vachel Barnes. He enlisted August 6, 1862 in Summerfield, OH (Noble County). He served as a private with the 92nd Ohio Vol. Infantry Co. D. He mustered out with his company on June 10, 1865.

Ted L. Barnes

On July 13, 1865 he married Margaret Ann Smith in Noble County. They had seven children. Ca 1870 the family moved to Wirt County, WV where Vachel died May 20, 1887 from lung disease contracted during the war.

Ted Barnes served in the U.S. Air Force from January 1962 to October 1966 with 376th Bomb Wing SAC and 62nd Military Airlift Command. Ted and his wife Pat live in Marietta, OH. Pat is a senior vice president in the DUV - Elizabeth Rector Buell Tent #19 of Marietta, OH. Their son Army Sgt. Jeffrey L. Barnes is also a member of Brooks Grant Camp #7. Their daughter Joan L. Barnes Hoff is a member of Elizabeth Rector Buell Tent #19.

WARREN E. BARNEY, joined Anna M. Ross, Camp #1, Philadelphia, PA, December 16, 1991.

Warren E. Barney   *Martin M. Barney*

He bases his right to membership on Pvt. Martin M. Barney, who served from February 15, 1864 to January 29, 1866. Pvt. Barney served with Co. K 112 PA Vol. and 2nd PA Heavy Artillery. Pvt. Barney belonged to GAR Post W.B. Hatch Post 37, Camden, NJ. He served in various forts in defense of Washington D.C., but was captured at Bermuda Hundred, VA and taken to Richmond, VA as a P.O.W. December 15, 1864. He was paroled at Cox's Wharf, VA, February 5, 1865.

MICHAEL T. BARRY, was born on May 7, 1963, in Chicago, IL. He currently resides in Lake Forest, CA. He has been a member of the Sons of Union Veterans, Phil Sheridan Camp #4, Department of California and Pacific since December 1992.

His connection to the Grand Army of the Republic comes from his great-great grandfather Morris Welch. He was born on October 9, 1838, in Waterford County Ireland. Morris immigrated to the United States during the summer of 1860, finally settling in Chicago, IL.

On October 17, 1863, he volunteered as a private Co. F, 89th Regt., Illinois Infantry. After several weeks of preparation in Chicago, he was ordered to report to the regiment. On November 17, 1863, he arrived at Chattanooga, TN. While assigned to the 89th Illinois and the Army of the Cumberland, he participated in the following major engagements; Missionary Ridge, the Atlanta campaign, Franklin and Nashville.

On June 10, 1865, he was transferred to Co. F, 59th Regt. Illinois Infantry and remained in active duty until mustered out of service December 8, 1865.

Morris Welch died on February 19, 1929, and is buried at the National Cemetery, Rock Island, IL.

RONALD L. BAYLES, JR. & SALLY ANN WRIGHT-BAYLES, Ron joined the David D. Porter Camp #116, in 1994. His wife Sally, is the great-granddaughter of Sgt. Phillip M. Wright, Bugler, Co. I, 1st North Carolina Cavalry, which was assigned to the command of General J.E.B. Stuart, for most of the conflict. Both are involved in family tree research and have located at least eight family members who served in the Civil War, six of which were killed in action, including Pvt. David Franklin, Co. G, 72nd Infantry Regt., Illinois Volunteers, (Ron's great-great-grandfather on his dad's mothers side of the family) who died in battle during the siege of Vicksburg, MS, in May-June, 1863. Pvt. Franklin is buried in the Vicksburg National Cemetery, Section A., Grave #9738.

Ronald L. Bayles, Jr.   *John H. G. Bayles*

A survivor of the war, Sgt. John Henry Gennings Bayles, Co. C, 35th Infantry Regt., (1st Irish), Indiana Volunteers, born December 17, 1844, in Athens County, OH, to William Bayles and Mary Boyer-Bayles. Moved to Cooks Corner, Porter County, IN, sometime in 1846. Two brothers, David and Leander, three sisters Rebecca, Sarah and Mrs. Samuel Alyea. Sgt. Bayles met his wife Augusta Ann Curtis-Bayles, in Cooks Corner, IN. At the age of 16 years and ten months, John enlisted in the Army on October 22, 1861. He reenlisted as a veteran volunteer on December 16, 1863, at Shell Mound, TN. He was discharged at the end of the war while stationed with his unit at Victoria, TX. Sgt. Bayles, was wounded in combat on two occasions. Once in the battle at Stones River, TN, December 30, 1862 - January 3, 1863, and again in "the battle above the clouds" on Lookout Mountain, November 23-24, 1863.

After the war he purchased a farm in the village of Furnessville, Porter County, IN. His children were Lilly May, Francis (Frank), John, Lucy, Nelson, Margret, Catherine, Edna, Cleveland and Richard. Retired on Horse Prairie Avenue in Valparaiso, IN, where he passed away April 14, 1926.

SAMUEL J. BEHRINGER, Jr., joined the Sons in 1992 and is a member of an Ohio Camp.

He bases his right to membership on his ancestor, Pvt. Ignatz Behringer, 106th Ohio Vol. Infantry, Co. E. Ignatz was a German emigrant and a tailor in Cincinnati's German community. He joined the 106th OVI, which was known as the "4th German Regiment," one of six regiments comprised entirely of German emigrants recruited in the State of Ohio. He enlisted on August 23, 1864, at the age of 44 and was discharged on June 29, 1865. In the latter years of the war after his enlistment, the 106th OVI was attached to the 4th Army Corps and did valuable service guarding railroads and conducting numerous expeditions against guerrillas and bushwackers in KY, TN, and AL.

After his discharge, Ignatz returned to tailoring in Cincinnati which he continued until his death on October 19, 1873. Ignatz has about 358 direct descendants in approximately 37 states which include a former Speaker of the Ohio House of Representatives and numerous community and civic leaders, attorneys, law enforcement officers, teachers, businessmen and industrial engineers.

DUANE A. BENELL, joined the SUVCW July 8, 1993, Phil Sheridan Camp #4, Cal-Pacific Dept. His claim to membership is based on Pvt. James Benell, Civil War ancestor enlisted August 18, 1862 and discharged June 25, 1865, serving with the 126th Regt. Ohio Infantry He belonged to Solomon Duncan Post No. 618, New Bedford, OH.

Duane A. Benell

James Benell, a farmer born October 8, 1842 in Baltic, Tuscarawas County, OH, enlisted in Co. G, 126th Regt. Ohio Infantry on August 18, 1862 at Baltic, OH. He was 19 years old. The 126th was a three year regiment mustered into United States service on September 4, 1862, at Camp Steubenville, OH. He took part in 17 battles, including The Wilderness, Spotsylvania, Cold Harbor and Mine Run, before being captured July 9, 1864 by troops of CSA General Jubal Early at the Battle of Monocacy, MD. He was imprisoned at Danville, VA, where those captured at Monocacy were taken. He was exchanged on February 28, 1865, rejoined his regiment near Petersburg, VA in March, and was mustered out near Washington, DC on June 25, 1865. He was a charter member of Solomon Duncan Post No. 618 at New Bedford, OH. He died in the National Military Home in Dayton, OH on July 19, 1921.

BRIAN BLACK, joined the Orlando A. Somers Camp #1 in Kokomo, IN on November 28, 1992.

Brian Black   *John Black*

He bases his right to membership on Pvt. John Black. John Black joined Co. A 8th KY CAV. September 6, 1862, and was discharged September 23, 1863. He belonged to the Sanderson GAR Post, New Albany, IN. While in the service, John contracted a camp illness, for which he later received a pension.

LARRY C. BLACKETT, joined the Sons in 1986 as Member-at-Large. His Civil War ancestor, Sgt. Marvin Bogart (aka) Boget, served in MI 22 Co. I, from August 15, 1862 through June 26, 1865.

Marvin Bogart aka Marvin Boget, was born March 17, 1840 in Greenfield Township Michigan to Henry VD Bogart and Jane Swift. He was the great-great grandson of Revolutionary War Patriot Mindert Van der Bogart survivor of Valley Forge, and the seventh generation grandson of Harmen Van der Bogaert, immigrant to America 1630. Marvin was the first cousin to Mrs. Clara Ford, Henry's wife and enjoyed their friendship his entire life which was to last 98 years. Married Sarah R. Kimmis December 31, 1866 having five children with her.

Larry C. Blackett *Marvin Bogart*

With a respectable education, teaching school from time to time, he enlisted in the Michigan 22nd under Col. Moses Wisner in August of 1862. Leaving Pontiac, MI, in party with the famous "22nd Cow Bell". He became very sick in Lexington, KY (with most of the company, Col. Wisner died there), promoted to sergeant July 26, 1863. First and only major battle, September 20, 1863 Chickamauga, GA, was in the famous stand to hold off the confederacy, allowing General Thomas and the entire Union Army, to retreat, being captured and sent to Belle Isle, VA as a prisoner of war, then on to Andersonville to spend the remainder of the war. He survived and upon returning home, taught school and farmed for the remainder of his life, some 73 more years, living in the same home he was raised in. Learned to drive at the age of 85 years, with a car that was the gift of Henry Ford (Henry also loaned him his chauffeur to teach him). Marvin fell out of an apple tree he was pruning at age 84 breaking his hip; he raised the apple trees as part of his cash crop. While he was recuperating, Henry came to give him the car; they also enjoyed airplane rides over the city together. Marvin was the last member of the Northville GAR post and the second to last survivor of the Mich 22nd. At his death, his daughter donated the "Cow Bell" to the State of Michigan, it had been carried through the war, then rung at every gathering until his death in 1938. Today that bell can be viewed at the Wisner Museum in Pontiac, MI. Henry Ford and family were part of the many hundreds to attend Marvin's funeral July 10, 1938.

RICHARD H. BLUM-BRO BLUM, recently joined the Order as a member-at-large Department of New York, he is also a member of the 121st Infantry Regt., 1st Corps of Gettysburg's Friends of the National Park where he has spent the past six Memorial day weekends, decorating memorials of the local units that participate in the battle.

Richard H. Blum

Richard bases his right to membership to his great-great-uncle Cpl. Henry Fical, Co. F, 97th Regt., NY Infantry who received wounds at second Bull Run, Bro Blum and his wife Violet who also is an auxiliary member, resides in Herkimer, NY.

DONALD J. BOEHM, joined the Son's of the Union Veterans of the Civil War on January 3, 1992 as a member-at-large. A former member of the North-South Skirmish Association, he has been a long time Civil War student.

Donald J. Boehm

Don claims his right to membership on his grandfather, Herman Boehm, who enlisted on January 11, 1862 at Dunkirk, NY in Co. B of the 14th U.S. Infantry Regulars, and was discharged January 11, 1865 at Ft. Trumbull, CT.

Pvt. Boehm saw action at Gaine's Mill, Fredericksburg, second Bull Run, Chancellorsville and Gettysburg, plus numerous skirmishes. Three times he was wounded, the most serious at Gettysburg where a ball entered his left side and exited his right side.

Pvt. Boehm was a member of the William O. Stevens G.A.R. Post 393 in Dunkirk, NY. He died September 14, 1900.

Brother Boehm and his wife Shirley reside in Jamestown, NY.

NED P. BOOHER, joined Camp No. 1, Orlando A. Somer Camp September 11, 1982. He has served as the Camp Commander.

He bases his right to membership on his ancestor, 1st Lt. Samuel S. Martin (Commissary Officer of the Reg.). Samuel joined the 11th IN Cav. Co. M January 1, 1864, and was discharged on September 19, 1865. He served briefly in a 3-month Ohio regiment in early

Ned P. Booher *Samuel S. Martin*

1862. 1st Lt. Martin belonged to GAR Post, R.C. Kise Post No. 437 (Darlington, IN). He was on detached service in the Huntsville, AL area when his regiment took part in the Battle of Nashville under Thomas.

RONALD T. BOWERS, was born in Baker City, OR on May 26, 1932, where he has lived most of his life.

His grandfather was Pvt. Charles Bowers who served from January 1, 1862 to March 21, 1865 with Co. F, 60th Indiana Volunteers. He was a member of the Grand Army of the Republic.

Charles Bowers

Ron joined the Sons in Portland, OR and was department secretary-treasurer until the department disbanded. He is now a MAL in New York. He belongs to the Ladies of the Grand Army of the Republic and a charter member of the National Museum of Civil War Medicine.

His wife, Nancy, died July 22, 1993. She was department president, three years of the Oregon Department, Ladies of the GAR.

JOHN A. BRADEN, (in kepi), was born in Detroit in 1953. He is currently a research and appellate attorney residing in Fremont, MI. Braden is a member of the Henry Plant Camp No. 3, (Grand Haven).

Braden is a great-great-grandson of John Braden (born in New York City in 1829). The last-named Braden emigrated to Michigan before serving with the 15th U.S. Infantry during the Mexican War.

John A. Braden *John Braden*

Braden was a machinist in Detroit when, in September, 1861, he enlisted in Co. C, 5th Michigan Infantry He was promoted through the ranks, finally attaining the rank of first lieutenant of Co. G.

Braden was wounded twice and appeared in practically every major battle fought by the Army of the Potomac. He resigned his commission in October, 1864, married, and fathered nine children. Braden died in 1895 and is buried at Elmwood Cemetery in Detroit.

ELLIS S. BRANCH, was born April 8, 1925. He joined the SUVCW August 7, 1988, and enlisted as a private in the SVR in 1990. Appointed District Chaplain of the 3rd Military District with rank of Major, October 15, 1991, he requested to be transferred from Member-at-Large to the newly formed Camp No. 1, West Point, Kentucky, July 10, 1995. Ellis was a WWII combat infantryman with the 313th Infantry Regiment, 79th inf. Div. He participated in D-Day and Utah Beach in Normandy; later he was assigned to the 618th Medical Detachment. He is now a retired school administrator and counselor in private practice.

Ellis S. Branch   *Paul A. Neff*

He bases his right to membership on his great granduncle, Paul A. Neff. Paul was a German emigrant who enlisted in the Union Army on August 15, 1862. He was Regimental Bugler, Trumpeter, and Chief Musician of Co. D, 8th Reg., KY Vol. Cav. Their most famous accomplishment was their pursuit of John Hunt Morgan and his first capture in Ohio in 1863. Paul was discharged at Russellville, Kentucky on September 23, 1863 and died February 12, 1907. He and his wife, Louisa who died October 6, 1908, are buried in Cave Hill Cemetery in Louisville, KY.

MARK LOWELL BRECKNER, joined Phil Sheridan Camp No. 4 in March 1994.

He bases his membership on Pvt. Cyrus Sellers. Cyrus, who was involved in the siege of Mobile, was drafted in Co. I, 8th IL Infantry in 1864, and was discharged on September 26, 1865. Mark Breckner is also related to several other civil war veterans: Philo A. Castle, 1st Lt. (Co. A, 4th WI Cavalry), Lewis Castle (Co. A, 4th WI Cavalry), and Alonzo L. Castle (Co. H, 13th WI Regiment Infantry).

THOMAS P. BRESEE, joined the U.S. Navy on July 27, 1970. Boot camp was at Great Lakes, IL for 15 weeks. He then was assigned to the USS *O'Callahan* DE 1051 at Long Beach, CA. Later overseas to the Philippines, Japan and Vietnam. Discharged to Reserves July 1970 for four years. He was honorably discharged in 1974.

He joined Lincoln Camp 100, Department of New Jersey, October 4, 1993. Thomas P. Bresee's great-grandfather, William Henry Bresee, joined Co. D, 134th NY Infantry volunteers. In July of 1862 boot camp was at Middletown, NY, then he moved south by train to Washington, D.C. Later that year moved south to Virginia.

On May 1863 they participated in the battle of Chancellorsville, VA. Then off to Gettysburg, PA, where he was wounded on the first day of the battle, late afternoon July 1, 1863. He was at a field hospital for a couple of days, then was moved to a Washington, D.C. hospital by train. Later, moved to Newark, NJ hospital for rehabilitation. He was discharged on January 30, 1865.

ERROL C. BRIGGS, Col., USAR, was born January 29, 1943. Joined Joshua L. Chamberlain Camp, Barre, VT, No. 69, Department of Maine, in February 1991.

Civil War ancestor: Joseph Henry Briggs, (born at Woodstock, ME on June 25, 1824, died April 4, 1904), a private in Co. H, 13th Maine Volunteers from December 1861 to January 1864, then Co. H, 30th Maine Veteran Volunteers until discharge at Savannah in August 1865. Served at Ship Island, MS, the Texas coast, Louisiana (the Red River Campaign), the Shenandoah Valley in Virginia, and Georgia. Member of G.A.R. Post 158.

ANDREW D. BRINKMAN, joined the Round Rock, TX SUVCW Camp March 1995. He has one great-great-great-grand-uncle and two great-great-great-grandfathers who served in the Union Army (Patrick McCabe; James Dunse, 21st CT Infantry; and Joseph Segar, 1st NY Light Artillery).

Andrew D. Brinkman

Private Patrick McCabe was born in Ireland in 1822. He emigrated to Port Henry, NY, and was a boatman on Lake Champlain hauling iron ore and supplies to Troy, NY. He married Catherine McClure and had seven children before he enlisted at age 41 in the 93rd New York Infantry, Co. A on December 21, 1863.

He was wounded May 5, 1864 at the Wilderness, and fought at Cold Harbor, Petersburg, Weldon Railroad and Fort Sedgwick. The 93rd was a part of the 2nd Corps which pursued General Lee to Appomattox. Patrick was discharged June 29, 1865 and was in GAR Post 102 at Port Henry, NY.

HENRY JOSEPH BRINKMAN, joined the Austin, TX SUVCW Sam Houston Camp #3 in May 1995. He has a great-grandfather, Joseph Segar, and a great-granduncle, Patrick McCabe, who served in the Union Army.

Private Joseph Segar was born in Quebec, Canada in 1822. He emigrated to Port Henry, NY in 1842 and was a boatman (along with Patrick McCabe) hauling iron ore and supplies to Troy, NY.

He enlisted at age 42 in the 1st New York Light Artillery Btry. H on August 18, 1864.

He participated in the battles of Peeble's Farm, Weldon Railroad (December 1864), and in the Appomattox Campaign.

Patrick McCabe was in Co. A, 93rd New York Infantry

Henry Brinkman is William G. Brinkman's father. (See William G. Brinkman bio)

ROBERT H. BRINKMAN, joined SUVCW February 1995 and is secretary-treasurer of the Round Rock, TX camp. He has two great-great-great-grandfathers and one great-great-granduncle who served in the Union Army (James Dunse; Joseph Segar, 1st NY Light Artillery; and Patrick McCabe, 93rd NY Infantry).

Corporal James Dunse was born in Glasgow, Scotland in 1831. He emigrated to Springfield, MA in 1853 and was a manufacturer. He married Isabella Potter and had four children before he enlisted August 13, 1862 in the 21st Connecticut Infantry, Co. I.

Robert H. Brinkman

His regiment participated in the battles of Fredericksburg, Drewry's Bluff, Cold Harbor, Petersburg and Fort Harrison September 29, 1864. James was injured during the charge on Fort Harrison. His unit marched into Richmond on April 3, 1865. He was discharged June 16, 1865 and was in GAR Post 79 in Connecticut.

WILLIAM G. BRINKMAN, joined SUVCW September 29, 1994 and is commander of the Round Rock, TX camp. He has two great-great grandfathers and one great-great granduncle who served in the Union Army (Joseph Segar; James Dunse, 21st CT Infantry; and Patrick McCabe, 93rd NY Infantry).

Private Joseph Segar was born in Quebec, Canada in 1822. He emigrated to Port Henry, NY in 1842 and was a boatman on Lake Champlain hauling iron ore and supplies to Troy,

William G. Brinkman

NY. He married Sophia McClure and had seven children before he enlisted at age 42 in the 1st New York Light Artillery, Btry. H (August 18, 1864).

His battery was sent to the front with the infantry to break up the rebel charge at Peeble's Farm on September 30, 1864. Joseph's battery participated in the Weldon Railroad fight in December 1864, and was selected to go with Generals Sheridan and Warren to get ahead of General Lee at Appomattox. Joseph was discharged May 30, 1865 and was in GAR Post 102 at Port Henry, NY.

CARL ALAN BROOKSHIRE, joined the SUVCW on August 20, 1992.

He bases his right to membership on Pvt. Thomas Jefferson Brookshire. Pvt. Brookshire enlisted December 29, 1863, Co. E, 9th Indiana Cavalry Volunteers, serving in Kentucky, Tennessee, Mississippi, and Alabama. During the Morgan Raid, he served in the State Troops, Co. B, 110th Indiana Infantry. On August 28, 1865 Tom was discharged at Vicksburg. He married his childhood sweetheart, Clementine Akers, and they relocated near Fairmount, IN, where Tom was active in the Hackleman Post, No. 238, G.A.R. Tom died November 1, 1922, and is buried in Park Cemetery, Fairmount, IN.

Carl A. Brookshire   *Thomas J. Brookshire*

Carl Brookshire entered the ministry in 1955, later devoting his time to teaching. Carl is also affiliated with the Sons of the American Revolution, and has established 16 ancestors as Indiana pioneers.

ELLSWORTH W. BROWN, joined Sumner H. Needham Camp #21 Lawrence, Massachusetts on January 10, 1994. He has served as Commander and re-activated Camp #21.

He bases his right to membership on Pvt. George Albert Bailey, 26 Mass. Co. A. Pvt. Bailey enlisted on October 22, 1861. He was killed at the battle of Winchester, VA on September 19, 1864. His body was never recovered, but his name is etched on the family stone in West Parish Cemetery in Andover, Mass. and on the marble tablets of Post 99 in the Memorial Hall Library in Andover, Mass.

MICHAEL BUB, a resident of Mississippi County, MO, was born February 26, 1968 in St. Louis, MO. He and his wife Tammy, with their two daughters, Chastina and Catherine, are members of the Nazarene Church. Michael joined the Sons in February of 1994 as a member of the William T. Sherman-Billy Yank Camp 65 in St. Louis, MO. Mr. Bub is the great-great-grandson of Captain Robert Bruce Bartleson. In August 1862, Mr. Bartleson enlisted in the 109th Illinois Volunteer Infantry, serving a few months in this regiment as a lieutenant in Co. K. While at Holly Springs, the remaining 11 companies were placed under arrest for indications of disloyalty and soon after, were "disgracefully" discharged from service. Bartleson, along with the remainder of his company, were transferred to the 11th Illinois Volunteer Infantry As being promoted a captaincy in Co. F, Robert Bartleson served in that capacity until mustering out with the regiment July 14, 1865.

Michael Bub   *Robert B. Bartleson*

Robert Bruce was not the only Bartleson to hear his countrys' call-seven of his eight brothers also served to uphold the stars and stripes. His twin brother William, who was wounded at Fort Donelson, enlisted with his younger brother Alonzo, in the 18th Illinois Volunteer Infantry Alonzo died of disease in 1861. Warren K. served with the 1st Illinois Cavalry. James, Edwin, Aratus, and John Wool Bartleson enlisted with Co. I, 81st Illinois Volunteer Infantry Captain James and John were both captured at Guntown; John being sent to Andersonville where he endured all the many hardships incident to a soldiers life in prison. Living a long, full, productive life, John Wool Bartleson died April 18, 1944 and is believed to have been the last living survivor of Andersonville.

DANIEL BUNNELL, joined Phil Sheridan Camp #4 in 1992. He has served as Commander of Phil Sheridan Camp No. 4, Senior Vice Commander of Department of California and Pacific.

Daniel Bunnell   *Joseph Foust*

He bases his right to membership on Pvt. Joseph Foust. Pvt. Foust enlisted September 26, 1864, in Co. H, 66th Regiment, OH Infantry commanded by Capt. Robert Simpson. He lost his hearing due to an explosion during the battle of Savannah, Georgia, and contracted rheumatism. He was honorably discharged June 3, 1865. Joseph had three brothers that also served. His youngest brother, Henry, served with the 21st Ohio and fought in the battle of Chickamunga. General Thomas left three regiments on Snodgrass Hill to cover his retreat, including the 500 men of 21st Ohio. The 21st fought until they ran out of ammunition, and then made a bayonet charge down the hill. Henry was captured, and later died of pneumonia.

JEFFRY CHRISTIAN BURDEN, became a member of Lincoln-Cushing Camp #2, Department of Maryland, on March 2, 1991.

His great-great-grandfather, 2nd Sgt. Milton Lingo, enlisted in Co. G, 22nd Iowa Volunteer Infantry, on August 11, 1862. He transferred to Co. I, 3rd Regt., Veterans Reserve Corps on April 30, 1864. He was discharged for disability on October 28, 1864. He belonged to the Washington County, IA GAR Post.

Jeffry C. Burden

The 22nd distinguished itself under Grant at Vicksburg and Sheridan in the Shenandoah Valley. However, the stories his mother remembers hearing from her mother, Milton's granddaughter, were about the hardships faced by Milton's wife and children in his absence on the family farm near Iowa City.

JAMES G. BURNS, JR., joined the Sons June 15, 1990, Phil Sheridan Camp #4.

His Civil War ancestor James Baker, private, served with Co. A, 6th WV Infantry He enlisted Feb. 14, 1865 and was discharged June 10, 1865. He belonged to "Headquarters Meade Post"

James Baker

James was the son of David Baker and Mary West. He was born in Marion Co., VA. James enlisted when he was old enough, after serving in the "Home Guard". During the war, while on guard duty, he caught a cold which caused him to go deaf in one ear, and gave him problems with his hip; severe enough that he had to walk with a cane. He was granted $17.00 a month disability pension. He joined the GAR in 1886. He, and one of his sons married into a families of "secessionists". His grandmother said there were interesting "discussions" when the families got together. James was proud about his role in the war, on his family tombstone is "James Baker, Co. A, 6th West Virginia Infantry" One of his treasures is a shiny GAR button from his coat, that has been passed down in the family, it was given to him by his mother, Frances (Baker) Burns.

WILLIAM BURNS, joined Ezra S. Griffin Camp #8 on June, 1992, Camp Guard.

William bases his right to membership on 2nd Lt. John R. Shields. John enlisted in NY 9th Regiment, Hawkins Zouaves Co. K. on May 4, 1861, and was discharged September 14, 1863. From a Regimental Journal at the Ward Museum, Alexandra, VA which contains the entire history of the 9th NY "Hawkins" Zouaves comes this paraphrase: "The commanding officer of K Co., while under intense fire and infantry attack, said to his brother officer, 'The smoke is heavy, I can't see where they are coming from.' He answered, 'See which way 1st Sgt. Shields is facing, that is where they will be.'"

John R. Shields

John retired from the NYC Fire Department. He died in 1924 at 82 years of age. Bronchial pneumonia did what cannon fire could not. Submitted for William Burns by his father, Tom Burns, member SUVCW Camp #8.

MILTON Y. BUTLER, joined Colegrove-Woodruff #22 Marshall, MI September 1, 1993.

He bases his right to membership on William Wallace Harness. Pvt. William Wallace, the name under which he fought, served with Co. I, 136th Illinois Vol. Infantry and Kentucky and Missouri Infantries. William enlisted June 1, 1864 and mustered out October 22, 1864.

Milton Y. Butler   *William W. Harness*

His division was shipped by cattle car without bathroom facilities to Gettysburg. When they stopped for fuel and water, women threw flowers and food to them. The train stopped at a rail spur 15 miles from Gettysburg on July 3, 1863. The division lined up and the company clerk took their personal possessions. He put their name and rank on their shirt. On the 4th the Company lined up for battle. The Commander said they would meet General Lee today and get ready to die. Word came that Lee was retreating. They marched 15 miles to the battlefield to bury bodies and burn the animals. Soldiers heaved up blood from the stench of death. Pvt. Wallace was 16 years old.

CHRISTOPHER DUFFY CAMERON, joined Appomattox Camp No. 2, Maryland Dept. April 23, 1994. He was a delegate to the National Encampment 1994 in Lansing, MI.

Christopher D. Cameron

He claims his right to membership on Edward W. Culin, Ordinary Seaman and Jacob Culin, his father, of Co. K, 26th Regiment, PA Infantry Edward Culin was discharged September 28, 1864. Christopher Cameron is fifteen years old and the son of John Clifford Cameron of Malvern, PA. He is descended from Edward W. Culin and his father Jacob Culin.

JOHN CLIFFORD CAMERON, joined the Appomattox Camp No. 2, Maryland Dept. on November 7, 1993. He served as Junior Vice Commander 1994, 1995 Camp Patriotic Instructor, and MD Dept. 1994-1995.

He claims his right to membership on Edward W. Culin, Ordinary Seaman and Jacob Culin, his father, of Co. K, 26th Regiment, PA Infantry Edward Culin was discharged September 28, 1864. He served in the Navy on the North Carolina, the William G. Anderson and was discharged from the U.S. *Savannah*. He is buried in the Chester Rural Cemetery in the Soldier's circle, Row 1, Grave #115. His father, Jacob Culin, enlisted on May 13, 1861. He is buried in the same, Row 1, Grave #7. He saw action at Peninsula, Bull Run, Centreville Heights. Jacob was in charge of the War Balloon and had 37 men under his command.

He was born at the ancestral homestead on Crum Creek in Ridley Township. The property was granted to Johan Van Culin an earlier Dutch/Swedish descendant before William Penn settled Pennsylvania. He also served in the Florida war against the Seminole Indians in 1837 as a Private.

MERLE "PETE" CARLSON, joined the Wm. T. Sherman Camp #93, Dayton, OH, in June 1994. He has served as Camp Commander.

Merle Carlson   *Henry W. Quigley*

Pete bases his right to membership on Pvt. Henry W. Quigley who was born August 27, 1843 in Lancaster County, PA. Pvt. Quigley served in 28th PA Vol. Infantry from October 11, 1861 to September 1862 and then was transferred to 147th PA Vol. Infantry Co. E. He was mustered out July 15, 1865 after Grand Parade in Washington, D.C.

He married Lydia Martin on December 11, 1867. Lydia was born in August of 1845, also in Lancaster County. Henry died May 4, 1932 and Lydia died on November 8, 1924 in Ludington, MI.

JACK W. CARMICHAEL, joined Phil Sheridan Camp No. 4, San Jose, CA on November 5, 1994. He served in the AAF from October 1942 to January 1946. He received a direct commission from civilian life in U.S. Army Reserve and served from 1949 to 1959. He was honorably discharged as a Captain. He is now retired as a public and private school administrator.

Jack bases his right to membership on two ancestors, Pvt. William W. Self and Sgt. Arthur Wellington Carmichael, Jr. Pvt. Self, of Co. C, 5th Regiment Mounted Infantry, TN Vol., enlisted on September 23, 1864. He was hospitalized at Cleveland, TN for six months during his service due to dysentery, and was discharged July 16, 1865. Pvt. Self died six months after he was discharged due to effects of dysentery.

Sgt. Carmichael of Co. I, 2nd Iowa Cavalry, enlisted, at the age of 20, on August 4, 1861. He was wounded in Mississippi by a mini ball in his right ankle. After the war, he followed his profession of a veterinary surgeon. He died in DeWitt, Nebraska, November 27, 1923.

JOHN K. CARMICHAEL, JR., joined Ben Harrison Camp 356 (Indianapolis) August 12, 1991, during 110th National Encampment at Indianapolis.

John K. Carmichael, Jr.   *Michael Ryan*

John bases his right to membership on his paternal great-uncle, Pvt. Michael Ryan. Pvt. Ryan joined Co. K, 19th Regiment, IN Volunteer Infantry (part of the famous Iron Brigade), February 1, 1864, and was killed in action June 18, 1864 in the Battle of Petersburg, VA, after only 4 months in service. He was 18.

BRIAN S. CARPENTER, SR., joined S.U.V.C.W. in 1993, Anna M. Ross Post #1 Philadelphia. He joined many others do, interested in his ancestors before him, learning more of his past and intend to hand it down to further generations.

His great-great grandfather, Joseph K. Norcross, was a senior vice commander in the

G.A.R. Post #8, Philadelphia, in 1879 (by orders escorted U.S. Grant to a reception), and in 1880 became post commander. He was in Philadelphia 65th Regt., 5th Calvary Co. A, Joseph enlisted February 1964. Medical records has him in and out of the hospital, and medically discharged at Germantown, PA March 1865.

He married Katie G. Snyder September 1867, having two sons and two daughters. He died of heart disease in 1913 and is buried in Northwood Cemetery Philadelphia, PA.

ROBERT G. CARROON, joined the Order in 1977 as a member of Henry Harnden Camp 32 in Madison, WI. In 1991 he transferred to Alden Skinner Camp #45, Rockville, CT, where he was elected Camp Commander in 1994. Bro. Carroon is currently junior vice commander of the Department of Connecticut. He has also served as commander of the Connecticut Commandery of the Military Order of the Loyal Legion of the United States and is currently Sr. Vice Commander-in-Chief of that Order.

Robert G. Carroon   *John Arbuckle*

Among his seven veteran ancestors Bro. Carroon bases his right to membership on his great grandfather, 1st Lieutenant John Arbuckle, Co. "B" 61st Ohio Volunteer Infantry. Lieutenant Arbuckle enlisted March 1, 1862 at Navare, Ohio and resigned his commission on November 2, 1864. He died at Maywood, IN, on March 15, 1905.

JAMES F. CARVER, joined the Sons June 1995, as member-at-large. His Civil War ancestor, Pvt. James Lee Wheeler, served in Co. B, 14th Regt., from October 10, 1861 to January 31, 1865. He belonged to Camp Wallace, Louisa, KY.

James F. Carver   *James Lee Wheeler*

James Lee Wheeler, a son of John Ramey Wheeler and Rachel LeMaster, was born November 21, 1841 in Blaine, Lawrence County, KY.

James Lee at the age of 19 rode his horse to Catlettsburg, KY and enlisted into the Union Army on October 10, 1861. His actual active duty began December 10, 1861 when James Lee mustered in at Camp Wallace in Louisa, KY as a private. He served in Co. B, 14th Regt., Kentucky Infantry.

James Lee would serve his country well until June 20, 1864, when at the age of 22 years, he was wounded at a battle in Altons. It would be 15 days later before James Lee would be admitted into the General Hospital (#1667) in Louisville, KY on July 5, 1864. James Lee suffered a severe flesh wound in an upper part of a thigh, a minnie ball was removed. James Lee shortly thereafter was transferred to the General Hospital in Ashland, KY. By November 1864 James Lee returned to active service.

James Lee Wheeler would marry his war bride, Mahala Angeline Sparks, in Blaine, KY on January 4, 1865, less than a month before his military discharge on January 31, 1865. James Lee lived a productive life until his death on January 19, 1921 in Webbville, Elliott County, KY.

IRVEN R. CASSIO, is a charter member of Henry Casey Camp No. 92 which meets in Washington Court House, OH. He is employed as a senior computer analyst. He is married to Caroline Gruber, and is the stepson of Robert E. Grim. He is a corporal in Co. C, 20th Ohio Volunteer Infantry which is the Sons of Veterans Reserve unit for the Henry Casey Camp.

Irven R. Cassio

He is the great-great-grandson of Private William Newcomb McFadden who served in Co. B, 187th Ohio Volunteer Infantry Irven is also the great-great-grandson of Private George Washington Hanes who served in Co. I, 7th Indiana Infantry and was discharged due to a medical disability. However, he enlisted again in Co. F, 25th Indiana Infantry

George Washington Hanes is buried at Edinburg, IN. William N. McFadden is buried at Lees Creek, Clinton County, OH.

WILLIAM T. CHAPMAN, joined the sons May 30, 1995 as national member-at-large. His right to membership is based on his grandfather, Sgt. George E. Chapman, Co. B, 173rd Regt., Ohio Volunteer Infantry Enlisted August 20, 1864; discharged July 5, 1865.

George Ed Chapman was born in Gallia County, OH on March 17, 1840. He was married and the father of two sons at the time he enlisted in the 173rd Regt. The 173rd Regt. participated in the Battle of Nashville December 15-16, 1864. The regiment then guarded prisoners at Nashville and also served at Columbia and Johnsonville. The regiment made several raids across Tennessee from Johnsonville and also guarded the railroads.

The regiment was ordered to Nashville on June 20, 1865 and on June 28, 1865 was mustered out of Federal Service, number 854 men. The regiment was sent to Camp Dennison, OH where it was paid and discharged on July 5, 1865.

After discharge he returned to his home and family on what was known as "The Devil's Nubbin" on the Levisa River in Lawrence County, KY. He established a mercantile business and later he and his sons added a sawmill which they operated until 1880. When the Gallup Post Office was established about 1878 he was appointed the first postmaster. He purchased a small tract of land near the forks of Griffith Creek and erected a store building in which the post office and a general merchandise store were located. His store at the Devils Nubbin was removed to the new location.

William T. Chapman

After his first wife died in 1885, he resigned from his postmaster position at Gallup and moved to Clifford on the Tug River where he became postmaster at that place. He married my grandmother, Mary E. (Branham) Maynard, at Louisa, KY on November 24, 1886 who was a Civil War widow of Col. Maynard. His father, F.T. Chapman, was one of their four children.

During his lifetime, his grandfather was a veteran of the Civil War, a stonemason, merchant and mechanic. He died in Donithon, KY on September 22, 1910 and was buried there in the Chapman and Maynard family burial grounds. *Submitted by William T. Chapman, grandson July 27, 1995*

CHARLES L. CHRISTIAN, joined the Sons, Phil Sheridan Camp #4, on April 15, 1993. His Civil War ancestor was his great-grandfather, Pvt. Charles B. Smith, served with Co. D, 4th MN Infantry Enlisted April 11, 1862 and was discharged June 11, 1864. It is unknown to which GAR post Smith belonged.

Charles L. Christian   *Charles B. Smith*

He took sunstroke at the siege of Corinth, MS, May 1862. As a result he was assigned as a printer clerk to the Commissary-Quartermaster sergeant. He went back into the trenches in the rear of Vicksburg and his brigade was given the honor of being the first to march into that city on its surrender, July 4, 1863. Upon his discharge for disability July, 1864, he became the quartermaster agent on Island #98, north of Vicksburg. In 1865 he joined the 9th Vets. Res. Regt. in Washington, D.C. At the end of the war he got a clerkship in the war department and assigned as an assistant to General O.O. Howard in the Freedmens Bureau. This resulted in a friendship with the noted General that was prized by Charles until his death at Cloverdale, CA in 1924.

WILLIAM J. CLAYBORN III, joined the Colegrove-Woodruff Camp 22 in January 1994.

William bases his right to membership on two Civil War ancestors, Pvt. William J. Clayborn and 1st Lt. Dr. Charles J. Lane. Pvt. Clayborn enlisted in the 9th MI Infantry Co. E on August 30, 1864, and was discharged June 20, 1865. 1st Lt. Lane served from September 16, 1861 through January 8, 1862 and May 23, 1864 through February 28, 1866.

William J. Clayborn III   *Dr. Charles J. Lane*

Dr. Lane was the only surgeon and physician who served continuously on the two steamers, *Western Metropolis* and *Northern Light,* during the entire time they were in commission as hospital transports. During the administration of Presidents Harrison and Cleveland, he served as United States Pension Examining Surgeon.

LOUIS B. COATES, JR., joined the Jeremiah Smith, 4th U.S. Cavalry, 5th Military District SVR on March 25, 1994. Louis Coates served in WWII, his son served in the Vietnam War, and his grandson is currently in the U.S. Navy.

Louis B. Coates, Jr.   *Donald B. Coates*

He bases his right to membership on Pvt. William Green, Co. A, 106th Regt. IL Vol., who enlisted, at the age of 33, on August 15, 1862. He served continuously, in battles including the battle at Vicksburg. Immediately after Vicksburg, his unit advanced on Little Rock and was duty in Arkansas until the close of the war. Pvt. Green was discharged on July 24, 1865.

After his discharge, William Green, returned to his family and resumed farming. He had married Arrilda Jane Buchanan on April 7, 1853 and with her had ten children. On March 13, 1875, William died in a tragic wagon accident, having been run over and trampled in New Memphis, Bourbon County, Kansas.

LEO F. COHOON, PCC - Bro. Cohoon joined the SUVCW in 1985, helping to revitalize WA-BU-NO Camp #53 as commander in Mt. Pleasant. On the department level Bro. Cohoon has served as chaplain and color bearer. He currently serves as camp counselor.

From his four veteran ancestors, great-grandfather Clark Wright, Co. F, 12th Michigan Infantry Regt.; John Buckenberger, great-grandfather, 5th Independent Co. Ohio Volunteer Sharpshooters; great uncle Stephen Cohoon, 1st Michigan Eng. and Mech; great uncle Sgt. Benjamin A. Cohoon, who enlisted, September 9, 1861 at Jackson, MI. Mustered in September 23 1861, at Fort Wayne, MI, Co. K, 9th Corp., 8th Regt., Michigan Vol. Infantry, Bro Cohoon bases his right to membership on his great uncle Sgt. Benjamin A. Cohoon who was discharged in accordance with G.O. No. 77 from the War Department dated April 28, 1865. Mustered out at Camp Chase, OH, June 13, 1865. He was a member of Ralph Ely Post #150, G.A.R. Shepherd, MI. He died August 28, 1917, about two months after his 50th wedding anniversary.

Bro. Cohoon and his wife Rose reside in Shepherd, MI.

DALE COLLIER, joined the Sons, Ohio Dept. Camp #12, as life member #246 on April 19, 1990. Mr. Collier lives in Tiffin, OH.

His father, Harry Judd Collier served in Co. F, 140th Illinois Infantry.

CHARLES W. CORFMAN, joined Given Camp #51, Wooster, OH, in August of 1973 and has held the offices on Camp Commander, Treasurer, Dept. Commander, National Site Committee Chair, Commander-in-Chief, and Commanding General SVR.

Charles W. Corfman

He bases his right to membership on Pvt. Christian Curfman of the 37th Iowa. His enlistment is unknown. Pvt. Curfman was discharged April 2. 1862.

ARTHUR J. COSTIGAN, joined the Abraham Lincoln Camp 100 on April 26, 1980 in Hightstown, N.J. He has held the office of Vice Camp Commander.

Arthur bases his right to membership on his grandfather Pvt. Kyran Edward Costigan of Co. G 47th NY State Militia. Pvt. Costigan was mustered in June 18, 1862 (Fort McHenry, MO), and was mustered out September 1, 1862 (Brooklyn, NY). Pvt. Costigan belonged to GAR Post G.K. Warren Post 286.

Arthur J. Costigan   *Kyran E. Costigan*

Kyran left his home, the Williamsburg section of Brooklyn, NY at the age of 16 to enlist in the militia for 3 months with complete tour of duty at Fort McHenry. Official records show Costigan to be age 19, when in fact he was 16, and that his first name was Ryan (this could have been an alias). Pvt. Costigan who was born at Oxford, MA on February 10, 1846, died in Englewood, NJ February 11, 1911 and is buried in Old Calvary Cemetery, Queens, NY.

JOHN W. COTHERN, joined the Sons February 1, 1994, member-at-large (soon to be charter member Camp #1, Memphis, TN).

George W. Cothern, Civil War ancestor with rank of private in Co. K. Served with 1st Alabama Cav. He enlisted November 1, 1863 and was discharged May 16, 1865.

"The 1st Alabama Cavalry was composed mostly of men from the northern portion of that state and their love and devotion for the union and the old flag was not excelled by any who wore the blue." ("Alabama Tories", The First Alabama Cavalry, U.S.A., 1862-65, page 43, William Stanley Hoole, 1960, Confederate Publishing Company, Inc., Tuscaloosa, AL). George W. Cothern was born in Henry County, GA ca 1835 and was living in Madison County, AL when he joined the 1st Alabama Cav. The 1st Alabama Cav. was with General William T. Sherman on his march to the sea. George W. Cothern was wounded at the Battle of Monroe's Crossroad in North Carolina on March 10, 1865. His wound disabled him and subsequently led to his discharge. After the war he returned to Madison County, AL and moved to Cross County, AR sometime in the 1890s.

BRADLEY SCOTT COX, born July 30, 1967 in Washington Court House, OH, became a charter member of Henry Casey Camp #92, Department of Ohio, in August 1992, serving the camp as historian and color bearer.

Bradley S. Cox   *Charles Schoonover*

Brad is the third great-grandson of Charles Schoonover, a private in Co. E, 33rd Regt., Ohio Volunteer Infantry, enlisting on September 3, 1861 at Camp Morrow, near Portsmouth, OH. He participated in the Battle of Perryville, and was captured on September 20, 1863 at the Battle of Chickamauga while serving under General Thomas. Family history states he was sent to Libby Prison. After being paroled at City Point, VA, on April 30, 1864, he spent time at hospitals in Annapolis, MD and Columbus, OH. He was discharged on September 14, 1864 at Columbus. He reenlisted with the 194th Regt., Co. H, on February 17, 1865 and was honorably discharged on October 24, 1865.

GREGORY DAVID COX, born November 20, 1964 in Washington Court House, OH, is a charter member of Henry Casey Camp #92, Department of Ohio, having joined in August 1992. Greg has served the camp as junior vice commander and senior vice commander.

Gregory D. Cox

Greg is the great-great-great-grandson of Pvt. Robert D. Taylor, who enlisted in Co. C, 1st Regt., Ohio Volunteer Heavy Arty., on June 22, 1863 at Portsmouth, OH. During December 1863 and January 1864, he was detached doing guard duty at Cincinnati, OH. Forming a part of the 1st Brigade, 4th Div., Army of the Cumberland, the regiment saw service mostly in Tennessee, North Carolina, Virginia, Georgia and South Carolina. Robert was discharged on July 25, 1865 at Knoxville, TN, by orders of the War Department. At 28 years of age, Robert was five feet, three inches, with grey eyes, dark hair and a dark complexion.

RONNIE DAVID COX, has been an associate member of Henry Casey Camp No. 92 since the camp was organized in Washington Court House, OH in 1992. He is currently serving as chaplain of the Henry Casey Camp. He is a retired fireman and is a veteran of the United States Army. He is a corporal in Co. C, 20th Ohio Volunteer Infantry The 20th O.V.I. is the Sons of Veterans Reserve Unit for the Henry Casey Camp.

Ronnie D. Cox

The camp is named in honor of Cpl. Henry Casey who received the Congressional Medal of Honor while serving with Co. C, 20th Ohio Volunteer Infantry at Vicksburg during the Civil War.

SHAWN ALAN COX, born on October 7, 1972 in Washington Court House, OH, became a charter member of Henry Casey Camp #92, Department of Ohio, in August of 1992. He served as camp color bearer from the formation of the camp through 1994 and is currently in 1995 serving as camp senior vice commander.

Shawn A. Cox　　*Hillory L. Wilcoxon*

Shawn is the great-great-great-grandson of Pvt. Hillory Lyles Wilcoxon, who enlisted in Co. E, 33rd Regt., Ohio Volunteer Infantry, on September 12, 1861 at Camp Morrow near Portsmouth, OH. From November 1862 until January 9, 1864, he served with the detached Pioneer Brigade, 1st Bn., Co. D. He was then transferred to the 94th Regt., Co. F, arriving January 28 and serving until April 3, 1864 when he returned to the 33rd Regt. He was discharged near Villenow, GA, upon the expiration of his term of service on October 10, 1864.

ROBERT COLIN CRAIG, is a charter member of the Orlando A. Somers Camp No. 1 of Kokomo, IN. He is the son of Dr. Reuben A. Craig and Jo Emily Schwartz Craig and the son-in-law of Past Commander-in-Chief Allen W. Moore and Barbara Tiley Moore. Brother Craig holds two degrees from Purdue University and is employed as an engineer at Delco Electronics. He is the great-great-grandson of Pvt. Thomas J. Ferguson.

Thomas J. Ferguson enlisted in the 24th Light Artillery, Indiana Volunteers from Carroll County, IN, on September 27, 1862, and was discharged on August 3, 1865. He was born August 6, 1843, and died November 17, 1933.

ROBERT H. CRAWFORD, joined as a National Member-at-Large as a re-enactor on April 19, 1995. He bases his claim to membership on Captain John Jacob Belsterling, of Co. C, 88th PA. He enlisted September 13, 1861 and died in action at Second Bull Run, VA August 30, 1862.

On January 4, 1862, an elegant silk regimental flag was presented to the 88th Pennsylvania Regiment by his Honorable G. Grow, the Speaker of the House of Representatives. It is said that during this gala affair, Captain and Mrs. Belsterling conceived the last of their five children.

 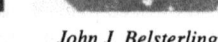
Robert H. Crawford　　*John J. Belsterling*

Unfortunately, Captain Belsterling never lived to see the birth of his daughter, Mary Emma. She was born 6 days after her father was killed. Twenty-three years later Mary Emma married Robert H. Crawford.

FRANK KEVIN CULLEN, joined Ben Harrison Camp 356, Indianapolis, on August 20, 1994.

Frank bases his right to membership on his Civil War ancestor Lt. Henry H. Dudley. He enlisted in Co. C 13th Maine Vol. Infantry in April of 1861, and was promoted to Sgt. December 4, 1861. In September 1863, he was commissioned as a 2nd Lt. with the 20th Regiment Infantry Corps De Afrique, which was later called 91st U.S. Colored Infantry. His commission was signed by General Nathaniel Banks. He served at Fort Macomb and New Orleans. Dudley was injured in June 1864 while he and his men were pulling a picket boat from a bayou. Dudley was discharged in August 1864.

The Dudley family settled in Louisville, KY in 1876. Henry died there on June 6, 1909, at 75 years of age, and is buried in Cave Hill Cemetery.

JAMES ROLAND CYPERT, joined the Sons, General John Gibbon Camp No. 19, Chino, CA on July 25, 1994. His Civil War ancestor is Cpl. L.M. Teters, 45th Regt., who enlisted on August 10, 1864 and was discharged on July 10, 1865. He belonged to GAR Post St. Louis, MO.

James R. Cypert　　*Lafayette M. Teters*

According to Union Army Certificate of War Service records on file in the Missouri State Archives and the Rolls in the Office of the Auditor of the United States War Department, his great-grandfather, Cpl. Gilbert Du Motier Marquis De Lafayette Monroe "Lafe" Teters (circa 1845 to June 2, 1883) enlisted in the Union Army as a private on August 10, 1864; he was 19 years of age and weighed 94 pounds. Private Teters was of Cherokee descent. His commanding officer at this time was Capt. Portchard. On the day of his enlistment he was mustered into the 45th Regt. (Infantry), Co. F at Warrensburg,

MO. After a period of infantry training at Warrensburg, MO, Pvt. Teters moved with his regiment to Jefferson City, MO in anticipation of a rumored Confederate attack on that city. Private Teters was "wounded in action" at the Battle of Jefferson City, MO on October 7, 1864 during the assault on that city by the Confederate General Sterling Price. Unfortunately, the family has not been able to ascertain the extent of his wounds. Family tradition says that "Private Teters", during the heat of the battle, saw a Co. F comrade get shot and drop the American flag. Private Teters ran, picked up the flag and rallied Co. F to fight on. After this battle the 45th Regt. remained in Jefferson City, MO until December 1864 and then moved on to Nashville, TN. Private Teters participated in the Battle of Nashville with his regiment on December 15 and 16, 1864. The regiment then moved on to Spring Hill, TN where Pvt. Teters was assigned garrison and guard duty until January 5, 1865. On January 11, 1865 Pvt. Teters was involved in a military operation near Sugar Loaf Prairie, AR. Private Teters was promoted to the rank of corporal on March 20, 1865 by Capt. H.C. Donnohue. Corporal Teters was relieved from duty at St. Louis, MO on July 10, 1865. On February 22, 1869 he married Miss Susan Angeline Nave in Cole Camp, Benton County, MO. Their eldest son, Clayton Monroe Teters, was born on December 18, 1869. Clayton Monroe Teters is the grandfather of James Roland Cypert. Clayton Monroe Teters married Mary Catherine Wright on November 4, 1900 in Fairfield, Benton County, MO. Their eldest daughter, Dorothy Lear Teters, was born on October 21, 1902 in the Indian Territory (now Oklahoma). Dorothy Lear Teters is the mother of James Roland Cypert. Corporal Teters became a police constable in Golden, MO after the Civil War. He was taken captive by horse thieves and killed in the line of duty on June 2, 1883 in Golden, MO.

James Roland Cypert (October 18, 1946) is the great-grandson of Cpl. Lafayette Monroe "Lafe" Teters. Mr. Cypert is a veteran of the Vietnam War, having served in the United States Navy aboard the USS *Valley Forge*, LPH-8.

During his 18 months in Vietnam Mr. Cypert participated in the following combat operations: Dagger Thrust, Double Eagle, Blue Marlin and Harvest Moon. Mr. Cypert was awarded the National Service Medal, Vietnam Service Medal, (two Bronze Stars), Vietnam Campaign Medal (with device), and the Battle Efficiency "E" Ribbon.

Mr. Cypert is a member of the Sons of Union Veterans of the Civil War, Sons of the American Revolution, Veterans of Foreign Wars of the United States and the American Legion.

Mr. Cypert's paternal and maternal ancestors have fought in the American Revolution, War of 1812, Civil War (Union and Confederate), World War I, World War II and the Korean War. Mr. Cypert is a veteran Los Angeles police officer. On September 27, 1968 he married his childhood sweetheart, Judith Lynn Crosier. They have four children: James Dylan, Julie Kathleen Diane, Joelle Ranae and Jeannette Michelle. These children are the great-great-grandchildren of Cpl. Lafayette Monroe "Lafe" Teters.

GEORGE DARLEY, claim to membership to the SUVCW is his father, Pvt. Benjamin Darley, who served with Co. K, 2nd Illinois Artillery.

His brother, Robert, was for a short time superintendent of the American Military Cemetery at Cambridge, England.

George Darley lives in Jacksonville, FL.

AUGUSTUS PLUMMER DAVIS, was born in Gardiner, ME on May 10, 1835. As a youngster he loved the sea. This may be the reason why at age 14 he sailed to California during the gold rush. Later he joined the U.S. Navy and was discharged in 1855 after five years of service at the age of 20. He later served as a volunteer subordinate officer of the French Navy during the Crimean War. As of this date, French Naval Archives have not found records of his service.

On November 12, 1861, he was mustered as captain of Co. F, 11th Maine Infantry for three years. On February 4, 1863, he tendered his resignation after receiving a surgeon's certificate that read as follows:

"Headquarters, Suffolk, VA. Medical Director's Office, February, 4, 1863. I have carefully examined Capt. A.P. Davis, Provost Marshal of the Post and find that he has tubercular deposits in the right lung with plursitic adhesions on that side. In consequence, I believe exposure incedent to field service will very soon assuredly break down his health. D.W. Hand, Surg. and Med. Director, Peck's Division."

Davis was breveted a major for faithful service, effective March 13, 1865.

After his resignation, he returned to Maine. However, illness acquired during the war compelled him to move to a more suitable climate-Pittsburgh, PA. He was engaged in the insurance business for many years. Davis married Nancy E. Fulton of Derry, PA, on June 22, 1876.

Augustus P. Davis

On November 12, 1881, the 20th anniversary of his enlistment in the Union Army, he formed a camp of the Sons of Veterans. This was Davis Camp #1 of Pittsburgh. Later, the camp was designated as Davis * Camp, as it was the first camp of the Order. Davis Camp still holds its meetings in Soldiers' and Sailor's Memorial Hall and owns the original charter, leather flag, seal and meeting book. The seal is quite unusual, as it has a lion in the center.

At the second national encampment, Davis was invested with the rank of Past Commander-in-Chief and received $200 for expenses. He was instrumental in the adoption of our badges and ribbons. At the fifth national encampment he was appointed ordnance officer. He was to keep regalia within regulations, supply ribbons at cost, and badges at $6 per dozen. In 1907, Mrs. Davis sold all the remaining ribbon to the order for $100.

A.P. Davis died May 1, 1899 at 6:00 a.m. at his home at 6335 Howe St. in Pittsburgh. *The Pittsburgh Commercial Gazette* read: "Major Augustus P. Davis, age 64, a prominent member of the Grand Army of the Republic and the originator of the "Sons of Veterans" died at his home yesterday morning after a short illness. For many years Mr. Davis was engaged in the insurance business. He was a member of the Loyal Legion, Union Veterans Legion, Knights of Pythias and Masonic Order." The same day, the *Pittsburgh Press* ran the following: "A mass meeting of the Sons of Veterans of Pittsburgh, Allegheny and vicinity is called to meet tonight at 7:30 p.m. in the Armory of Co. A, 14th Regt., in old City Hall to take suitable action regarding the death of Major A.P. Davis." John Seiferth, Past Colonel of Pennsylvania and oldest member of Davis Camp issued the call.

Davis was buried in Pittsburgh's Allegheny Cemetery, 4734 Butler St., Section 28, Lot 35. His mausoleum has been marked with a bronze tablet honoring him as the founder of the Sons of Union Veterans of the Civil War. His wife Nancy died June 13, 1912, and was laid to rest in the tomb with her husband.

CAMERON P. DAVIS, joined the Colegrove-Woodruff Camp 22, September 1992. He has served on the Camp Counsel and as a Patriotic Instructor.

Davis bases his right to membership on Pvt. Hiram Blake, of the 25th Michigan Infantry. Pvt. Blake enlisted in August of 1862 and was discharged in June of 1865. He participated in the Atlanta campaigns which included, Battle of Ressaca, Rocky Face, GA, Cassville, GA, Kennesan Mt., GA, Nick-A-Jack Creek, GA, among others.

ROBERT WARREN DAVIS, joined the Governor William Dennison Camp #1 January 6, 1978. He has held the offices of Camp historian, department of Ohio Chief of Staff, and GAR Highway Officer.

He bases his right to membership on two ancestors, Pvt. Henry L Althen of the 95th Ohio C Co. and Cpl. Francis Davis, of the 55th Ohio A Co. Pvt. Althen enlisted on August 19, 1862 and was discharged August 14, 1865. He served at Vicksburg, MS, Richmond, KY, where he was held prisoner of war from August to October of 1862. Cpl. Davis served from McDowell, VA, Bull Run, VA (2nd Battle), Chancellorsville, VA and Gettysburg, PA. Promoted to Corporal prior to January 10, 1863. Cpl. Davis was in a Cleveland OH hospital from October 31, 1863 until discharged on September 27, 1864.

WILLIAM K. DAVIS, joined Harpers Ferry No. 6 July 4th, 1992.

He bases his right to membership on three Civil War ancestors. His great-grandfather, Anson F. Davis, was acting master and pilot, U.S. Navy, Volunteer Officer. Davis, who belonged to the North Atlantic Blockading Squad, enlisted February 5, 1864 and was discharged June 15, 1865. He was the pilot of the double turret iron clad *Monadnock*. Davis died August 2, 1893 and is buried in the Benjamin Davis Cemetery at Davis, NC Carteret County.

William K. Davis   *Anson F. Davis*

His maternal great-great-great-grandfather, 1st Sergeant Joseph D. Thach with Co. G 9th TN was stationed with the East Tennessee Campaign and in operations in the Cumberland Gap. He enlisted April 7, 1863 and was discharged July 29, 1865. 1st Sergeant George W. Burchett, his maternal great-great-uncle, served with the 12th KY Infantry from September 29, 1861 through July 24, 1865. He was one of 24 chosen as pall bearers for President Lincoln.

JERRY M. DEIBEL, Ed.D, (S.A.R.), Jeremiah Smith Camp #1, Newalla, OK (March, 1993).

His great-grandfather, Ireneus B. Snavely enlisted in the Union Army for a period of one year March 10, 1865, at Lafayette, IN. He was assigned as a private to Co. B, 154th Regt., IN Volunteer Infantry The 154th Regt. left for the front by train, April 30, 1865 from Indianapolis, IN. The regiment traveled to Parksburgh, WV, then to Steven's Station in the Shenandoah Valley, VA, in May, 1865, and from June 27 at Opeguan Creek until Aug. 4, 1865, where the regiment was mustered out Aug. 4, 1865 at Steven's Station, VA. The 154th lost one enlisted man in service, and 40 enlisted due to disease.

Jerry M. Deibel   *Ireneus B. Snavely*

Ireneus was a successful participant in the Cherokee Strip Land Run, Sept. 16, 1893, the opening of Oklahoma Territory for settlement. He claimed the SW 1/4 of Section 20, Township 29, Range 1 East of Indian Meridian. At this location, he and his wife Sarah reared their family of six sons, and two daughters. His grandfather, Howard Snavely, was the fifth son, and seventh child. Ireneus and Sarah later moved to 305 Cherokee in Enid, OK, until his death Jan. 5, 1916. Their house at 305 Cherokee Ave. is still standing in Enid, OK, as of March 30, 1995. He was a member of the Enid, OK GAR.

Jacob L. Snavely, his great uncle, joined the Union Army Aug. 14, 1862, as a private in Co. I, 86th Indiana Volunteer Infantry Regt. for a period of three years. He was discharged March 5, 1863, for disability in Gallatin, TN. Jacob Snavely's service record shows, "treated Nov. 30 to Dec. 6, 1862, gunshot". Private Jacob Snavely was shot in the foot during the advance to Murfreesboro, TN. The 86th was in reserve at Perryville, and participated in the Battle of Stones River, Nashville, and many other engagements of the war.

Upon recovery, Jacob joined older brother, Ireneus Snavely, in the formation of the 154th Indiana Regt. and served in Co. B from March 20, 1865 to May 25, 1865. Jacob Snavely observed that his service in the 154th Regt. towards the end of the war in the Shenandoah Valley as "picking blackberries all summer". After the war Jacob and his wife Mary homesteaded in western Kansas where they farmed. Jacob Snavely became Probate Judge for Haskell County, KS, for many years. He died Nov. 16, 1919, at Sublette, Haskell County, KS. G.A.R. membership unknown. *Submitted by Jerry M. Deibel*

PIERRE J. DePEYSTER, Brother DePeyster, a patriotic member of Stewart-Hope Camp No. 126 joined in 1994. His conviction to the honorable cause of the war and his pride in his veteran ancestry brought him to this worthy order. Brother DePeyster bases his membership on his great-great-grandfather.

John Y. Maier, born in Wurtemburg, Germany in 1827 and a veteran of the German Infantry. He entered America in 1855 and married in 1857 to Christina Deitz.

Pierre J. DePeyster   *John Y. Maier*

Mustered in Rome, NY on December 18, 1863 in Co. F, 24th Regt., New York Cavalry. His company was in some of the hardest fighting around Petersburg. A charge at The Battle of the Crater, he was wounded in his leg from which he never fully recovered. He continued his service fighting on the Appomattox Campaign. He was honorably discharged at Clouds Mills, VA, July 19, 1865.

He died February 28, 1906 a man devoted to his family and country.

WILLIAM J. DEVER JR., joined the Phil Sheridan Camp #4, Calif-Pacfic, San Jose, CA on October 21, 1992. Mr. Dever is a WWII veteran and is retired from the Treasury Department.

William J. Dever, Jr.-1945   *William J. Dever, Jr.*

Mr. Dever bases his right to membership on Pvt. Peter Woll and his son, Pvt. Martin Woll. Peter was a member of Co. H, 5th Michigan Infantry, and enlisted February 1, 1864 and was killed in action at the siege of Petersburg, VA on June 16, 1864. Martin Woll served in Co. E 26 MI Infantry from August 8, 1862 until July 1, 1865.

JERRY BARKER DEVOL, senior vice commander of the newly-formed Brooks-Grant Camp No. 7, Middleport, OH. Served in USAF, 1951-1955, during Korean Conflict, with NATO forces, in Aerial Photography Squadron. Later with occupation forces in Germany. Commissioned, lieutenant, USNR, intelligence, during Vietnam conflict, 1967. Served in active reserves, naval intelligence until discharge, 1980. Reenlisted USAR, combat engineers, 1980. Volunteer, U.S. Army, 1990, for Persian Gulf War. Commander, 318th Quartermaster Detachment, Log Base Echo, near Hafir-Al-Batin, Saudi Arabia, 1991. Participated in liberation of Kuwait, 1991. Honorably discharged and retired, 1992, captain, USA, 35 years of service.

Captain Devol was a longtime member of the Military Order of the Loyal Legion, Ohio Commandery.

Jerry B. Devol   *Gordon B. West*

Among numerous Union Civil War ancestors, Capt. Devol's nearest were: 1). Great-grandfather Wilhelm Ludwig "Lewis" Theis, first lieutenant and commanding officer, "Paxton's Guards", Co. D, 4th Regt., West Virginia Volunteer Cavalry, 1863-64. He participated in the action at Medley Farm, Grant County, WV, January 30, 1864, when his company, guarding a wagon train, was surprised by Rosser's brigade; 2), Great-grandfather Alexander Donaldson, Private, Co. B, "Round-Heads", 100th Regt., Pennsylvania Veteran Volunteer Infantry 1861-1865; This regiment participated in most of the important engagements including Fredericksburg, Bull Run, Antietam, Vicksburg, Wilderness, Spotsylvania, Petersburg, and Cold Harbor. Private Donaldson was wounded at Sharpsburg, 1862. The 100th P.V.V.I. was among those regiments sustaining the highest casualties of the war; 3) great-great-uncle Gordon Battelle West, captain and regimental quartermaster, 77th Regt. Ohio Veteran Volunteer Infantry, 1861-1866. Enlisted as a private, "Union Blues", Co. B, 18th Regt., Ohio Volunteer Militia, in the three months service, April-August 1861. Reenlisted three years 77th O.V.I. While sergeant major of the 77th, wounded severely at Shiloh, Pittsburg Landing, TN, April 6,

1862, musket ball passing through his chest narrowly missing the heart. Returned to regiment after months of recuperation in Cincinnati hospital. Died, Soldier's home, Los Angeles County, CA, 1932, last surviving officer, 77th O.V.V.I.

Captain Devol's grandfather Dr. John Walter Donaldson was an officer in major E.C. Dawes Camp No. 2, Sons of Veterans, Marietta, OH.

GARY ALAN DICKEY, D. Min., Ph.D, joined the Sons, Phil Sheridan Camp #4, California in 1993. His Civil War ancestor was William Gibson Dickey of 121 Pennsylvania Volunteers (1842-1886). He enlisted August 23, 1862 and was honorably discharged June 2, 1865. He was wounded at Battle of Five Forks April 1, 1865 during the siege of Petersburg. He died 21 years later from bomb fragments lodged near his spine which eventually poisoned him.

Gary A. Dickey *William G. Dickey*

Following the Civil War he moved his family from Venango County, PA to Kansas and homesteaded a farm in Ottawa County. He married Tobitha Francelia Gibbons (1844-1940) on December 24, 1867. He was associated with the GAR Post at Salina, KS as were other members of related families. She was awarded his Civil War pension over a period of 54 years.

JUSTIN LEE DINGMAN, is Life Member #107, Membership-At-Large, and joined April 1, 1979.

Justin L. Dingman *Albert Dingman*

He bases his right to membership on Pvt. Albert Horace Hibbard Dingman, Co. G 9th Regiment, IN Volunteer Infantry. He enlisted February 13, 1864 in Valparaiso IN by Captain Joshua Healy. Shortly after he joined, between March 1 and April 9, 1864 he came down with the measles in Nashville. He was only 16 years old at the time. He was a drummer boy during his military career. He was discharged September 28, 1865 at Camp Stanley, TX.

DR. GARY E. DOLPH, CC, DC, joined the Order on March 17, 1990 on the recommendation of PCinC Allen W. Moore as a member of the Orlando A. Somers Camp #1 in Kokomo, Indiana. Starting in 1992, Gary has served four consecutive terms as camp commander. Starting in 1993, Gary has served as Indiana department commander. At the national level, Gary has served on the History and Encampment Site Committees.

Dr. Gary E. Dolph

Gary bases his right to membership on his great-great-grandfather, Sgt. Alfred A. Collins, who enlisted on December 11, 1861 in Co. A, 107th Pennsylvania Infantry Sgt. Collins was crippled from a leg wound received on July 1, 1863 at Gettysburg and was discharged on March 28, 1864. Other relatives who served include: Pvt. Samuel Dolph (Co. D, 61st Pennsylvania Infantry), crippled by a neck wound received at Fair Oaks on May 31, 1862; Pvt. Nathaniel Goodrich (Co. I, 46th Pennsylvania Infantry); Pvt. Samuel Fenn Goodrich (Co. B, 177th Pennsylvania Infantry); Pvt. James Ogden (Co. G, 141st Pennsylvania Infantry), missing in action on November 6, 1862; Cpl. John Ogden (Co. G, 141st Pennsylvania Infantry), killed at the Boydton Plank Road on October 27, 1864; Pvt. William Ogden (Co. E, 179th Pennsylvania Infantry); and Pvt. Henry S. Whiting (Co. H, 187th Pennsylvania Infantry), died of disease at Summit House Hospital in Philadelphia.

LEO DORRINGTON, joined the Sons December 13, 1994, member-at-large, Mass Department. His Civil War ancestor, Pvt. Hugh Dorrington, enlisted June 11, 1861, serving with Co. E, 9th MA Regt., and was discharged June 21, 1864.

Leo Dorrington

Hugh served at Gettysburg and Cold Harbor among other battles. He became a leather tanner in Boston, MA and passed the trade on to his son (Andrew Dorrington-his great-great-grandfather) who founded his own firm in Massachusetts. He died in 1911 (born in 1828).

There is no known photography of him in Leo's possession. One of the proudest moments of Leo's life was when he went to Gettysburg and stood on the same ground Pvt. Dorrington's unit held on July 2, 1863. Leo likes to feel he is continuing in his spirit. Leo has been in the military (U.S. Army) for 25 years (September 1969) and served in Saudi Arabia in Desert Storm/ Shield.

DANIEL STEPHEN DOYLE, SUVCW, was born in Guelph, Ontario, Canada and became a member of the Austin Blair Camp No. 7 Department of Michigan, located at Jackson, MI on November 8, 1993. His great-grandfather, Stephen Hadfield, enlisted in the GAR on August 30, 1864 in Co. D, 53rd Regt. Pennsylvania Volunteers and served as a private in the infantry until his honorable discharge on June 30, 1865. In 1914 Mr. Hadfield attended the 48th National Encampment held in Detroit, MI between August 31 and September 5. He died in 1936 at the age of 95 and is buried in Saint Joseph's Cemetery in Guelph. At the time of his death Daniel was eight years old. The only account he has of his great-grandfather's life during the war is from an interview Mr. Hadfield gave Mr. A.E. Byerly, D.D. published in the *Guelph Daily Mercury* on March 2, 1934. The following is condensed from that article:

"One of the remarkable old men of Wellington County and the only soldier of the United States Civil War to live in Guelph, Stephen Hadfield, at the age of 93, possesses a keen memory of the events of 1864 and 1865 when the North and South fought their final battles and he enjoys the distinction of being one of the few survivors who were present at the surrender of General Lee to General Grant.

Daniel S. Doyle *Stephen Hadfield*

One incident he recalls was at the fierce but short battle of Hatcher's Run, where he was one of a company 32 strong, when in a charge he realized that he was the only man for some distance standing. Wondering what the trouble was, he looked about, and those who were not dead or dying were on the run down hill. There was nothing for him to do but to turn and run also.

His company was one that besieged Petersburg during the winter of 1864 and 1865. Earthen breastworks guarded the men on both sides of Petersburg but at times the men would call a halt or truce and exchange sugar for tobacco, and have some conversation back and forth before hostilities started again.

On April 2, 1865 he recalls the Southern troops evacuated Petersburg and started their retreat. The Northern soldiers followed.

A few more days and the war was over. General Grant's Army marched up from Farnville to Appomattox Court House where General Lee was making his stand. Mr.

Hadfield's company was located near a cross road, and there on the 8th of April 1865, they saw General Sheridan and cavalry pass along the road between their lines. That night they slept in the field just off the road leading into Appomattox and their breakfast consisted of what they had in their haversacks, without coffee.

About 9 or 10 o'clock that historic morning of the ninth, a man was seen by Mr. Hadfield to come from Lee's troops with a white flag, and word was soon passed around that Lee was negotiating with General Grant. A man went from Grant's army into the camp of Lee. After his return Grant himself came along in a carriage drawn by four horses and entered Appomattox Court House and about midday it was announced the war was over.

The aged veteran could still see clearly those closing hours of the war and never forgot the time he shook hands with Abraham Lincoln, the one and only time he saw the President. This occurred at a place on the Potomac River when Mr. Lincoln shook hands with a few of the men who were marching by.

WILLIAM T. DOYLE, was born and raised in Pittsburgh, Pennsylvania. After being discharged from the Marine Corps he relocated to Los Angeles, CA, and became a deputy sheriff with the Los Angeles County Sheriff's Department. After retiring from the sheriff's department he became the owner/operator of a private investigation/body guard service.

He married Susan Holm and had one son, Matthew, from that marriage and along with Susan, raised two sons, Edward and Gregory, from a previous marriage.

He joined SUVCW, Phil Sheridan Camp #4, Cal-Pac, on January 17, 1993.

William T. Doyle   *William Williams*

He is a member of the National Society of Sons of the American Revolution and serving as the vice-president of the San Fernando Valley Chapter. He has eight proven ancestors that served as soldiers during the Revolutionary War.

On July 3, 1863, in the city of Pittsburg, PA, William Williams volunteered for service in the U.S. Army and was appointed to the rank of captain, Co. A, 1st Bn., Pennsylvania Volunteer Cavalry (six month service), which he was authorized to organize by Major General Brooks, after a request from Gov. Curtin of Pennsylvania, due to Confederate troops in force advancing upon the border and headed towards Gettysburg.

On, or about, the first day of November, 1863, while in command of a squad of scouts in search of deserters, William Williams was fording the Yohoghany River at Broad Ford Crossing near the town of Broad Ford, PA, south of Uniontown, PA, when the horse he was riding stumbled and fell with him, throwing Capt. Williams into the river.

Being some 12, or 13 miles from his camp, near Uniontown, Capt. Williams returned to his camp in his wet condition, and due to the weather being quite cold, he took a severe cold which settled in his eyes. Later in his life Capt. Williams became totally blind, as a result of his exposure to the cold when he was thrown from his horse.

On December 29, 1863, in the city of Pittsburgh, PA, Capt. Williams was mustered out of the service with his unit, due to the term of his enlistment expiring.

At some later date William Williams volunteered again with the Union Army. From information obtained from letters, on August 2, 1864, he was attached to the Upper Military Div. of the Mississippi, A.Q.M. Department, where his title was general superintendent of Corrals and Transportation, and evidence seems to show that he was in that position as late as August 11, 1864.

PAUL R. DRAKE, joined the Sons as a member-at-large, Ohio Department on May 1, 1995.

Paul R. Drake   *Oscar W. Midlam*

He bases his membership on his Civil War ancestor, Pvt. Oscar W. Midlam, of 55th O.V.I., who enlisted on November 12, 1861, and was discharged December 20, 1864. He belonged to GAR Posts Cooper, Marion OH and Robbins, Upper Sandusky, OH. Midlam was captured by Jackson's troops at Chancellorsville and escaped that night. He was at the cemetery during the battle of Gettysburg. Attended 50th reunion of GAR-UCV at Gettysburg on July 1, 2, 3, 1913.

ROBERT M. DRUCKEMILLER, joined James B. McPherson #66 October of 1993. He has held the officer of camp commander.

Robert M. Druckemiller   *Thomas Sparks*

He bases his right to membership on Corporal Thomas Sparks of 9th Battery IN Light Artillery. He enlisted December 20, 1861 and was discharged January 27, 1865. The 9th Indiana Light Artillery was one of the Artillery units under General Lew Wallace during the second day battle of April 7, 1862 at Shiloh. Among others, he participated in the following actions: siege of Corinth, Bolivar, TN, Grant's central Mississippi campaign, campaign against Roddy's forces, pursuit of Forest, Meridian campaign, Red River campaign, battle of Pleasant Hill, battle of Nashville, and the pursuit of Hood.

Corporal Sparks was ordered home on January 25, 1865. However, he never made it to Indiana. He was killed January 27, 1865, in Johnsonville, TN, when the steamer *Eclypse*, on which he was being transported, blew up. Out of seventy officers and men, only ten escaped unhurt.

ALAN R. DUKE, is a member of Anna M. Ross Camp #1, Philadelphia, PA.

He bases his right to membership on 1st Lt. Charles Wilson Duke of the 19th PA Vol. and 90th PA Vol. Lt. Duke enlisted April 27, 1861. He was the first Union officer killed at the Battle of Fredericksburg, VA on December 13, 1862. He had just returned from the hospital in Alexandria, VA prior to the battle.

Alan R. Duke   *Charles W. Duke*

His valor in leading Co. K against the Confederates was recognized by the poem written by William Fayette, Drummer, Co. C, 90th Regiment, PA Volunteers. This poem was published. Alan Duke retired from DuPont after 40 years of service, and has a strong interest in archeology and history.

WALTER KENNY DUNN, joined February 6, 1986 as a Member-at-Large.

He bases his right to membership on his great-great-grandfather, Corporal John Henry Crooks. He was born in Baltimore County, Maryland and was a descendent of Col. Henry Crooks (War of 1812), Captain John Owings (War of 1812) and 1st Lt. Joshua Owings (American Revolution). John Henry Crooks enlisted August 14, 1862. He was a member of Alexander's Battery, Baltimore Light Artillery and saw action in the Battle at Antietam

Walter K. Dunn   *John H. Crooks*

and Gettysburg. He was discharged June 17, 1865. Walter Kenny Dunn is a veteran of WWII and a member of many military history groups.

FREDERICK A. DURLING, joined SUVCW May 1, 1981. His Civil War ancestor was Frederick E. Durling, Pvt., Co. K, 137th Infantry, Regt., enlisted August 20, 1862, Caroline, served, August 29, 1862, Binghampton, NY.

Frederick A. Durling

Participated in various battles including Chancellorsville and Chattanooga. Guard duties, General George S. Greene's Headquarters, 3rd Brigade, 2nd Div., 12th Army Corps of the Potomac at Acquia Landing. While at Guard House (May 12, 1863) the building collapsed and plate supporting roof, fell upon him causing severe internal injuries. Sent to Fairfax Seminary General Hospital, near Alexandria, but transferred to Chesnut Hill Hospital, Philadelphia, on June 18, 1863.

When his Brigade began its march June 13, 1863, he was unable to go with his company. The brigade march ended in Gettysburg, and joined the well-known battle of July 1863.

Filed application for pension April 11, 1867, number 120792. Pensioned September 12, 1867, Certificate 84920, retroactive to June 9, 1865. Died February 3, 1910. Ithaca, NY. Survived by five sons and five daughters.

DESMOND G.I. DUTCHER, joined the Sons, Col. George Willard #154, Albany, NY on May 15, 1986. Mr. Dutcher is a member of the Pearl Harbor Survivors Association. He was stationed with the U.S. Navy at Pearl Harbor on December 7, 1941. He is also a Vietnam veteran serving with the U.S. Coast Guard. He lives in Oswego, NY.

He bases his right to membership on his father, Pvt. Hiram P. Dutcher, of Co. D, 184th NYSV.

LAWRENCE I. DUTCHER, joined the Sons, Sidney Camp #41, Ithaca, on October 18, 1993. Mr. Dutcher is a retired school teacher and lives in New Paltz, NY.

He bases his right to membership on his father, Pvt. Hiram P. Dutcher, of Co. D, 184th NYSV.

ROBERT F. DYER, JR, MC, USAR joined the Sons Lincoln-Cushing Camp in 1978, and has served as Camp Commander, and was a candidate for National Surgeon General.

He bases his right to membership on his Civil War ancestor, General Philip Sheridan, who entered the Civil War in 1861 as a captain. His able leadership of campaigns in Tennessee caused General Grant to appoint Sheridan commander of cavalry in the Army of the Potomac in 1864. From August to October, as commander of the Army of the Shenandoah, Sheridan drove the Confederate Army in Virginia out of Shenandoah Valley, and then pillaged the area so that it could not be used to supply the Confederates. Sheridan became a major general in the regular army in 1864 and took part in the advance of Grant's army on Richmond in 1865. He was instrumental in General Lee's surrender.

Philip Sheridan

After the war Sheridan commanded American forces on the Mexican border (1865-1867) and was appointed military governor of Texas and Louisiana (1867).

JAMES EDWARD EDMUNDSON, joined the Lincoln-Cushing Camp #2 November 10, 1984.

He bases his right to membership on Pvt. Joseph Kennison and Corporal John G. Whigham. Joseph Kennison was born on February 18, 1832, in Fayette County, PA. He married Eliza Rebecca Kiger, and they had fifteen children. Joseph's grandfather, also Joseph Kennison, was an early settler in what is now Fayette County.

James E. Edmundson   *Joseph Kennison*

Joseph enlisted in the 14th Pennsylvania Volunteer Cavalry, Companies D and E, at the Town of Greensburg, February 24, 1864. His regiment participated in numerous battles, many in the Shenandoah Valley of Virginia. Some of the more well-known battles were Winchester, New Market, Kernstown and Cedar Creek. In April 1865, Pvt. Kennison and members of his company were camped at the Fairfax Courthouse. Coincidentally, one hundred and thirteen years later, Joseph's great-great-grandson, James Edward Edmundson, an officer with the Fairfax County Police department, gave testimony in traffic and criminal cases at the same courthouse. Pvt. Kennison mustered out of service on August 24, 1865. He died December 8, 1907, and was buried at the small cemetery at the Haydentown Christian Church, Fayette County, PA.

Interestingly, Joseph used the spelling "Kinison" when he signed his enlistment papers. The military records used Kennison and his family has used the spelling since his death. The spelling "Kinison" was used on his headstone.

Corporal Whigham and his younger brother, Robert, initially enlisted in the 58th Regiment of the Pennsylvania Militia, Company D, from June 27, 1863 until discharged on August 14, 1863. John later enlisted with the 116th Pennsylvania Volunteer Infantry, Company I and served from February 23, 1864 through January 24, 1865. He fought in the battles of Spotsylvania, The Wilderness, Cold Harbor, and Petersburg. He was wounded as his regiment charged the Confederate entrenchments surrounding Petersburg, and was discharged due to the severity of his injury. Corporal Whigham was born in Allegheny County, Turtle Creek, Pennsylvania, on July 7, 1842. He married Sarah Curry on March 20, 1867. He died April 29, 1915, in McKeesport, PA and is buried in Richland Cemetery, Dravosburg, PA.

CHARLES GORDON EDWARDS, Membership-At-Large of SUVCW October 27, 1978. Transferred to U.S. Grant Camp Number 100, Cincinnati, OH June 1993 when the camp was reactivated by himself as commander.

Born Kittanning, Armstrong County, PA, February 2, 1930, graduated from Kittanning, Pennsylvania High School 1948, sergeant United States Air Force October 1948 until August 1952. Evening school University of Cincinnati five and a half years, majoring in business administration, while working full-time and raising a family. Retired from the National Underwriter Company, a publishing company for the insurance industry, after 27 years. Married first to Cynthia (Morgan) deceased and have two sons, Richard and Dale. Currently married to the former Mary Sexton (birth surname Nienaber).

Past President Cincinnati Chapter, Sons of the American Revolution, Past Commander West Hills Post 788 American Legion, currently Secretary General Sons of Indian Wars.

Charles G. Edwards   *William Cathcart*

Charles bases his membership on his great-grandfather, Pvt. William Cathcart, Pennsylvania Volunteer Infantry, 11th Regt. Reserves (40th Volunteers), Co. K, who enlisted at Brookville, PA on June 7, 1861 and rendezvoused at Camp Wright, near Pittsburgh, PA. He was honorably discharged at Pittsburgh, PA June 13 1864.

William Cathcart was born June 18, 1837 vicinity of Oakland, Armstrong County, PA - married Elizabeth Miriam V. Anthony April 14, 1870, died August 5, 1915 at Kittanning,

Armstrong County, PA of mitral heart lesion - buried Oakland Cemetery, Armstrong County, PA. He was the son of Alexander Cathcart and Martha Devers.

August 1861 detailed as a Teamster. While driving team from Washington, D.C. to Tennallytown, MD in September 1861, he was injured by a horse falling on him, breaking the joint of his left foot, disabling him from duty. He was treated in the regimental hospital.

November or December 1861 he got dumb ague and was hospitalized in the Pierpont Hospital at Camp Pierpont, near Langley, VA.

At the Battle of Gaines' Mill, VA on June 27, 1862 (Peninsular Campaign), Pvt. Cathcart was Captured with most of his regiment on June 28, 1862 he was incarcerated in Libby Prison. A few days later, the enlisted men were separated from the officers and transferred to Belle Isle, a sandy island in the James River. On August 5, 1862, a cartel was agreed upon and the men were paroled and sent to Aiken's Landing and there furnished transportation to Harrison's Landing.

In November 1862 Private Cathcart was detailed as ambulance driver.

BILL G. EFFLE, joined the Sons March 1993, Phil Sheridan Camp #4, California Pacific.

His Civil War ancestor, was Pvt. Nicholas Effle, who entered the service from Croghan, Lewis County, NY, on August 21, 1863. He was 20 years of age, height 6 feet, 1 1/2 inches, grey eyes, brown hair. He enlisted in Co. A, 20th Regt., New York Cavalry.

Bill Effle   *Nicholas Effle*

His unit left New York, September 30, 1863 and served with McClellan Cavalry, 22nd Corps, October 1863 at Portsmouth, VA, in Department of Virginia; in Heckman's Div. 18th Corps, from January 1864 in the defense of Portsmouth, VA; in the district of East Virginia, Department of Virginia and North Carolina, from April 1864; in 1st Brigade, Kautz's Div., Cavalry, Army of the James, from December 3, 1864. Mustered out July 31, 1865.

Nicholas served in area of Camp Getty near Portsmouth, VA in fall of 1863. While on scout in January 1864 at Gaines Mill, near Suffolk, VA Nicholas was thrown from his horse, as the Rebels drove a Union regiment from the area. Breaking his breast bone, and requiring him to be sent to the Regimental Hospital at Portsmouth, VA.

He rejoined his company at Hickory Grove, NC and took part in Campaign of Carolinas, March 1 through 26, 1865. And Appomattox Campaigns, VA April 1 through 9, 1865. Taking part in the following engagements, Battle of Five Forks, VA, The Fall of Petersburg, Deep Creek, Rice's Station, Burke's Station and at Appomattox Court House.

Nicholas was granted a pension from the injury received while thrown from his horse of 12 dollars per month. He was born August 9, 1843 France (Alsace/Lorraine) of German descent, died April 9, 1910 Omaha, NE. Buried Greenwood Cemetery Creighton, Knox County, NE. He and his wife Mary Hentges homesteaded in Verdigre Knox County, NE in 1879.

LUTHER E. EIKLOR, joined the Sons on July 27, 1974, S.F. Smith Camp #193, Halsey Valley. Luther is a member of the DAV and WWII veteran. He lives in Barton, NY.

His claim to membership is based on his Civil War ancestor, Pvt. William H. Randall of Co. C, 161st N.Y.S.V.

PAUL W. ELDER, Brother Elder joined the order in 1992 and is a member of Oliver Tilden Camp #26, Dept of New York, whose members meet at the 7th Regt. Armory in New York City.

Paul W. Elder

He receives his right to membership from his great-great-grandfather, Stephen H. Pine, a private of Co. F, 132nd New York Volunteer Infantry, who also served as post wagon master. Stephen Pine was a stage coach driver living in New York City at the time of his enlistment in 1862. Born in the early 1820s, he left a wife and two children when he was killed in an accident on May 26, 1864 during the federal occupation of New Bern, NC. Stephen Pine is buried in New Bern National Cemetery. This chapter of his family's history was discovered by Paul and with the assistance of cemetery personnel, the grave marker was replaced in 1992. The photograph shown here was taken Memorial Day, May 30, 1994.

WILLIAM W. ELDRIDGE, joined the Sons, Camp Lt. Nathaniel Bowditch Camp #30, in September of 1994. His basis for membership is his ancestor, Pvt. Michael Littleton. Served with 7th Massachusetts Volunteer Regiment. Enlisted June 15, 1861 and was discharged on June 27, 1864. He belonged to William H. Bartlett Post #3 Taunton, MA.

The Eldridge brothers, William and Joseph, members of SUVCW Camp 30 Department of Massachusetts, and being re-enactors in the 5th Massachusetts Btry., Co. E, Light Artillery, Army of the Potomac, Inc., are the proud descendants of their maternal great-grandfather Michael Littleton.

Michael was born on March 17, 1837 in Ireland, County of Clare. He enlisted in Taunton, MA June 15, 1861 as a private in Co. C, 7th Massachusetts Vol. Regt. and was discharged as a private June 27, 1964. He served the full term of his three year enlistment.

His first battle was on May 5, 1862 at Williamsburg, VA. He also took part in the battles of Fair Oaks, Malvern Hill, Chantilly, Antietam, Fredericksburg 1st and 2nd, Gettysburg, Mine Run, Wilderness, Spotsylvania, and Cold Harbor.

William W. Eldridge

He was never wounded, never in the hospital, nor was he ever taken prisoner. His most intimate comrades were Peter Dyer, Gustavus T. Fisher and William C. Cahoon. He said there was no very important event in his Army life, and that he was glad to have served his adopted country for three years.

On March 14, 1868 Michael married Catherine J. Mackey, a lovely Irish immigrant. They raised a fine, God-fearing family on their farm on Glebe Street in Taunton, MA. They had one son and seven daughters, one of whom was their maternal grandmother Anna Littleton Carr. Michael and Catherine both passed away within a few months of each other in 1910.

HARRY DE FOREST EVELIEN, joined the Sons July 27, 1974, S.F. Smith #193, Halsey Valley, NY. He held office of commander of Camp #193.

His Civil War ancestor, Alfred Evelien, private, served with Pennsylvania State Volunteers.

A WWII veteran member of VFW. He lives in Ithaca. He and his wife Ruth, are the main supporters of the GAR Hall in Halsey Valley.

EDWARD P. FAHEY, joined the Order in 1992 as a member-at-large. Edward bases his right to membership on his grandfather, Pvt. Edward Fahey, who enlisted in Easthampton, MA August 12, 1862 in Co. B, 1st Regt., Massachusetts Volunteer Cavalry. He was Captured on May 10, 1864 at Beaver Dam Station, VA and confined to Libby Prison in Richmond. He was then sent to Andersonville Prison, GA and after being exchanged he was discharged March 18, 1865. He was a member of the Abraham Lincoln Post No. 4, Department of Colorado and Wyoming, GAR. He died December 19, 1927.

Bro. Fahey and his wife Mary reside in San Antonio, TX.

PHILIP FAZZINI, joined the Capt. John P. Bruck #96 Hamilton, OH camp on March 8, 1993.

He bases his right to membership on Pvt. Ziba P. Sayre of Co. H, 4th Ohio National Guard Regiment. He enlisted July 2, 1863. Ziba P. Sayre was married twice and had at least three sons and three daughters. He adopted William Moore Sayre as his son. While Ziba P. Sayre

Philip Fazzini   *Ziba P. Sayre*

was discharged October 4, 1865 for being "overage," William, who belonged to Co. K. 66th O.V.I., died of wounds June 16, 1864 near Pine Knob, Georgia. William is buried in the "unknown" section of the National Cemetery at Marietta, Georgia (apparently, identification was lost).

In 1979, W.M. Sayre's Civil War letters were privately transcribed by a great-great-grandnephew.

KARL FELDMEYER, was born in Franklin County, PA. He joined SUVCW Camp #6 in May of 1993. He is the grandson of Kenneth Dile of Mont Alto, PA, and the great-great-grandson of Private Samuel Dile of Co. A, 101st Pennsylvania Volunteer Infantry Samuel enrolled October 22, 1861, at Pittsburgh and was mustered into service on November 17, 1861, at Harrisburg, PA.

Karl Feldmeyer   *Samuel Dile*

He was wounded at the Battle of Williamsburg, VA, on May 5, 1862. After serving in many battles and skirmishes, he was discharged on December 31, 1863. He reenlisted January 1, 1864, as a veteran. On April 20, 1864, after holding off a sustained enemy attack from all sides for three days at Plymouth, NC, Samuel and his regiment were Captured. He was imprisoned at Andersonville, GA. He was paroled at Wilmington, NC, on February 22, 1865, and was discharged on June 25, 1865 at Roanoke Island, NC. He died on November 13, 1916, and is buried in Newbloomfield, PA.

REV. RAYMOND J. FERRICK, of Saint Michael's Church, Smithfield, RI, has been a member of Elisha Dyer Camp No. 7, Department of Rhode Island since September 19, 1990.

Father Ferrick has served as chaplain of Camp 7 and has held the post of Department Chaplain since 1994.

He is the great-great grandson of two Union Veterans of the Civil War: Pvt. John G. Thurber, Jr., who served in Co. C of the 1st Rhode Island Volunteers from April 17, 1861 until the regiment was mustered out after the battle of Bull Run on August 2, 1861.

He is also the great-great grandson of Pvt. George L. Greene, who served in Co. K of the 51st Mass Volunteers from August 25, 1862 to July 27, 1863.

George Green was a member of the George H. Browne Post 25, Providence, RI and served as post commander from 1899-1900. He also served as department commander, Department of Rhode Island, G.A.R. from 1906-1907.

WILLIAM "ROO" FLECK, joined the Sons in 1994, Camp 120, Washington, PA. His Civil War ancestor was Corporal August Funk who served with Co. K, 74th Penn. Vol. Infantry. Enlisted September 3, 1861 and discharged October 17, 1864. He belonged to GAR Post Pittsburg.

William Fleck

August Funk was born in Prussia in 1837, and immigrated to the USA in 1858-1859. He settled in the Pittsburgh area and in the summer of 1861 married Anna E. Alt, a German immigrant from Hesse. August joined the 74th Pennsylvania Voluntary Infantry Regt. in September of 1861. His highest rank was corporal, and he was listed as a ambulance driver on at least two occasions during his service. He was a member of the G.A.R. in Pittsburgh. He died in 1900 at the age of 63.

FRANK A. FOIGHT III, Colonel in Sons of Veterans Reserve; born Cleveland, OH, July 12, 1927; grew up in Lakewood and Fairview, graduate Fairview High. Enlisted in Army Air Corps on August 3, 1944. Served in Guard and Reserve until July 1987, in Retired Reserve to July 1992. Graduated from Texas Christian University in 1958, graduate work at North Texas, WVU, N.W. Missouri State, and Shepherd College, WV. Active duty during WWII, Korea, and Vietnam.

Frank A. Foight III

Joined SUVCW Camp 2 in Washington, DC in April 1988, founded Harper's Ferry WV Camp 6 in spring of 1989; Adjutant General of Sons of Veterans Reserve, 1989-1994; Senior Aide-de-Camp to commanding General since August 1989. Served four terms as camp commander, one as department commander, Department of Maryland; Past National Chaplain, Past National Americanism and Education Committee chairman. Currently serves as Camp Vice-Commander, Harper's Ferry Camp #6.

Ancestor was Cpl. John G. Foight who served with 4th Pennsylvania Volunteer Heavy Artillery in the defenses of Washington during 1864 and 1865. Later a Pennsylvania State Senator, famous as the founder of good roads in the state. When he came out of the RR Station in Cleveland in November 1946, enroute home from World War II, the GAR was marching past the station, one of their last conventions ever. He will always remember them.

PAUL E. FOSTER, joined Gov. Wm. Dennison #1 OH on September 1, 1994.

He bases his right to membership on his great-grandfather John Oliver Foster (b.1842) and his great-uncle William Wesley Foster (b.1837), both of whom volunteered with the Ohio Vol. Infantry, 185th Regiment, Co. E, Heavy and Light Artillery on February 13, 1865. Their parents came to Ohio in 1837 from Staffordshire, England. They mustered in together at Camp Chase, OH by Wm. P. Richardson, Brevet Brigadier General U.S. Volunteers. John held the rank of Private for one year and Wm. was appointed Corporal in February and Sergeant in August 1865.

Paul E. Foster   *John O. Foster*

They were under orders to report to General Thomas at Nashville, TN but General Palmer obtained permission to retain the regiment in Reg. headquarters, Eminence, KY. They were scattered to Mt. Sterling, Shelbyville, LaGrange, Greensburg, from Owensboro to Cumberland with the Fifty-Third Kentucky. They mustered out September 26, 1865. John went home to his wife Almira and two children, and died in 1876. Wm. Died in 1907.

Paul E. Foster and his two brothers volunteered before Pearl Harbor in the Army/Air Corps.

VICTOR I. FOX, joined the Sons March 12, 1995, Camp Ben Harrison #356.

His Civil War ancestor, James w. Phipps, private, enlisted along with his brother Julius. They were assigned to Co. F. James dressed out in a gray suit with a gray hat. He was armed with a enfield smooth-bore musket. He left for Baltimore from Indianapolis on July 31, and arrived on August 3. He and his regiment were assigned to guard vessels. On February 19 it was ordered to the front. He left on an expedition with General Butler to the Gulf. James' regiment was the only Indiana regiment on this expedition. It was also the first regiment to enter the city of New Orleans with its band playing Piccayune Butlers coming, coming. He was in a number of small engagements, the largest to be the battle of Baton Rouge.

Victor I. Fox

He was Captured at the battle of Brasher City and was prisoner for five days before being paroled. James lost his equipment and arms and was charged $12.09 for this loss. The 21st Regt., was reorganized in February 1863 into the 1st Regt. Heavy Artillery.

IVAN E. FRANTZ, SR, joined the Capt. Edgar Monroe Ruhl #33, York, Dept. of PA in September of 1941. He has held many offices at the Camp level, including color guard, junior vice commander, commander, council, guide, secretary, and treasurer. He has also held many offices at the Department level, including patriotic instructor, council, secretary-treasurer, junior vice commander, and senior vice commander. At the National level he has been chairman and co-chairman of the GAR Remembrance Day Committee, recorder to the National Military Affairs Committee, Aide-De-Camp to Commanding Officer of National Military Department, Personal Aide to Commander-in-Chief, and Chairman of the National Headquarters Fund Committee.

Ivan E. Frantz, Sr.   *Samuel L. Baldwin*

He bases his right to membership on his great-grandfather, Pvt. Samuel L. Baldwin, who was mustered into the 117th PA Volunteers Regiment, 13th PA Cavalry, on September 16, 1863. He was mustered out July 14, 1865. On a pension application, he claimed that during his term in the Union Army, he was kicked by a horse, which resulted in back pains years later.

During 1995, Ivan Frantz and his two sons will have 100 years of continuous membership in Capt. Ruhl Camp #33; 54 years for Ivan, Sr., 26 years for Ivan Jr., and 20 years for Karl.

IVAN E. FRANTZ, JR., joined the Sons June 1969, Pennsylvania Department, Encampment, Harrisburg, PA.

He held offices: Capt. E.M. Ruhl, Camp #33, York PA - Camp Council, Camp Jr. Vice Commander, Camp Sr. Vice Commander, Camp Commander. Pennsylvania Department, SUVCW - Chaplain, Chief of Staff, Patriotic instructor, secretary/treasurer, Department Junior Vice Commander, Department Sr. Vice Commander, Department Council.

Civil War ancestors: paternal great-great grandfather: Pvt. Samuel Baldwin, Co. D, 13th PA Cav. (117th PA Vol. Regt.). Enlisted September 16, 1863. Discharged July 14, 1865. It is not known if he belonged to G.A.R. He did apply for and receive pension based on injury to back and foot.

Maternal great-great-grandfather: Pvt. John Staub, Co. D, 7th PA Vol. Infantry Enlisted August 27, 1861. Discharge date is unknown. It also is not known if he belonged to GAR. His name is on Pennsylvania Memorial at Gettysburg, indicating he was still on regimental muster roll at time of Battle of Gettysburg.

EDWARD R. FREDERICK, joined the Sons, Col. William Hardy Link Camp #12, in April 1995 and held office as camp color bearer.

He bases his membership on his Civil War ancestor, Pvt. Benjamin Frederick, who served with Co. E, 48th Indiana Infantry. He enlisted on December 3, 1861 and died in service on August 8, 1862.

FRANCIS R. FREDERICK, joined the Sons in June 1975, was a member-at-large 1975-1994, and joined the Col. Wm H. Link Camp #12 in 1995. Held offices as council and guide (camp).

He bases his membership on his Civil War ancestor, Pvt. Benjamin Frederick, who served with Co. E, 48th Indiana Infantry. He enlisted on December 3, 1861 and died in service on August 8, 1862.

The 48th Indiana Infantry Regiment was formed in Goshen, IN in December 1861, with Norman Eddy as colonel. It left for Fort Donelson in February where it arrived the day after its surrender. The 48th moved to Georgia and engaged in siege of Corinth. He died at Camp Cedar Creek near Corinth, GA from illness.

ROBERT WILLIAM FREDERICK, of Georgia, joined the Sons based on his great-great-grandfather, Private Adam Frederick who enlisted in the GAR on August 17, 1864. He was mustered into Co. K, 7th Pennsylvania Volunteer Cav., 1st Brigade, 2nd Div. Cav., Army of the Cumberland, as a private. The 7th Pennsylvania was part of Mintys Brigade and served in the campaigns of the Western Armys.

Adam Frederick

In the fore part of February 1865, while marching from Gravely-Springs, AL and Nashville, TN through cold and inclement weather, Pvt. Frederick suffered severe frostbite. He was finally honorably discharged in Macon, GA in August 1865 due to the close of the war.

Private Frederick also had a brother, Cpl. John Frederick, who served from 1861-1864 in the 74th Pennsylvania Infantry and was wounded at Gettysburg.

Private Frederick was married to Hannah Aldinger Frederick. They had three children: William, Ida, Dora.

MICHAEL FULLER, joined the SUVCW in 1994, Camp General. William T. Sherman, Billy Yank Camp No. 65, St. Louis, MO. His Civil War ancestor Alonzo Green Fuller, private, Unit 24th Iowa, Co. F. Enlisted August 21, 1862, medical discharge, January 11, 1865. GAR Post Logan County, Oklahoma.

Michael Fuller

Alonzo was a farmer living in Mt. Vernon, IA with his wife and two children before the Civil War. He enlisted in the Iowa Temperance Regt. at Camp Strong, Muscatine, IA. New Enfield rifles, Captured from the C.S.A., were issued to the men. He participated in Expeditions along the White River, and General Bank's Red River Expedition (Battles of Sabine Crossroads and Pleasant Hill). Embarked on the "Star of the South" to Alexandria, VA, then joined Sheridan's campaign in the Shenandoah Valley. Wounded in the ankle by a bursting shell at the Battle of Winchester, VA. He was treated at hospitals in Frederick City, Philadelphia, and Davenport. Returned to Iowa, moved to Missouri, then homesteaded near Stillwater, OK during 1891. Died at the home of his daughter in 1903 at the age 78 years. Buried near Hallett, OK with his military service noted on the tombstone.

JAMES H. GAFFNEY, has been a member-at-large of SUVCW since 1977. James H. Gaffney of Silver Spring, MD was a lawyer in government service with the Interstate Commerce Commission when he retired as an administrative law judge. Also, he had been commissioned in the U.S. Army Reserve in 1939, and subsequently retired as a lieutenant colonel.

He bases his membership on his great-grandfather, Cpl. Lucius Graham, who was mustered into Co. F, 49th Illinois Volunteers Regt. in December 1861. In February 1862, he saw action in the battle for Fort Donelson, in which General Grant issued the ultimatum "No terms except immediate and unconditional surrender", resulting in the surrender of

James H. Gaffney   *Lucius Graham*

14,000 Confederates. And in April 1862, he was Captured at the battle of Shiloh and marched away by the retreating Confederates. Later, he was paroled near Washington, D.C. where he died of fever October 25, 1862, and he is buried there in the cemetery adjacent Soldiers Home.

CHARLES R. GAMM, joined the George A. Custer Camp #1 on September 30, 1985.

Charles R. Gamm

He bases his right to membership on Corporal Madison Koontz of the 119th IL Volunteer Infantry. Corporal Koontz enlisted on August 8, 1862 and was discharged August 26, 1865. Mr. Gamm has been a Civil War Reenactor since 1975 and has been in two movies, North and South-Book II, and Gettysburg.

RAYMOND LEROY GARLAND, joined the Lone Star Camp #1 March 1, 1995.

He bases his right to membership on Pvt. Russell Garland, of the 2nd TN Infantry Regiment. He enlisted August 10, 1861. Russell Garland enlisted at Kingston, TN and participated in battles of Wildcat Mountain, Mill Spring, Stone's River, Cumberland Gap, Carter's Station, Blue Spring, and Rogersville, in Kentucky-Tennessee area. He was captured by the confederates November 6, 1863 and was imprisoned at Belle Isle, VA, Andersonville, GA, and Florence, SC until he was paroled March 1, 1865. After his discharge on March 15, 1865, he returned to his home in Stocton's Valley, TN and then moved his family to Savoy, TX. He drew a military pension for loss of sight. He died in Savoy.

THOMAS J. GAUGHAN, joined the Sons June 26, 1993, Camp Lt Ezra S. Griffin, Camp No. 8, PA Div., Sons of the Veterans of the Civil War.

Pvt. Philip Thomas, was born in Ireland 1841, arrived in Philadelphia USA, 1853. From Philadelphia he traveled inland to Ashland, Schuylkill County, PA, where he resided until 1862, working in and around the coal mines. By 1862 he traveled to Scranton, PA to join his mother, Mary Loftus Thomas. The same year, he enlisted with the Pennsylvania Volunteers, and joined the Army of the Potomac at Washington, DC. He engaged in his first battle in Virginia. Later as his outfit was proceeding to the Gettysburg Campaign, and in a battle at Winchester, VA, he was shot off his horse, injured and hospitalized in the Federal City.

DAVID C. GEORGIA, Brother Georgia joined the Order in 1992 and is a member of David C. Caywood Camp #146, Ovid, NY. Brother Georgia bases his right to membership on his great-grandfather, Pvt. Joseph Patrick. Pvt. Patrick enlisted on Aug. 1, 1864 in Btry. C, 1st New York Light Arty. After about two months of service Pvt. Patrick became ill and spent much of his remaining time in the army in the hospital. According to later accounts, Pvt. Patrick acquired a "rupture" soon after enlisting. He was discharged May 14, 1865. In old age, Joseph Patrick lived for a short time in the Soldiers and Sailors Home in Bath, NY. He died July 27, 1924.

Brother Georgia resides in Trumansburg, NY and is employed by Cornell University, Ithaca, NY.

GARY L. GIBSON, PDC, Bro. Gibson joined the Order in 1978 as a member-at-large. In 1985, he helped to organize Benjamin Pritchard Camp #20, in Kalamazoo. Gary served two terms as camp commander. From 1990-1992, he served as Michigan Department Commander. On the national level, Bro. Gibson has served as chaplain, history book coordinator, chair of the Programs and Policies Committee, and patriotic instructor. In 1993, he was elected commander of the Central Region. Gibson currently holds the rank of lieutenant in the Sons of Veterans Reserve.

Gary L. Gibson   *Martin Horan*

Among his six veteran ancestors, Gary bases his right to membership on his great-great-grandfather, Sgt Martin F. Horan. Sgt Horan enlisted in Grand Rapids July 18, 1862, in Co. H, 4th Michigan Cav. He was discharged July 18, 1865, and was a member of Ruddock Post #224, GAR, in Cheboygan, MI. He died September 12, 1912.

Bro. Gibson and his wife Beth reside in Kalamazoo.

JOHN F. GILBERT, joined Philip Triem Camp #43, Salem, OH (19th OH Regiment) on January 31, 1989.

He bases his right to membership on Pvt. Elijah M. Daihl of the 130th PA Volunteers. Pvt. Daihl enlisted on August 10, 1862, and was killed September 17, 1863 at Antietam Creek, Maryland. The following is from a letter Pvt. Daihl wrote in 1863: "[We] expect to get into

John F. Gilbert   *Elijah M. Daihl*

[a] fight, but I don't believe we [shall] get in a fight soon, but I don't care how soon it comes for if I don't fight them, then tell me if God spares my life to come home again, you will see another kind of boy, but if I fall on the battlefield, I hope that I will meet you all in the promised land where parting is never known no more forever." This letter was written along the Leesburg Pike, fifteen miles from Washington. He was killed a month later.

Mr. Gilbert has had a strong interest in Civil War history from the age of five.

PAUL S. GILLETTE, joined the Phil Sheridan Camp #4, Cal-Pac, on November 11, 1994.

He bases his right to membership on Pvt. Thomas Hill, of the Co. F 2nd IL Cavalry. Pvt. Hill enlisted August 13, 1862. He was wounded twice in the battle of Holly Springs, MS, December 20, 1862, and returned to duty in March 1863, serving in Vicksburg campaign. He was discharged at Vicksburg on August 14, 1863 for "inability to endure fatigue due to gunshot wounds received in battle of Holly Springs."

STEVE GIMBER, joined Lyon Camp #10 New Jersey in November of 1981. He has held the position of Guard and camp historian. He was involved with re-establishment of the Baxter Camp #72 SUV and with cataloging GAR artifacts for the Vineland Historical Society.

Mr. Gimber bases his right to membership on Captain Fredrick L Gimber of the 109th PA Co. E. and Henry Gimber of 150th PA Vol. Co. F. Captain Fredrick Gimber enlisted in 1861 and was discharged in 1865, while Henry Gimber enlisted in 1862 and was discharged in 1865. Henry was captured during the battle of Gettysburg.

MAYNARD C. GOETHE, joined the Phil Sheridan Camp No. 4 in 1993.

He bases his right to membership on Sgt. Octave Jarvis of Co. B 15th MI Infantry Regiment. He enlisted on October 14, 1861, and was discharged on August 13, 1865. He was wounded on his right hand during the siege on

Maynard C. Goethe

Atlanta, Georgia. Goethe has another Civil War veteran ancestor, Alexander Duvall of Co. D, 9th MI Cavalry Volunteers. He enlisted on March 7, 1863 and was discharged on July 21, 1865.

DANIEL HAROLD GRABLE, born October 1, 1954, Neenah, WI. Resides in Oshkosh, WI. Moved to Spring Lake, MI. Member of Boy Scouts, Eagle Scout, Woodbadge recipient (as Scouter). Schools: S.L. H.S., Muskegon Community College (AA), Ferris State University (BS Retail Marketing). Church: First Christian (Disciples of Christ) Muskegon, offices: deacon, elder. Memberships: Grand Haven Genealogical Society: Henry E. Plant Camp #3 SUVCW, initiated September 22, 1993, offices: guard, secretary/treasurer.

Daniel H. Grable *William S. Baird I*

Ancestor: William Sidney Baird I, farmer, birth: January 28, 1846, Ida, MI; moved to Watson, Allegan County, MI. Service: Co. E, 28th Michigan Infantry, private October 17, 1864 and was discharged on June 5, 1866. Marriages: Almira Mason, Hannah Pickett, Effie Carpenter (outlived first two). Children: Hattie, Maude (first marriage); William II (second marriage). Residences: Hopkins; Gun Lake, Barry County; Martin, MI. Church: Congregational (Hopkins), offices: trustee, deacon. Memberships: GAR, Oddfellows. Wrote journal of military experiences. He died May 8, 1922.

Daniel has nine other Civil War veterans plus two veteran fringe relations (including President Rutherford B. Hayes).

DANIEL VERNON GRAVES, joined Gov. Crapo Camp No. 145, Flint MI, on November 5, 1992. He has held the offices of Camp Council, Camp Secretary/Treasurer, Junior Vice Camp Commander, and held the rank of Cpl. in the Camp Guard and SVR.

Daniel V. Graves

He bases his right to membership on Pvt. Valerous E. Graves of the 1st MI E&M Co. G. Pvt. Graves enlisted on August 21, 1864 and was discharged on June 6, 1865. He belonged to Harlow Pelton Post No. 453, Kingston, MI.

ALLEN BRUCE GRAY - May 11, 1993, Phil Sheridan Camp #4.

Benjamin Allen (great-great-grandfather), Colonel, 16th Wisconsin Infantry Regt., October 10, 1861, to July 7, 1863. Commanded 16th Wisconsin at Battle of Shiloh and sieges of Corinth and Vicksburg. Commanded 1st Brigade, 6th Div. at Battle of Corinth. The green regiment fought well at Shiloh, ending up to the rear of the Bloody Pond. Colonel Allen's horse was killed, as was a second when he attempted to mount. Allen was also wounded, and forced to leave the field. His wound never healed properly. Ultimately necessitating his medical discharge. After the war, the Benjamin Allen Post of the G.A.R. was established in Arkansaw, WI.

Allen B. Gray

Almon D. Gray (great-grandfather). Captain, Co. H, 16th Wisconsin, November 5, 1861. After the Battle of Shiloh and the siege of Corinth, he resigned September 8, 1862, for medical reasons.

DEWY G. GREEN, is a charter member of Henry Casey Camp No. 92 which meets in Washington Court House, OH. He is the brother of Gerald E. Green and Harold D. Green who are also members of this camp.

They are all great-great-grandsons of Pvt. Henry Ernest Schomburg who served in Co. D, 5th Ohio Volunteer Cav. and Co. I, 140th Ohio Volunteer Infantry This 5th O.V.C, served in the Shenandoah Valley. Private Schomburg is buried with his wife Jemmia Wait at Batterson Cemetery, Scioto County, OH.

Private Schomburg was born in Oselar, Hanover, Germany and came to the U.S. with his parents at age five. He was in the Civil War at age 19. After the war he worked as a farmer and operated a butcher business.

GERALD E. GREEN, is a charter member of Henry Casey Camp No. 92 which meets in Washington Court House, OH. Gerald is a great-great-grandson of Pvt. Henry Ernest Schomburg. Schomburg was a private in Co. D, 5th Ohio Volunteer Cav., and Co. I, 140th Ohio Volunteer Infantry

The 5th O.V.C. served in the Shenandoah Valley. Private Schomburg was 5'7" with hazel eyes and dark hair and a dark complexion. He died January 30, 1916 at the age of 70. He had nine children and worked after the war as a farmer and butcher.

JAMES GREEN, JR., joined Memphis Camp No. 1 on March 1, 1995. He bases his right to membership on his great-grandfather Cpl. John Fox, of Co. M, 6th TN Cavalry of the Union Army, who was born in Gibson County, TN. He enlisted on August 11, 1862, and was appointed as a Corporal on October 13, 1864 by order of Lt. Col. W. J. Smith. Cpl. Fox was mustered out July 26, 1865.

John Fox

After the war, John Fox returned to Tennessee to marry and start a family. Eventually, he moved his family from Tennessee to West Plains, MO, where he purchased 180 acres of land to start a farm. During this period of his life, he was elected Justice of the Peace for two eight-year terms and served as County Judge for two terms. John Fox retired and lived to be 75 years old.

JAMES GREEN III, joined Memphis Camp No. 1 on March 1, 1995. He bases his right to membership on his great-great-grandfather Cpl. John Fox, of Co. M, 6th TN Cavalry of the Union Army, who was born in Gibson County, TN. He enlisted on August 11, 1862, and was appointed as a Corporal on October 13, 1864 by order of Lt. Col. W. J. Smith. Cpl. Fox was mustered out July 26, 1865.

James Green III

After the war, John Fox returned to Tennessee to marry and start a family. Eventually, he moved his family from Tennessee to West Plains, MO, where he purchased 180 acres of land to start a farm. During this period of his life, he was elected Justice of the Peace for two eight-year terms and served as County Judge for two terms. John Fox retired and lived to be 75 years old.

ROBERT GREEN, joined the Memphis Camp No. 1 on March 1, 1995. He bases his right to membership on his great-grandfather Cpl. John Fox, of Co. M, 6th TN Cavalry of the Union Army, who was born in Gibson County, TN. He enlisted on August 11, 1862, and was appointed as a Corporal on October 13, 1864 by order of Lt. Col. W. J. Smith. Cpl. Fox was mustered out July 26, 1865.

After the war, John Fox returned to Tennessee to marry and start a family. Eventually, he moved his family from Tennessee to West Plains, MO, where he purchased 180 acres of land to start a farm. During this period of his life, he was elected Justice of the Peace for two eight-year terms and served as County Judge for two terms. John Fox retired and lived to be 75 years old.

CHRISTOPHER S. GRIM, has served as treasurer of Henry Casey Camp No. 92, since 1992. He is a charter member of this camp. He works as an audio-visual specialist at Miami Trace High School, Washington Court House, OH. He is married to Rona Rodgers and they have two daughters: Alicia and Felica.

Christopher S. Grim

He is the son of Max E. Grim and the great-great-grandson of Pvt. William F. Grim, Co. K, 8th Ohio Volunteer Cav. He is also the great-great-grandson of Pvt. Henry Ernest Schomburg, who served in Co. D, 5th Ohio Volunteer Cav., and Co. I, 140th Ohio Volunteer Infantry

He is the great-great-great-grandson of Pvt. John W. Rodgers, Co. G, 113th Ohio Volunteer Infantry He died at Camp Zanesville, OH on December 5, 1862.

DAVID W. GRIM, is a charter member of Henry Casey Camp No. 92. Henry Casey Camp was chartered in 1992 and meets in Washington Court House, OH. David works as a computer analyst and is married to Connie L. Parrett. He has four children: Debbie, Jodi (married to Curt A. Evans), Jeffery Scott and Kelli Michelle. He currently serves on the Henry Casey Camp Council and is a member of Co. C, 20th Ohio Volunteer Infantry, which is a Sons of Veterans Reserve unit.

David W. Grim

He is the great-grandson of Pvt. William F. Grim, Co. K, 8th Ohio Volunteer Cav. and Pvt. Henry Ernest Schomburg, who served in Co. D, 5th Ohio Volunteer Cav. and Co. I, 140th Ohio Volunteer Infantry

He is the great-great-grandson of Pvt. John W. Rodgers who served in Co. G, 113th Ohio Volunteer Infantry He died at Camp Zanesville, OH on December 5, 1862.

GEORGE DONALD HARRY GRIM, is a charter member of Henry Casey Camp No. 92. He served as patriotic instructor in 1992. He is married to Nerizza Tukay. A veteran of the U.S. Air Force, he has been an educator since 1966.

He is the great-grandson of Pvt. William F. Grim, Co. K, 8th Ohio Volunteer Cav. Private Grim's unit served in the Shenandoah Valley with General Phil Sheridan and saw action at the Battle of Cedar Creek.

He is also the great-grandson of Pvt. Henry Ernest Schomburg, Co. D, 5th Ohio Volunteer Cav. and Co. I, 140th Ohio Volunteer Infantry The 5th O.V.C. also served in the Shenandoah Valley.

He is the great-great-grandson of Pvt. John W. Rodgers who served in Co. G, 113th Ohio Volunteer Infantry He died at Camp Zanesville, OH on December 5, 1862 from the measles.

HAROLD MORGAN GRIM, is a charter member of Henry Casey Camp No. 92 which meets in Washington Court House, OH. He is also a member of Co. C, 20th O.V.I. which is the Sons of Veterans Reserve unit for Henry Casey Camp No. 92. He is the son of James L. Grim and is married to Lisa S. Butler. They have three children: Ethan M. Grim, Cales W. Grim and Daniel C. McColl IV.

He is the great-great-grandson of Pvt. William F. Grim, Co. K, 8th Ohio Volunteer Cav.,

Harold M. Grim

and Pvt. Henry Ernest Schomburg, who served in Co. D, 5th Ohio Volunteer Cav. and Co. I, 140th Ohio Volunteer Infantry

He is the great-great-great-grandson of John W. Rodgers who served in Co. G, 113th Ohio Volunteer Infantry He died at Camp Zanesville, OH on December 5, 1862.

JAMES L. GRIM, is a charter member of Henry Casey Camp No. 92 which meets in Washington Court House, OH. He is a veteran of the U.S. Air Force and has worked as a draftsman and surveyor at Fayette County Map office since 1968. He is married to Elenor Leach. He has four children: Cheryl (Robert L. Stout, Jr.), Harold M. (Lisa S. Butler), Jeri L. (David D. Wamsley) and Nellie M. (Arthur E. Taylor).

William F. Grim

Henry E. Schomburg

He is the great-grandson of Pvt. William F. Grim, Co. K, 8th Ohio Volunteer Cav. and Pvt. Henry Ernest Schomburg, who served in Co. D, 5th Ohio Volunteer Cav. and Co. I, 140th Ohio Volunteer Infantry

He is the great-great-grandson of Pvt. John W. Rodgers who served in Co. G, 113th Ohio Volunteer Infantry He died at Camp Zanesville, OH on December 5, 1862.

MAX E. GRIM, is a charter member of Henry Casey Camp No. 92 which meets in Washington, Court House, Ohio. He teaches vocational education and served 12 years as mayor of Bloomingburg, OH (1968-1980). He is a U.S. Air Force veteran and married to Carolyn McCray. They have one son, Christopher Scott Grim.

He is the great-great-grandson of Pvt. William F. Grim, Co. K, 8th Ohio Volunteer Cav. Private Grim was a member of GAR Miran Judy Post No. 480, Bloomingburg, OH. Private Grim is buried with his wife Martha Morgan at the Madison Mills Cemetery in Fayette County, OH.

Max is also the great-grandson of Pvt. Henry Ernest Schomburg who served in Co. D, 5th Ohio Volunteer Cav. and Co. I, 140th Ohio Volunteer Infantry Private Schomburg is buried with his wife Jemmia Wait at Batterson Cemetery in Scioto County, OH.

PAUL S. GRIM, is a charter member of Henry Casey Camp No. 92 which meets in Washington Court House, OH. He served as senior vice commander of the camp in 1992. He served as color bearer of the Ohio Department in 1993. Paul is a high school guidance counselor and is married to Linda Moore. He has two daughters: Amy Marie and Misty Jo. He is a U.S. Air Force veteran.

He is the great-grandson of Pvt. William F. Grim, Co. K, 8th Ohio Volunteer Cav., and Pvt. Henry Ernest Schomburg, who served in Co. D, 5th Ohio Volunteer Cav. and Co. I, 140th Ohio Volunteer Infantry

He is the great-great-grandson of Pvt. John W. Rodgers who served in Co. G, 113th Ohio Volunteer Infantry He died at Camp Zanesville, OH on December 5, 1862, but the site of his grave is unknown.

RAYMOND M. GRIM, JR., has served as secretary of Henry Casey Camp No. 92 which meets in Washington Court House, OH since 1992. He is a charter member of that camp. He is retired, and a former president of the Bloomingburg Village Board of Trustees of Public Affairs.

His great-grandfather was Pvt. William F. Grim, Co. K, 8th Ohio Volunteer Cav. He is also the great-grandson of Pvt. Henry Ernest

Raymond M. Grim, Jr.

Schomburg, who served in Co. D, 5th Ohio Volunteer Cav. and Co. I, 140th Ohio in Volunteer Infantry

He is also the great-great-grandson of Pvt. John W. Rodgers who served in Co. G, 113th Ohio Volunteer Infantry He died at Camp Zanesville, OH on December 5, 1862 from the measles.

ROBERT E. GRIM, joined the Ohio Department as a member at large in 1988, later transferred to Gov. William Dennison Camp No. 125 and in 1992 organized and chartered Henry Casey Camp No. 92. He holds dual membership, and has served as commander of Henry Casey Camp No. 92 since it was chartered.

Robert E. Grim

In 1994 he was elected commander of the Ohio Department, and elected to a three year term on the National Council of Administration.

He has been a high school teacher for 28 years. He currently teaches American history. He is president of the Society of War of 1812 in Ohio. He is a Past District Deputy Grand Master of the 8th District of the Grand Lodge of Free and Accepted Masons of Ohio, and Knight of the York Cross of Honour.

His great-grandfather was Pvt. William F. Grim, Co. K, 8th Ohio Volunteer Cav.

RODNEY R. GRIM, is a charter member of Henry Casey Camp No. 92 which meets in Washington Court House, OH. He served as junior vice commander of the camp in 1993. He is a sergeant in Co. C, 20th O.V.I. which is the Sons of Veterans Reserve unit for Henry Casey Camp. He is a United States Marine veteran and works as a lieutenant for the Ohio Department of Corrections.

Rodney R. Grim

Rodney is the son of Raymond M. Grim, Jr. He has six children: Rose Marie, Randa Kay (Robert S. Abbott), Rachael Lynn, Rodney Ray, Jr., Ronald C. R., and Magen Racine.

He is the great-great-grandson of Pvt. William F. Grim, Co. K, 8th Ohio Volunteer Cav.

and Pvt. Henry Ernest Schomburg, who served in Co. D, 5th Ohio Volunteer Cav. and Co. I, 140th Ohio Volunteer Infantry

He is the great-great-great-grandson of Pvt. John W. Rodgers.

WILLARD A. GRIM, the son of Raymond Morgan Grim, Sr. and Nellie Irene Schomburg Grim Looker, is a charter member of Henry Casey Camp No. 92 which meets in Washington Court House, OH. He works for the U.S. Department of Defense after retiring from the United States Air Force.

He is married to Cynthia Hurst. They have one son Paul William Grim. He has three stepchildren: John F. Hogan, Linda S. Hogan, and David W. Hogan.

Willard A. Grim *William F. Grim*

Willard is the great-grandson of Pvt. William F. Grim, Co. K, 8th Ohio Volunteer Cav. and Pvt. Henry Ernest Schomburg, who served in Co. D, 5th Ohio Volunteer Cav and Co. I, 140th Ohio Volunteer Infantry

He is the great-great-grandson of Pvt. John W. Rodgers who served in Co. G, 113th Ohio Volunteer Infantry He died at Camp Zanesville, OH on December 5, 1862.

GEOFFREY A. P. GROESBECK, joined the Davis (Star) Camp, PA, March 10, 1989.

He bases his right to membership on Bugler William Jay Groesbeck. Bugler Groesbeck, originally of Milton, NY, enlisted in the New York Independent Battery, 11th Co. (Albany, NY) on November 8, 1861 - only 13 days after its formation - at the age of 19. His company was mustered into service on January 6, 1862, and took part in some of the Civil War's fiercest battles, including Manassas Junction, Fredericksburg, Chancellorsville, Gettysburg, and Mine Run.

He was honorably discharged on January 22, 1864 in order to marry his fiancee, Mary Caroline Osborn, which he did on February 25, 1864. After only a few months respite, he re-enlisted in the 11th Company's Veteran Corps. He was a cousin of Major General James Groesbeck and a descendant of one of New York's oldest families.

ALBERT G. GROSS, joined the George Armstrong Custer #1 on May 1, 1993.

He bases his right to membership on Pvt. Joseph Smith of the 154th IL Volunteer Infantry. Smith enlisted on February 15, 1865 and was discharged June 19, 1865. He received a $100 bounty upon enlisting, and served mostly in Tennessee doing picket, guard, and garrison duty.

JAMES J. GUIDER, joined Lafayette Camp #140, New York in 1958 and eventually joined Lincoln Camp 100, New Jersey, of which he was a former Commander.

James J. Guider

He bases his claim to membership on his two great-grandfathers, Sergeant Thomas Howley, of the 28th Infantry Reg. Connecticut Volunteers, and Sergeant James Ellis, of the 15th New York Engineers Volunteers. Sgt. Howley enlisted September 10, 1862, and participated in the bloody 48 day siege of Port Hudson, Louisiana. He was discharged on August 28, 1863. Sgt. Ellis enlisted on September 2, 1862 and participated in Fredericksburg, Gettysburg, Wilderness Carolinas, and Appomattox. He was discharged July 2, 1865.

ROBERT NEIL "BOB" HALL, of Evansville, IN, joined Benjamin Harrison Camp No. 356 at Indianapolis on April 8, 1984. Hall, copy editor at *The Evansville Press,* was born February 22, 1948, in Hopkinsville, KY. He and his wife Ruth have a daughter, Renee, who was born January 20, 1981.

Robert N. Hall

Hall's great-great-grandfather was Pvt. William Washington "Wash" Shadoin of Princeton, KY. Shadoin was in Co. I of 48th Regt. of Kentucky Infantry Volunteers. He enlisted October 5, 1863, at Princeton. He suffered sunstroke and was discharged December 15, 1864, at Bowling Green, KY. Shadoin died July 23, 1882, at Salem, KY.

Hall's great-great-great-grandfather was Cpl. Fleming Crittenden "Critt" Gresham of Hopkinsville. Gresham was in Co. A of 25th Regt. of Kentucky Infantry Volunteers. Gresham enlisted October 15, 1861, at Henderson, KY and was shot and killed April 6, 1862, in Battle of Shiloh at Pittsburg Landing, TN.

WILLIAM J. HALPIN, Brother Halpin joined the Order in February 1992 as a member of the Jacob Ten Eyck Camp #154 in Albany, NY which changed its name in 1993 to the Col. George L. Willard Camp #154. He served as the Camp's junior vice commander in 1993 and is currently camp commander. Brother Halpin is also a reenactor with the 125th New York State Volunteers and a member of the Capital District Civil War Round Table.

William J. Halpin   *Martin Blessinger*

Brother Halpin is the great-grandson of Pvt. Martin Blessinger who enlisted in the 45th NYSV (Fifth German Rifles) in New York City on September 9, 1861. The unit was composed almost entirely of German immigrants. Martin was wounded at the Battle of Gettysburg. The 45th was consolidated with the 58th NYSV in June 1865, and he was discharged from that unit in October 1865. Martin is buried in the Lutheran Cemetery, Middle Village, NY.

HOBERT S. HALSEY, JR., joined the Lincoln-Cushing #2 Maryland Camp on April 24, 1993.

He bases his claim to membership on Pvt. James Milson, of Co. F 175 PA Infantry Pvt. Milson enlisted on October 16, 1862 and was discharged on August 7, 1863.

LOWELL V. HAMMER, PC-IN-C, Brother Hammer joined the SUVCW in 1975 as a member-at-large. After returning in 1983 from a U.S. Embassy assignment in Paris, he transferred to the Lincoln-Cushing Camp. He served as Camp Commander, Maryland Department Commander, National G.A.R. Highway Officer, Council of Administration member, and as a SVR Colonel before being elected commander-in-chief in 1991.

Lowell V. Hammer   *John B. Hammer*

Lowell's grandfather, great uncle and two great-grandfathers served in the Union Army. He joined the SUVCW on the service of his grandfather, John Beisel Hammer, who served in Co. D, 138th Regt., Pennsylvania Volunteers from 1862 to 1865, participated in 21 battles and engagements, was promoted to sergeant, and was wounded at the battle of the Wilderness and again at the Third Winchester. He was sheriff of Bedford County, PA from 1893 to 1896 and commander of the E.S. Wright Post No. 33 of the G.A.R. He died in 1917.

DAVID K. HANN, first joined the Sons in 1987. Co-founded Col. Louis R. Francine Camp #7 on December 28, 1990. He served as it's first commander and have served as secretary/treasurer. He has served in the New Jersey Department as secretary, senior vice commander, and will be the department commander this June. His ancestor is Charles Ellet Jr. He was the inventor of the "Ram Fleet" that saw service on the Mississippi River. Ellet was commissioned colonel, and on June 6, 1862 this "Ram Fleet" engaged the Confederates just below Memphis, sinking eight of nine Confederate ships. Mortally wounded in the knee by a pistol bullet, he died on June 21, 1862. For his services to the United States, Col. Ellet was given a state funeral at Independence Hall in Philadelphia, and is buried at Laurel Hill Cemetery in Philadelphia.

DOUGLAS MEIERE HARDING, (JVC), born June 23, 1932, Atlanta, GA. Joined early 1993 Oliver Tilden Camp #26, SUVCW, New York City. Took oath of membership April 26, 1993 at General U.S. Grant's Tomb, New York City. Elected junior vice commander 1994. Membership through Cpl. Joseph Edwin Harding (1842-1917) of Lewiston, ME. Served Co. K, 12th W. VA. Infantry USA. Fought seven battles, Captured Winchester, VA, imprisoned Danville, VA and Andersonville, GA. Member of O.M. Mitchell Post GAR, Atlanta, GA. Served as adjutant, Jr. and Sr. vice commander and 1892 as commander.

Douglas M. Harding   *Joseph E. Harding*

Stephen Edward Harding, born December 4, 1949, Atlanta, GA. Joined Oliver Tilden Camp #26, SUVCW, New York City in August 1994. Membership through Cpl. Joseph Edwin Harding of Lewiston, ME. Enlisted Wellsburg, VA, August 12, 1862, Co. K, 12th W.VA. Infantry, USA. Fought seven battles before being Captured at Winchester, VA, July 14, 1864. Imprisoned Danville, VA, transferred to Confederate Prison in Andersonville, GA. Mustered out June 16, 1865. Early GAR member transferring to O.M. Mitchell Post G.A.R., Atlanta, GA. Served in 1892 as commander.

KEITH GRAHAM HARRISON, Commander-In-Chief, SUVCW, of Holt, MI, was elected Commander-in-Chief of the Sons of Union Veterans of the Civil War on August 13, 1994 at the 113th National Encampment in Lansing, MI. Brother Harrison represents the fourth Michigan in the 114-year history of the Order and the first in the last 46 years to serve in the Order's highest office. The three other Commanders-in-Chief from Michigan were Perle L. Fouch, 1948; Urion W. Mackey, 1944; and Marvin E. Hall, 1892.

Commander-in-Chief Harrison has served the National Organization in several capacities including senior vice commander-in-chief, junior vice commander-in-chief, patriotic instructor, membership-at-large coordinator, and history book coordinator. Within his native state of Michigan, he has served as department commander for three years, senior vice commander for two years and is currently in his seventh term as department chief of staff. He is a charter member of Curtenius Guard Camp #17 of Lansing-Sunfield, which he organized in 1983, and a dual member in the U.S. Grant Camp #101 of Detroit. Within the Lansing-Sunfield Camp, he has served as camp commander, camp secretary, camp treasurer, and is currently serving his fourth term as camp historian. He also served two years as camp treasurer with the Detroit Camp. He has been a member of the Order since 1981 and a life member since 1986.

Keith G. Harrison

Commander-in-Chief Harrison traces his SUVCW eligibility back to 28 Michigan Civil War soldiers, including one great-great-great-grandfather (Capt. Joseph Harper, 12th Michigan Volunteer Infantry, Co. A), three great-great-grandfathers, eight great-great-granduncles, and 16 cousins. The Michigan regiments represented by his ancestors include the 1st, 2nd, 11th, 12th, 15th, 18th, 19th, 27th, and 28th Volunteer Infantries; the 4th, 8th, 10th and 11th Volunteer Cavalries; and the 13th and 14th Batteries. The regiment with the greatest number of his ancestors was the 12th Michigan Volunteer Infantry with three grandfathers, four uncles and one cousin. In 1862, the 12th Michigan went directly from Niles, MI to Pittsburg Landing, TN, two weeks before the Battle of Shiloh. During the ensuing battle, several of his relatives were Captured; luckily, however, none were killed.

Capt. Joseph Harper was born on December 19, 1805 in Pennsylvania and was a carpenter by trade. He came to Cassopolis, MI in 1835 and was one of the builders of the first and second courthouses in the new county seat. He later served the village of Cassopolis as president and the county of Cass as deputy sheriff, sheriff and justice of the peace. When war broke, he raised a company of men. He received his commission in September 1861. Following the Battle of Shiloh, he resigned his commission at age 56 on May 8, 1862 due to disability. His army experience greatly undermined his health and he was for two years thereafter a sufferer of chronic disease. In 1864, with a view to improve his health, he traveled to Montana and for three years followed mining. The experiment proved successful for upon his return to Michigan, his health was much improved. In 1881 he was chosen president of the Cass County Pioneer Society. Capt. Harper's political affiliation was Wig prior to the organization of the Republic Party, but changed in 1860 and remained devoutly Republican until his death. Capt. Harper died in Cassopolis at the age of 88 on August 28, 1894.

Commander-in-Chief Harrison currently holds two state government positions within Michigan. He is the director of the Office of Environmental Administration for the Michigan Department of Management and Budget, and holds an appointment from Michigan Republican Governor John Engler as executive director of the Michigan Environmental Science Board. He is a 1968 graduate of Cassopolis High School. He holds a bachelor of science degree (1972) in fisheries and wildlife biology from Michigan State University and a master of arts degree (1974) from Western Michigan University. He is licensed as a registered sanitarian and as a registered environmental health specialist, and is nationally certified as an ecologist. His professional research and work have resulted in more than 60 publications addressing a wide variety of environmental, environmental health, natural history, and resources management topics. He has been published in local, state, national and international societal journals.

Commander-in-Chief Harrison has been a Civil War reenactor since 1982 and has risen through the ranks. He is a member and former Captain of the 7th Michigan Volunteer Infantry, Co. B, Inc. and a major, currently serving as chief of staff, with the Cumberland Guard, a nationally-recognized Civil War reenactment association. Within the Sons of Veterans Reserve (SVR), he holds the rank of major and serves as chief of infantry for the Third Military District and as commander of the Michigan Department SUVCW Color Guard, SVR (30th Michigan Volunteer Infantry). He has participated in more than 500 reenactments, parades and ceremonies since 1982, and has served innumerable times at Civil War reenactments as an infantry company commander and battalion commander, and as overall Union army commander. Major Harrison is knowledgeable and well-practiced in Hardee, Casey and Coupee, and is competent in 1861-1865 U.S. Army company, battalion, division, brigade and army-level infantry drill and tactics. He participated in most of the 125th anniversary Civil War battle reenactments and is currently participating in many of the 130th anniversary reenactments. Major Harrison's years and reputations within the 7th Michigan and the Cumberland Guard have resulted in his name being commemorated in song.

Commander-in-Chief Harrison belongs to several historical, patriotic and civic organizations including, Military Order of the Loyal Legion of the United States, in which he has been the commander of the Michigan Commandery since 1986; Society of the War of 1812; Sons of the Revolution; Society of Colonial Wars; Society of Mayflower Descendants; and Honorable Order of Kentucky Colonels. He is also a Mason (Lodge No. 252 of Okemos, MI) and a charter member of the Civil War Masonic Association.

Commander-in-Chief Harrison has been married twice, his first marriage being to Linda (Dodson) Harrison in 1976 and his second to Jean (Whitmer) Harrison in 1990. He has one son, Nathan Lewis Harrison, who is a Junior Son of the Order. His interest in history and genealogy peaked with the birth of his son in 1983, when he wrote and published a 350-page genealogy, *The Ancestry of Nathan Lewis Harrison*. The book documents his son's ancestry to the year 938 AD and identifies more than 150 families and 1,700 individuals who preceded him.

NATHAN LEWIS HARRISON, of Haslett, MI is the son of Commander-in-Chief Keith Graham Harrison of the Sons of Union Veterans of the Civil War. He is a Junior Son within the Order and belongs to the Curtenius Guard Camp #17 of Lansing-Sunfield, MI. His ancestry traces back to 45 Michigan Civil War soldiers, including one great-great-great-great-grandfather (Capt. Joseph Harper, 12th Michigan Volunteer Infantry, Co. A - see biography of Keith Graham Harrison), four great-great-great-grandfathers, one great-great-great-great-granduncle, 13 great-great-great granduncles, and 26 cousins. The Michigan regiments represented by his ancestry include, the 1st, 2nd, 3rd, 4th, 5th, 6th, 11th, 12th, 14th, 15th, 18th, 19th, 27th, and 28th Volunteer Infantries; the 1st, 4th, 5th, 6th, 8th, 10th, and 11th Volunteers Cavalries; and the 1st Light Artillery, Btry. E and the 13th and 14th Batteries.

Nathan L. Harrison

In addition to the SUVCW, Brother Harrison is Junior member in the Michigan Commandery of the Military Order of the Loyal Legion of the United States and Sons of the Revolution, and a member in the Children of the American Revolution and Society of Mayflower Descendants. He currently attends Haslett Public Schools.

CHARLES OTIS HARTHY, was born July 15, 1937 in Hastings, MI, the only child of Otis Clark and Vesta Clare (Reid) Harthy. He graduated from Hastings High School in 1955 and Michigan State University in 1959. He married Mary Lou White on September 15, 1956 and five children were born to this union: Jeffery D., Laura J., Paul S., Julie A., and Linda M. There are five grandchildren. Charles joined Curtenius Guard Camp #17 in 1988 and transferred to Henry E. Plant Camp #3, in 1992, as a charter member and its first secretary-treasurer. He currently serves as historian and Genealogist. He is a life member of the Sons of the Revolution in the state of Michigan and is past master of Grand Haven Lodge #139, F&AM and Past High Priest of Corinthian Chapter #84, R.A.M. He is a long time member of the New York Central System Historical Society and has authored several articles for *The Headlight*, its quarterly publication.

Charles O. Reid, was born July 25, 1840 in Ash Township, Monroe County, MI. He was the son of Jasper Smith and Rebecca (Lowden) Reid. He enlisted in the Ninth Michigan Cavalry in St. Joseph County, MI on November 24, 1862 - his enlistment papers show the last name as Reed and until his death in the service, all records bear that spelling. He was mustered in at Coldwater, MI as a member of Co. F on March 12, 1863 as a private, for three years. He was transferred to Co. B of the 9th Regt. of Cavalry on May 1, 1863. Charles O. Reid died January 23, 1864 at Hospital #3 in Knoxville, East Tennessee of diarrhea. He is buried in the National Cemetery at Knoxville and his stone bears the name Charles Reed.

JAMES B. HAYWARD, joined the Sons July 13, 1994, national member-at-large. Civil War ancestor Jeremiah Kelly, private. He served with Co. E, Stone County Mo. Home Gds. Mustered in June 10, 1861; mustered out November 10, 1861. It is unknown if he belonged to a GAR, possibly Springdale, AR, Washington County.

James Hayward's great-grandfather liked to play the fiddle and when he came home on leave, he and some of his friends stopped off at a saloon before going, home, his wife found out about it, she went to the saloon and dragged him out by the ear. (He was 6' tall, she was 5'2"). In later years, when she was angry with him, she would remind him of the incident.

James B. Hayward   *Jeremiah Kelly*

After the war, Pvt. Jeremiah Kelly lived in Goshen and later on in Springdale, which are both in Washington County, AR, he was a farmer.

On January 3, 1898, he applied for a pension for his Union Army military service. His certificate number was 770040.

He was born on April 15, 1823 in Virginia and died in 1912 at Sonora which is near Springdale, AR in Washington County.

His wife, Jane Baker, whom he married on December 20, 1846 in Taney County, MO.

They became the parents of Elijah J., Missoura Ann, Virginia, Tennessee, Mary A. and Emma Jane.

Emma Jane Kelly married John Cleveland Hayward in 1896 at Goshen, AR. They became the parents of Brent Louis Von Hayward, Gayle, Vance, and Don R.

Brent Louis Von Hayward married Pasadena Hawkins on January 29, 1930. They became the parents of James Bert Hayward, writer of this bibliography, J.D. Hayward, Jerry Hayward, Joyce Grace Hayward-Harden and Opal Jeanette Hayward.

ROBERT WILLIAM HAZEL, joined the SUVCW May 2, 1993 as a member-at-large, and joined the James Birdseye McPherson Camp #66 on June 7, 1994. He has held the office of Junior Vice Commander and has been on its Council.

He bases his right to membership on seven Civil War ancestors, all privates: George Hazel (October 28, 1861-February 22, 1863) of Company E 72nd Ohio Vol. Infantry; Frank J. Bihm (October 31, 1862-May 16, 1865) of 5th Ind. Co., Ohio Vol. Infantry; Louis Bihm, older brother of Frank, (1862-1865); John Shook (February 20 through September 28, 1865) of Co. G 189th Regiment Ohio Vol. Infantry; Jacob Smith (October 19, 1861-January 3, 1863) of Co. E, 72nd Regiment Ohio Vol. Infantry; Joshua V. Smith (1861-1865) of Co. C 21st Regiment Ohio Vol. Infantry; Abraham V. Smith (August 22, 1862-May 30, 1865) of Co. C 21st Regiment Ohio Vol. Infantry. Abraham was taken prisoner of war during the Battle of Chickamanga on September 20, 1863. When he was released, he weighed only 63 pounds.

HYLON JOHN HEATON III, joined the Sons January 22, 1994, Gov. Crap Camp #145.

Ancestor Vignettes: George Elias William Beryl Heaton, sergeant, 28th Michigan Infantry, Co. F, great-grandfather of Hylon J. Heaton III, Gov. Crapo Camp No. 145.

George E.M.B. Heaton was born August 5, 1844, in Orleans County, NY. He volunteered for service in Co. B of the 13th Michigan Infantry on February 10, 1863. He was wounded on September 20, 1863 at Chickamauga Creek, TN and was hospitalized in Chicago, IL. He returned home to Fitchburg, MI to recover from his wound.

Hylon J. Heaton III   *George Heaton*

George E.M.B. Heaton reenlisted August 20, 1864 in Co. F of the 28th Michigan Infantry He entered as corporal. His father, Pvt. John C. Heaton, a wagon maker, enlisted with him. His brother, Pvt. Hylon (Hyler) E. Heaton also enlisted but in Co. C of the 9th Michigan Cav. George E.M.B. Heaton was injured a second time in the battle of Kingston, NC (called Wyse Ford). It was said that he lay trapped 26 hours under a breastwork timber during the battle. He gained the rank of sergeant before his honorable discharge June 5, 1866 at Raleigh, NC.

He wore a double truss the remainder of his life to correct the left inguinal hernia he received at Wyse Ford and died of surgery complication for a strangulated bowel the result of this hernia on March 3, 1922 in Boyne City, MI.

CLIFFORD HENKE, SVC, Bro. Cliff joined Oliver Tilden Camp #26, New York City in 1990 where he currently serves as senior vice commander. In addition, he is department GAR highway officer.

He is the great-grandson of Sgt Peter Eberhardt who served first in Co. D, 6th Regt., New York Militia, April to July 1861. Then on October 3, 1861 he enlisted in Co. D, 45th Regt., New York Volunteers. During his service, he was Captured on July 1, 1863 at Gettysburg and was a prisoner of war at Belle Isle, Richmond, VA until December 29, 1863 when he was exchanged. He was mustered out with his Company October 8, 1864 at Nashville, TN. He was a member of the GAR in Delaware, OH and later in Sheboygan, WI. Peter Eberhardt died February 13, 1927 in New York City and is buried in St. John's Cemetery.

Clifford Henke   *Peter Eberhardt*

Bro. Cliff is great-great-grandson of Pvt. Conrad Stoll of Co. B, 32nd Regt., Indiana Infantry Pvt. Stoll enlisted August 30, 1861 and took part in the Battle of Shiloh. He was discharged October 1, 1862 in Louisville, KY suffering a disability. He died November 29, 1869 in Columbus, OH.

Bro. Cliff is also related to Pvt. Conrad Stoll, Co. K, 18th Regt., Kentucky Infantry who was killed in action August 30, 1862 at the Battle of Richmond, KY.

Bro. Cliff is a veteran of the Korean War and is also a member of the American Legion, American Ex-POWs and the BPO Elks. He resides in Middle Village, NY.

ROBERT M. HENSLEY, joined January 6, 1981 as a member-at-large. He was born April 24, 1929 in Pittsburg, KS. He served in the Marines from 1947 to 1950, and retired from Texaco after 38 years. He lives in Tulsa, OK and enjoys bicycling and genealogy.

He bases his right to membership on Sgt. Henry G. Thomas of Co. B 22nd KY Vol. Infantry He was born in Argalite, KY on March 28, 1836. Sgt. Thomas enlisted November 9, 1861 and was discharged on January 20, 1865. After participating in several engagements with the Confederate forces, Henry was wounded at the battle of Champion Hill, MS on May 16, 1863 while charging the enemy. Even though wounded, he helped several other members of his regiment who were more seriously wounded to safety. He died on August 21, 1921 in Southpoint, OH.

Robert M. Hensley   *Henry G. Thomas*

ROBERT REID HEPLER, JR., was born in Alhambra, CA and now resides in Temple City, CA. He has been married for 27 years, has two children and one granddaughter.

Mr. Hepler went into the U.S. Army in September of 1967 where he completed basic training at Fort Ord, CA. He then went to Fort Knox, KY for his A.I.T. training where he received orders for Vietnam, assigned to I-troop, 11th Armored Cav. Regt., Xuan Loc. He was transferred to the 11th Air Cav. in Bien Hoa where he served the remainder of his tour. Mr. Hepler was shot down while on a combat mission near the Cambodian border, narrowly escaping Capture. His commanding officer Col. George S. Patton, the son of the late World War II General Patton, was able to effect a rescue.

Sgt Hepler's awards and medals include: Distinguished Flying Cross, Bronze Star with Valor, 11 Air Medals with Valor, two Army Commendation Medals with Valor, Republic of Vietnam Gallantry Cross with Palm, Republic of Vietnam Campaign Medal, Good Conduct Medal, National Defense Service Medal, Combat Infantryman's Badge and Flight Wings.

Robert R. Hepler, Jr.   *Andrew W. Hepler*

Mr. Hepler is a General contractor and owns his own business, Oakridge Building Contractors. He is also licensed in plumbing, electrical, concrete, drywall and insulation trades. He is an artist, sculptor and photographer. His Bronzes include "Hugh Hefner" and California Plaine Air Artist "Karl Albert". His works have been sold in both the United States and Canada. He has photographed both the 1992 and 1994 Playmates of the Year. He has been featured in the Orange Coast Magazine, *Artist Artsembles*, the 11th U.S. Cav. Blackhorse, book of poetry *Tears of Fire*, and is listed in the *Encyclopedia of Living Artists in America.*

Mr. Hepler is a member of the American Legion, the 11th Armd. Cav. Regt., 11th Air Cav., Decanso Gardens, Huntington Library & Art Gallery, Sons of Union of Veterans of the Civil War, Akron Society of Artists and the Gene Autry Museum.

In his spare time Mr. Hepler enjoys windsurfing, sailing, skiing, bungie jumping, juggling, golfing, aerobatics, kayaking and skydiving.

His Civil War ancestor, Pvt. Andrew W. Hepler, who served with Co. E, 10th Iowa. Enlisted October 15, 1864, discharged August 15, 1865. He belonged to General Sheridan's Post No. 452, Springville, IA.

Dr. Andrew W. Hepler was born in Ohio on July 29, 1848. At the age of 10 he moved with his family to Iowa. On October 15, 1864, at the age of 16, he enlisted in the Union Army in Davenport, IA. He then joined Co. E, 10th Iowa in Kingston, GA. He took part in General Sherman's famous march to the sea and on April 29, 1865 was among Union Army personnel who took part in the Grand Review in Washington, DC. The 10th Iowa sustained the loss of six officers and 95 enlisted men. An additional 134 enlisted men died from disease or other non-battlefield related circumstances.

Andrew was discharged as a private on August 15, 1865 in Little Rock, AR. His Captain was Montgomery Cooper. He saw action in over 15 skirmishes and battles during his enlistment, these included: The Siege of Savannah, GA; Campaign of the Carolinas, Columbia, Bentonville, Goldsborough, Raleigh; and the Surrender at Bennett's House, Durham Station, NC.

Andrew married Eugennia A. Heustis October 13, 1884 in Maquoketa, IA and was the father of two children.

After the Civil War Andrew became a doctor, served as a city councilman and was mayor in Wyoming, IA. He also belonged to General. Sheridan's Post No. 452 G.A.R. and the Free and Accepted Masons Springville Lodge No. 139.

Dr. Hepler was so moved by his Civil War experiences that he decided to lecture on the Civil War. His lectures included over 100 Stereopticon glass lantern slides of the Civil War that were hand colored by his wife Eugennia.

Dr. Hepler and his family moved to Los Angeles, CA in 1919 where he died July 23, 1921 at the age of 73. He was buried in the Sawtelle Veterans National Cemetery in Los Angeles.

KENNETH DAY HERSHBERGER, joined Lincoln-Cushing Camp No. 2, Maryland Dept., on August 21, 1991. At a Camp meeting in Washington, D.C., on September 12, 1991, he was obligated with two other Sons. He has served as Camp Secretary, Junior Vice Commander, and Senior Vice commander. In 1995, delegates to the Maryland Dept. Encampment elected him to the post of Dept. Senior Vice Commander. At the national level, Mr. Hershberger has served as Assistant National Membership List Coordinator. He was Camp Organizer for the James A. Garfield Camp No. 1, which began operating on April 1, 1995, with Mr. Hershberger as Camp Commander.

He bases his right to membership on his great-grandfather, Pvt. James Harbison Hershberger. At age 20, he mustered in with Co. D, 6th PA Heavy Artillery, on August 30, 1864. The company spent most of its time at several of the forts surrounding Washington, D.C., serving as replacements for the artillerymen General Grant converted into infantrymen for the march on Richmond. Pvt. Hershberger mustered out with his company on July 13, 1865.

RICHARD A. HILL, joined the Sons as a Member-at-Large on September 8, 1991.

Richard A. Hill

He bases his right to membership on Pvt. Henry William Premo of Co. B, 12th Regt. WI Infantry Volunteers. He was enlisted on November 29, 1861 and was mustered out on July 16, 1865. Private Premo served in Missouri, Kansas, Kentucky and Tennessee prior to being attached to XVII Army Corp, which was engaged in Grant's Central Mississippi Campaign in the fall of 1862. He participated in the Coldwater River Expedition, sieges of Vicksburg and Jackson, Mississippi, Harrisonburg Expedition, and the Meridian Campaign. Private Premo served with General Sherman during the Campaign for Atlanta, March to the Sea, Siege of Savannah, and the Campaign of the Carolinas. He participated in the Grand Review, Washington, D.C., May 24, 1865.

THOMAS H. HILLERY, joined the Sons on August 22, 1994 as a member-at-large. Dept. of Massachusetts. He has served three terms of the Board of Assessors, Sudbury, MA. He holds the title of Worshipful Master, Charles A. Welch Lodge, Ancient Free and Accepted Masons. Thomas holds a BA in economics with honors from Clark University (1985), and has served on Clark's University Alumni Council. He is a Jonas Clark Fellow (1992-date). Harvard University, ALM Religion, 1995, and is a writer for the Dorchester News.

He bases his claim to membership on Pvt. Michael Canty of Co C 26th Regiment, MA Vol. Infantry He enlisted, at age 35, on October 15, 1861. He was stationed at New Orleans, July 1862-1863, was on extra duty as a mason from July 25-August 21, 1862. He served detached service, New Orleans, March 23-April 30, 1864. Nearly two-thirds of his regiment re-enlisted at Franklin, furloughed March 23, returned to New Orleans May 20, 1864. Pvt. Canty was present with regiment in August, 1864, Shenandoah Valley; heavily engaged Winchester, VA September 19, 1864, regiment loss 46, company C loss 3. Mustered out in Boston, MA November 7, 1864. Died Brookline, MA November 9, 1891.

DAVID HILLS, bases his right to membership on his father, Pvt. Thomas Hill of the 45th Pennsylvania Volunteers. His sister B. Durfee lives in Elmira, NY and he lives in Tioga, PA.

JAMES R. HODGSON, joined the Sons December 22, 1992, Lone Star Camp #1. Held offices as founder of Lone Star Camp #1. Civil War ancestor Robert Hodgson, private, Co. F, 10th Wisconsin Infantry Enlisted September 22, 1861 to November 3, 1864.

James R. Hodgson   *Robert Hodgson*

Robert was the first American born Hodgson of their family. He was born at Rocky Ford, IL on January 3, 1843 while his family was immigrating from Newcastle, England enroute to Wisconsin.

Robert was 18 when he enlisted with the "Grant County Patriots" at Lima, WI. He spent most of his enlistment in Kentucky and Tennessee guarding the railroads. He also spent a great deal of time hospitalized with diarrhea, fever, bronchitis, and a complete hernia. He did participate in the battle of Stones River in Murfreesboro, TN under the command of Phil Sheridan. After the battle, in Murfreesboro, he returned to Regimental Hospital and later sent to hospital in Nashville where he was transferred to the Invalid Corps, and eventually became part of the Veterans Reserve Corps.

After the war, he returned to Platteville, WI for a time and eventually moved to Iowa. He had two sons, Clarence Richard and James Harvey. He died in Baxter, IA on June 1, 1881.

SCOTT W. HOLMES, joined the Joshua Lawrence Chamberlain Camp No. 20, Dept. of Maryland on February 17, 1995.

Robert J. Holmes

He bases his right to membership on Musician Robert J. Holmes of the 16th Regt. Connecticut Volunteer Infantry. He enlisted on August 14, 1862. Three weeks after being mustered into service, the 16th participated in the battle at Antietam. After being engaged at Fredericksburg and Suffolk, VA, the 16th went to Plymouth, NC. After a three day defense of Plymouth in April 1864, the garrison there was forced to surrender to an overwhelming number of the enemy.

The entire regiment (except Co. H) was taken prisoner and sent to prisons in the south. The enlisted men went to Andersonville, where a large number of them died. In September, most of the 16th (who survived to that point) were transferred via Charleston to a prison in Florence, SC. Beginning in December 1864, for a several month period, prisoners were paroled and returned to Union lines. Robert J. Holmes spent the remainder of the war in recovery, and was discharged on July 5, 1865.

TODD D. HOLTON, joined the Austin Blair Camp #7, Jackson, MI on July 13, 1992. Mr. Holton is active as a Civil War re-enactor (the 1st MI Light Artillery 3rd Battery). He is thankful his wife Faith is a very understanding person as his research takes him to distant places and requires many hours away from home. He submits this as a historical record for his three sons, Nathaniel, Philip, and Thomas.

Todd D. Holton   *Francis Kingsbury*

S. Ebenezer Shoff   *Lewis Ostrander*

Mr. Holton bases his right to membership on eight Civil War ancestors: Pvt. Francis Kingsbury (Co. H 15th MI Vol. Infantry, wounded in Shiloh, TN), Pvt. George W. Ostrander (Co. K 15th MI Vol. Infantry), Pvt. Lewis H. Ostrander (Co. F. 14th OH Vol. Infantry, P.O.W. Andersonville, GA), Pvt. James Ostrander (Co. F. 14th OH Vol. Infantry), Gilbert Ostrander (3rd Ohio Cavalry, wounded at Shiloh, TN), twin brothers Pvt. S. Ebenezer Shoff (Co. D 85th New York Vol. Infantry, wounded Ft. Monroe, VA) and Joel Elaezor Shoff (Co. E 104th New York Vol. Infantry), and William H. Palmer (Co. G, 1st MI Light Artillery Battery G).

DON R. HOPKINS, joined the Memphis Camp No. 1 on March 1, 1995. He bases his right to membership on his great-grandfather, Corporal John Fox of Co. M 6th Tennessee Cavalry. Fox enlisted on August 11, 1862 and mustered out July 26, 1865.

JAMES ROBERT HOPKINS, Mount Vernon, OH, SUVCW, Ohio Department McLaughlin Camp #12, March 15, 1989. Reorganized General Henry B. Banning Camp #207, April, 1991.

Great-grandfather Daniel Simpson Hopkins, born August 13, 1845, Hopkins Mill, Greene County, PA. Enlisted at New Brighton, PA February 29, 1864, Co. A, 140th Pennsylvania, Vol. Served from The Wilderness through Petersburg, being under fire every day for five weeks. Honorably discharged July 7, 1865. He died January 3, 1921, Ohio.

Great-granduncle John W. Hopkins, born December 6, 1839, Hopkins Mill, Greene County, PA. Enlisted March 1861, Co. F, 1st Pennsylvania, Cav., Army of the Potomac. Battles: Fredericksburg, Cedar Mountain and second Bull Run. Honorably discharged December 6, 1862, disability. He died July 25, 1901, Ohio.

MICHAEL R. HORGAN Jr., joined the Col. Louis R. Francine #7 Camp (S.U.V.), Hammonton, New Jersey in January, 1993. He has served a Vice-Commander and as the New Jersey Department Junior Vice-Commander. Mr. Horgan has worked at the *Star-Ledger* newspaper in Newark, New Jersey since 1962. He and his wife Ellen have five children.

Michael R. Horgan, Jr.   *John S. Maxwell*

Horgan bases his right to membership on his maternal great-grandfather, John S. Maxwell of Amsterdam, NY, who enlisted in the Navy as a Landsman in 1864 and served until the end of the war. He served on the *Vermont, A.D. Vance, North Carolina, Genessee, Baltic,* and the *Morgan*. In June of 1906, Maxwell was elected Commander of the New York State Grand Army of the Republic, the first Commander to come from the Navy. He was frequently a delegate to the GAR National Encampment.

JOHN HOTTENSTEIN, bases his right to membership on his father, 2nd Lt. Justin Hottenstein, of the 20th IL Infantry. Justin's widow, Enos, after his death in 1928, married Charles Tillman and Chester Divelbliss. When she died on November 15, 1985, she left 5 sons, 2 daughters, 23 grandchildren, and 19 great-grandchildren. She lived in Humbolt, MO. Mr. Hottenstein is a retired school teacher in Grandview, MO.

JOSEPH HARRY HUBBARD, Bro. Hubbard joined the Order as a member-at-large in 1994. He's a member of Oliver Tilden Camp #26, Sons of the Union Veterans of the Civil War, NY, NY.

Mr. Hubbard bases his right to membership on his great-grandfather, Sgt William S. Ely. Sgt Ely enlisted in New York City on May 27, 1861 in Co. H, 31st Infantry, 1st NYV. The 31st Regt. of Infantry, also known as the Montezuma Regt., the Baxter Light Guards and the First New York Union Volunteers was accepted by the State on May 21, 1861; organized and recruited in New York City, except Co. I, which was recruited at Williamsburgh; and mustered in the United States service for two years.

The regiment, under Col. Calvin E. Pratt, left the State on June 24, 1861; served at and near Washington, DC from June 26, 1861; in 2d Brigade, 5th Div., Army of Northeastern Virginia, from July 13, 1861; in Franklin's Brigade, Division of Potomac from August 4, 1861; in Newton's Brigade, Franklin's Div., Army of the Potomac from October 15, 1861; in 3d Brigade, 1st Div., 1st Corps, Army of the Potomac, from March 13, 1862; in 3d Brigade, 1st Div., 6th Corps, Army of the Potomac from May, 1862; in Light Brigade, 6th Corps, during the Chancellorsville Campaign in May 1863. The regiment took part in the following engagements: Fairfax Court House, Blacksum's Ford, Bull Run, Munson's Hill, Springfield Station, West Point, Seven Days' Battle at Gaines' Mill, Garnett's and Golding's Farm, Glendale and Malvern Hill; Burke's Station, all of Virginia; Crampton's Pass and Antietam of Maryland and Fredericksburg, Franklin's Crossing and Marye's Heights and Salem Church of Virginia.

Sgt Ely was not among the 211 members of the 31st Infantry who did not return. He was mustered out and honorably discharged under Col. Frank Jones, on June 4, 1863 in New York City from Co. I, 31st Infantry, 1st N.Y.V. William died on April 15, 1912 and is buried in the Denison Cemetery in Stonington (Mystic), CT.

Bro. Hubbard and his wife, Nancy LaRue (Kendall) Hubbard reside on Staten Island, NY.

ROGER BRYANT HUNTING, joined Sons of Union Veterans August 1, 1993, member Army of the James Camp 1865. He served in the Army Air Force in the South Pacific in WWII and his father, Elmer R. Hunting, served in the AEF in France in WWI. His great-grandfather Charles F. Bryant was mustered in to Co. K, 33rd Mass Infantry Regt. August 8, 1862 and mustered out near Washington D.C. June 11, 1865. He served with his company at, among others, the battle of Gettysburg, July 1-3, 1863. Thereafter, on July 17, while as a corporal, rounding up stragglers in Louden County, VA, he was taken prisoner. He was held, successively in Libby, Belle Isle and Pendelton prisons. Was paroled; returned to his home in Sharon, MA and when he recovered his health, rejoined his regiment which had been part of Great Sherman's Army in its march from Atlanta to the Sea, in or near Columbia, SC.

Roger B. Hunting   *Charles F. Bryant*

He was part of the Grand March through Washington after the Confederate surrender. He returned to his home in Sharon where he served as postmaster for over 40 years, while very active in Kingsley Post 94 of the GAR.

PAUL L. AND PAUL M. IMMEL, are the grandson and great-grandson, respectively, of George Immel. They joined the Brooks-Grant Camp #7, Ohio Department, S.U.V. in 1994. Paul L. was born on July 23, 1926; and his son, Paul M. on March 27, 1955. Both visited the monuments honoring the 92nd O.V.I. at Chickamauga, GA in 1989.

Their Civil war ancestor, George Immel was born on August 26, 1844 in Bebra, Hesse-Cassel, Germany; and died on January 27, 1914 in Marietta, OH. He enlisted on August 11, 1862 in Co. F, 92nd Ohio Volunteer Infantry Regt. and mustered out with the company near Washington, DC on June 10, 1865. George was an active member of Buell Post, G.A.R.

Bro. Paul L. and his wife Betty reside in Marietta.

BERTRAM ISAACS, was born April 30, 1909 and joined Camp #26, May 20, 1925. During WWII he served in the Civil Defense League. He served as department secretary-treasurer from 1953 to 1974. In 1968 he was given the honorary title of PDC. He lives in Ft. Lauderdale, FL.

Bertram's father, Julius was born 1876 and joined the SUV in 1892. In 1918 he was appointed honorary colonel by NYC Mayor Hylan to welcome home the troops. In 1927 he was appointed adjutant General of the GAR. In 1928 he was elected secretary of the New York Department SUV and served until his death on Jan. 20, 1953. In 1948 he was granted the title of PDC.

Bertram's grandfather, Isidore Isaacs, was born in 1847 and served under the name Theodor Barwood. Serving in Co. F, 59th NY and Co. I, 12th NY Cav. He was New York Department Commander GAR in 1921 and Jr. Vice CinC in 1919. He was a founder of the Hebrew Veterans Union now known as the Jewish War Veterans. He died Feb. 18, 1924.

STEPHEN T. JACKSON, joined the Ben Harrison Camp #356 in Indianapolis on April 29, 1990, where he currently serves as camp commander. Brother Jackson also serves as the Indiana Department senior vice commander.

Stephen T. Jackson

Among his 14 veteran ancestors, Steve bases his right to membership on his great-grandfather, Pvt. William L. Jackson. Pvt. Jackson enlisted in Connersville, IN, August 10, 1862 in Co. G, 84th Indiana Infantry He was discharged on June 14, 1865. He died June 14, 1907.

Brother Jackson and his wife Janene reside in Anderson, IN.

NELS A. JACOBSON, joined the Sons as a member-at-large on August 2, 1993. His Civil War ancestor was, Pvt. Nelson James Smith, who served with Co. G, 28 Wis. Vol. Infantry. He enlisted on August 21, 1862 and was discharged on August 23, 1865. It is unknown if Nelson James Smith belonged to a GAR post.

Nelson J. Smith

JON DAVID JEHU, joined the Sons, Sydney #41, Ithaca, on February 10, 1991. His Civil War ancestor was, Pvt. Harvey Wilbur, of the 25th New York Cav.

Harvey Wilbur married Mary Snyder in 1888 when she was 18. After he died in 1911 she married John Snyder and he died in 1936. She lived to 1980, age 110 at NYS Veterans Home Oxford. She was the last widow put on the pension for the Civil War.

JOHN DAVID JENKINS, PCC - Bro. Jenkins joined the General George H. Thomas Camp #19, Lancaster, PA October, 1988 and served as camp commander during 1992 and 1994. Jenkins also served as Pennsylvania graves registration officer 1994-1995 and served on the national level as chairman of the Publications Committee, 1991 to 1993.

Jacob Klepper   *Andrew Good*

Between his two veteran ancestors, J.D. bases his right to membership on his great-grandfather Jacob Klepper who enlisted in Co. G, 138th Pennsylvania Volunteer Infantry September 9, 1862 and fought in numerous battles and was wounded in the hip, abdomen and thigh on July 9, 1864 at the Battle of Monocacy. Eventually taken to the Army Hospital in Philadelphia, he was nursed by his sister, Elizabeth Klepper Davidson for nine months. He died July 6, 1912 in his 71st year.

J.D.'s other veteran ancestor was great-grandfather Andrew Good who served as a private in the 27th Pennsylvania Emergency Regt. whose only engagement was June 28, 1863 at the Columbia/Wrightville Bridge (Lancaster/York Counties) where advance elements of the Army of Northern Virginia were stopped. He died July 10, 1922 in his 91st year.

ANDREW L. JOHNSON, joined the order in 1990. He is hopeful that a camp can be organized in Minneapolis, MN where he now lives so he can become more active in the SUV. His membership is based on the service of his great-great-great-uncle George Wesley Bennett who served in Co. D, 111th New York Volunteer Infantry His unit was engaged at Gettysburg on July 2 in action at the Wheatfield where Bennett was wounded in the leg. He subsequently received a head wound while under fire on Cemetery Ridge on the morning of July 3. He was discharged for disability on October 31, 1863. He married and moved to Michigan where he died on May 4, 1878 at Pottersville, MI.

ANDREW M. JOHNSON, joined the order on June 30, 1990. Served in all elected offices of the Lincoln-Cushing Camp in Washington, DC area and all elected offices in the Maryland Department. He served as department commander in 1993 and is currently serving a second term as secretary/treasurer. He has been elected to a three year term on the National Council of Administration. Served as a major in the SVR as Washington, DC liaison. Among his ancestors, he bases his membership in the SUV on Wesley Bennett, a great-great uncle and a private in Co. A, 112th New York Infantry Regt. from July 31, 1862 to his death from fever on October 26, 1864 at Jones Landing, James River.

CLAYTON R. JOHNSON, joined the order in 1990. Travel around the United States has prevented active participation but he hopes to join a new camp in Minneapolis, MN. His claim to membership in the order is through his great-great-great-uncle John Annis Bennett, private, Co. G, 29th Indiana Volunteer Infantry Bennett served from September 15, 1861 until his Capture on September 20, 1863 at the Battle of Chickamauga. John Annis Bennett died at Andersonville Prison Camp on November 15, 1864. He is buried at the National Cemetery there in Section H, Grave 12,019.

JAY WILLIAM JOHNSON, became a member of Orlando A. Somers Camp No. 1 of Kokomo, IN, on April 24, 1993. He is the son of Professor James L. and Janice Gieseke Johnson. A graduate of Purdue University, Brother Johnson is engaged in farming. He is the son-in-law of Past Commander-in-Chief Allen W. Moore and Barbara Tiley Moore. He is the great-great-grandson of Pvt. Williamson Haworth.

Williamson Haworth enlisted in Co. A, 79th Regt. of Illinois Infantry on July 14, 1862, and was discharged on March 10, 1863. Pvt. Haworth was born October 30, 1845, in Vermillion County, IL, and died on August 19, 1920, in Elwood, IN. He was a member of the Elwood GAR Post #61. He is buried in the Elwood City Cemetery.

CRAIG A. JONES, age 32, resident of Nixa, MO. One son, Matthew, age five. Sell beverage Co2 systems for P.G. Walker, Springfield, MO. Hobbies include metal detecting, and Civil War reenacting. Member and past editor of the Civil War roundtable of the Ozarks. Charter member of Phelps Camp #66 of SUV, Springfield, MO, October 1, 1994.

Descendant of Thomas Gold, born 1819 in Lincoln County, TN, and died 1894 in Stone County, MO. Enlisted August 14, 1862 in Springfield, MO, Co. G, 8th Missouri Cav. (Union). Participated in the battles of Cane Hill, AR, November 28, 1862, and Prairie

Craig A. Jones

Grove, AR, December 7, 1862 under the command of General James Blunt. Attached to General Fredrick Steele's expedition to Little Rock, AR, August through September 1863. Action at Bayou Fourche and capture of Little Rock, September 10, 1863. Discharged due to chronic diarrhea at Brownsville Station, AR, July 28, 1864.

MYRON ELLIS JONES, JR., joined Camp Dennison #125 on May 12, 1992 and transferred to Brooks-Grant Camp #7 as a charter member on July 11, 1994.

He joined through his great-great-uncle, Thomas Jones. Thomas was born in Gallia County, OH in 1846 to Levi Campbell and Nancy (Rife) Jones. Thomas enlisted at Fayetteville, WV with the 91st OVI on October 25, 1863 under Capt. Richard Blazer's Co. B. His enlistment papers say he was 5'7", light complexioned and hair, and grey eyes. He paid the supreme price on the first day of battle, charging the C.S.A. forces at Opequon, VA, the 19th of September 1864.

Myron E. Jones, Jr.   *Thomas Jones*

Thomas' brother, Henry, died February 1862 while serving with the 53rd O.V.I. His grandfather, Thomas, served in the war of 1812. His great-grandfather, James Martindale, was an officer in the Revolutionary War with the South Carolina Militia under Col. Brandon.

Thomas left behind sisters Lovina, Mary Ann, Sarah and Libbie and brothers Eli, James and Jonathan.

JAMES JOYCE, joined the Sons September 1993, Admiral Foote Camp #17. His Civil War ancestors:

Pvt. Michael Ryan served with Co. E, 17th Conn. He enlisted August 9, 1862 until January 19, 1865. Fought at the Battle of Gettysburg. Was on sick call just before the battle but left the field hospital against the advice of the surgeon to join his unit for the campaign. He received a shell splinter in the right hip on the second day fighting that he later claimed caused him rheumatism in his right leg.

James Joyce

Michael Ryan   *John S. Cunningham*

Sgt. John Cunningham served with Co. A, 1st D.C. Cav. Enlisted July 1, 1863 to October 26, 1865. For unknown reasons he joined under an alias of John Scott. Two months before Appomattox he was sentenced to three months in prison for disrespect to his superior officer. After hard campaigning he lost his temper and told a LT Lakin to "kiss my ass" and then challenged him by saying "I am as good a man as you, get off here, God Damn you and I'll lick hell out of you". This may be why he was left out of the regimental history.

JOHN F. JUDGE, JR., joined the Sons March 19, 1994 (14th birthday). Sumner H. Needham Camp #21, Lawrence, MA. Held office as secretary/treasurer Camp #21.

Civil War ancestor: James Walsh, private, served with 6th Mass, Co. I. Enlisted August 31, 1862-May 31, 1863. He belonged to GAR Post 146, Lawrence, MA.

Although James Walsh's birth certificate is unobtainable, his age is given as 18 on his discharge, (which would make his year of birth 1844) but on pension records and marriage certificate it is given as 1851. Family legend is that he lied about his age to enlist.

CHARLES A. KALLDIN, JR., joined as a Member-at-Large May 4, 1990 and transferred to Lone Star Camp #1, Arlington, Texas on December 3, 1994.

He bases his right to membership on Pvt. George Vogt of Co. D, 45th Regt. NY Infantry (Enlisted September 20, 1861 - Discharged October 1, 1865). Pvt. Vogt belonged to Gen. Jas. McQuade Post, No. 557, Dept. of New York, GAR. He participated in operations in Shenandoah Valley, including the battles of Cross Keys, Cedar Mountain, Waterloo Bridge, White Sulphur Springs, Gainsville, Groveton, Second Bull Run, Chancellorsville and Gettysburg, where he was wounded on July 1, 1863 between McLean's Barn and Cemetery Hill. After a stay at Satterlee U.S.A. General Hospital, he returned to his unit and took part in battles of Wauhatchie and Chattanooga.

Pvt. Vogt re-enlisted at Lookout Valley, January 4, 1864: then engaged in demonstrations at Rocky Faced Ridge and Dalton: Battles of Resaca, New Hope Church, Dallas, operations about Marietta and against Kenesaw Mountain. The 45th was ordered to Nashville July 6, 1864, where he remained on Military Guard Duty until discharged. The 45th NY Consolidated with 58th NY on June 30, 1865, and was discharged October 1, 1865.

Vogt was born in Bavaria and became a US Citizen on October 15, 1866. He married Anna Maria Zimmermann November 15, 1868. They had one daughter and five sons. He died September 29, 1894 and is buried in Calvary Cemetery, Queens, NY.

DENNIS KELLY, joined the Gen. Philip H. Sheridan Camp #2 Department of IL on March 4, 1995.

Dennis Kelly   *George I. Vastine*

He bases his right to membership on his great-great-grandfather, Pvt. George Vastine of the 81st OH Vol. He enlisted August 7, 1862 and was discharged July 13, 1865. Pvt. Vastine was with General W.T. Sherman during his famous Atlanta campaign plus the "March to the Sea" and Carolina campaigns of 1864-65. His unit was part of Greenville Dodge's XVI Corp. (McPherson's Army of Tennessee). After the Atlanta campaign his unit was attached to General J. A. "Black Jack" Logan's XV Corp. Some of the major engagements that George fought in were: Kennesaw Mountain, Resaca, Atlanta, Jonesboro and Bentonville.

After the campaigns of 1864-1865, George returned home to where it was said that his physical appearance changed so much that his mother did not even recognize him. He died November 2, 1888.

JOSEPH V. KELLY, joined the Abraham Lincoln 100 on March 10, 1994.

He bases his right to membership on Pvt. Martin Joyce of B Co. 9 Conn. Infantry. He enlisted on October 4, 1861 and was discharged August 3, 1865. He belonged to the GAR Post of Meriden Connecticut. The 9th Connecticut was an all Irish unit. Kelly served in 5 states.

MARK ALLEN KETTLER, joined the Sons, General William T. Sherman - Billy Yank Camp No. 65, St. Louis, MO, on December 8, 1993.

He bases his membership on two Civil War ancestors. The first is Cpt. Christian Hermann Kettler, who served with Co. H, 2nd Infantry Regt., U.S. Reserve Corps, Missouri Volunteers. Enlisted February 18, 1862 and discharged September 3, 1862. He belonged to GAR Post Red Bud, IL; Omaha, NE and Milwaukee, WI.

On April 25, 1862 granted five days leave of absence from General John M. Schofield to escort his son, who was seriously wounded at Pittsburg Landing, back to his family in Waterloo, IL. In the summer of 1862 he developed rheumatic fever and chronic diarrhea; was reported near death while in a hospital at Rienzi, MS. By July, he tendered his resignation and requested sick leave. Due to his illness, he had to be hauled to an ambulance when his unit was ordered to St. Louis, MO in August 1862. Died January 12, 1899. The Milwaukee, WI post of the Grand Army of the Republic officiated at his funeral.

Mark A. Kettler   *Christian H. Kettler*

Mark's second Civil War ancestor is, 1st Sgt. Gottfried Vollrath Kettler, who served with Co. A, 43rd Regt. Illinois Volunteer Infantry. Enlisted August 19, 1861 and discharged December 14, 1865. Promoted to corporal on January 1, 1862. Seriously wounded at the Battle of Pittsburg Landing. Sent to hospital at Savannah, TN, thence to Mound City Hospital, where his father came to collect him and take him home to his family in Waterloo, IL. Did not return to his regiment until April 1, 1863, at which time he was court-martialed for desertion and demoted. Reenlisted on February 27, 1864. Promoted to first sergeant on January 1, 1865.

THOMAS F. KING, joined the William Tabor Camp #162 on August 14, 1993. He has served as Secretary, treasurer, and guard.

He bases his right to membership on Pvt. Thomas Burns part of MA Vol. Militia 6th Inf, Regt. and 8th Battery Light Artillery from April 16, 1861-August 2, 1861 and June 6, 1862-November 29, 1862. He belonged to Benjamin Butler Camp #32. When his unit was passing through Baltimore, MD at the beginning of the war, they were attacked by a mob of people and two of his comrades were killed.

RUSSELL W. KIRCHNER, joined Orlando A. Somers Camp #1 Kokomo, IN on January 23, 1993. He has served as Junior Vice Commander and Senior Vice Commander.

Russell W. Kirchner   *Carroll C. Kirchner*

He bases his right to membership on Sgt. an Carroll Charles Kirchner of Co. C 4th Cavalry, 64th Regiment, PA Vol. He enlisted August 26, 1861 and was discharged September 11, 1864, and belonged to GAR Post #28, Indiana, Pennsylvania.

The Pennsylvania 64th Regt., 4th Cavalry participated in many engagements including the Battle of Gettysburg. The PA monument at Gettysburg Battlefield has C.C. Kirchner's name inscribed.

ARTHUR PAUL KIRMSS, was born October 19, 1946 in Brooklyn, NY.

He joined Capt. Oliver Tilden Camp #26, New York City, on April 15, 1983, serving as sergeant at arms, secretary, and presently, as musical director and editor of *Billy Yank*, the camp newsletter.

Arthur P. Kirmss   *Ernest Wagner*

Brother Kirmss is an historic-style hand engraver and performs Early American songs.

His great-grandfather, Ernest Wagner, Co. H, 13th New Jersey Volunteers, enlisted August 14, 1862, Newark, NJ. Ernest fought at Antietam, Chancellorsville, Gettysburg, Atlanta, and the Carolinas, mustering out June 7, 1865.

He joined his regiment's Veteran association in 1887, attending Gettysburg's 25th anniversary, July, 1888. Joining U.S. Grant Post #327. He was, by 1909, post commander, then state aide-de-camp of New York, by 1912, attending Gettysburg's Fiftieth Reunion, 1913. He died September 21, 1921, and reposes in Cypress Hills National Cemetery, Brooklyn.

PHIILIP KISSEL, joined the Oliver Tilden Camp #26 in December of 1994.

John Kissel

He bases his claim to membership on Pvt. John Kissel of Co. I 20th NY Infantry (1861-1863). Pvt. Kissel was later put on detached service to the 1st NY Artillery. A John Kiston was also a member of Co. I and often used John Kissel's name.

CHRISTOPHER R. KLENK, joined the Abraham Lincoln #100 December 3, 1994. He was born on April 22, 1936 in Cheektowaga, NY. He worked with the Boy Scouts of America for a profession and retired on May 1, 1992. He was a member of the N.Y.S. Air National Guard and the Air Force Reserve (Air Police). He had four children and five grandchildren.

Christopher R. Klenk   *Garrett S. Snell*

He bases his right to membership on his great-grandfather, Pvt. Garrett S. Snell of the 37th IL Infantry (September 27, 1862-June 10, 1865). He belonged to the Buffalo, NY GAR Post. Garrett served along with his brothers Burton and Milton in I Co. The 37th IL was know as "Fremont Rifles" and as the "IL Greyhounds." All three brothers participated in the Siege of Vicksburg and a monument for the 37th stands at Vicksburg upon which their names are engraved.

JAMES R. KLIPSTEIN, Sr., joined Harpers Ferry Camp #6 on July 24, 1994. He was a Civil War reenactor in the 1960s with Co. C, 2nd MD Cumberland Continentals Vol. Infantry.

James R. Klipstein, Sr.   *Joseph Crawford*

He bases his right to membership on his great-grandfather, Pvt. Joseph Crawford of Co. D 2nd MD P.H.B. Vol. Infantry (August 9, 1861 to September 29, 1864). Pvt. Crawford was a member of GAR McPherson Post #20. He came to America from Bavaria, Germany at the age of 10, first to Cumberland, MD Allegany County, then moved 20 miles south west to the town of Barton and labored as a coal miner most of his life. He joined the Union Army in Piedmont VA (now WV), and spent most of his time guarding C&O canal and B&O railroad. He went on General Hunter's raid to Lynchburg, VA, June 2 to June 18, 1864.

CHRISTOPHER G. KNIGHT, Bro. Knight became the fourth generation of his family to belong to General George H. Thomas Camp #19, Lancaster, PA in 1994. He lives in Lancaster and is a newspaper photographer. His membership is derived from great-great-grandfather William J. Knight who was a private in Co. G of the 126th Pennsylvania Volunteer Infantry He later enlisted as a wounded veteran in Co. L, 21st Pennsylvania Cavalry which was dismounted and became Co. L, 182nd PVI.

DOUGLASS ROBERT KNIGHT, joined the Anna M. Ross Camp #1, Philadelphia, PA on December 5, 1990. He transferred to Charles H. Bond Camp #104 in Malden, MA. At this camp he served as Junior and Senior Vice Commander, MA Dept. Patriotic Instructor and National Aide. He then transferred to the William Tabor Camp #162 in Methuen, MA. At this camp he served as Camp Organizer, Camp Commander, MA Dept. Council and National Aide.

Douglass R. Knight   *John L. D. Hopkins*

He bases his right to membership on two Civil War ancestors, Pvt. John L.D. Hopkins of Co. A, 58th MA Infantry, and Pvt. John H. Knight of Co. I, 60th MA Infantry. Pvt. Hopkins enlisted December 22, 1863 and participated in the Battle of Wilderness, after which he was promoted to Corporal. He fought at the Battle of the Crater, and was one of 18 men of the 58th to return to Union lines. He was wounded during the Battle of Spotsylvania. He was captured during the Battle of Poplar Springs. He died in a POW camp in Salisbury, NC on February 10, 1865. Pvt. Knight enlisted on July 16, 1864 and was honorably discharged on November 30, 1864. He performed guard duty in Baltimore, MD and Indianapolis, IN.

GLENN B. KNIGHT, Bro. Knight joined the General George H. Thomas Camp #19, Lancaster, PA in 1992, unaware that he was the third generation of his family to belong to that camp. The following year he was elected camp commander and then joined the staff of the Department of Pennsylvania as graves registration officer. As the 1994 department commander he was appointed as a national aide for fund development and was later elected department senior vice commander.

Knight is a former Marine and an Air Force retiree who is presently executive director of the Lancaster County Historical Society, where Camp #19 holds its meetings. He is a native of and lives in Lititz, PA with his wife, Beverly, who is chaplain of the Pennsylvania Department, Auxiliary to the SUV.

His right of membership derives from Pvt. William J. Knight, Co. L, 21st PA Cav., his great-grandfather.

GLENN F. KNIGHT, Bro. Knight first joined General George H. Thomas Camp #19, Lancaster, PA in the 1930s. As a teenager he was seeking the adventure of military service, not knowing that his father had previously been a member of the same camp. He dropped out of the order and served in the World War II where he earned the technician fifth class rank with service in coast artillery, artillery and infantry. He saw combat in the South Pacific. Returning to Lancaster County he worked as a lithographer until his retirement. Now living in Silver Springs, FL with his wife Dorothy, he rejoined Camp #19 when his son, Glenn, became Camp Commander in 1993. He is now a life member.

Bro. Knight's veteran ancestor was his grandfather, Pvt. William J. Knight who enlisted from Chambersburg in Co. G, 126th Pennsylvania Volunteer Infantry, was wounded at Fredericksburg and reenlisted in Co. L, 21st Pennsylvania Cav.

JOHN B. KNIGHT, Bro. Knight became a member of General George H. Thomas Camp #19, Lancaster, PA in 1926. His occupation was listed as laborer but in his lifetime he had worked on the railroad, operated steam boilers and even played in a band. Born in Franklin County, PA he had migrated east into Lancaster and died in Lititz, just north of Lancaster.

His father, Pvt. William J. Knight, served first with Co. G, 126th Pennsylvania Volunteer Infantry and was wounded at Fredericksburg. He returned home to Chambersburg, PA following his release from hospital and he was at home during the battle at Gettysburg. A month after the Gettysburg unpleasantness he enlisted in Co. L, 21st Pennsylvania Cav., which was from time-to-time dismounted and became Co. L, 182nd PVI. He served through the end of the war and was mustered out with his company.

ROGER M. KNOX, joined the Phil Sheridan Camp #4, San Jose, CA on April 25, 1994. As a reenactor, Mr. Knox is enlisted in the U.S. 4th Regiment Regulars, 5th Corps, and wears his great-grandfather's 5th Corps Maltese Cross (the Corps insignia) to commemorate Private Knox's service.

Roger M. Knox   *James M. Knox*

He bases his right to membership on his great-grandfather Pvt. James M. Knox who enlisted on August 11, 1862 and was mustered in on September 2, 1862. He served for three years under Capts. Daniel S. Knox, and George Stowe, and Cols. John McLane and Strong Vincent. The Regt. was assigned to 3rd Brigade, 1st Div., 5th Corps, and engaged at: Yorktown, Second Bull Run, Antietam, Fredericksburg, Mud March, Chancellorsville, Aldie, Middleburg, Gettysburg, and Wilderness. He was wounded at Fredericksburg where he was slightly wounded when a minie ball grazed his temple. After the Wilderness, he was transferred to Co. E, 83rd Regt, PA Vol. Infantry, under Capt. Peter Grace and Col. C.P. Rodgers and engaged at: Spotsylvania, North Anna, Petersburg, Weldon Rail Road, Hatcher's Run, Five Forks, and Surrender of General Lee.

The 83rd PA fought at Little Round Top in Gettysburg, and Pvt. Knox's name is inscribed on the monument to his regiment at the battlefield site. This battle, which is a main scene in *Gettysburg* and was important in holding the hill on the Union's left flank, was important to the Union victory.

He was honorably discharged on May 29, 1865 by reasons of close of war. He was a member of GAR Bayard Post Chapter 22, Olean, NY.

ROBERT L. KRASCHE, joined the Army of the James Camp #1864, Dept. of Maryland on February 1, 1980, and is Life Member #177. He has held the offices of Secretary, Treasurer and Commander of Colorado Springs Camp #5 Dept. CO and WY, and also Secretary, Commander of Dept. of CO and WY.

Robert L. Krasche   *Jonathan Houghton*

He bases his right to membership on Corporal Jonathan Houghton, of Co. C 17 IL Cavalry from November 8, 1863 to November 23, 1865. He was a member of J.W. Guthrie Post 252, Dept of Iowa, Woodward, IA. His Company was the first Union troops to arrive following the massacre of 110 Missouri Union troops at Centralia, MO by guerrilla leader "Bloody Bill" Anderson. Companies C and D chased Anderson for the next 18 days, resulting in several skirmishes. His regiment's chief scout (and spy) was William "Wild Bill" Hitchcock. His regiment was sent to Kansas to protect against Indians after the war. Eight of the Regiment's men froze to death in a blizzard enroute from Ft. Larned to Ft. Leavenworth to be mustered out of US service in November 1865.

CHRISTOPHER KRECOTA, joined the John T. Crawford Camp #43 on February 12, 1995. Eight year old Christopher has been the camp's mascot for six years and was the first junior member. He has spoken at schools and talked about what kind of toys the children played with during the war. He participates as an reenactor with his parents and two brothers.

Christopher Krecota   *Tobias Stiveson*

He bases his right to membership on Pvt. Tobias Stiveson of Co. K 76th Reg. PA (July 13, 1863-June 2, 1865). Tobias was wounded during the war. He died May 19, 1898 at the age of 79 years, 1 month, and 20 days.

DARRIN KRECOTA, joined John T. Crawford camp #43 in September 1989. He has served as Senior Vice Commander and flag bearer. Darrin carries the 78th flag in parades and was at the 130th Anniversary of Gettysburg Battle and Remembrance Day Parade. He helps the camp replace soldier's tombstones in Armstrong County, PA.

Darrin Krecota

He bases his right to membership on Pvt. John A. Walker of Co. D 62nd Regt. PA Vol. John was born where the Crooked Creek Lake is today in Pennsylvania. Pvt. Walker was paid by his brother-in-law to do his service duty. He enlisted July 24, 1861 and was killed July 2, 1863 in a wheat field in Gettysburg, PA. He is buried in Section D Grave 77 at Gettysburg.

JASON KRECOTA, joined the John T. Crawford Camp #43 on August 11, 1989 at the age of 13. He has served as Patriotic Instructor and Junior Vice Commander. Jason has spoken at schools and historical societies on the life of a drummer boy and a soldier. He participated in the 130th Anniversary of Gettysburg, Remembrance Day Parade. He is pictured on the cover of Servants General Store catalog. He participated in the movie *Gettysburg, Johnson Island - The Documentary*. He is a B flat trumpeter and principle drummer for the 105th Wildcat Regimental Brass Band out of Indiana, PA. Recently, Jason participated in the launching of the Civil War Coin Set in Philadelphia, PA.

Jason Krecota *Peter Beal*

He bases his right to membership on Pvt. Peter Beal of Co. B 78th Regiment PA Vol. who enlisted on February 27, 1864 and was discharged on September 11, 1865.

THAYNE C. LA BANTA, joined the Austin Blair Camp No. 7 in 1929. He has served as Dept. Commander.

Thayne C. La Banta *Derick D. Banta*

He bases his right to membership on his father, Pvt. Derick D. Banta of the 76th Vol. Infantry (1862-1865). Pvt. Banta later changed his name to Dean LaBanta. At 18, he was a drummer in the fife and drum corps. Banta's base was in Kankakee, IL. He saw action at Vicksburg and after the war, in 1886, formed the First Regiment of New York, an independent state militia of over 1200 men. He was a member of Edward Pomeroy Post 48 - GAR, Jackson, MI. After the war he became a chemist. He also wrote a publication titled "De La Banta's Advice to Ladies," a 380-page guide book on lady's etiquette. Derick was 60 when Thayne was born.

IVAN DEAN LANCASTER, joined Ben Harrison Camp in the early 1970s. He has served as Camp Commander, and was twice Department Commander of Indiana. He is also a member of the Military Order of the Loyal Legion of the United States.

Ivan D. Lancaster

He bases his right to membership on his great-grandfather 2nd Lt. Nathan Elliott from Ohio and his great-great-grandfather, William H. Collins of Indiana 33rd, who died at Cumberland Gap.

SCOTT M. LANGSTON, joined the Lone Star Camp #1 in 1994 and has served as Camp Chaplain.

He bases his right to membership on Pvt. Charles F. Trotter of the 25th KY Infantry and the 17th KY Infantry. He enlisted on October 15, 1861 and was discharged on January 23, 1865. He participated in the following battles: Fort Donelson, Shiloh, Chickamauga, Missionary Ridge, Atlanta Campaign, and Franklin. On May 27, 1864 he suffered a gunshot wound to the forehead at Pickett's Mill, GA and did not return to duty until September, 1864.

RICHARD F. LEE, joined at Curtenius Guard #17, Sunfield, MI on July 27, 1993. He is a charter member at Gilluly-Kingsley #120 Howell, MI, April 1994, where he has served as Camp Commander. He was elected Michigan Dept. Secretary in June 1995. Richard was born in February of 1931 in Detroit, MI. He enlisted in the USAF in 1952 and was an aerial photographer on a B-36 inter-continental bomber, SAC during the Korean War. He later taught at Durfee, Ruddiman and Pelham Middle Schools in Detroit. He married Elizabeth A. Bootz in August of 1963.

Richard F. Lee *Amos Lee*

Richard bases his right to membership on his great-grandfather Pvt. Amos Lee of Co. B 87th IN Infantry. He enlisted on December 15, 1863 and was discharged on July 21, 1865. Also, Richard's great-grandfather, 2nd Lt. William T. Edwards of Co. C 132nd IN Infantry served from May 18, 1864 to September 7, 1864.

JAMES TRACY LEWIS, joined as a member-at-large, Dept. of Massachusetts on December 5, 1994. He was born on December 10, 1928. He is a veteran of the Korean War.

He bases his right to membership on Pvt. Daniel Lewis of Co. E 37th Regiment, Mass. Vol. He was born on July 4, 1835. He enlisted on July 15 1862 and left for Washington in September of 1862 under the direction of Col. Edwards. When he arrived at Camp Chase, was assigned to Briggs Brigade, Casey's Div. of Reserves. He participated in the battle of Fredricksburg VA, Salem Church, VA, and Gettysburg, PA. He was wounded at Gettysburg with a gunshot wound in the right hand with the loss of a thumb. While confined to hospitals at Fort Schyler, NY and Providence Rhode Island, he did hospital work. He was honorably discharged in July of 1865.

REV. RAYMOND A. LIEBER, joined as a member-at-large on October 7, 1974.

Rev. Raymond A. Lieber

He bases his right to membership on Oscar Curtis of Co. B 160th NY Regt. He was a wagoner, and was a prisoner of war at Andersonville, where he had to dig for food and water.

WALTER LININGER, bases his right to membership on Pvt. Henry F. Lininger of Co. K 3rd Regiment, Potomac Home Brigade, Maryland Infantry. He enlisted on March 1, 1864 and was discharged on May 29, 1865.

Henry F. Lininger

Pvt. Lininger ran away from home at age sixteen to enlist. He had only been in the army a little over four months when he was a part of the small army under General Lew Wallace at the Battle of Monocacy, July 9, 1864. He died June 30, 1930 at the age of 83 and is buried in St. Jacobs Cemetery, Smithfield, PA.

DAVID LONG, joined Phelps Camp 66 of Springfield, Missouri in July of 1994 when it was formed. He is a Charter Member and has served as Senior Vice Camp Commander.

He bases his right to membership on his great-great-great-grandfather Joseph Calvin Long of the 24th Missouri Infantry, Co I (83). Although he did not see any combat, he gave his life to disease one year after joining the army.

Other great-great-great-grandfathers that served were William K. Reed, Co. A 1st AR Cavalry; Levi Knight Co. H 8th MO Cavalry; Reubin Smith Co. B 2nd KS Cavalry, David Worley and John Worley, Co E 3rd IA Cavalry; Levin Caffey Co. A 73rd MO Militia; Lawson Scrivener, Dallas County MO Home Guard; and Thomas Cook, 1st AL Cavalry. David Long has numerous other great uncles and cousins that also served.

CLAYTON J. LONGVER, joined J.S. Durgin #7 in 1985. He has served as Treasurer at J.S. Durgin #7 and Secretary-Treasurer of the New Hampshire Department.

He bases his right to membership on Pvt. Issac Langevin of the 5th NH Vol. Infantry He enlisted in 1861 and was discharged in 1862 for disability. He also enlisted in Vermont in Co. C 8th VT Infantry.

MARTIN W. LOWERY, SR., joined the sons, Gov. William Dennison Camp #125, Dept. of Ohio on April 11, 1990. He held the offices of Camp Senior Vice Commander and Camp Council. The following also joined Camp #125: Martin W. Lowery, Jr. (June 1, 1990), Norman S. Lowery (February 11, 1992), Robert L. Lowery (June 30, 1992), and William R. Lowery (June 30, 1992).

(l. to r.) William R. Lowery, Robert Lowery, Norman S. Lowery, Martin W. Lowery, Jr., and Martin W. Lowery, Sr.

They base their right to membership on their Civil War ancestor, Pvt. Leonard Lowery, Co. A of the 63rd Regt. OH Vol. Infantry. He enlisted on September 15, 1861 and was discharged on July 8, 1865.

Leonard Lowery

Leonard's Company assembled at Marietta, OH and on February 18, 1862, the 63rd Regt. left to go westward to join the Army of Mississippi. They fought with the western armies throughout the war. They were assigned mostly with the 16th and 17th Corps under Sherman and Grant. He was wounded in North Carolina, shot accidentally in the right hip by his own Sergent King.

ALAN R. LOOMIS, Junior Vice Commander-in-Chief, Brother Loomis joined David D. Porter Camp #116, Valparaiso, IN, in 1979. He has served as camp secretary/treasurer, two terms as camp commander, department secretary/treasurer, three terms as department commander, National G.A.R. highway officer, and as a member of the National Program and Policy Committee. In addition, he served as the General chairman of the 110th National Encampment, SUVCW, (125th anniversary of the 1st G.A.R. National Encampment) held in Indianapolis, IN, in 1991. He is presently serving as Department G.A.R. highway officer, commander of the Central Region Conference, and junior vice commander-in-chief.

Alan R. Loomis   *James A. Latimer*

Alan bases his membership on one of his maternal great-grandfathers, Sgt. James A. Latimer, who was one of four ancestors that served in the Union Army. Sgt. Latimer enlisted October 14, 1861, in Co. K, 39th Illinois Volunteer Infantry He reenlisted January 1, 1865, and was present with his regiment at Appomattox Court House on April 9, 1865. He was discharged December 6, 1865, and was a member of Joseph Woodruff Post #281, G.A.R. Marseilles, IL, following the war. He died March 18, 1895, at Danway, IL.

RICHARD LUFKIN, joined A. A. Sherman Camp Uxbridge, MA in April 1988. He is presently Camp Commander and has served as Junior Vice Commander and GAR Highway Officer, Dept. MA.

He bases his right to membership on Pvt. Sylvester of the 8th MA who enlisted in June 1862 and was discharged in July of 1865. He was a member of Lynn Massachusetts GAR. The 8th MA followed the 6th MA through Baltimore riots.

JOHN P. LYNCH, JR., Bro. Lynch joined the Order in 1994 and belongs to the Oliver Tilden Camp #26 in New York City. John bases his membership on his great-grandfather, James A. Lynch. James A. Lynch enlisted in the U.S. Navy in 1864 and achieved the rank of captain of the Tops while serving aboard the USS *Brooklyn*. He served with the *Brooklyn* during the famous Battle of Mobile Bay with Admiral Farragut. James A. Lynch was born on September 14, 1837 in Akron, OH but returned to his fathers 150 acre farm after the war in Erie, PA.

John P. Lynch, Jr.

James also spent 22 years at sea before and after the war, traveling four times around the world.

He and his wife Julia travelled with their sons James M. and Frank E. Lynch across Pennsylvania during the Oil Excitement running saloons and boarding houses. They then settled in Croton, NY around 1885 opening up a saloon and hotel during the construction of the Croton Reservoir. James A. Lynch died on October 12, 1904 and is buried in St. Patrick's Cemetery, Verplancks, NY. He is presently survived by three generations of John P. Lynch's residing in Pearl River, NY.

STEPHEN DOUGLAS LYNN, was born on September 24, 1964 in Madisonville, KY, the son of Douglas Ray and Martha Ruth Clayton Lynn. He is married to the former Sandra Jeanne Wilkerson and is an attorney practicing in his hometown of Dawson Springs, KY. Steve joined the SUVCW in 1992 and is a member of the Fort Duffield Camp No. 1 of West Point, KY. He has four direct ancestors

Stephen D. Lynn   *William R. Goodaker*

who served the Union cause during the Civil War: Cornelius Alexander Brown, William Riley Goodaker, Aaron Purdy, Jr. and Joseph T. Thomason.

Cornelius Alexander Brown, was born in Henderson County, KY on May 7, 1842, the son of Obadiah and Matilda Sights Brown. He married Mary Brown after the war and had at least seven children. On August 13, 1862, he enlisted in Co. H, 8th Kentucky Cavalry in Henderson, KY. This unit was a part of the forces that pursued and captured CSA General John Hunt Morgan during his raid into Kentucky, Indiana, and Ohio in July 1863. He was mustered out of the service in Russellville, KY on September 23, 1863 with the rank of corporal. He died on December 12, 1912 and is buried in Shady Grove Cemetery in Poole, KY.

William Riley Goodaker, was born in Caldwell County, KY on May 25, 1840, the son of Lewis and Mary Townsend Goodaker. He married Rebecca Caroline McGregor and had one son, William Bayliss Goodaker. On August 15, 1863, he enlisted in Co. C, 48th Kentucky Mounted Infantry and was mustered in to service at Princeton, KY on October 26, 1863 along with his brothers, Lewis and David Goodaker, and brother-in-law, James McGregor. He soon contracted the measles and died in Princeton, KY on November 24, 1863. He is buried in the McGregor-Goodaker Cemetery in Caldwell County, KY.

Aaron Purdy, Jr. was born in Hopkins County, KY about 1842, the son of Aaron and Elizabeth Bradshaw Purdy. He married Martha Jane Chappel and had one daughter, Nancy Elizabeth Purdy. In 1864, he enlisted in the 17th Kentucky Cav. He soon contracted the measles and was brought home by his father where he died in 1865.

(On September 9, 1883, the only son of William Riley Goodaker and the only daughter of Aaron Purdy, Jr. married.)

Joseph T. Thomason was born on February 11, 1841, the son of John and Martha Turner Thomason. He married Winfred Jackson. On August 13, 1863, he enlisted in Co. C, 48th Kentucky Mounted Infantry and was mustered in to the service on October 26, 1863, in Princeton, KY. He was mustered out of the service on December 15, 1864 in Bowling Green, KY. After the death of his first wife, he married Jane Purdy. He had at least 12 children. He died on June 21, 1921 and is buried in the Boyd-Jackson Cemetery in Caldwell County, KY.

JAMES T. LYONS, became a member of the Curtenius Guard Camp #17 on April 24, 1984. A veteran, he served with the 25th Infantry Div. in Korea. He served as National Secretary from 1989 to 1994, Michigan Department Commander in 1988 and 1989, and Commander of his Camp in 1986, 1987 and 1988. He has been active in a variety of hereditary societies including the Society of the Cincinnati in New Hampshire.

He bases his membership on his great-grandfather, Erastus Ruthven Winter, who served in Co. H, 35th Regt., Wisconsin Volunteer Infantry. He enlisted December 23, 1863 and was mustered out as a corporal on May 15, 1866 at Brownsville, TX. He felt that his most

James T. Lyons   *Erastus R. Winter*

important service was in the capture of the city of Mobile and his frontier service in Texas during 1865 and 1866. He entered the E.B. Wolcott Post No. 1, Milwaukee, WI June 28, 1899. He served as post commander in 1908.

THOMAS EDWARD MADAN, joined as a member-at-large in the Dept. of MA on June 3, 1995.

He bases his right to membership on Sgt. George H. Pierce of the 32nd Mass. Vol. Co. E. He was born September 12, 1831 in Rochester, MA. He enlisted on February 26, 1862 at Fort Warren, MA. He was wounded with the loss of his index finger on July 2, 1863 at Gettysburg, PA. He transferred September 12, 1863 to the Veteran Reserve Corps and re-enlisted April 11, 1864. He was promoted to Sergeant July 1, 1865 and was mustered out November 21, 1865 as of Co. F 21st V.R.C.

EDWARD T. MAGUIRE, joined the Hartsuff Camp #50, Rockland MA in September of 1990. He has served as senior vice commander.

He bases his right to membership on Sgt. James Maguire of the 2nd Mass He enlisted on April 11, 1861 and was discharged July 26, 1865. He was a member of GAR Chipman Post 89, Beverly, MA. He served both in the east (12th Corps) and the West (20th Corps) missing only 5 months service after being wounded at the Battle of Gettysburg.

DONALD NELSON MALLORY, joined SUVCW July 23, 1981. Abraham Lincoln Camp No. 6, Department of New York; transferred to Anna M. Ross Camp No. 1, Department of Pennsylvania.

Civil War ancestor: Otto F. Schmidt, private, Co. H, 140th New York Vol. Enlisted August 21, 1862. He was honorably discharged July 8, 1865.

Donald N. Mallory   *Otto F. Schmidt*

The 140th New York Volunteer was recruited from Monroe County, NY. They saw action at Fredericksburg in December 1863, at Chancellorsville in May 1863, at Gettysburg in July 1863 and beginning with the Wilderness Campaign, they took part in 13 successive battles during the spring and summer of 1864, suffering a total of 460 casualties. They retained their distinctive Zouave uniforms long after most regiments had abandoned them for the standard Union issue. Otto was wounded during the Wilderness campaign and spent several months in the U.S. Army Hospital at 65th and Vine St. Philadelphia, PA. He returned to his regiment and was mustered-out June 3, 1865 near Alexandria, VA.

GARY RICHARD MALONEY, born October 25, 1969, Pittsburgh, PA. He joined SUVCW in 1995, and is a member of the Davis Camp, Pennsylvania Department. He graduated May 18, 1995 with an associate degree in Corrections Administration. He currently interns with the Allegheny County Sheriffs Department. His hobbies and interest include role playing and Civil War History. He enrolled through the service of Pvt. William C. Marshall, Co. E, 9th Illinois Cav.

William C. Marshall married Charlotte E. Rainey. Mrs. Marshall died November 28, 1860 in Logansport leaving William with three daughters: Ella, Callie and Cora. He enlisted in Capt. Ira R. Gifford's company on September 10, 1861 in Logansport, IN. He participated in skirmishes on May 29, 1862, near the junction of the White and Black Rivers, AR, and June 12, 1862 at Waddell's Farm, near Village Creek, AR.

RONALD JOSEPH MALONEY, January 15, 1964, Pittsburg, PA. He joined SUVCW in 1993 and is a member of the Davis Camp, Pennsylvania Department. He will graduate in 1996 with a masters degree in Archival and Editing Studies, and he currently works as a professional genealogist. He enrolled through the service of Pvt. William Robert M. Hoysradt, Co. H, 91st New York Infantry Regt.

William Robert M. Hoysradt married Ella Marshall in 1867 and he enlisted September 15, 1864. His regiment participated in the battles of Boydton Plank Road, March 29, 1864, Gravelly Run Church, April 1, 1864, and this regiment was assigned to stayed and received the arms of the enemy after their surrender at Appomattox Courthouse. He was mustered out of service July 3, 1865 near Washington, D.C. and was granted a pension April 6, 1893.

JOHN R. MANN, PCC - Brother Mann joined the Order in 1990 as a member of Austin Blair Camp No. 7, Jackson, MI. He served as camp commander in 1993.

John had five ancestors that fought in the Civil War. His great-grandfather, Jacob Presler served in the 88th Indiana Infantry, Co. H. Jacob had two brothers, Samuel and Simon, who served in the 21st Ohio, Co. F. Both died in service. Another brother, George, served in the 178th Ohio Infantry, Co. G.

John bases his membership on another great-grandfather, Robert Mann. Robert enlisted as a private in the 111th Ohio Infantry, Co. F, on August 15, 1862. He was 33 years old at the time, was married and had four children. He managed to survive three years of war without any major wounds, mustering out on June 27, 1865. Robert died in Hicksville, OH on August 20, 1893.

KENNETH L. MARLIN, joined the Sons March 29, 1993, General Samuel R. Curtis Camp #82. Held offices as camp junior vice commander, camp commander, secretary/treasurer.

His Civil War ancestor, Pvt. John Dooley was born January 13, 1841 in Morgan County, IN. He went to Iowa with his mother and younger brother in 1858 and settled in Warren County.

He enlisted at Carlisle, IA on August 23, 1861 and served as a private with Co. B of the 10th Regt. of Iowa Volunteers. He reenlisted and was re-mustered on February 1, 1864 at Huntsville, AL. Private Dooley mustered out August 15, 1865 at Little Rock, AR.

Kenneth L. Marlin   *John Dooley*

Some of the involvement of the Iowa 10th included: skirmish near Charleston, MO, campaign of New Madrid, Siege of Corinth, Battle of Iuka, Battle of Corinth, Campaign in Mississippi, Yazoo Pass Expedition, Vicksburg Campaign, Battle of Champion Hills, The Jackson Campaign, March to Tennessee, Battle of Missionary Ridge, March to Savannah, March through the Carolinas and move to Arkansas.

During his furlough he returned to Warren County, IA and married Nancy Ann Wheeldon on July 18, 1864.

His pension records document the harsh conditions that soldiers suffered during the war. He sustained a hearing loss from measles and was hospitalized a number of times.

He died January 19, 1920 in Carlisle, IA.

The chair being held by Ken Marlin was made by John Dooley.

JOSEPH R. MARSDEN SR., joined Gettysburg Camp #112 in 1984.

He bases his right to membership on his great-grandfather Pvt. William L. Marsden of Co. A, 2nd Regiment D.C. Infantry (President's Guard). He enlisted on January 28, 1862 at age 50, though he said he was 40. He was discharged on May 19, 1864 due to disability and overage.

LARRY J. MARSHALL, joined the John T. Crawford Camp #43 on September 9, 1990.

He bases his right to membership on great-great-grandfather Pvt. Aaron Burnhiemer of Co. D 78th Regiment PA Vol. Infantry (October 12, 1861-November 4, 1864). The "Fighting 78th" was attached to McCooks Division, Army of the Cumberland, and saw action at Nashville, Stones River, Tullahoma, Chickamauga, and Lookout Mountain. The regiment was mustered out at Kittanning by Lt. Ward, US Army, on November 4th, 1864 and were paid on the 5th.

Larry J. Marshall   *Aaron Burnhiemer*

He returned to his home in Rayne Township and took up farming, where he married Sarah J. Butterbaugh and raised 10 children. He died of a sudden illness on September 26, 1916 and was buried in the Dunkard Cemetery, now known as Ruffner Cemetery, Tanoma, PA.

DR. DAVID G. MARTIN, born February 8, 1949. Joined SUVCW February 9, 1979. Member of Abraham Lincoln Camp #100, the State Camp of New Jersey; NJ Dept. Commander, 1993-1995; NJ Dept. Sr. Vice Commander, 1991-1993; Commander, Lincoln Camp #100, 1980-1982; Secretary-Treasurer; Lincoln Camp #100, 1982-present; Captain commanding NJ Brigade, S.V.R., 1989-1992; Sergeant, commanding Co. F, 14th NJ Vols., 1988-present; member, company of military historians; instructor in Latin, the Peddie School, Hightstown, NJ; head editor, Longstreet House Publishers; author or editor of over 30 Civil War books including: *Regimental Strengths and Losses at Gettysburg, Confederate Monuments at Gettysburg, Jackson's Valley Campaign* and *Gettysburg July 1*.

Dr. David G. Martin   *George Martin*

Great-grandson of George Martin, born March 14, 1843, Warwick, England emigrated to America in 1851. Enlisted March 2, 1862 in 8th Michigan Btry. (his older brother William enlisted in the same unit on November 12, 1861).

Served at Island No. 10, Fort Pillow, Holly Springs, Port Gibson, Big Black Ferry, Jackson, Champion's Hill, Vicksburg, Clinton, and Meridian.

Reenlisted February 27, 1864, served at Big Shanty, Kennesaw Mountain, Nickajack Creek, Peachtree Creek, siege of Atlanta, Jonesboro, Lovejoy's Station and Nashville.

Mustered out July 22, 1865. Resided near Highland, MI, after the war, then Cass City member of Milo Warner GAR Post (number not known). Died June 27, 1913, buried at Cass City, MI.

RAYMOND D. MARTIN, joined the Sons January 22, 1993, as a member-at-large. He bases his membership on, Cpl. Henry Martin, of Co. F, 116th O.V.I. Cpl. Martin enlisted on August 18, 1862 and was discharged on June 17, 1865. He was a member of GAR Post Moss Run Post #455 Ohio.

Henry was promoted to corporal in 1864. His battle list includes Winchester, Piedmont, Fisher's Hill, Morefield, Halltown, Snicker's Gap, Lexington, Stanton, Lynchburg and Hatcher's Run. In 1863, he was captured at Romney, VA by McNeils men, and held until the next day, when he was paroled and he went home. After being exchanged he rejoined his command at Winchester, VA in 1863. He was honorably discharged at Richmond, VA June 17, 1865.

Raymond D. Martin

Henry also had three brothers, Jacob, Robert and John A., who served in Co. F, 116 OVI. Jacob was present at Lee's surrender. Robert was wounded at Piedmont, taken prisoner at Stanton, VA and died at Florence Stockade, Florence, SC February 1865.

EDWARD G. MAX, Brother Max joined the order in 1993 as a member in General George H. Thomas Camp #19, in Lancaster, PA. Ed resides in Honey Brook, PA. He is captain of the 121st Co. D living history program.

Edward G. Max   *William Ford*

Ed bases his right to membership on his great-great-grandfather William Ford who enlisted as a private in the 121st Pennsylvania Volunteers on August 31, 1862. William Ford was wounded near Shepardstown, VA on October 28, 1862 and was discharged on January 7, 1863. Ed also has seven other ancestors who served during the Civil War in 1861-1865.

DONALD P. MAXWELL, JR., joined as a member-at-large on November 14, 1994. He bases his right to membership on several Civil War ancestors. The Maxwell family were among the first pioneers to settle in Fairfield, Jefferson County, Iowa, in 1849. The patriarch, Benjamin Maxwell served as a private in Co. F, 3rd IA Cav., from September 4, 1861 to September 14, 1862, when he obtained a medical discharge after injuring his wrist falling from his mount "pursuing rebels" in Mexico, MS.

Donald P. Maxwell   *Harvey C. Maxwell*

Abner B. Maxwell   *William W. Maxwell*

Benjamin misstated his age by ten years to qualify for service. Apparently, he was not the only one to do so, as referenced by the famous Iowa regiment nickname of "The Gray Beards".

Benjamin had three sons who also served:
1. William Whistler Maxwell, of Co. F, 3rd IA Cav. who mustered in on August 30, 1861.
2. Pvt. Abner B. Maxwell, of Co. F, 3rd IA Cav., who served from August 30, 1861 to September 19, 1864.
3. 2nd Cpl. Harvey Clayton Maxwell, Donald Maxwell's great-great-grandfather, who served with Co. G, 30th Iowa Infantry, from September 14, 1862 through June 5, 1862. He marched over 3000 miles from Keokuk, Iowa, to Vicksburg on to Atlanta and Savannah, participating in major battles at each. He was wounded by a musket ball in the head at Vicksburg during the same attack in which the Regimental Colonel was killed. He was mustered out of service at Washington, D.C., and thankfully returned to Iowa by rail. Of the 1,132 original members of the 30th Regiment, over half died or were wounded during the War.

During a Maxwell family reunion in 1919, celebrating Harvey Maxwell's 76th birthday, a granddaughter affectionately remembers him telling the story that "the reason he was bald" was because of his war injury. . . a "cannonball" which "just barely grazed" the top of his head on May 22, 1863 in Vicksburg.

RALPH WALTER MCBRIDE, joined the George Armstrong Custer Camp #1 on July 9, 1993.

Ralph W. McBride   *Andrew B. Chew*

He bases his right to membership on Pvt. Andrew Bennett Chew of Co. H 27th IL and Co. G 9th IL. Pvt. Chew was born on April 20, 1830 in Jefferson County Illinois. He married on March 23, 1864 in Carbondale, IL while on leave. He served from August 26, 1861 to July 9, 1865, with a re-enlisted in January of 1864. He was a veteran volunteer and when he re-enlisted with Company G, he served under General Sherman in the Atlanta Campaign, and the Battles of Franklin and Nashville in Tennessee. He participated in the Grand Review in May 1865 in Washington DC. He was a carpenter and farmer by trade. Chew died July 5, 1912 and is buried in Murphysboro, Illinois City Cemetery.

DENNIS C. MCCLOSKEY, joined Anna M. Ross Camp #1, Philadelphia, PA in November 1986.

Dennis C. McCloskey   *Charles M. Wills*

He bases his right to membership on 2nd Lt. Charles M. Wills of Co. H 121st PA Vols. He enlisted on August 28, 1862 and was discharged on June 6, 1865. He was wounded at Spotsylvania Courthouse on May 10, 1864. He was captured and taken prisoner October 1, 1864 at Poplar Grove Church, VA. He spent time at Libby Prison and Salisbury, NC and was paroled February 24, 1865.

CLARK D. MCCULLOUGH, joined Abraham Lincoln Camp #100, Highstown NJ on June 1, 1994. A new member of the Civil War Trust and a member of the Cumberland County Historical Society, and A.P.C.W.S. Friends of the National Parks at Gettysburg. He is a Vietnam Veteran.

He bases his right to membership on three veterans: Capt. Hugh W. McCullough, Co. I, 9th PA Cav. who enlisted on August 24, 1861 and was killed in action; Captain John J. McCullough of 4th PA Co. C who enlisted on September 16, 1861 and died while in the service from typhoid fever on August 27, 1862 at a hospital at Bedlow Island, Ft. Wood, N.Y.; and Corporal Leonidas McCullough of the 4th PA Co. C who enlisted on September 16, 1861 and was discharged on April 9, 1862. Leonidas was discharged for medical reasons when his horse refused to make a jump, which caused him to strike the saddle pommel and thus resulting in a ruptured hernia. Reported on sick call, and found unfit for duty by a surgeon, he was ordered discharged by Capt. John J. McCullough, who was his older brother.

KEITH MCDANIEL, Bro. McDaniel joined the order in 1994 Brooks-Grant Camp Middleport. Keith bases his right to membership on his great-great-grandfather, private John Taylor. Private Taylor enlisted in Lawrence County, OH. August 12, 1864 Co. H, 91st O.V.I., he participated in the Dublin raid with General Crook 1864, including the battle of Clodys Mountain also that year General Hunters attack on Lynchburg, VA. He was wounded at the battle of Steves Depot, VA on July 20, 1864 he died of these wounds August 10, 1864 at Gen. Hospital Cumberland, MD and is buried at Antietam National Cemetery. Bro. McDaniel lives in Jackson, OH with his wife and three children.

JACK R. MCELROY, born June 4, 1950 at Sandpoint, ID. Occupation Hospital Stationary Engineer, at Sacred Heart Medical Center, Spokane, WA. Mr. McElroy joined Col. George L. Willard Camp #154, Albany, NY formerly (Jacob H. TenEyck) on June 18, 1993. Jack was sponsored by Commander William Halpin. Geographic location keeps Mr. McElroy from being an active member of his camp, but he believes our Civil War heritage must be preserved.

Jack R. McElroy   *Charles Horn*

Among his two veteran ancestors. Jack bases his right to membership on his great-great-grandfather Pvt. Charles Horn. Pvt. Horn enlisted in New York, September 9, 1861, in Co. B, 45th New York Vol. Infantry He was wounded July 1, 1863 at the battle of Gettysburg, PA. Pvt. Horn was honorably discharged October 1, 1865. He was a brick mason by trade and a member of the GAR. Born in Germany April 8, 1839, died February 5, 1905. Buried at Seneacquoteen Cemetery, Valley, ID.

Mr. McElroy his wife Gayle and children reside at Sandpoint, ID.

BRADLEY MCGOWAN, joined the Grenville M. Dodge Camp 75, Iowa in April 1991. He has served as Dept. Patriotic Instructor for Iowa.

Bradley McGowan

He bases his right to membership on Pvt. Anderville E. Bolton of Co. I 2nd IA Cav. He enlisted on May 17, 1864 and served through September 19, 1865. He was only 16 years old when he enlisted. He had two brothers and two cousins who all enlisted in Co. H 24th IA Infantry on the same day, August 11, 1862.

RALPH F. MCGREGOR, Bro. McGregor joined the order in 1994 as a member-at-large. He is the son of Arnold Bert McGregor whom is a veteran of World War II.

Among his veteran ancestors, Ralph bases his right to membership on his great-great-grandfather, Daniel C. Reed. Daniel C. Reed enlisted August 30, 1862, as a private in Co. I, 142nd New York, St. Lawrence County Regt. He was taken prisoner on September 29, 1864, at Chaffin's farm, VA. He was taken to Libby Prison at Richmond, VA, and finally to Salisbury Prison at Salisbury, NC. There he died and was buried February 5, 1865, in one of those 18 trenches dug in an abandoned corn field outside the Confederate Prison stockades. Salisbury National Cemetery encompasses this mass grave site, now a grassy expanse marked by a head and foot stone for each trench which reads "unknown U.S. Soldier".

Ralph F. McGregor   *Daniel C. Reed*

In memory of Daniel C. Reed and the approximate 3940 known prisoners of war buried in these trenches, Ralph has requested that a plaque be erected at the Salisbury National Cemetery listing their names, as they are known. U.S. Soldiers whom gave their life for their country.

Daniel C. Reed wife Irena Amanda Majors, a descendent of Revolutionary War soldier George Majors, filed application for pension no. 86-568 and widow pension No. 55-363 was issued commencing February 4, 1865.

Brother McGregor and his wife Pamula reside in Brewerton, NY.

GLENN WAYNE MCKELVEY, Bro. McKelvey joined the Order in 1992. He was initiated into membership in General George H. Thomas Camp No. 19 in Pennsylvania, and presently serves as a member of Council.

Glenn W. McKelvey

Among his two veteran ancestors, Wayne bases his right to membership on his great-great-grandfather, Pvt. Thomas P. McKelvey of Co. E, 11th Regt., Pennsylvania Vol. Infantry Thomas enlisted February 20, 1862. He was wounded at Antietam and spent seven months in a hospital, and was also wounded in the first day of battle in Gettysburg. He was paid a bounty of $100.00 when he reenlisted with the same unit in April of 1864 in Culpepper, VA, being promoted to corporal.

Having been wounded seven times, he was discharged March 27, 1865 near Hatchers Run, VA. He died in September 1914.

Brother McKelvey, his wife Beverly, and two daughters live in Holtwood, PA.

PAUL WILLIAM MCKIBBEN, joined the Orlando A. Somers Camp No. 1 at Kokomo, IN, in 1993. He is a great-great-grandson of Pvt. James A. McKibben. Bro. McKibben was born January 26, 1947 in Kokomo, IN, to Lowell and Delvigne (Geinemann) McKibben. Educated in the Kokomo Public Schools, he attended Indiana University-Kokomo. He served two years in the U.S. Army in Southeast Asia. He served 13 years with the Kokomo Fire Department and presently is a volunteer at the Kokomo Library in the Genealogy Department.

James A. McKibben, along with his brothers-in-law, Jerome Armacost and David W. Fee, enlisted in the 52nd Indiana Volunteer Infantry on December 23, 1863 at Castleton, Marion County, IN. While at camp in Indianapolis, he contacted typhoid fever and died on February 18, 1864. He is buried in the Soldier's Section of Crown Hill Cemetery in Indianapolis. On February 27, 1864, Pvt. Armacost and Fee were transferred to the 52nd Indiana Volunteer Infantry reorganized. They were mustered out at Montgomery, AL, September 10, 1865.

ROBERT V. MCKNIGHT, was initiated on October 14, 1969 and is a past (and last) commander of Dayton Camp No. 5 past commander of Lincoln Camp No. 100 and past commander of the New Jersey Department (1988-1990). He is also a veteran of the Korean War with one Battle Star.

Private Egbert V. VanZandt, a great-grandfather of Robert V. McKnight, served from May 11, 1861 to June 22, 1863 in Co. F of the 38th Regt. of New York Infantry His G.A.R. Post is unknown, but it would have been somewhere around Pearl River, NY where he died on June 15, 1890 at the age of 50.

Robert V. McKnight   *Egbert V. VanZandt*

Egbert mustered in (and out) at East New York then took part in the defense of Washington. He saw action with the 38th at Fairfax Courthouse, 1st Bull Run, Munson's Hill, Yorktown, Williamsburg, Fair Oaks, Jourdan's Ford, Glendale, Malvern Hill, Centreville, Groveton, 2nd Bull Run, Chantilly, Fredericksburg, and Chancellorsville. Their total loss was 482.

In the Williamsburg Campaign[1], "... the 38th made a brilliant dash down the road, taking rifle pits by the flank. The charge was a complete success and the Confederates were driven from their position." At Chantilly [2] "... and by means of a bayonet charge ... the 38th ... drove the Confederates back for a considerable distance, and held the field for the night.

The location of Egbert's grave remains unknown.

Sources: [1]*Pictorial History of the Great Civil War* by John Laird Wilson 1878, pg. 218, [2]*Pictorial History of the Great Civil War* by John Laird Wilson 1878, pg. 303.

MICHAEL W. MCMILLAN, joined Governor Crapo #145 in July 1994. He has been the camp color bearer.

He bases his right to membership on Corporal David Loomis of 14th MI Infantry Co. K. He was enlisted on January 7, 1862 and was discharged on April 24, 1863. Corporal Loomis was a member of WA-BU-NO GAR Post #150 and fought at Stones River on January 3, 1863 under Brig. General James G. Spears, where two men were killed and five wounded.

ALBERT L. MCMULLIN, born December 4, 1919 in East Petersburg, PA. Remembers Adam Long, Civil War veteran (one of three in town of less than 1,000 residents) visiting their school on occasion. In 1937 his father took him to visit Fort Delaware to see where his grandfather served in Civil War. In 1938 Memorial Day parade he marched as a member of Pennsylvania National Guard as several Civil War veterans rode in 'top-down' touring cars.

On July 3, 1938, he attended final reunion of "Blue & Gray" at Gettysburg, PA. His National Guard unit was federalized September 16, 1940. Served in Africa and Italy during WWII. Remained in service, retiring as first sergeant in 1966 after 26 years. Then 19 years with E.I. DuPont & Company. Married Corinne Guy in December 1944. They have three children, three grandchildren and a great-granddaughter, born on Memorial Day May 30, 1984.

Albert L. McMullin   *James McMullin*

Also a member of Sons of the American Revolution. He joined the Sons April 16, 1992, Appomattox #2, Department of Maryland and served as camp commander in 1993.

His Civil War ancestor, James McMullin, private, was born March 26, 1835 in Port Penn, DE. Served in Co. H, 5th Delaware Regt. at Fort Delaware on Pea Patch Island, DE. An old family story tells us that he was recruited while coming out of church with his pregnant wife. Upon returning home in August

1863, he met his son for the first time who was walking and talking. Fort Delaware is less than 10 miles from Port Penn. James McMullin was elected to the Delaware State Senate in 1890 and died in office on January 23, 1893. Discharged August 6, 1863.

THEODORE C. MCQUADE, joined the Sons January 4, 1991, member-at-large, New York Department. His Civil War ancestor was Col. James McQuade, who served with 14th NYSV. He became Major General of U.S. Volunteers on March 13, 1865. He enlisted on April 13, 1861 as captain of Co. A, 14th NYSV.

Another ancestor John F. McQuade of the 14th NYSV has GAR Post #14, of Utica, NY named after him. It was chartered on April 5, 1879. Theodore McQuade lives in Utica, NY.

DAVID R. MEDERT, joined Governor William Dennison #125 on July 17, 1988. He organized and recruited the Camp which now has 89 members. He has served as Camp Commander, Camp Treasurer, Dept. Jr. Vice-Commander, Dept. Jr. Commander and National Jr. & Sr. Vice Commander-in-Chief. He was born on February 29, 1928. He served in the 82nd Airborne Division and retired from the Ohio Highway Patrol as a 1st Lieutenant with 28 years service. He was a 32nd degree Mason and past President of the Arthur St. Clair Chapter of the Sons of the American Revolution.

David R. Medert

He bases his right to membership on Corporal Jacob Medert of Co. D, 106th Ohio Volunteer Infantry. He enlisted on August 15, 1862 and served through to his discharge on June 29, 1865. Cpl. Medert served in the Western Theater of Operations and was involved in the battle of Hartsville, TN on December 7, 1862 where he and his brother, Louis Medert, were captured by Confederate forces. They were paroled and exchanged and served with the 106th for the remainder of the war.

STEPHEN A. MICHAELS, Camp Commander - Bro. Michaels joined the Order in 1993 as a member-at-large in the Ohio Department. In 1994, he transferred to the Wisconsin Department and helped reorganize the C.K. Pier Badger Camp #1, in Milwaukee. In 1995, he was elected camp commander.

Steve bases his right to membership on his great-great-great-grandfather, Pvt. William Howard Wilson. Pvt. Wilson, a Mexican-American War veteran, enlisted at Camp Dennison, OH, on December 19, 1861, in Co. G, 48th Ohio Volunteer Infantry He was wounded at Shiloh and later received a dis-

Stephen A. Michaels

ability discharge on January 26, 1863. He was a member of the GAR in Ohio. Wilson died from complications from his war service on June 13, 1886.

Bro. Michaels, his wife Danielle, and four children reside in Franklin, a Milwaukee suburb.

WAYNE G. MIESEN, JR., joined the Joshua Lawrence Chamberlain Camp 20, Dept. of Maryland on November 11, 1993, and has served as patriotic instructor.

He bases his right to membership on Pvt. Joseph H Dennis of the 29th NJ Infantry Volunteers. He enlisted on September 20, 1862 and was discharged on June 30, 1863. Pvt. Dennis, while working on the forts surrounding Washington D.C., contracted typhoid fever and was hospitalized in Washington, D.C. and Philadelphia. This resulted in his losing his hearing. He obtained a partial disability pension from the government after his discharge. He continued his occupation of house painter while living in Red Bank N.J.

DANIEL HARLAN MILLER, joined the Fort Duffield Camp #1 (former Member-at-Large) on March 11, 1994.

Daniel H. Miller

He bases his right to membership on his great-great-grandfather, Corporal Hiram K. Chapman of Co. K, 5th Ky Volunteer Cavalry. He enrolled on October 3, 1861 and was mustered in on June 17, 1862 at Shelbyville, TN. He was a resident of Rock Bridge, Monroe County, KY. Many relatives and farming neighbors served in this cavalry company, which was made up of Southern Kentuckians. This cavalry unit served under General Buell in KY, TN, NC, and GA. Corporal Chapman transferred to Co. L, 3d KY Cavalry on April 9, 1865. He is buried at the Skaggs Creek Cemetery, Near Tompkinsville, Monroe County, Kentucky, along with James M. Chapman, his first cousin, and Henry R. Strode, both of whom were in his company.

GEORGE H. MILLER, JR., joined the Lincoln-Cushing Camp No. 2 on December 8, 1966 and has served as Lincoln-Cushing Camp Commander (1970-1971) and Maryland Department Commander (1970-1971).

George H. Miller, Jr.,

He bases his right to membership on Pvt. Andreas Gieselmann of Co. D Battalion 48, IA Infantry. He enlisted on May 5, 1864, served for a hundred days and then was discharged on October 20, 1864. Pvt. Gieselmann started receiving a Civil War pension in 1907 and died in 1928.

GEORGE SCOTT MILLER, JR., life member Oliver Tilden Camp #26, New York. Brother Miller has two great-grandfathers who served. Corporal John H. Miller, Co. B, 80th New York Infantry He enlisted August 20, 1861. Wounded at Gettysburg, PA July 1863. Discharged September 5, 1864. Born March 26, 1844, died June 17, 1909. Buried Croton on Hudson, NY. Private Isaac Kanoff, Co. K, 124th New York Infantry Enlisted August 9, 1862. Wounded and taken prisoner at Chancellorsville, VA May 3, 1963. Paroled May 13, 1863, and wounded at Spotsylvania, VA, May 14, 1864. Discharged May 29, 1865. Born July 1834-died June 20, 1897. Buried Wallkill Cemetery, Middletown, NY. Brother Miller and his wife the former Nancy E. Messenger, and their two children Laura E. Miller and Scott Burton Miller reside in Goshen, Orange County, NY.

Both veterans were discharged for disabilities and received pensions for life.

JOSHUA A. MILLER, was born in Jackson, MI, August 9, 1985, son of Kristi and Gary Miller. His mother, Kristi, is the daughter of Brother Max D. Miller and his wife, Darlene. Joshua is a student in Western School District, Jackson County, MI.

At the 1994 National Encampment, a recommendation was made and passed to allow Juniors, ages 8-14, to join the S.U.V.C.W. His grandfather, Bro. Max D. Miller, sponsored him for membership. On August 27, 1994, during

Joshua A. Miller   *Peter Campbell*

the Civil War Muster in Jackson, MI, he was initiated as the first junior in the Austin Blair Camp #7. He was initiated by Commander-in-Chief, Keith Harrison.

Brother Miller has attended several meetings and looks forward to participating on work projects involving registration and restoration of Civil War veteran's graves.

He bases his right to membership on his great-great-great-grandfather, Elias F. Pierce (refer to Brother Max D. Miller's lineage). Also, great-great-great-grandfather, Pvt. Peter Campbell is claimed through his grandmother, Darlene Miller. Pvt. Campbell enrolled in Co. D, 10th Michigan Vol. Infantry September 29, 1864 in Midland, MI. He was mustered out at Washington, DC on July 11, 1865. He died February 28, 1910 at the age of 88.

Joshua resides with his mother at 170 S. Sandstone Rd., Jackson, MI.

MAX D. MILLER, was born February 11, 1935 in Jackson, MI to Allen and Edna Miller. February 11 was also the birthday of the ancestor under whom he joined the S.U.V.C.W. He attended a one-room school through grade eight and graduated from Jackson High School in 1952. He always had an interest in the Civil War due to stories and artifacts that were handed down through the family.

Brother Miller joined the S.U.V.C.W. in November, 1993 in Jackson, MI at the Austin Blair Camp #7. He was elected to the Austin Blair Camp Council in 1995; was a delegate to the 105th Michigan Department Encampment at Lansing, MI, on June 11, 1994 and to the 113th National Encampment in Lansing on August 12-14, 1994.

Miller bases his right to membership on his great-grandfather Elias F. Pierce. Pierce mustered into service at Detroit, MI on August 20, 1862 as a private in Co. I, 4th Michigan Vol. Cav. The regiment was assigned to the Cav. Div., Army of the Cumberland until November 1864, then to the Cavalry Corps, Military Div. of Mississippi.

Max D. Miller *Elias F. Pierce*

Pvt. Pierce was involved in many actions with the 4th Michigan. During the Battle of Stones River he had his horse shot from under him. During December, 1863 he was on courier duty between General Grant's and General Burnside's headquarters. On May 10, 1865, Pierce participated in the capture of Jefferson Davis at Irwinsville, GA; he received $500 as his share of the reward in the capture of Davis. He ended his service as orderly at General Grant's Headquarters in Nashville. Pierce was honorably discharged July 1, 1865. The family story goes that he returned home and spent a month sleeping in a tent in the family yard until he could get used to a bed. Pierce was a member of the Edward Pomeroy GAR Post #48 at Jackson, MI. He died in 1925 at the age of 82.

Other Civil War ancestors are:

1. Great-grandfather, Pvt. Ansel Reardon, who mustered in Co. G, 6th Regt. Michigan Heavy Arty. Vol. on February 9, 1864. He died of typhoid fever at the age of 39 on October 10, 1864 at Barrack's General Hospital, New Orleans, LA. He is buried in the National Cemetery at Chalmette, LA.

2. Great-grandfather, Pvt. German Miller, enlisted in Co. K, 180th Ohio Vol. Infantry on October 1, 1864. He was honorably discharged in Charlotte, NC on July 12, 1865. He died in 1920 at the age of 86.

3. Great-Grand Uncle Cpl. Cyrus Pierce, enlisted in Co. K, 26th Michigan Infantry, October 23, 1862. Mustered out June 4, 1865.

4. Great-Grand Uncle Darius Pierce, mustered March 14, 1865, in Co. E, 20th Infantry Transferred to Co. K, 2nd Infantry Mustered out July 28, 1865.

Brother Miller and his wife, Darlene, reside at 180 S. Sandstone Rd. in Jackson, MI.

SCOTT BURTON MILLER, joined Oliver Tilden Camp #26, Dept. of NY on July 10, 1995. His father George S. Miller, Jr. is also a member of Camp #26.

He bases his right to membership on Pvt. Isaac Kanoff of Co. K 124th NYVI. He enlisted on August 9, 1862 and served through May 29, 1865. He belonged to the Gen. Lyon GAR Post #266 at Middletown, NY. He was wounded May 3, 1863 at Chancellorsville, VA and was captured in action. He was paroled May 13, 1863 and was again wounded in action at Spotsylvania, VA on May 14, 1864. At Columbian Hospital, Washington, D.C. he was discharged for wounds and received a pension of $17 per month.

JOSEPH WILLIAM MILLS, joined the Orlando A. Somers Camp #1 on August 5, 1982 and has served as Senior Vice Commander, Junior Vice Commander, Chaplain, Department Chaplain, and Patriotic Instructor.

He bases his right to membership on Pvt. William Mills of Co. B 156th Ohio Vol. He enlisted in May of 1864 and was discharged in September of the same year. Two of Joseph Mills' great-grandfathers also served: Joseph Shewmon Co. H, 93rd Regiment Ohio Infantry and Peter Swoveland, Co. H, 4th Regiment, OVC.

GUY DARYL MINOR, joined the Alden Skinner Camp No. 45 on June 18, 1992. He has served as Junior Vice Commander, Senior Vice Commander, Department of CT Historian, and National Aide.

He bases his right to membership on Pvt. Samuel Kimball Ellis of the 25th Regiment CVI. He enlisted on September 2, 1862 and was discharged on August 21, 1863. He was a member of Burpee GAR Post No. 71, Chaplain, Commander 1898. From a document dated July 3, 1863, Pvt. Ellis writes, "We attacked Port Hudson at two points, but were beaten back with great loss. The battle still rages and omnipotence

Guy D. Minor *Samuel K. Ellis*

still holds the stakes in equal balance. This is the 25th day of the siege and we are still stuck outside the fortification. Last Sunday we made a general assault we got inside three times but for want of support were driven back. Men were mowed down on our right and left. It was a wonder how I was preserved. I have been in four direct assaults on the breastworks, several skirmishes and yet not a scratch have I received!"

RICHARD L. MIX, joined the SUVCW, Anna M. Ross Camp No. 1, Philadelphia, PA on January 1, 1988.

He has several ancestors who fought in the Civil War. His great-great-grandfather on his father's side, Cpl. Amasa H. Mix, served with Co. G, 13th Regt., PA Militia and Co. K, 15th Regt., NY Engineers, between June 16, 1863 and June 13, 1865. Amasa was a member of Ingham Post No. 92-GAR Canton, PA.

Richard L. Mix

His great-great-grandfather on his grandmother's side, Pvt. Samuel J. Randall served with Co. I, 203rd Regt. Infantry and Co. G, 76th Regt. Infantry from March 4, 1865 to July 18, 1865.

Luther W. Randall, Samuel's brother, with Co. G, 8th PA Cavalry, enlisted in 1861 and served for three years. He re-enlisted in 1864 and was wounded in the Battle of Wilderness and taken prisoner on September 16, 1864. He was transferred from Libby Prison to Salisbury, NC where he died on January 18, 1865 from pneumonia.

Capt. Howard S. Randall, Samuel's brother, served with Co. G, 4th Regt., MO Vol. Infantry of the Confederate from January 1, 1862 to June 8, 1865.

MARK E. MONROE, joined Phil Sheridan Camp #4 CA and Pacific in November 1991. He was born in Columbus, OH on July 4, 1945 and served his country in the Vietnam Era, from June 1965 until October 17, 1969. He served in the Selected Naval Air Combat Ready Fighter Squadrons as an Aviation Ordnanceman to the rank of Aviation Ordnanceman, 2nd Class.

Mark E. Monroe   *William J. Monroe*

He bases his right to membership on Pvt. William James Monroe of the 4th Oneida Regiment NY Vol. Infantry who enlisted on August 8, 1862. Pvt. Monroe engaged the enemy at such battles as Suffolk, Fort Sumter, City Point, Swift Creek and Arrowhead Church, Drury's Bluff, Bermuda Hundred, Cold Harbor, Petersburg, Fair Oaks, Chafin's Farm, and Fort Fisher. He was mustered out of service on June 8, 1865 at Raleigh, NC.

Mr. Monroe is also related to George Nixon I, who served in the Revolutionary War, George III, who enlisted in the Union Army 73rd Ohio Infantry and was killed in the Battle of Gettysburg and to the former President of the United States, Richard M. Nixon.

ALLEN W. MOORE, PCinC - Brother Moore joined the Order in June 1981 as a member of the Ben Harrison Camp #356 at Indianapolis, IN. He served two years as camp commander and six years as secretary-treasurer. In 1982 he reorganized the Orlando A. Somers Camp #1 at Kokomo, IN, and served as camp commander for five years. From 1983-1985, he served as Indiana department commander. On the national level, he has served as junior vice commander-in-chief, senior vice commander-in-chief, and commander-in-chief 1993-1994. Bro. Moore is a life member.

Allen W. Moore   *Cornelius F. Whitehouse*

His great-great-grandfather Cornelius F. Whitehouse (1831-1913) enlisted at Mt. Eden, KY, on August 16, 1862, in Co. B, 15th Kentucky Volunteer Infantry for three years along with his younger brother Harrison J. Whitehouse. He received a medical discharge on December 14, 1863, after contracting typhoid fever in Tennessee.

HARRISON GERALD MOORE IV, was born on October 23, 1962 in Charleston, WV. He is a professional opera singer, having received his bachelor of music degree from Houston Baptist University in 1987. In 12 years of singing Harrison has performed over 600 performances of opera from Seattle to New York. He is starting graduate school in the fall of 1995 at Rice University.

Harrison joined the Sons of Union Veterans of the Civil War in March 1993 as a member-at-large. In July 1994 he helped establish and became a charter member of Lt. Cmdr. Edward Lea USN Camp No. 2 in Houston, TX, the second camp in the state of Texas. Harrison serves as the camp chaplain, and looks forward to seeing his brother, Frank Sidney Moore (March 26, 1967) join the camp this year.

Harrison G. Moore, IV

The ancestor from whom Harrison derives his right of membership is his great-great-grandfather, William Moore (1829-1894). William served as a private in Co. K, 63rd Ohio Volunteer Infantry, enlisting on December 5, 1861 and being mustered out on January 12, 1865 by reason of expiration of term of service. Serving with William was his brother, Harrison G. Moore (1831-1865) for whom Harrison, his father, grandfather, and great-grandfather were named. William served as company cook, Pioneer Corps, and regimental teamster. He was present with his company at the sieges of New Madrid, Island No. 10, and Corinth; and at the battles of Iuka and Corinth. At the start of Sherman's Campaign he was assigned as divisional teamster for the 16th Army Corps (later amalgamated into the 17th Army Corps, Army of the Tennessee) and saw service at Atlanta and its environs as well as the March To The Sea. William was mustered out at Beaufort, SC on January 12, 1865. He died in 1894 at his farm in Ohio.

Harrison Moore's other ancestors in the war were great-great-grandfather Philip Walter (1836-1911) of Co. H, 32 Ohio Infantry, and great-great-granduncles George Walter, 36th Ohio Infantry; and Henry C. Walter, Co. D, 23rd Ohio Infantry and survivor of Andersonville.

JERRY J. MOORE, joined the Order in 1995 and is a member of the General Philip H. Sheridan Camp No. 2 at Naperville, IL. He holds no office. Brother Moore is an archaeologist, having worked for Illinois State University, University of Illinois and University of South Carolina, at this time he has put his work on hold to attend to family matters. He is co-author and author to many archaeological reports and has been an illustrator to several international journals on archaeology and cultural history.

Among his many veteran ancestors, Jerry Moore bases his right to membership on his great-grandfather, Pvt. George W. Moore. Private George W. Moore was born January 7, 1839 in Iroquois Co. IL. He enlisted on July 24, 1862, at Kankakee, IL, Co. A, Illinois 76th Infantry Regt. Volunteers. He served at the Siege of Vicksburg, MS, from May 21, 1863 to July 4, 1863, he was wounded on April 9, 1865 at the Battle of Blakeley, outside of Mobile, AL, on

Jerry J. Moore   *George W. Moore*

the last day of the war. The 76th was the first to hoist the regiment colors on the Rebel ramparts. He was discharged August 18, 1865. He died November 25, 1905, Iroquois County, IL.

JARED WESLEY MORAVEC, Harvey Tuttle's great-great-great-great-great-grand nephew, joined the Sons of Union Veterans of the Civil War as a member-at-large on August 4, 1994.

Jared W. Moravec

At the young age of 19, Harvey Harrison Tuttle enlisted in the army. He joined the 44th Ohio Volunteer Infantry on September 25, 1861. His term of enlistment was three years during which time he served as a corporal in Co. F. While serving in this regiment, he saw action at Lewisberg on May 23, 1862. In October of the same year, Cpl. Tuttle had three fingers on his left hand blown off as a result of an accidental discharge of a gun while on picket duty. On December 27, 1862, he was discharged due to disability. After attending Wittenburg College for a little over a year, he reenlisted on May 11, 1864 in the 146th Ohio National Guard for a 100 day term. During this period, he served as second lieutenant of Co. D. After the war, he was a member of Mitchell Post, G.A.R. He died in 1913 at the age of 71.

FREDERICK JOHN MORGANTHALER II, born May 5, 1978 in Hammond, IN. Presently resides in Billings, MT. He joined the SUVCW, January 23, 1995. He held position as camp organizer. Presently only member in the state of Montana.

Frederick J. Morganthaler   *Henry Compliment*

His was the great-great-grandson of Pvt. Henry Compliment who was born about 1837, and enlisted on August 3, 1862. He enlisted in Green Township, Scioto County, OH. Served with 91st Ohio Volunteer Infantry, Co. F, 8th Corp. Fought in Lynchburg and Winchester. Stationed in Virginia and West Virginia, mostly in Shenandoah Valley. He fought with cousin (Pvt. Charles Compliment, 91st Ohio Infantry, Co. F) and died on November 29, 1872.

After some very successful encounters, the 91st engaged at Lynchburg on June 17-18, 1864. Heavy reinforcements by the rebels caused the 91st to retreat. During the two week forced march under heavy rains and harassment by the rebel infantry and cavalry, Henry contracted pneumonia and later came down with chronic dysentery. This eventually lead to his death.

The date that the picture of Henry Compliment was taken is unknown. The frame that the picture was in has two American flags on each side and is inscribed "The Union Forever".

ROBERT E. MORRIS, is a charter member of Henry Casey Camp No. 92 which meets in Washington Court House, OH. He works as a computer installer. He is first sergeant of Co. C, 20th Ohio Volunteer Infantry which is the Sons of Veterans Reserve Unit of Henry Casey Camp. He is a U.S. Army veteran.

Robert is married to Barbara A. Scott and they have three children: Rochelle, Tracy and Scott.

Robert E. Morris

He is the great-grandson of Pvt. William Newcomb McFadden who served in Co. B, 187th Ohio Volunteer Infantry He is also the great-grandson of Pvt. George Washington Hanes who served in Co. I, 7th Indiana Infantry and was discharged due to a medical disability. However, he enlisted again in Co. F, 25th Indiana Infantry

George Washington Hanes is buried at Edinburg, IN. William N. McFadden is buried at Lees Creek, Clinton County, OH.

ANDREW MOSIER, joined the Gilluly Kingsley Camp #120 on April 27, 1994. He has served as color bearer, guide, and historian.

He bases his right to membership on Pvt. Tobias Mosier of Co. F, 144th IN Inf. He enlisted on August 12, 1864 and was discharged on January 17, 1865.

JAMES A. MUETING, SR., joined the Sons, Camp General George Armstrong Custer, Camp #1, Department of Illinois on February 9, 1991. He held offices as Camp Patriotic instructor and camp senior vice commander. He is currently camp commander Department of Illinois, and current secretary-treasurer. He is on the National committee for fraternal relations.

Civil War ancestor: Julius John Graves, private. He served with Co. H, 8th Illinois Volunteer Infantry, Co. A, 132nd Illinois Volunteer Infantry

Served 8th Illinois Volunteer Infantry, April 1, 1861 to July 24, 1861, 132nd Illinois Volunteer Infantry, May 14, 1864 to October 17, 1864.

GAR Post: Gratehouse Post No. 181, Humphrey, NE.

Interesting fact: Julius John Graves served in the same regiment in the Civil War that James A. Mueting, Sr., went to WWII with, the 132d Infantry Regt. This was the start of James' military service. James went on to become a lieutenant colonel in the Army of the United States and was retired in the grade of colonel from the Illinois ARNG.

THOMAS ALLEN MYERS, joined the Sons March 8, 1993, national member-at-large. His Civil War ancestor: Albert Young, first sergeant, served with Co. H, Pennsylvania, 200th Volunteers. He enlisted September 12, 1862 and was discharged May 30, 1865. He belonged to unknown GAR post in York, PA.

Albert Young served two relatively brief tours of military duty. In both instances under the same captain Jacob Wiest. In September 1862, when a Confederate invasion of Pennsylvania appeared imminent, he was sworn into service, fully armed and equipped, and drilled from the 12th to the 24th of the month and then disbanded; the danger had been averted by the technical victory of the Union Army at Antietam. For some reason the Home Guards were not re-activated the following summer when an actual invasion took place in York, PA. Then on August 9, 1864 he was enrolled, again as a private, in Co. H, 200th Pennsylvania Volunteers. Only 18 and one of the youngest men in the company, he received a warrant as first sergeant on September 1, 1864, and so served until the war ended. He was honorably discharged at Alexandria, VA on May 30, 1865.

DAVID ALLEN NAVORSKA, joined the Lone Star Camp #1 on April 13, 1995. He was born on August 29, 1944 in Cleveland, OH to Clarence Albert and Lela Rose (Bowles Ebel) Navorska. On June 3, 1967, David married Betty Katherine Meyer, who was born June 16, 1946 in Buffalo Center, IA to Carl and Gertie (Sleper) Meyer. Their daughter, Katherine Denise was born August 4, 1974 in Irving, TX.

David bases his right to membership on Pvt. William Edward Hill, born March 28, 1842, Bushey Heath, Bushey Parish, Hertfordshire to Thomas and Mary Ann (Cullen) Hill. He immigrated to Delta, OH in 1858 with Mary and three sisters. Thomas had died in 1851.

William enlisted at the first call for volunteers as an hundred-day man. He re-enlisted on May 27, 1862 in Co. I, 87th OH Vol. Inf. On June 27, he was transferred to Co. D, 85th OVI. He was captured and "paroled" at Harper's Ferry September 15, 1862. He was sick with typhoid fever at Delaware, Ohio, October 3, 1862. He then proceeded to his home in Delta, OH.

David A. Navorska *William E. Hill*

He re-enlisted in 1983 to Co. F, 86th OVI and then re-enlisted again on February, 13, 1864 into the 6th OH Volunteer Cavalry at Cleveland. His horse was shot from under him June 24, 1864. His service ended June 27, 1865 at Petersburg, VA at war's end.

On July 17, 1865, William married Salmah Alwood, who was born August 17, 1842, in Delta, OH to Ephriam Kelly and Elizabeth (Salsberry) Alwood. The couple moved to Elkland Township, Tuscola County, MI in October 1865.

They produced seven children. Salmah died May 20, 1891 in Cass City, where she is buried. That year, William returned to Delta, to live with his mother and sister, Eliza. William died March 6, 1923 in Toledo, OH and is buried in Greenlawn Cemetery, Delta, near his mother and sisters Mary and Eliza.

In Michigan, Private Hill was with the Milo Warner GAR Post and in Ohio he was with the McQuillin GAR Post.

WILLIAM BENJAMIN NEAL, M.A.T., retired history teacher and life member, was mustered into Appomattox Camp No. 2, Maryland Department on April 16, 1992. He was elected camp senior vice commander in 1993 and has been serving as camp commander since January, 1994. He is presently serving as Commander of the Maryland Department and has helped establish the General Torbert Camp of Milford, Delaware. Bill has recommended 30 Brothers who have joined his camp including his uncle James R. Neal, Sr., who is, also, a life member, his cousin James R. Neal, III and his half-brother James W. Neal. He was co-chairman of the 1995 and 1996 Wilmington Memorial Day Parade Committee.

Bill's great-grandfather Cpl. William Charles Neal enlisted November 11, 1862 in Co. I, 6th Delaware Infantry Regt. and was honorably discharged September 5, 1863. Bill has two additional Delaware ancestors who served in the war his great-great-grandfathers Sgt. William Henry Righter (Wrighter) and William Henry Todd.

William B. Neal *William C. Neal*

The only known Civil War story about William C. Neal occurred immediately after the war. He was hired as a teacher in the state of Virginia, but, when it was discovered that he fought for the Union, he was fired.

William B. Neal has a master's degree from Harvard University and was the first president of both the Delaware Genealogical Society and the Maj. Peter Jaquett Chapter, of the Delaware Society Sons of the American Revolution. He is listed in the Herediary Society Blue Book.

CAPTAIN ROLAND D. NEISS, JR., USAF - Brother Neiss joined the Order in 1991 as a member-at-large, while stationed in Iceland during the Gulf War. Upon reassignment to the Buffalo Military Entrance Processing Station as operations officer in late 1991, he joined Chaplain Philos G. Cook Camp #223, Buffalo, NY. While there, he served as camp chaplain and was appointed National Aide and Delegate to the 1993 Department Convention. In 1994, Brother Neiss was reassigned overseas and transferred to David C. Caywood Camp #146, Ovid, NY, with his relatives. Brother Neiss became a life member of the Order in 1994.

Among his five veteran ancestors, Brother Neiss bases his right to membership on great-great-grandfather, Pvt. Thomas Sarsfield. Pvt. Sarsfield enlisted on August 21, 1861 in Co. A, 89th New York Volunteer Infantry He was discharged on November 10, 1864 due to wounds received in battle. He was a member of Treman Post #572, GAR, Trumansburg, NY. He died September 16, 1905.

Brother Neiss currently resides in Bachelor Officer Quarters, Akinci Airfield, Turkey.

ROLAND D. NEISS, SR., Brother Neiss joined the Order in 1992 and became a life member of David C. Caywood Camp #146, Ovid, NY, in 1994. Among his four veteran ancestors, Brother Neiss bases his right to membership on his great-grandfather, Pvt. Thomas Sarsfield, Co. A, 89th New York Volunteer Infantry In the assault on Petersburg, VA, on June 18, 1864, Pvt. Sarsfield suffered a gunshot wound to the neck and a light flesh wound in his left side. The ball entered "at the neck and passed out between the shoulder blades, somewhat towards the left side of the back". He was transported to Satterlee USA General Hospital, West Philadelphia, PA and discharged a few months later for disability. Pvt. Sarsfield's neck wound left his left arm paralyzed for the remainder of his life.

Brother Neiss resides in Trumansburg, NY and is employed by Cornell University, Ithaca, NY.

SHAWN D. NEISS, joined the Order in 1992 and became a life member of David C. Caywood Camp #146, Ovid, NY, in 1994. Among his five veteran ancestors, Brother Neiss bases his right to membership on his great-great-great-grandfather, Pvt. Delos Taft. Pvt. Taft enlisted on August 7, 1862 in Co. I, 117th New York Volunteer Infantry. He served with the regiment in all engagements and was discharged on June 8, 1865. In spring 1863, Pvt. Taft severed his right thumb from his hand in a woodcutting accident. According to later accounts, he was chopping wood when members of his company, who were wrestling or engaged in a scuffle, bumped his arm. Pvt. Taft was a member of Skillin Post #47, GAR, Rome, New York. Delos Taft died February 6, 1916.

Brother Neiss currently resides in Trumansburg, NY and is employed by Tompkins Community Hospital.

ALLEN M. NELSON, joined the Sons as a member-at-large NY on June 1, 1990. He is a resident of Sanford, FL.

He bases his right to membership on his father, Pvt. George H. Nelson of the 1st VT. Vol. He belonged to Chamberlain GAR Post #1, St. Johnsbury. He joined the 1st Vols. at age 16 and fought in many battles, including Gettysburg. At the 75th Anniversary of the Battle of Gettysburg in 1938, Pvt. Nelson was one of 5 Vermont veterans there. His son, Allen, was his official escort. He died January 2, 1942, at the age of 96.

LTC. HOWARD E. NORRIS, JR., USAF (RET) joined the William Tabor Camp #162 May 28, 1994. He is the Recorder for the Massachusetts Commandery of the Military Order of the Loyal Legion of the United States.

He bases his right to Sons membership on Capt. William T. Wiggins Co. C 49th NY Infantry. He enlisted on August 1, 1861 at NYC. On May 5, 1864, he was shot through the head while leading his men on at the Wilderness. He was buried on the battlefield. Two years later in 1866 those who buried him could not find the grave due to the growth of the underbrush and trees.

ROBERT CHARLES NUTT, who has been a member since September 9, 1994, Lt. Nathaniel Bowditch Camp #30 Massachusetts, is the great-great-grandson of William Nutt who enlisted May 25, 1861, in Co. I, 2nd Regt., Massachusetts. William was made a corporal and then sergeant on August 11, 1861.

Robert C. Nutt   *William Nutt*

William was a very capable drill-master, and was detailed early in the service to instruct officers and men. His regiment lost nearly half its men and more than half its officers in the Battle of Cedar Mountain and from that time until March 1863, he was acting first sergeant. At the Battle of Antietam a third of the regiment was killed or wounded. He was commissioned March 5, 1863, second lieutenant, and in May, first lieutenant, Co. F, 54th Regt., under Col. Robert Gould Shaw.

William was transferred to Co. D, 55th Regt. and commissioned captain, May 31, 1863; major, November 23, 1864; lieutenant colonel, June 25, 1865; and brevet colonel to date March 13, 1865 for gallant and meritorious service. He served with the 55th at the surrender of Fort Wagner, Honey Hill, James Island, and the siege of Charleston. He was mustered out in August 29, 1865. He commanded the survivors of the 54th and 55th Regts. at the dedication of the Shaw Memorial, Boston.

SGT. MAJ. THOMAS E. O'BRIEN, U.S. Army, Ret., joined the SUVCW November 5, 1976, Lincoln-Cushing, Camp No. 2. Civil War ancestor: John Cooney, private. Served with Co. A, 63rd Regt., New York Volunteers, Irish Brigade.

Enlisted August 7, 1861. Killed in action September 17, 1862.

John Cooney was born in 1835. Married Margaret Miller October 28, 1854. They had three children, two boys and one girl. On September 17, 1862, while under the command of Capt. Joseph O'Neill, Co. A, he was killed in action at Bloody Lane at Antietam, MD. His remains were never recovered but it is assumed that he is buried in Antietam National Cemetery along with the 1,836 unknown Union soldiers.

GEORGE WILLIAM O'HALLORAN, born May 13, 1930, descendant of Jacob Herrlinger, brother of John, son of William and Katherine, native of Kings County. Tilden Camp Member (three years) officer in Jacob Herrlinger Memorial Unit (captain) by trade a master craftsman, antique furniture restoration. U.S. Army and reserves (corporal) Korean War. Like Jacob and John he was in field artillery. Attainments include founding member, then supervisor of Community Film Workshop, field director, Apple Shop Crafts Center, Whitesburg, KY, organizer Federal Grant, Indian Workshop (Santa Fe), script writer CBS documentaries, first assistant director to John Cassavetes, mayoral consultant for the arts to Mayor John Lindsay of New York.

George W. O'Halloran

Hobbies include artistic attainments. A cousin, Lois La Marche, Ansonia, CT, a nurse supervisor, a descendant of Jacob, is a medical officer (captain) of the Herrlinger Unit. George was a pioneer worker in Federal Equal Rights programs of various administrational efforts to improve the status of the poor.

JOHN DENNIS O'HALLORAN, O.S.J., REV., FR., was born in Kings County, NY, September 8, 1928 to Katherine Frances (Herrlinger) and William Harold O'Halloran. Descendent of Jacob Herrlinger (b. 1823) Pvt. B Co. 4th Regt. 1st Division, N.G.S. NY Light Artillery who served at Gettysburg, New York City (Draft Riots), and Washington, D.C. Enlisted June 4th 1862 to wars end. Died in New York and was buried in the family plot on April 28, 1871 at Lutheran Cemetery, Middle Village, NY.

Father O'Halloran served in the Field Artillery, also in the B Battery of 816 FA Battalion 190th Group, Sunbury, PA (Bucktails). He was ordained in 1962 and is presently chaplain of many groups including the Oliver Tilden Camp #26, NYC. He is active in Knights Orders in Europe, Australia, and America, as Grand Master (House Orders of the Family, an ancient Irish noble line of which he is presently Prince of Don) St. John of Jerusalem (Malta) St. Gereon and others. He is an Ambassador Plenipotentiary with high military and naval ranks. As a Colonel (presented by the Governor of Louisiana for services rendered organizing parish (county) historians and with the rank of Honorary State Historian) he activated his ancestors old unit as a memorial to him and celebrates mass on the family plot twice a year for all veterans. These masses are attended by SUV and Confederate units as joint ventures. Reconstructed units also join in.

John D. O'Halloran *Jacob Herrlinger*

Jacob Herrlinger is patron of the Jacob Herrlinger Memorial Unit which is supported by, but independent of, the SUV. The unit is available for commemorative services in the New York area. Fr. O'Halloran, due to his service in Louisiana, has numerous ties to Confederate as well as Union units and holds rank in both army and naval groups as well as Marines. He also serves the 69th Regiment, NY as a member and in a clerical role.

DAVID B. ORR, born August 26, 1921 in Pittsburg, PA. Eldest son of John Edward Orr and Dorthy Marie Hilterman Orr. Deceased August 23, 1992. Joined SUVCW April 29, 1981. Member of Davis Camp, Department of Pennsylvania. Member Pennsylvania Commandery, Military Order of the Loyal Legion of the United States.

Camp offices: Historian, graves registration officer, junior vice commander, senior vice commander, camp commander, camp secretary.

Department offices: Chr. Department Encampment Committee (four years), General chairman three Department Encampments Department Historian, chief-of-staff, patriotic instructor, department junior vice commander, department senior vice commander, department commander, department commander at the time of his death.

National Offices: National Historian (seven years).

Civil War ancestors: Peter Paul Gallisath, private Cos. L and F 5th Pennsylvania Cav. Enlisted August 19, 1861. Discharged May 8, 1865 by reason of wounds. Member GAR Post 3, Pittsburgh, PA. Wounded three times, left hip, left lung, right thigh during the Petersburg campaign.

Bardele Gallisath, Capt. Co. F, 5th Pennsylvania Cav. Enlisted August 19, 1861. Discharged December 25, 1865. Wounded in lower right leg during the Petersburg campaign which resulted in amputation of the leg. After a prolonged hospital stay was assigned to the General Court Martial Board in Pittsburgh. Following his discharge he opened a tavern in Pittsburgh. On the anniversary of the amputation of his leg he would hang his artificial leg from the sign outside the tavern and all drinks were free all day. He continued this practice until his death. Member of GAR Post 3 Pittsburgh, PA.

An additional 135 uncles and cousins are known to have served the Union cause.

NATHAN L. ORR, born August 26, 1977 in Pittsburgh, PA. Eldest son of Donald Paul Orr and Joyce Ellen Leslie Orr.

Senior, Seton LaSalle High School, Pittsburgh, PA. Joined SUVCW August 26, 1994. Member of Davis Camp, Department of Pennsylvania. Member of the Pennsylvania Commandery, Military Order of the Loyal Legion of the United States. He held office as junior vice commander.

Civil War ancestors: Peter Paul Gallisath, private Cos. L and F 5th Pennsylvania Cav. Enlisted August 19, 1861. Discharged May 8, 1865 by reason of wounds. Member GAR Post 3, Pittsburgh, PA. Wounded three times, left hip, left lung, right thigh during the Petersburg campaign.

Bardele Gallisath, Capt. Co. F, 5th Pennsylvania Cav. Enlisted August 19, 1861. Discharged December 25, 1865. Wounded in lower right leg during the Petersburg campaign which resulted in amputation of the leg. After a prolonged hospital stay was assigned to the General Court Martial Board in Pittsburgh. Following his discharge he opened a tavern in Pittsburgh. On the anniversary of the amputation of his leg he would hang his artificial leg from the sign outside the tavern and all drinks were free all day. He continued this practice until his death. Member of GAR Post 3 Pittsburgh, PA.

Martin P. Schaeffer, sergeant Pennsylvania Militia of 1863. Unit was federalized during the Gettysburg campaign to protect the federal arsenal in Pittsburgh and to man the fortifications along the Allegheny, Monongahela and Ohio rivers. In later life he held the offices of constable, justice of the peace, and chief of police of Allegheny City, PA all at the same time. He was known to have boasted that he didn't care how anyone voted as long as his boys were counting the votes.

An additional 135 uncles and cousins are known to have served the Union cause.

RICHARD D. ORR, born October 13, 1948 in Pittsburg, PA. Eldest son of David Bernard Orr and Bernadette Elizabeth Wetter Orr.

B.Sc. Pennsylvania State University 1970; M.Sc. Idaho State University 1972. Employed by Allegheny County Health Department as environmental health administrator.

Joined SUVCW April 29, 1981, member of Davis * Camp, Department of Pennsylvania. Member of the Pennsylvania Commandery, Military Order of the Loyal Legion of the United States.

Camp Offices: junior vice commander, senior vice commander, camp commander, camp secretary, camp treasurer.

Department offices: chief-of-staff, patriotic instructor, department junior vice commander, department senior vice commander, department commander, chairman Department Council.

National offices: National Membership-at-Large coordinator (three years), national counselor (eight years), life membership coordinator (six years), chairman committee on the Constitution and Regulations (three years), chairman Special 1999 Blue-Gray Investigatory Committee (three years), General chairman 1992 National Encampment, National Treasurer (six years).

Civil War ancestors: Peter Paul Gallisath, private Cos. L and F 5th Pennsylvania Cav. Enlisted August 19, 1861. Discharged May 8, 1865 by reason of wounds. Member GAR Post 3, Pittsburgh, PA. Wounded three times, left hip, left lung, right thigh during the Petersburg campaign.

Bardele Gallisath, Capt. Co. F, 5th Pennsylvania Cav. Enlisted August 19, 1861. Discharged December 25, 1865. Wounded in lower right leg during the Petersburg campaign which resulted in amputation of the leg. After a prolonged hospital stay was assigned to the General Court Martial Board in Pittsburgh. Following his discharge he opened a tavern in Pittsburgh. On the anniversary of the amputation of his leg he would hang his artificial leg from the sign outside the tavern and all drinks were free all day. He continued this practice until his death. Member of GAR Post 3 Pittsburgh, PA.

Martin P. Schaeffer, sergeant Pennsylvania Militia of 1863. Unit was federalized during the Gettysburg campaign to protect the federal arsenal in Pittsburgh and to man the fortifications along the Allegheny, Monongahela and Ohio rivers. In later life he held the offices of constable, justice of the peace, and chief of police of Allegheny City, PA all at the same time. He was known to have boasted that he didn't care how anyone voted as long as his boys were counting the votes.

An additional 135 uncles and cousins are known to have served the Union cause.

ROBERT J. ORR, born January 12, 1954 in Pittsburg, PA. Youngest son of David Bernard Orr and Bernadette Elizabeth Wetter Orr. Employed by Grinnell Fire Protection Equipment Co. as district manager of the Columbus, OH office.

Joined SUVCW February, 1983. Member of Davis * Camp, Department of Pennsylvania. Camp Offices: guard, guide, color bearer, History Committee, Graves Registration Committee.

Civil War ancestors: Peter Paul Gallisath, private Cos. L and F 5th Pennsylvania Cav. Enlisted August 19, 1861. Discharged May 8, 1865 by reason of wounds. Member GAR Post 3, Pittsburgh, PA. Wounded three times, left hip, left lung, right thigh during the Petersburg campaign.

Bardele Gallisath, Capt. Co. F, 5th Pennsylvania Cav. Enlisted August 19, 1861. Discharged December 25, 1865. Wounded in lower right leg during the Petersburg campaign which resulted in amputation of the leg. After a prolonged hospital stay was assigned to the General Court Martial Board in Pittsburgh. Following his discharge he opened a tavern in Pittsburgh. On the anniversary of the amputation of his leg he would hang his artificial leg from the sign outside the tavern and all drinks were free all day. He continued this practice until his death. Member of GAR Post 3 Pittsburgh, PA.

Martin P. Schaeffer, sergeant Pennsylvania Militia of 1863. Unit was federalized during the Gettysburg campaign to protect the federal arsenal in Pittsburgh and to man the fortifications along the Allegheny, Monongahela and Ohio rivers. In later life he held the offices of constable, justice of the peace, and chief of police of Allegheny City, PA all at the same time. He was known to have boasted that he didn't care how anyone voted as long as his boys were counting the votes.

An additional 135 uncles and cousins are known to have served the Union cause.

JEROME L. ORTON, joined Col. George L. Willard Camp #154 on June 5, 1969. He served as commander for four years. On the department level he has held every office except historian. In 1980 he was elected as New York Department Commander. Nationally he has served as historian on several occasions and is currently chairman of the real sons and daughters committee. He is a private with Co. E, 148th NYSV, the oldest re-enactors unit in New York State. He also belongs to the SR, SAR, S and D of the Pilgrims and Sons of Spanish War Veterans.

His wife, Lorraine, served two years as New York Department president, Woman's Relief Corps and national historian. They currently live in Syracuse, NY.

Among his Civil War ancestors was Benjamin Orton who served in Co. K and B, 77th NYSV. Enlisting at Saratoga, NY on August 14, 1862 and mustered out on June 16, 1865.

RICHARD OTHMER, is a member of Camp #154 NY. Mr. Othmer is from Kent, NY.

He bases his right to membership on his great-great-grandfather, Pvt. Stephen Eismann of the 46th NY Vol. Inf. Reg. Pvt. Eismann joined on February 29, 1864 in NYC and served as 2nd Brigade Bugler until July 28, 1865.

RON OWENS, joined the Sons November 9, 1993, national member-at-large.

Civil War ancestor: Amariah Crosley, was born in Clay County, IN, on April 10, 1842. On August 10, 1864, at the age of 22, he enlisted as a private in the Union Army for one year. He enlisted at Rockport, MO. His enlistment papers describe him as being a farmer, 5'6" or 5'7" tall, with a dark complexion, black hair and black eyes. On September 17, 1864, he was mustered into Co. I of the 43rd Missouri Infantry at St. Joseph, MO.

His unit served in central and northern Missouri during the last eight months of the war, mostly against guerilla actions by Confederate General Sterling Price's raiders. During this period they were involved in half a dozen combat actions at Booneville, Brunswick, Glasgow, Little Blue River and the Star House near Lexington, MO. The unit was mustered out of service at Benton Barracks, MO on June 30, 1865. They had 11 men killed in action and 53 died from disease during their service.

Bennett Crossley, was born January 6, 1840, in Clay County, IN. Enlisted on August 13, 1862, he was assigned to Co. E, 93rd Illinois Infantry His brothers John, Nathan, David and Amariah would also serve. Under General Grant, they moved to Mississippi and in May, were in the battles of Port Gibson, Champion Hill, Big Black River and Vicksburg.

Transferred under Sherman, they fought at Chattanooga and Missionary Ridge, then Allatoona and Atlanta, GA. On October 7, 1864, Crossley went on sick call, suffering "enteric fever, lung disease and chronic diarrhea". Sent home, he was discharged on June 23, 1865. His health permanently broken, he only succeeded in getting a pension in February of 1897, nine months before his death. This was how the spelling of his surname changed. Originally spelled "Crosley", his military records spelled it "Crossley". He had to spell it that way to receive his pension. He died on November 25, 1897, in Seward, OK.

David Cushman Crosley was born November 7, 1845, in Clay County, IN. He enlisted in Co. D, 12th Missouri Cav. on October 5, 1863, three weeks after his older brother Nathan. Moving to Tennessee in August 1864, they marched to Oxford, MS, fighting skirmishes at the Tallahatchie River, Hurricane Creek, Abbeville and Oxford. In November they pursued Nathan Bedford Forrest's cavalry, fighting at Shoal Creek, Lawrenceburg, Campbellville, Lynnville and Duck River. In December, they fought at Nashville and pursued the retreating Army of Tennessee.

After five months scouting in Mississippi and Alabama, they returned to Missouri in May of 1865. Like many others with three year enlistments, Crosley considered his enlistment up when the Confederacy surrendered and went home. He was listed as a deserter on June 15, 1865. The company mustered out on April 9, 1866. On March 16, 1885, he was honorably discharged after Congress passed an act of amnesty for these men. He died December 24, 1932, in Lawrie, OK.

Nathan Crosley was born on April 10, 1837 in Clay County, IN. On September 15, 1863, at the age of 26, he enlisted as a private in the Union Army at Rockport, MO, for three years. On October 23, he was mustered in under Lt. J.H. Rickard's company, Co. D of the 12th Missouri Cav. at St. Joseph, MO. His enlistment papers state he is a farmer, 5'6" or 5'7" tall, with a fair complexion, blue eyes and sandy hair.

His unit remained on duty near St. Louis until June 1, 1864, when they moved to Memphis, TN. There they were transferred to be a part of the 1st Cav. Div., 1st Brigade, District of West Tennessee. Nathan Crosley was discharged at La Grange, TN, on July 31, 1864, on a surgeon's certificate of disability. He saw no further service and was mustered out at Fort Leavenworth, KS, on April 7, 1866. He died on June 28, 1899, in Seward, OK.

BERNARD T. PARK, joined Given Camp 51 in July of 1994. He has served as Junior Vice Commander Given Camp 51, Ohio Dept. GAR Highway Officer, Patriotic Instructor, and Graves Registration officer.

Bernard T. Park

He bases his right to membership on William Anderson who was a Sergeant with the 84th OVI Co. H and a Corporal with 163rd Regiment OH National Guards, Co. I. He served in the Valley of the Shenandoah, on the Peninsula, in the operations on the James River, Petersburg and Richmond, in the Battle of Moncaray, and in the trenches of Washington. He fought in the Battle of Look Out Mountain with the 84th O.V.I

LOUIS PARKER, bases his right to membership on Pvt. Tilly G. Sanford of Co. D, 2nd IA Cavalry. He enlisted on August 2, 1864 and served through to his discharge on October 3, 1864. He belonged to the Custer Nole Post in Tacoma, WA. Tilly's daughter, Alma Parker, is alive at age 98 in Tacoma. Louis lives in Steilacoom, WA.

BRIAN L. PARTRIDGE, joined the Sons on August 1, 1993, as a member-at-large.

He bases his membership on Pvt. Jacob Niebels, of Co. E, 4th MN Infantry/4th MN Regt. Band, who enlisted at Fairabult, MN on October 1, 1861 and was mustered in at Fort Snelling November 27, 1861. With the cold setting in, he spent the winter months at the fort. On April 20, 1862 the steamboat *Sucker State* docked at the fort and took six companies, including the regimental band, south. The men had to disembark at Dubuque and perform a dress parade through town. They embarked again (same boat) on their journey south, stopping again at Davenport, IA and marched through town to a park with temporary housing for Iowa troops. It was here they did battalion drills while their boat crossed the rapids. They embarked the same boat stopping again at Keokuk, IA for supplies before arriving in St. Louis on April 23. They stayed here until May 2 before a new boat took them onto Tennessee.

He was later discharged and was re-enlisted on January 1, 1864, with his final discharge on August 5, 1865. He was a member of the Stanton GAR Post.

ROGER A. PATZ, Brother Patz joined the SUVCW in 1995 as a member of the David D. Porter Camp #116, Department of Indiana. He resides in Cedar Lake, IN and is employed as the deputy chief of police for the Cedar Lake Police Department. He served as Indiana State president of the American Federation of Police

Roger A. Patz

1989-present. He is also serving a second four year term as a member of the Board of Education, having served as president for three years.

Bro. Patz bases his right to membership on his great-great grandfather, Pvt. Peter Mager. Pvt. Mager enlisted in Co. D of the 83rd Indiana Infantry on October 15, 1862 at Indianapolis, IN, and was discharged August 8, 1863 at Camp Sherman, MS. He was injured at the Siege of Vicksburg. He died February 10, 1902 in St. John, IN where he is buried.

MICHAEL ANDREW PEARSON, became a member of the Ben Harrison Camp No. 356 of Indianapolis, IN, on September 27, 1992, and is a life member. He is the son of Harry L. Pearson and Betty Jo Dollar Pearson. A graduate of Northwestern Technical College, he owns Pearson Auto/Diesel. He is the son-in-law of Past Commander-in-Chief Allen W. Moore and Barbara Tiley Moore. Brother Pearson is a great-great-grandson of Pvt. James M. Boles.

James Marten Boles enlisted as a private in the 25th Light Arty., Indiana, on September 9, 1864 and was discharged on July 20, 1865. He was born April 8, 1846, in Brown County, OH, and died September 26, 1917. He was a member of the Jacob Stahl GAR Post #227 at Hartford City, IN, where he is buried.

DONALD R. PERRY, joined the Order in 1991 as a member of Ben Harrison Camp No. 356 in Indianapolis. His right to membership is based on his great-great-grandfather Pvt. Alexander C. Gilliland who enlisted at Hartsville, IN June 12, 1862 in the 15th Indiana Light Arty. and was discharged June 30, 1865 at Indianapolis. He died April 7, 1904 and is buried in the Hartsville Baptist Cemetery. Bro. Perry and his wife Jill reside in North Vernon, IN.

DANA PETERSON, joined the W.T. Camp 162 in 1993 and has served as chaplain. Mr. Peterson served in WWII.

He bases his right to membership on his great-grandfather, Pvt. Thomas Musson of the 14th Mass. Inf. He was born in Belfast, Ireland and resided in Taunton, Massachusetts before his service and in Fall River after his service. He enlisted in 1860 and was discharged on June 28, 1863. His daughter stated that Musson performed some brave act in conflict, but there was not a written record of said act.

CAPT. P. MICHAEL PHILLIPS, USA, joined Sons, Joshua Lawrence Chamberlain, Camp 20 in January 1994.

Civil War ancestors: Pvt. William Norton, Co. L, 3d PA Cav., enlisted August 19, 1961, discharged May 29, 1962; Cpl. John Reiley, Co. L, 3d PA Cav., enlisted August 22, 1961, discharged August 24, 1964; Pvt. James Reiley, Co. L, 3d PA Cav., enlisted August 22, 1961, died April 1, 1963; and Pvt. Thomas Reiley, USMC, USS *Keystone State,* enlisted August 23, 1961, KIA January 31, 1963.

GAR Posts: (Norton) Unknown, Sebastian County, AR.

P. Michael Phillips

Interesting Stories: The Nortons and Reileys lived together in the small Irish mining community of Mt. Laffee, overlooking Pottsville, PA, and the four of them went to Pottsville with the intention of enlisting in the Union Army. Thomas backed out, deciding to travel to Philadelphia to enlist in the Marines; he was killed in action at Charleston, SC, during a battle with the CSS *Palmetto State* and CSS *Chicorra.* Norton had the misfortune of having his horse fall on him at Port Tobacco, MD, and was discharged as a result of his injuries; he returned to Mt. Laffee to marry the Reileys' sister, Mary , and it is from this union that Michael Phillips is descended. John and James served at the battle of Kelly's Ford, the first major cavalry engagement of the war, and were present near the site of the death of Maj. John Pelham. James died of disease a few weeks later in their camp at Potomac Creek, VA. John was promoted to corporal, and was mustered out upon the inactivation of his regiment, in August, 1864.

DONALD E. PICKRELL, joined the Sons March 26, 1991, General Benjamin Pritchard Camp #20, Kalamazoo, MI. He held offices as camp treasurer, and camp secretary.

His great-grandfather was William J. Flowers and he enlisted in the 62nd Ohio, Co. K, on October 19, 1861 as a private. He was honorably discharged on September 1, 1865. He received a pension up until his death in December 1909.

In his military papers it stated that he had a severe sunstroke while at Folly Island, and his friends carried him over to the only tree on the island and placed him under the tree. He also got typhoid fever, and after the war was never in good health.

In 1994 he was able to locate his grave in New Lexington, OH and has a veterans headstone placed on his grave.

JOHN C. POLLARD, joined the Phil Sheridan Camp #4 on November 17, 1994.

He bases his right to membership on Pvt. Michael Pollard of A Co. 9th IL Cavalry. He enlisted on September 1, 1861 and was discharged on December 5, 1862. He was disabled during 1862 March to Helena, Arkan-

John C. Pollard

sas, which was called by Brigadier General J.N. Reece to be "one of the most famous marches of the Civil War."

JOHN R. POOLE, joined the order in 1983 as a member-at-large. In 1994 he joined the Ben Harrison Camp #356 in Indianapolis, IN. John bases his right to membership on his great-grandfather Pvt. Alfred H. Price. Pvt. Price enlisted September 20, 1861 in Co. C, 31st Indiana Volunteers.

John R. Poole

He was honorably discharged December 8, 1865 in Texas. Pvt. Price was discharged with the rank of sergeant. He served as a courier on the staff of General Sheridan. Among other battles, Pvt. Price fought at the Battle of Shiloh. Bro. Poole is single and resides in Terre Haute, IN.

GEORGE CARVILLE PORTER, joined the Lincoln-Cushing #2 on March 2, 1990. He has held office at the Department level in Maryland and at the national level in Washington DC.

George C. Porter

George A. Porter *Asbury J. C. Hughes*

He bases his right to membership on two Civil War ancestors. First his grandfather George A. Porter (alias Seeger) of Co. B, 1st Regiment Maryland Vol. Cavalry, who enlisted on March 11, 1864 and was discharged on August 8, 1865.

His second Civil War ancestor was his great-grandfather Asbury John C. Hughes who was a staff sergeant with the Artillery. He was born on July 1,1827 and died December 8, 1891. George's grandfather Hughes was 7 years old when he carried his lunch to his father, Asbury John C. Hughes, at Stemmers Run, where he was guarding the railroad bridge (B.W.P Railroad at that time). It was about five miles going and coming from the log cabin.

HARRY L. PORTER, joined Memorial Camp #300, York, PA on March 12, 1995. Harry enlisted in the USNR on March 22, 1943 and served as an electrician's mate. He served on several vessels, including a two year stint on the USS *Yo* 115 in Eniwetok, the Marshall Islands and the South Pacific. He was honorably discharged on April 26, 1946 at the USN Personal Separation Center in Bainbridge, Maryland.

Harry L. Porter   *William H. Porter*

He bases his right to membership on his grandfather Pvt. William H. Porter of the 142nd PA Vol. Co. H. He enlisted on August 13, 1862 and served through to his discharge on May 29, 1865. He belonged to the William F. Kurtz GAR Post #104, Connellsville, PA. Pvt. William H. Porter was called Billie "The Spy Catcher" by the Captain of the 142nd, Capt. Dushane.

DAVID LEE PRESHUR, joined S.F. Smith #193 Halsey Valley on September 9, 1992. David lives in St. Petersburg, FL.

He bases his right to membership on Pvt. Elisha Blanchard of Co. D of the 85th NYSU who enlisted on October 1, 1861.

BOBBY W. PRIEST, joined and was a charter member for Fort Duffield Camp No. 1 on July 26, 1994.

Charles Sipes

He bases his right to membership on Pvt. Charles Sipes of Co. I, 13th KY Vol. Infantry. He enlisted on October 16, 1861 and was mustered out on January 12, 1865. Charles served his term in the Union Army and returned home shortly after his discharge, but due to continued hostilities, he enlisted in the Kentucky State Militia for one year or the duration of the war. He served in Co. A, Green River Battalion.

JOSEPH J. PUCCIARELLI, presently commander of Oliver Tilden Camp No. 26, in New York, Bro. Pucciarelli joined the Sons of Union Veterans in 1988 and served as its treasurer and senior vice-commander. In 1994, he was in charge of the annual General Grant ceremony. He is a member of the New York State Department Council, a department aide and a noncommissioned officer in the Sons of Union Veterans Reserve.

Joseph J. Pucciarelli   *John J. Curtin*

Brother Pucciarelli's ancestors include his grandfather, John J. Curtin and granduncle, Daniel Curtin. John enlisted in the Union Navy as a cabin boy in July 1863. He served on the USS *Emma* during the war. He was a member of a New York GAR Camp until his death in 1904. Daniel, John's brother, served with the 9th New York Militia (83rd New York Volunteers). He was killed in September 1862 at Antietam, MD. Joe and Catherine Pucciarelli live in Rockville Center, NY.

WILLIAM E. RADABAUGH, JR., joined Henry Casey Camp No. 92 in October of 1992. He has served as Junior Vice Commander, Parliamentarian, and Camp Councilman.

William E. Radabaugh   *Rudolph LeBeau*

He bases his right to membership on Pvt. Rudolph LeBeau of Co. B 26th Regiment OH Vol. Inf. He enlisted on June 14, 1861 and was discharged on April 27, 1864.

JONATHAN W. RADABAUGH, joined Henry Casey Camp No. 92 in October of 1992. He has served as Camp Councilman.

He bases his right to membership on Pvt. Rudolph LeBeau of Co. B 26th Regiment OH Vol. Inf. He enlisted on June 14, 1861 and was discharged on April 27, 1864.

SEAN F. RALSTON, joined Gillaly Kingsley #120 on April 27, 1994. He has held the positions of Camp Graves Registration Officer, Committee Member, and Chaplain.

He bases his right to membership on his great-great-great-grandfather, Pvt. John Ralston of Co. E, 44th Ohio Vol. Infantry, who enlisted September 16, 1861. In January of 1864, he re-enlisted into the newly formed, Ohio 8th Volunteer Cavalry. He was killed in action at the Battle of Martinsburg, WV, September 18, 1864.

Orrin D. Kingsley

Sean had several other Civil War ancestors including his great-great-grandfather, Corporal Orrin D. Kingsley of Co. D 24th MI Vol. Infantry. Kingsley enlisted on August 13, 1862 and was mustered out on June 30, 1865 as First Sergeant. His brother Samuel R. Kingsley served in the same company and was wounded at the first day of Gettysburg. Pvt. Andrew Ralston, brother of John, enlisted with Co. E 110 OH Vol. Infantry on August 15, 1862 and served until the close of the war. He served under General Sheridan and was at Appomattox for the surrender of Lee. Abraham Davis, Sean's great-great-great-grandfather, enlisted as a private in Co. E of the 19 OH Vol. Infantry on September 12, 1861, and was discharged on March 29, 1865, on a surgeons certificate of disability as a veteran.

JOHN L. RAYE, has been a member of the Sons for about five years and is associated with Alden Skinner Camp #45 in Rockville, CT. John is the Author of *Island Sacrifice*, a book about his great-grandfathers' Civil War experiences. John has helped produce *Foothills For Freedom*, a documentary about Northwestern Connecticut and the Civil War that has been seen on C.P.T.V.

John has two great-uncles who were in the Civil War, Moses Gove and James Rae (Raye) and a great-grandfather, Henry Wadsworth. Henry Wadsworth joined the 9th Maine Vol. Regt., as a private at age 19 in September of 1862. He fought in many battles including, Bermuda Hundred campaign, Cold Harbor, Petersburg, and Fort Fisher. He was honorably discharged in June 1865 as Adjutant of his regiment, with small pox. Although not expected to live, he survived until 1934 and was the last living member of Meade Post 63, Eastport, Maine.

TODD JAMES REBILLOT, joined the Sons September 26, 1986. He is in the process of transferring from member-at-large to C.K. Pier Badger Camp #1, Milwaukee, WI.

He bases his membership on Edwin G. Swift, who was born on December 21, 1826, in Geneseo, NY. His parents were Zebulon and Abigail (Perkins) Swift.

Louisa Billick was born on October 10, 1830, in Geneseo, NY. Her parents were William and Sarah (Marsch) Billick. Her line of descent is as follows: Johann Arnoldt Billig (circa 1700), Emmanuel Billig (1750), George Arnold Billig (1778), William Billick (1802).

Edwin Swift and Louisa Billick were married on November 20, 1848, in Winnebago County, IL. The officiant was Numan Campbell, justice of the peace. Their children were as follows: Oscar (1849), L.V. (1850), Orville (1851), Alpheus (1855), Adalaska (1857), Kenneth (1858), Essie (1858-1859), Adalbert (1860), Ella (1862), Ulysses (1866), Elmer (1869), and Arba (1872). Ella has been discussed in the previous generation.

Edwin Swift served valiantly during the Civil War. His first term of duty was from April 30, 1861 until July 30, 1861. He served as a private, in the 11th Regt., Illinois Infantry His second term of duty was as follows:

Todd J. Rebillot

Second lieutenant, Co. B, 74th Regt., Illinois Infantry September 1862-May 1865. In June of 1864, Edwin was wounded (shot in the face), at the battle of Kennesaw Mountain. He was sent to the hospital on June 27, 1864, returning to active duty in July 1864, at which time he assumed command of the company. He was taken prisoner at Jonesboro, GA, on September 1, 1864, and transmitted to "Libby Prison", until his release on April 23, 1865. In May of 1865, he was promoted to first lieutenant; however, he was honorably discharged on May 15, 1865, as a second lieutenant. He was once again promoted to first lieutenant, on May 31, 1865, as a result of special war department order #28. It is interesting to note, that the war records describe Edwin Swift as 5'9", dark hair, dark eyes, and light complexion.

Edwin Swift was a carpenter by trade, and owned land in Pecatonica, Winnebago County, IL.

Edwin Swift died on February 9, 1897, in Pecatonica, IL, at 7:30 a.m. The cause of his death was neuralgia of the heart.

Louisa Swift died on January 26, 1917, in Pecatonica, IL, at 4:00 a.m. The cause of her death was pneumonia.

Both Edwin and Louisa Swift are buried in the family lot, located in the Pecatonica Cemetery, Pecatonica, IL.

It is interesting to note, that Edwin's father, Zebulon Swift, served in the War of 1812, and that Edwin's grandfather, David Swift, served in the American Revolution.

RICHARD REED, joined the Sons October 28, 1993, H.E.K. Hall #28 Chelsea, VT. He served as VT Department junior vice commander and camp council.

He bases his membership on Cpl. Josiah Reed who served with 5th Vermont. He enlisted August 18, 1862 and served until June 19, 1865. He belonged to Pixley Post #102 Enosburgh Falls, VT.

Richard Reed   *Josiah Reed*

He took an active part in principal battles including: Fredericksburg, Gettysburg, Wilderness, Cold Harbor, Petersburg, Cedar Creek, Spotsylvania, and Winchester.

Although he was never wounded, Cpl. Josiah Reed did contract typhoid fever.

Once a man rowing with him in a boat was killed, and on another occasion in the midst of the battle, he crawled to a creek for a drink of water. On his return found a bullet hole through his cap he left behind. Once he held General Sheridan's horse for him, while the General went on an errand.

Josiah died on January 10, 1932 in St. Johnsbury, VT, at the age of 87. He was one of the last members of Chamberlin Post #1 St. Johnsbury, VT.

JOHN H. REEVES, Brother Reeves joined the Order as a life member in 1980 in the Oliver Tilden Camp No. 26 in New York City. He was a Vietnam veteran from September 15, 1972 and was honorably discharged on September 14, 1975. He became disabled in June 1976 in a fire, losing his left lung, but instead of giving up he started volunteering as the B.P.O. Elks #1 Representative at the NYVAMC and has put in over 17,000 hours helping disabled veterans.

His great-great-grandfather, William Beck (1822-1881), served as a private with the Army of the Eastern Shore, MD from August 29, 1862 and was honorably discharged on June 15, 1865. He died May 6, 1881 in Baltimore.

Also, his great-great-grandfather, James Bates (1816-1896), was the founder of the Bates Foundry in Baltimore, MD and built the first automatic elevator in the U.S. in 1846. He also helped the U.S. Government during the Mexican War and the Union forces with war supplies - cannons, rifles, ammunition, etc. He became a major in the Mounted Rifleman Unit, where he was sent to Oregon starting in 1853 and was there in Salem, when Oregon became a state in February 1859. During the Civil War he was a major in the 45th U.S. Infantry and was promoted to lieutenant colonel as commander of the first colored infantry unit, the 109th, in 1863. After the war he went back to Oregon in 1866 and stayed about eight years more fighting the Indians. When he went back to Baltimore, the city gave him the contract for lighting the streets and he invented the Bates pot belly stove, which are still in use. He died January 8, 1896 and is buried in the vault of his father John Bates at Greenmount Cemetery in Baltimore.

DAVID DONALD REHKOPF, joined Curtenios Guard #17 on September 29, 1992 and has served as a Camp Guard.

He bases his right to membership on Pvt. George Lincoln of the 8th MI Cavalry. He enlisted on June 13, 1864 and was discharged on August 14, 1865. He was a member of the George Walker GAR Post #256.

ROBERT RIPLEY, joined the Sons January 27, 1991 as member-at-large. Enlisted and served three years during WWII in the Army Air Corp including 29 months in Pacific Theatre.

His Civil War ancestor was Sgt. Sylvester Ripley, of Co. D, 126th (11th Cav.) Regt., Indiana Volunteers. He enlisted December 19, 1863 and was discharged September 19, 1865. The last few months of his great-grandfather's service was on the Santa Fe Trail. As a result of this experience he was motivated to return to Kansas from Indiana immediately after discharge. He operated a trading post on the Santa Fe Trail at the Cimarron Crossing on the Arkansas River until 1868. He then relocated to Butler County, KS and raised his family. Union service in the Civil War includes two other great-grandfathers and four great-grand uncles.

STEPHEN D. ROBISON, joined Lot Smith Camp #1 in July 1994 and was a Charter Member. He has served on the Camp Council.

He bases his right to membership on Pvt. Harley Ingersoll Colegrove of Co. A IL 20th. He was mustered in on June 15, 1861 and was discharged on June 3, 1864. He served most of his term on detached duty in Quartermaster's Department in Jackson, Tennessee.

DOUGLAS W. RONALDSON, joined L.A. Tifft Camp No. 15 on September 24, 1980.

He bases his right to membership on Sgt. Nelson S. Cole, who enlisted on May 18, 1861 in Brattleboro, VT. He served for three months and was assigned to Company C, 2nd Regiment Vermont Volunteers. Sgt. Cole participated in many battles and engagements which included: Bull Run, Golden Farm, Savage's Station, White Oak Swamp, Antietam, Fredericksburg, Marye's Heights, Salem Heights, Gettysburg, Funkstown, Rappahannock, Wilderness, Spotsylvania, North Anna, Cold Harbor and Petersburg. His company was relieved from the front on June 19, 1864 and they were mustered out on June 29, 1864.

The official statement of losses of the 2nd Vermont Volunteers were: 4 Officers killed in action, 134 Enlisted killed in action, 2 Officers died of wounds, 80 Enlisted died of wounds, 139 died from disease, 22 died in Confederate prisons not of wounds, 3 died by accident, and 1 was executed, with a total of 385 deaths.

WILLIAM ROSE, joined the Sons in December 1992 at E.D. Baker Camp 101 Department of Pennsylvania. He was the charter camp commander.

He bases his membership on Pvt. Serle Brown, who served with Co. I, 35th P.V. and Co. D, 18th VRC. He enlisted on October 8, 1861 and was discharged on May 29, 1964.

PERCIVAL R. ROYSTON, joined the Sons in April of 1994, at Oliver Tilden #26.

His Civil War ancestor was Sgt. Major Theo. E. Royston, who served with 11th Michigan Cav., 3 Bn. Eng. He enlisted on August 25, 1864 and was discharged on April 21, 1901.

His enlistment took place at Hillsdale, MI at the age of 16, as a substitute for Henry Kellog. He saw action in Virginia, Kentucky, Tennessee, West Virginia, South Carolina, and North Carolina. Retired in 1901 while stationed at Ft. Tottere, NY.

JAMES MITCHELL RULEY, is the son of the late Joseph Austin Ruley and Blanche Elizabeth (Mitchell) Ruley. He joined Governor William Dennison Camp No. 1, Department of Ohio, Sons of Union Veterans in 1993. Born in Honolulu, HI in 1960, he has resided in Springfield, OH since childhood. He received a B.S. degree in Engineering Physics from Wright State University in 1982, and an M.S. in Aeronautical Engineering from Air Force Institute of Technology in 1988. He is currently employed by the U.S. Air Force as an aerospace engineer. His hobbies include Civil War reenacting, photography, home improvements, and flying model airplanes.

James M. Ruley   *John Mitchell*

Capt. John Mitchell was the great-grandfather of James M. Ruley. A native of Ayreshire, Scotland, he emigrated with his family to Washington County, OH in 1841 at age six. He became a naturalized citizen in 1856. He joined Co. F, 73rd O.V.I. in October 1861, and became a 2nd lieutenant in November 1861. He served with this unit through the second battle of Bull Run, and was wounded on duty near Washington on September 3, 1865. This wound resulted in his honorable discharge on December 23, 1865. In 1864, Mitchell recruited Co. H of the 148th O.V.I. and served as its captain from May 17 to September 14. He died March 16, 1914 and is buried in Veto Cemetery, Veto, OH.

HORACE RUMSEY, bases his membership on his father Pvt. Horace Rumsey, who served with 148th NYSV. Mr. Horace Rumsey lives in Waterloo, NY.

EUGENE E. RUSSELL, joined the Sons October 26, 1961, Charles H. Bond Camp #104 Massachusetts. He held offices as camp commander, Massachusetts Department and Commander-in-chief.

Eugene E. Russell   *David H. Cheever*

He bases his membership on Sgt. David H. Cheever, who served with 17th Regt., MA. Sgt. Cheever enlisted on July 22, 1861 and was discharged on February 23, 1964. He belonged to Gen. E.W. Hinks Post No. 95.

Eugene E. Russell joined the SUVCW 100 years after his grandfather's enlistment in the Civil War.

JEREMIAH RAY RUSSELL, was born November 1, 1979, Pt. Pleasant, WV, son of Daniel Ray and Leah Jane (Van Meter) Russell. He attends Meigs Local High School. He belongs to Calvary Bible Church; Star Grange #778; Meigs County Pomona Grange; the Degree of Flora. He joined as charter member of Brooks-Grant Camp No. 7 Sons of Union Veterans of Middleport, OH, which formed in January, 1995. He was delegate to the 1995 Ohio Department. He is joining the Sons of Veterans Reserve.

Jeremiah R. Russell

He joined on his third great-grandfather's brother, Andrew J. Biram, who served as a corporal in Co. C, 63rd Ohio Volunteer Infantry from October 8, 1861. He was medically discharged April 1, 1863. He reenlisted in Co. I, 186th Ohio Volunteer Infantry on February 12, 1865. He was mustered out with his company on September 18, 1865. He is buried in Biram Cemetery, Meigs County, OH.

JOHN C. RUTHERFORD, joined Phelps Camp #66 of Springfield, MO, as a charter member on July 13, 1994, and serves as camp secretary-treasurer. Mr. Rutherford is the great-great-great-grandson of Capt. DeWitt Clinton Wadsworth of Companies C&I, 24th Ohio Volunteer Infantry Regt.

Capt. Wadsworth mustered in as a second lieutenant on June 3, 1861. Corresponding with relatives from Nashville, TN, in 1862, Wadsworth included a drawing of President

John C. Rutherford

Andrew Jackson's Hermitage, where the 24th Ohio camped. Wadsworth was discharged September 21, 1863 upon death from wounds, but a year went by before his family learned about it. During the summer of 1864, seven year old DeWitt Clinton Wadsworth, Jr., while walking along the streets of Sandusky, OH, met a recently discharged soldier from the 24th Ohio. The soldier remarked that DeWitt Jr., bore a striking resemblance to a Capt. Wadsworth of his regiment. Was the boy a relative? After confirming that Capt. Wadsworth was his father, DeWitt Jr., inquired if the soldier had any news of his father's whereabouts. The soldier then affirmed what the family had long feared: DeWitt Clinton Wadsworth Sr., had died during the Battle of Chickamauga.

WILTON A. RYDER, joined the Sons May 20, 1961, member-at-large. He held offices at Philip Sheridan Camp, Department of Florida, Bradenton, FL (no longer active). He was told by his father, that his grandfather was wounded at the second battle of Bull Run (August 30, 1862).

His Civil War ancestor was William Washburn Ryder who enlisted May 20, 1861 as a private in Co. F, 17th New York Volunteers from Ossining, NY. He was 17 years old at the time of enlistment. On August 30, 1862 he was wounded in the hip by a dum dum bullet at the battle of Second Manassas (Bull Run) and lay on the battlefield for 17 hours until assisted from the field by two of his comrades. He was mustered out of service on June 2, 1863 and returned home where he was later commander of Morrell post, GAR and active there until his death on November 24, 1922. He was a blacksmith in Ossining for many years.

GARY SALLADE, joined the Gov. Dennison #125 in November 1992. Gary was with the 1st Bn., 26th Marines in Vietnam. He has been a Physician's Assistant at the VAMC in Chillicothe, Ohio for the past 20 years. He is married to Brenda and they have one son, Scott, and two daughters, Shelby and Ashley.

Gary Sallade   *J. F. N. Householder*

He bases his right to membership on his great-great-grandfather 2nd Lt. J.F.N. Householder of Co. F 125th PVI. He enlisted on August 16, 1862 and served through May 15, 1865. He belonged to GAR Post Huntingdon Co. PA. JFN's diary states he was tilling a field and "took a notion to enlist." He was in the Army 30 days before the 125th PVI marched into the W. Woods at Antietam. He was promoted to 2nd Sgt. after Antietam, 1st Sgt. after Fredericksburg, and 2nd Lt. after Kanes Mills. His nine month enlistment expired just prior to Chancellorsville.

ERIC T. SAMPSON, joined the Sons in 1993, Joel Serfoss #273, and has held office as junior vice commander.

His Civil War ancestors were his great-great-grandfather's. William K. Synder, private, served with 31st Regt. He enlisted September 3, 1862 and it is not known when he was discharged. He belonged to Post 384. There is no information known of Civil War ancestor, George Washington Heims.

Both of his great-great-grandfather's fought in the battle at Gettysburg.

BRICE FRANKLYN SCALLEY, is a life member of Sheridan Camp #1. Brice was born in Alliance, Ohio and is a historian of military orders and heraldry, Zouaves, Cavalry, flags and bands.

He bases his right to membership on his great-grandfather Cpl. Madison Trail of Co. G 6th Ohio Vol. Cav. 1861-1863 and was a private in Co. F 155th Ohio Volunteer Infantry-Ohio National Guard 100 days service. He was a prisoner of war after being captured guarding ambulances. He was saved by an African American man who found him unable to walk and carried him to a train going home. He was an Officer of Alliance, Ohio GAR Post.

Brice's great-grandfather, James Gallaher also served in the Union Army with his two brothers. Brice's great-grandmother, Victoria Trail, served as Postmistress at Berlin Center, OH during the Civil War and would give out letters at night when people rapped upon the house window.

JOSEPH R. SCHAAF, SR., became a member of the John T. Crawford #43 Camp, PA, on November 14, 1994. Schaaf served 26 years with the Pennsylvania State Police and retired in January 1994 with the rank of corporal. He is married to the former Nancy Robison (DUV) and the father of one son.

Benjamin Diebler (Diveler) mustered in April 20, 1861, to serve three months with Co. K of the 8th Regt. PVI. He reenlisted in the 11th Pennsylvania Cav., Co. L on September 27, 1861, for a three year term. Cpl. Diebler was captured at Stoney Creek, VA on June 29, 1864 and was sent to Andersonville Prison for over nine months before his release on April 29, 1865. After his discharge on June 5, 1865, he returned to his farm in Brookeville, PA where he died on February 14, 1891.

GERALD P. SCHEIB, joined Phil Sheridan Camp H 4, Cal-Pacific on March 31, 1994. He was born on December 26, 1937 and is an artist, with a career as a high school art teacher.

Gerald P. Scheib   *William T. Scheib*

He bases his right to membership on Pvt. William Tecumsch Scheib. He enlisted and was mustered into service in Company H, 16th Iowa Infantry on January 1, 1862. During the battle of Shiloh, his regiment was ordered to retreat. He was so busy fighting that he did not hear the orders and found himself alone. While he ran to the Union lines he was wounded on his hand and a ball had lodged itself into the back of his head. Despite this wound, he only took one week off before rejoining his Company. He received another wound to his hand and arm in the battle of Corinth. While he was getting medical treatment, the Union lines retreated, and despite his wounds, he again had to run to prevent capture. Pvt. Scheib was discharged, on January 13, 1863, due to the severity of his wounds. He received an $18 pension from the government each month. Both William and Gerald Scheib were school teachers.

RICHARD CARL SCHLENKER, born April 29, 1923, Wilkes-Barre, PA. Son of Raymond John Schlenker and Elsie Keiser Schlenker. Moved to Washington, DC area 1941.

Affiliated with SUVCW November 30, 1974 Lincoln-Cushing Camp #2 Washington, DC, Maryland Department. Served as camp commander; department commander three terms; many national committees and top three offices; 15 years as Washington Representative; commanded Sons of Veterans Reserve as brigadier general. Mrs. Richard C. Schlenker served as national president of auxiliary to SUVCW 1982-1983 as well.

Richard C. Schlenker

His WWII service involved three years Regimental Hq. Co., 104th Infantry Regt., 26th Infantry Div. Four battles European Theatre. Ten years U.S. Army Reserve.

Member of nine hereditary, 12 Masonic, 13 history and general and eight veteran organizations.

Descendant of Pvt. Daniel B. Schlenker, Co. G, 167th Pennsylvania Militia, Berks County, PA. Served October 22, 1862 through August 12, 1863 mostly Suffolk, VA area. Member of Hermany Post 606, Lehigh County, PA (GAR).

V. DEAN SCHWARTZ, M.D., was born on May 11, 1924 in Leonardville, KS. Following high school graduation he attended the University of Kansas and Yale University, culminating with the degree Bachelor of Science in Medicine and the Doctoral degree in medicine, both from the Kansas School. He practiced family medicine in Wichita, KS, for 45 years. Additionally he was medical director of Health Services for St. Francis Regional Medical Center in Wichita from 1967 until his retirement in 1994. Military service included AUS, Medical Department, 1943 to 1946, and Medical Corps in Korea and Japan, 1951 to 1953, inactivated as a captain. On January 8, 1948 he married Eileen Ruth Bonicamp. Four children were born to the union. In addition to membership in SUVCW (1995) he is a past president of the Kansas Society Sons of the American Revolution and present commander of the Kansas State Commandery of the Military Order of the Loyal Legion, among other hereditary societies.

V. Dean Schwartz   *Rudolph Niehenke*

Rudolph Niehenke, leaving a German ship's company in New York City, Rudolph (NMI) Niehenke immediately joined the United States Army on November 8, 1847, for duty in the Mexican War. He was discharged on July 3, 1849. Fifteen years later Fort Leavenworth, KS was threatened by General Sterling Price and his Missouri Militia. The Kansas governor activated a militia of 17,000. Niehenke, having had prior military service, was commissioned a captain on August 3, 1864. His unit, Co. I, 17th Regt., Kansas State Militia, was assigned to reinforce Fort Riley against anticipated Indian attacks. Seventeen days later, Price having been defeated in Missouri, the militia was mustered out.

BRUCE SCHWEMMIN, joined the Sons April 27, 1994, Gilluly-Kingsley Camp 120. He held office as junior vice commander.

His Civil War ancestor was Oliver H. Perry, born at Flushing, Genesse Co., MI, December 8, 1844; enlisted at Saginaw, Saginaw County, MI, August 28, 1862, as private in Co. C, 7th Michigan Cav.; taken prisoner October 8, 1863,

Bruce Schwemmin   *Oliver H. Perry*

at Utz Ford, Robison River, VA, confined in Libby, Pemberton, Belle Isle, and Andersonville prisons; released at Baldwin, FL, April 28, 1865; mustered out at Camp Chase, OH, June 20, 1865, and honorably discharged.

Oliver married Sallie M. Goyer, January 21, 1875, daughter of Richard C. Goyer, 16th Michigan Infantry Oliver worked as a prison guard at Ionia State Prison and in later years lived with his son before passing away January 30, 1924 at Whitmore Lake.

KEVIN SCHWEMMIN, joined the Sons April 27, 1994, Gilluly-Kingsley Camp 120. He held office as patriotic instructor.

His Civil War ancestor was Oliver H. Perry, born at Flushing, Genesse Co., MI, December 8, 1844; enlisted at Saginaw, Saginaw County, MI, August 28, 1862, as private in Co. C, 7th Michigan Cav.; taken prisoner October 8, 1863, at Utz Ford, Robison River, VA, confined in Libby, Pemberton, Belle Isle, and Andersonville prisons; released at Baldwin, FL, April 28, 1865; mustered out at Camp Chase, OH, June 20, 1865, and honorably discharged.

Kevin Schwemmin   *Oliver H. Perry*

Oliver married Sallie M. Goyer, January 21, 1875, daughter of Richard C. Goyer, 16th Michigan Infantry Oliver worked as a prison guard at Ionia State Prison and in later years lived with his son before passing away January 30, 1924 at Whitmore Lake.

KURT SCHULZE, joined the SUVCW January 1992, Gov. Crapo Camp No. 145, Department of Michigan. He held office as member of the Camp Council (current position).

Civil War ancestors name: George Swift, private, Co. I, 21st Michigan Infantry Regt. Enlisted September 6, 1864 and died January 28, 1865.

George Swift served with Gen. Sherman's Army. He participated in the "March to the Sea". He died at Savannah, GA on January 28, 1865, and is buried in Beaufort, SC.

PAUL EDWARD SCULL, born August 17, 1949, entered the United States Air Force 12 days after graduating from high school. He served with the 306th Bombardment Wing (SAC) as an administrative specialist, rank of staff sergeant, served stateside, Turkey and Okinawa. He enlisted in July 1968, and was discharged on July 7, 1978 (ten years service). Paul joined Lyon Camp #10 SUV on August 29, 1994, serving in the position of company chaplain. He also belongs to the 14 New York State Militia "Red Legged Devils", Co. A, as company chaplain. He is an ordained minister of the Assemblies of God and has a Master of Arts degree in Christian counseling in psychology. He teaches two courses for the Vineland Adult Education - "Genealogy for Fun" and "Finding Your Military Ancestors. Paul married Eileen P. Tarozzi on March 1, 1969, and they have two children Michael and Amie. He is currently assistant pastor.

Paul E. Scull   *William F. Wellman*

He bases his right to membership on Pvt. William Francis Wellman, who served 2nd Co. Sharp Shooters, MA Volunteers. He enlisted on August 11, 1862 and was discharged on October 17, 1864. He belonged to Lyon GAR Post #10 Vineland, NJ. He was daily drummer of his company October-December 1863.

KENNETH EUGENE SEGUIN, joined the Sons, Lone Star Camp #1, on December 22, 1992.

He bases his right to membership on Pvt. John Gustave Beck and Pvt. Andrew Jackson Christy. Pvt. Beck served with 14th New Jersey Infantry Regt. He enlisted August 6, 1862 and was discharged June 18, 1865. John Beck (1831-1896) enlisted at Freehold, NJ; participated in battles of the Wilderness, Spotsylvania, Cold Harbor and Monocacy; captured by Confederates July 9, 1864. Imprisoned at Danville, VA until February 22, 1865. Moved to Ohio after the war. He died at National Home for DVS, Dayton, OH. Buried in Dayton National Cemetery; reinterred Caledonia, OH, during 1910s.

Kenneth E. Seguin

John G. Beck   *Andrew J. Christy*

Pvt. Christy, served with 14th Ohio Infantry Regt. He enlisted September 4, 1861 and was discharged July 11, 1865. Andrew Christy (September 9, 1844-April 4, 1920) enlisted at Napoleon, OH; participated in battles of Wildcat Mountain, Mill Springs, Chickamauga, Missionary Ridge, Kennesaw Mountain, Jonesboro, and March to the Sea; returned to Ohio after the war; died at Wauseon, OH; buried at Forest Hill Cemetery, Napoleon, OH.

LAURENCE E. SEITS, Ed.D, JVC, initiated into Camp #1 of the Illinois Department April 16, 1991, Seits transferred to Illinois Camp #2 in 1995 now serving as junior vice commander and Illinois Department GAR liaison chair.

Seits' grandfather, Pvt. Henry Seits of Co. C, 31st Indiana Infantry, served between September 5, 1861 and September 15, 1864.

Henry Seits, born in Dauphin County, PA, was the son of Karl and Matilda Seitz. The family moved to near Terre Haute, IN, before 1850. Henry married first Lydia Andrews (Andrus), second Rebecca Alward. He died in 1910 in Waveland, IN.

Laurence E. Seits

Brother "Larry" Seits, a retired teacher and Air Force veteran, is also a member of the SAR, the Pilgrim Society, the Huguenot Society, the Plainfield (IL) Masonic Lodge #536, the Order of the Eastern Star, the Scottish Rite, the American Legion, and the GAR (Post 20) Hall Memorial Society. His hobbies include gardening and genealogy. Larry and wife Linda Seits live in Aurora, IL.

MARVIN R. SEYMORE, joined the Henry Casey Camp No. 92 Sons of Union Veterans of the Civil War, as an associate member, when it was organized in Washington Court House, OH in 1992. He currently serves as a member of the camp council of administration.

Marvin, who is a United States Air Force veteran, works for the local government as a water treatment specialist. His wife Katie, is a public school teacher.

Marvin R. Seymore

Marvin serves as quartermaster sergeant in Co. C, 20th Ohio Volunteer Infantry which is the Sons of Veterans Reserve unit for the Henry Casey Camp.

JAMES H. SHAW, joined John T. Crawford Camp #43, Pennsylvania SUVCW on February 14, 1993.

He bases his membership on his Civil War ancestor, Peter Everly. Peter Everly (February 17, 1808-May 28, 1900), his great-great-grandfather enlisted in the Union Army on July 29, 1862, age 54, at Bruceton (Mills), Preston Co. (W) VA, Co. H, 3rd Regt. PHB (Potomac Home Brigade) MD Infantry Vols. This outfit called the "West Virginia Snake Hunters" formed March 29, 1862 with Capt. William Alpeus Falkinstine (1827-1900) as the C.O. (Note: Peter Everly 20 years older than his C.O.) Peter captured at Harpers Ferry, September 15, 1862, made a prisoner of war, sent to Alexandria, VA, instead of being imprisoned. He was paroled and again took up the fight and was discharged, as a private on June 14, 1864, of disabilities and "totally unfit for the Veterans Reserve Corps".

James H. Shaw

Peter and his wife Margaret Brandon Everly/William Brandon Sgt. War 1812/Alexander Brandon, Sgt. Rev. War./had 13 children of which three sons served in the Union Army - one of which was his great-grandfather William H. Everly (1846-1939) a private Co. A, 6th Regt. WVA Cav. The two older sons of Peter were, Abasalom, Co. C 6th WVA Cav. Vol. and John Gribble Everly, Pvt. Co. B 4th Regt, WVA Vol. Cav. In addition there were ten other Everly's (all related) 14 in all that served in the Union Army during the Civil War.

BYRD SHEPHERD, was born on February 22, 1937, in Harlan County, KY. He married Miss Marylou Jackson and they have two children. Byrd served nine years in the U.S. Army and 15 years in the U.S. Air Force, retiring in 1980 as a captain. He spent one tour in Vietnam with MACV from April 1964 to April 1965. Byrd graduated from Chaminade College in Honolulu. He holds membership in the Vietnam Veterans of America, the American Legion, the Retired Military Police Association, the Air Force Photo Mapping Association, and Counterparts, an Association of Southeast Asia advisors.

Byrd joined the Sons on March 1995. He is in the General George A. Custer Camp #1 in Illinois. His Civil War ancestor is Pvt. Hiram Fee of the 47th Kentucky Volunteer Mounted Infantry. Hiram enlisted on October 5, 1863, and died on December 17, 1863.

STEPHEN L. SHIELDS, joined the Sons, James A. Garfield #142 Camp, on August 9, 1993. He has held office as camp patriotic instructor.

His Civil War ancestor was Sgt. John L. Shields. Shields served with the 8th MD Vols. He enlisted August 15, 1862 and was discharged May 31, 1865. He was wounded May 8, 1864

Stephen L. Shields

at Laurel Hill, Spotsylvania. John L. Shields joined as a corporal, but was promoted to sergeant in February 1865. Mustered out at the end of the war. He belonged to GAR Post in Baltimore, MD.

RONALD S. SHINN, joined Austin Blair Camp #7 in Jackson, MI on November 9, 1992. He is also a member of the 14th Ohio Volunteer Infantry.

Ronald S. Shinn

His Civil War ancestor is his great-great-uncle Jacob B. Speaker who served as a private in the 14th Ohio Veteran Volunteer Infantry. He enlisted on August 21, 1861 in Defiance, OH. He fought in the battles of Shiloh, Siege of Corinth, Hoovers Gap and Chickamauga. With the optimism of youth he set a letter to his sister, his great-grandmother, Henrietta C. Speaker telling her that he had been granted a (30) day furlough and would be coming home after the battle of Chickamauga was finished. Unfortunately, he was mortally wounded on the first day of battle September 19, 1863, and died of his wounds September 26, 1863. He is buried at the National Cemetery in Chattanooga, TN.

ROBERT H. SHOOK, of Lockport, NY, joined the organization February 18, 1984, and is a member-at-large. His membership is based on his great-grandfather, Pvt. John H. Rockwell, who enlisted in Co. H, 30th Indiana Volunteer Infantry on December 1, 1863. John received a $100 bonus and a $300 bounty, more than a good year's pay. He was 18 and of medium height. John's baptism came at Tunnel Hill on May 7, 1864, near Ringgold, GA. By October the Regimental strength was so reduced that it was reorganized into a battalion, and John was transferred to Co. C. On November 25, 1865, he was mustered out at Victoria, TX. When asked why he didn't join the cavalry and ride, John said that then he would have

Robert H. Shook   *John H. Rockwell*

to take care of this horse first and last. John rarely talked of the war; never of combat; and led many Memorial Day parades. He died May 31, 1935.

RONALD GARTH SHULL, joined the Sons on March 30, 1993 and is a member of Curtenius Guard Camp No. 17, Dept. Of MI. He has served on the Camp Council.

Ronald G. Shull

He bases his right to membership on Pvt. Solomon Shull, born December 23, 1846, of 133rd Regiment Ohio Volunteer Infantry - National Guard. He enlisted on May 2, 1864 and died August 4, 1864 at Fortress Monroe, VA.

SAMUEL A. SIBILSKY, joined the Sons January 1995, Gov. Crapo Camp No. 145, Department of Michigan.

He held offices as musician and camp color guard.

His Civil War ancestors name was Hulbert E. Palmer (third great-grandfather). He served as first sergeant, Co. C, 24th Ohio Vol. Infantry He enlisted April 1862 and was discharged November 1864.

Samuel Sibilsky

Hulbert saw action at Shiloh, Stones River, Perryville, Murfreesboro, Chickamauga and Chattanooga. He enlisted as a private, was promoted to corporal, then became first sergeant of his company. After one engagement, he was briefly the commanding officer of his company, as all commissioned officers had been killed or wounded. He ended his service term as a recruiting sergeant for his regiment.

STEPHEN SIEMSEN, is a SUV life member with Lincoln-Cushing Post #2, Washington, D.C. He bases his membership on his Civil War ancestor, Perry Schermerhorn, Pvt, who was born in New York in 1843 and moved to Iowa with his parents in 1857. He enlisted in Co. C, 2nd Bn., 12th U.S. Infantry on March 24, 1862. Following initial training at Fort Hamilton, NY, Perry went on to participate in the battles of South Mountain, Antietam, Fredericksburg, Chancellorsville and Gettysburg as part of the Army of the Potomac's Second Div., V Corps before being medically discharged with 100% disability on March 30, 1864.

Stephen Siemsen

Although immediately eligible for a pension, Perry refused government "charity" when he returned to Iowa. He married Harriet Hoisington in 1865 and they had five children before Harriet's untimely death. He moved to Verndale, MN with his four youngest children in 1875. Unable to work due to his wartime disability, Perry finally accepted his Veteran's Pension in 1880. He remained a member of G.A.R. Post 102 in nearby Wadena until his death in 1897.

For almost a century Perry rested in an unmarked grave until Stephen Siemsen, a direct descendant, located his burial site after a four-year search. In July 1994, Perry's descendants placed a veteran's headstone on his final resting place.

JAMES ALAN SIMMONS, joined Lone Star Camp #1 in April of 1995. He was born in Texas to James and Julia Simmons, on October 23, 1961. Continuing four centuries of family military tradition, James was commissioned a Second Lieutenant in the U.S. Air Force, following graduation from TCU in 1983. Flying the F-4 Phantom II in the Tactical Air Command, James Alan served as an Instructor and Staff Officer, and was promoted to Captain in 1987. In 1991 he was hired as an American Airlines Pilot, and was married to Robyn Renee Lewis.

James A. Simmons   *James M. Simmons*

He joined the SUV to honor his four great-grandfathers and ten great uncles who served in the Ninth Kentucky Vol. Inf. Regt. The Ninth was in service from November 1861 to December 1864 and saw action at Shiloh, Stone's River, Chickamauga, Missionary Ridge, and the Atlanta Campaign.

His grandfather, James M. Simmons, was a Pvt/1st Sgt/2nd Lt of Co. K, then Capt. of Co. G. His grandfather, Moses L. Norvell, was 1st Lt. of Co. E, and died of measles on March 31, 1862. His grandfather Robert W. Barbour was a private in Co. E, and was wounded at Stone's River. His grandfather Samuel Piercy was a Private in Co. E, and was a POW.

CODY RANDOLPH SMITH, was born November 25, 1984, Gallia County, OH, as the son of Lawrence Randolph, Jr. and Heidi Jill (Ashley) Smith. He tied as the first junior in the Ohio Department by signing the charter of Brooks-Grant Camp No. 7 of Middleport, OH, which was founded by his paternal uncle, Keith Ashley. His paternal grandfather was Robert Drew Ashley, life member of the S.U.V.

Cody Randolph Smith

He is the third great-grandson of Cpl. William Ashley of Co. I, 36th Ohio Volunteer Infantry enlisting August 13, 1861. He was discharged January 19, 1864, due to illness after having been in the Invalid Corps. He is buried in Letart Falls Cemetery, Letart Falls, OH.

He resides in Chatfield, OH.

DOUGLAS E. SMITH, DVC, Bro. Smith joined the Order in 1990 as a member of the Albany, NY Camp #154. In 1991 as camp commander and department patriotic instructor, he served as department chairman for the 125th anniversary of the NYGAR-Memorial Ceremonies. While serving two terms as camp commander and currently secretary/treasure, camp membership has quadrupled to be the second largest state camp. Doug currently serves his department as senior vice commander.

Douglas E. Smith   *Daniel Smith*

Among his three veteran ancestors, Smith bases his right to membership on his great-great-grandfather Sgt. Daniel Smith. Sgt. Smith enlisted in Springfield December 18, 1863, in Co. B of the 24th NY Cav. He was disabled by artillery fire June 30, 1864 during the mine explosion before Petersburg. He was discharged with his unit July 13, 1865.

Bro Smith and his wife Marianne reside in Altamont, NY.

E.D. SMITH, Bro. Smith joined the Order in January 1995, as a member of General Philip H. Sheridan Camp No. 2, Naperville, IL, Department of Illinois.

E. D. Smith

Among his known veteran ancestors, Bro. Smith based his right to membership on his great-grandfather, Capt. Lawrence B. Smith, Co. H, 100th Ohio Volunteer Infantry, who enlisted July 19, 1862 but resigned November 27, 1862 by reason of disability. Bro. Smith also lists his great-great-uncle, Lt. Col. Albert B. Smith, Co. H, (later Co. E), 100th Ohio Volunteer Infantry, who enlisted July 30, 1862 and who was mustered out August 1, 1865 by order of the War Department. Lt. Col. Smith served as a line officer in the battles of Franklin, Nashville, Knoxville and Atlanta (Utoy Creek). Later, he was assistant-commissary-mustering for the Army of the Ohio and Department of North Carolina for the 23rd Army Corps.

Bro. Smith's grandfather, E.D. Smith, MD, of Fort Wayne, IN was state commander (Indiana) of the SUVCW in the 1920s.

CLARENCE "BUZZ" SMITHCORS, joined Lyon Camp #10, New Jersey on August 23, 1987 and has held the offices of Secretary/Treasurer and Sr. Vice Commander. He was involved in re-establishment of Baxter Camp #72 SUV. He help establish and organize the GAR room in the Vineland Historical Society and worked on the displays. He was involved with Open House at the Vineland Historical Society, the Camp research project to locate graves of Civil War veterans, Open House at the Millville Historical Society and with cataloging GAR articles. He participated in the flagpole dedication at the Oak Hill Cemetery on July 9, 1995.

He bases his right to membership on Pvt. Alexander Bryson of Co. D 4h NJ, who enlisted in April 1861 and was discharged in July 1861. He only served three months and was stationed in Virginia. He developed a kidney ailment and was discharged.

JAMES L. STAHL, joined D.D. Porter Camp #116, in September of 1994. He bases his membership on his Civil War ancestor, Pvt. Huston Stahl, of Co. K, 74th Ohio Vol. Infantry. He was reared on his father's farm in Tuscarawas County, OH, attended common schools and received a liberal education as a boy.

Not long after the outbreak of the rebellion, Huston joined for duty and enrolled at Tippecanoe, OH. Several weeks later, he mustered-in at Camp Chase at the age of 19, on February 11, 1862. His company was under the command of Capt. Robert P. Findley, a dedicated soldier, officer, and leader of men.

After serving two years in the 74th Ohio, Huston veteranized for three years service, which extended him to the close of the war.

Throughout his enlistment, Huston participated in 17 battles, and had several hair-breath escapes from harm and capture. He was wounded at Goldsboro, and at Stones River, 13 round balls pierced his clothing, but he escaped the confrontation with only minor wounds, the loss of two haversacks and a canteen.

Fortunately, Huston was never taken prisoner, but at the Battle of Peach Tree Creek, he was able to capture two rebel soldiers at the risk of losing his life, having to knock one of the men down with the butt-end of his musket in order to take him.

Huston spent 20 days on the skirmish line at Bentonville, and it was during this service, word was received of Lee's surrender. He was discharged on July 10, 1865.

Following the war, Huston returned to farming, moving to Harrison County, OH. He married Elizabeth Smith in 1867 and together they had four sons and two daughters, the eldest being Charles Grant Stahl, James Stahl's great-grandfather, who was well into his nineties when James had the pleasure of meeting him.

James Stahl's children's names are James Eric, Jason Ryan, Joshua Patrick and Jorie Elizabeth.

GREGORY JOHN STERIO, joined C.O. McCann Camp #199 of Seneca Falls, NY on May 24, 1984. Currently he is color bearer of the camp. He is a sergeant with the 8th Virginia Cav. He belongs to the Sons of Spanish War Veterans.

His great-great-grandfather, James Delancy, was a member of the 82nd Ohio Vols.

His mother, Lorraine Orton served as New York Department president, Woman's Relief Corps and national historian from 1993-1995. He is the step-son of PDC Jerome Orton of New York.

He currently lives in Syracuse, NY.

DALE STEWART, joined Ben Harrison Camp 356, Indiana on November 4, 1992.

He bases his right to membership on great-grandfather Pvt. Thomas Stewart of Co. D, 192nd PA Infantry. He enlisted on February 11, 1865 and was discharged on August 10, 1865.

Dale Stewart   *Thomas Stewart*

HOWARD STREETER, joined Colgrove-Woodruff Camp #22 MI on January 22, 1991 and has served as Chaplain. He bases his right to membership on Linus T. Squire of Company H, 11th MI Vol. Infantry, who enlisted on August 24, 1861, age 24, as a Sergeant. By the end of his enlistment he had the rank of 1st Lt. Adjutant.

The regiment took part in many engagements in Tennessee and Georgia, including the siege of Atlanta. The Brigade held one of the hills on Mission Ridge, and while covering the approach to Roseville, against a superior force, they were the last to leave the field. He was mustered out on September 30, 1864.

Howard Streeter   *Linus T. Squire*

After the war, he went back to Tennessee in 1867, married Emma who he met on a campaign. She died in 1869 and he came home to Michigan. He left for Washington, D.C. in 1870 and went to work for the Post Office. He married Susan in 1872 and along with her, graduated from Howard University in 1889 as a Doctor. She practiced medicine, while he went to work for the Pension Dept. to help the boys in the blue.

TY JASON STREETER, joined Colegrove-Woodruff Camp #22 on June 2, 1994 at the age of 14.

He bases his right to membership on Linus Truman Squire of Company H, 11th MI Vol. Infantry, who enlisted on August 24, 1861, age 24, as a Sergeant. By the end of his enlistment he had the rank of 1st Lt. Adjutant.

Ty J. Streeter   *Linus T. Squire*

The regiment took part in many engagements in Tennessee and Georgia, including the siege of Atlanta. In one of his letters, he wrote where they had to lay down at Stone River so the battery could fire over them. He went on to tell that for days after the firing he could not hear. He was mustered out on September 30, 1864.

Ty Streeter has in his possession, the inkwell that Linus used for writing his reports and also his spurs, saber and Spencer carbine.

FREDERICK M. STUEWER, joined the U.S. Grant Camp #101 in 1993. He bases his right to membership on John B. Waltz of the 22nd Michigan Infantry. He enlisted as a private and was discharged as a Corporal. John Waltz enlisted on August 29, 1862, at the age of 37 years, nearly twice that of many others. He was called "little grandpa" by the family. He was refused at his first attempt to enlist because he was too short. He went home and put lifts in his shoes and was then accepted. It is said that his musket was taller than he was.

John was captured September 20, 1863 at Chicamauga, GA-Snodgrass Hill. He had been part of Graingers Reserve Corps. He was among the last to enter the battle and along with his comrades among the last in combat. As a prisoner, he arrived at Richmond on September 29, 1863.

He was hospitalized at Danville, VA on April 22, 1864. The story is that he swallowed large amounts of chewing tobacco to make himself deathly ill. He was paroled at City Point, VA on April 30, 1864 and returned to his regiment on May 15, 1864. Fortunately, this parole occurred prior to the opening of Andersonville, where many of the 22nd Michigan Infantry died and are buried.

JOSEPH E. STUMP, is a member of George Armstrong Custer #1, Illinois.

He bases his right to membership on his father, Pvt. Henry B. Stump of Co. B 2nd Missouri Cavalry and Co. M 12th Illinois. He enlisted with Company B on January 21, 1862 through September 27, 1862. He was with Company M from December 4, 1863 until his discharge on January 19, 1866.

Retired farmers, Mr. And Mrs. Stump for the 65th wedding anniversary built a chapel at the park which marks the geographical center of the lower 48 states. This is across the road from their home in Lebanon, KS.

WILLIAM B. SUDELL, Bro. Sudell joined the Order in 1991 as a member of the Anna M. Ross Camp #1 in Philadelphia, PA, basing his right to membership upon his great-great-grandfather, Sgt. William Benson. Benson enlisted in Co. A, 13th Pennsylvania Volunteer Cav., the *Irish Dragoons,* on July 11, 1862. Captured at the battle of Second Winchester, he spent two months in Libby Prison until he was paroled. He then rejoined his regiment, and was discharged in May, 1865.

Dissatisfied with life in the textile mills of Manayunk after all he had seen and done in the war, Benson set out for the gold fields of California early in 1868. Shortly after arriving at Sacramento he contracted smallpox, and died in October, 1868 at the age of 24.

William B. Sudell

Bro. Sudell, an instructor at Thomas Jefferson University and health care management consultant, resides in Glenside, PA.

CHRIS SULLIVAN, joined the Lyon Camp #10 New Jersey on November 10, 1981 and has served as Commander and Secretary/Treasurer. He was involved in re-establishment of Baxter Camp #72 SUV. He helped establish and organize the GAR room in the Vineland Historical Society and worked on the displays. He was involved with Open House at the Vineland Historical Society and with cataloging GAR articles. He participated in the flagpole dedication at the Oak Hill Cemetery on July 9, 1995.

JAMES FITZ SULLIVAN, joined as a member-at-large New York on May 11, 1990. He bases his right to membership on his father, James P. Sullivan of Co. K, 6th WS Vol, "the Iron Brigade."

Mr. Sullivan was only 5 when his father died in 1906. He was a veteran of WWII. He served in the Navy, mainly in the New Hebrides. He served as National Commander of the Seabee Veterans of America. Mr. Sullivan lives in Holiday, Florida.

ROBERT E. SULLIVAN, JR., joined SUVCW Russell A. Alger Camp-at-large (Michigan) No. 462 on June 22, 1994. Civil War ancestors: great-great-uncles John and Henry Lamb (their youngest brother, Benjamin Franklin Lamb, had a daughter, Marie M. Lamb, who had a daughter, Gloria M. Sullivan, who was Robert Sullivan's mother). These two young brothers grew up at 237 Catherine St. (current day Madison St.) in Detroit, within short walking distances of the pre-Civil War Detroit homes of then Lt. Ulysses S. Grant (lived in Detroit from 1849-1851) and then Capt. George G. Meade (lived in Detroit from 1857-1861). Grant and Meade later led the Union to simultaneous victories at Vicksburg (Grant) and Gettysburg (Meade).

Robert E. Sullivan, Jr. *Henry C. Lamb*

Cpl. John Lamb (born July 18, 1844) had enlisted in Detroit at the age of 18 in Co. A (Capt. Robinson's Co.) Provost Guard, Michigan Infantry on December 19, 1862. He served at the provost marshal's office - Detroit Barracks, from May-July 1864. He was then detached to go north! - to Marquette, MI, "to suppress a riot." On January 3, 1865, he was detached to Savannah, GA (General William T. Sherman had just captured Savannah on December 21, 1864).

Cpl. Henry C. Lamb (born August 4, 1847) had enlisted in Detroit at the age of 17, in the same company as his brother John. Henry served on daily duty at the Detroit Barracks and it appears from his military records that he was never detached from his unit. Both brothers mustered out with honorable discharges on May 9, 1865 at Jackson, MI. John moved to Grand Rapids and worked in the furniture-making business. He died on April 6, 1915 and is buried at Oak Hill Cemetery, Grand Rapids. Henry became a doctor and remained in Detroit. He died on November 14, 1891 and is buried at Elmwood Cemetery, Detroit.

HERMAN SYNDER, joined the Joel SerFoss #273 in August of 1923. He is presently Commander Emeritus. He was Treasurer for 25 years and Commander for 3 years.

He bases his right to membership on his grandfather, Pvt. William K. Synder of the 31st Regiment, who enlisted on September 3, 1862. He was a member of the GAR Post #384. He fought in the battle at Gettysburg during his nine month term of enlistment.

LAWRENCE R. TATRO, married Karen Pinkerton, 1966, Wabash, IN (descendant of Civil War veteran Elisha W. Pinkerton, Co. C, 34th Regt., Indiana Vols. Infantry). They have two daughters. He's been a postman at the Northampton, MA Post Office for 28 years. Served two four year tours with the U.S. Air Force, 1958-1966, Europe and Pacific. Belonged to the Revolutionary War group, 6th Mass. Regt for eight years - in 1975 went on the "Arnold March to Quebec." Belonged to the Civil War Reenactment group, 10th Mass. Vol., Infantry for four years. Member of American Legion Post 344, Department of Massachusetts.

Lawrence R. Tatro *Amede B. Tatro*

His Civil War ancestor, Landsman Amede B. Tatro (Tetreau), served in the U.S. Navy. Enlisted September 3, 1864 and was discharged August 2, 1865. He belonged to Ezra Batcheller Post 51 Dept. of Massachusetts, North Brookfield.

Amede told Lawrence's father, his grandson, of serving on the USS *Brooklyn,* South Atlantic Squadron, and picking up an Enfield musket from the war in Charleston, SC , that had made it through the blockade. It is still in their family today. Also of two of his brothers that had served and how their French Canadian names had been altered. One, an Edward Tathroe, (Tetreau), Pvt. Co. C, 9th Regt., RI Vol. Infantry and second, Treffler Tetro, (Tetreau), Pvt. 1st Btry and 2nd Btry., VT Vol. Light Artillery.

MICHAEL L. TAYLOR, joined the Sons April 20, 1995, in the Gilluly-Kingsley Camp No. 120.

His Civil War ancestor, Sgt. David Taylor Roberts, served with Co. H, 14th WV Infantry He enlisted September 1, 1862 and was discharged June 27, 1865.

David recuperated from an unknown disease in August of 1864 at the U.S. Hospital in Parkersburg, WV, and on April 1, 1865 went on detached duty at Patterson Creek, Mission unknown, but more on his service record being researched still. He had two Confederate cousins.

CHARLES J. TEN BRINK, joined the Sons, Colegrove-Woodruff Camp #22, Marshall, MI, on September 1, 1993.

His Civil War ancestor, Pvt. Abraham Evans, Btry. C, 1st Michigan Light Arty., enlisted September 20, 1861 and was discharged February 27, 1863. He belonged to Joe Hooker Post #26, Hart, MI.

Abraham Evans

Abraham's wife Mary, 18, accompanied him to war, leaving their two year old son with her mother. While the 3rd Btry. was encamped at Corinth in the summer of 1862, she made herself useful by cooking and sewing, and helped nurse the soldiers after the battles in Northern Mississippi that fall. Abraham's heart condition, aggravated by the rigors of military life, cut short his service as a teamster for Battery C. After spending several months in a hospital in St. Louis, he was mustered out on a surgeon's certificate of disability and Abraham and Mary returned to their families in Michigan.

JOHN C. THIEL, joined the Sons, Col. Henry Harnden #2, on May 7, 1994.

His Civil War ancestor, Pvt. Lyman Webster, served with the 75th Illinois Infantry. He enlisted on August 12, 1862 and was discharged on May 2, 1863. He belonged to GAR Post in Elgin, IL.

John C. Thiel *Lyman Webster*

He saw action in the Ohio, Kentucky and Tennessee Campaigns, Perryville, KY (Goodings Brigade), and at Murphysboro, TN. He was taken prisoner on December 31, 1862, and sent to Belle Island Prison. He escaped during prisoner exchange about January 21, 1863. Pvt. Webster was sent to hospital at Annapolis, MD and was given a medical discharge in May of 1863.

KARL MICHAEL THOMAS, joined the Orlando A. Somers #1, Indiana, and was initiated on April 29, 1995.

He bases his right to membership on his great-great-grandfather James Redd of Co. B, 59th Indiana Infantry. He was mustered in on February 8, 1865 and was discharged on July 17, 1865. Joseph Redd, Mr. Thomas' great-great-uncle, also served in the war. He enlisted into the Co. D, 57th Indiana Infantry Regt. on October 11, 1861 and was discharged on November 21, 1865. Mr. Thomas' father, Lew Michael Thomas, is also in the SUVCW, as a member of Orlando A. Somers #1, Indiana

LEW MICHAEL THOMAS, joined the Sons, Orlando A. Somers, #1 Indiana, on January 21, 1995.

His Civil War ancestor is Pvt. James Redd, who served with 59th Indiana Infantry He enlisted on February 8, 1865 and was discharged on July 17, 1865.

Lew M. Thomas

James Redd was 17 when he enlisted. His brother Joseph Redd was 16 when he enlisted and served from October 11, 1861 to November 21, 1865 in the 57th Indiana Infantry as a brigade and regimental pioneer.

KENNETH C. THOMSON, JR. currently a member of the S.U.V. bases his membership on his ancestor, James Lewis Hix. James was a first lieutenant in Co. C, 5th Tennessee Volunteer Cav. enlisted September 2, 1862 in Nashville, TN for three years. He resigned May 12, 1865 for personal reasons.

Lt. Hix was born September 22, 1832 in Bedford County, TN the son of John Collins Hix and his wife Ellender "Nellie" Stewart. He was the grandson of William Hix and Sarah Collins and of William Stewart and Margaret Yates.

Kenneth C. Thomson, Jr.   *James L. Hix*

On May 4, 1854 he married Huldah Ann Holt who was born November 28, 1836 in Bedford County, TN the daughter of Jordan Cain Holt, Sr. and Margaret Wilhoite. She died August 16, 1883.

James and Huldah were the parents of eight children: Jordan Holt, Margaret Eleanor, Elizabeth Frances, John Collins, William Isaac, Benjamin Hiram, Lucy "Ludie" and Charles Albert.

Their son Benjamin Hiram Hix 1869-1936 married Nancy Hoge Baucom 1867-1961 and had a son Harold Tillman Hix, 1897-1986 who married Martha Lorelle Frakes 1899-1981. Harold's daughter, Jane Rogers Hix, married Kenneth Calvin Thomson, Sr. and their son was Kenneth C. Thomson, Jr. is currently a member of the S.U.V.

James Lewis Hix died January 3, 1906 in Nashville, TN and was buried in Shelbyville, TN.

ROGER TIEMAN, joined the Sons, George A. Custer #1, on February 19, 1994. He was born near Greenwood, WI, September 29, 1942. He spent the first 23 years of his life on a dairy farm in that area. He served in the U.S. Army Finance Corps from 1965-1967. After leaving the Army, he attended the University of Wisconsin-Eau Claire where he served as treasurer of the Veterans Club and graduated from there magna cum laude in May, 1971.

Mr. Tieman married Linda Tumm on June 17, 1972. He was registered as a certified public accountant in Illinois in October, 1974. He held various accounting positions with three major corporations before starting his own public accounting practice, Tieman & Associates, in 1992. Mr. Tieman has two sons, Gregory, born in 1979 and Joshua, born in 1982. He has been a resident of Lake Zurich, IL since 1974.

Roger's Civil War ancestor is Frederick Tieman, who was born in Germany and came to the United States with his parents in 1846. They were living in Round Top, TX at the start of 1861. He married Mary Giesee on January 13, 1861, one month before Texas seceded from the union.

Frederick Tieman enlisted in the Union Army at Cairo, IL on December 17, 1862. He served with the 12th Illinois Cav. during the Chancellorsville and Gettysburg Campaigns. After that, he spent the rest of the war with the 12th Illinois in Louisiana and Texas, eventually being discharged from the Army in Houston only about 100 miles from his pre-war home. Because of his service in the Union Army, he was not welcome in Texas after the war, and moved to Englewood, IL (now part of Chicago), where he lived until his death in 1892. Frederick Tieman was the father of five sons and one daughter.

RANDAL L. TOOKER, joined the Curtenius Guard Camp #17 Michigan Department in 1991 in memory of his great-great-grandfather, Daniel Dickerson Tooker.

Daniel was born in New York where he was a sea captain before moving to Michigan. On August 18, 1862 at the age of 34 and with a wife and four children at home his loyalty and patriotism for the United States of America convinced him to enlist as a drummer in Co. B, 17th Michigan Infantry Less than four weeks later they would become known as the "Stone-Wall" Regt. for their gallantry at the battle of South Mountain. Three days later they again were thrown into battle at Antietam. It was after Antietam that Daniel lost his last battle. Here, from his diary is part of the entry for October 12, 1862; "Am terribly reduced so that I can hardly sit up or write. Am a mere skeleton. I over did myself 2 weeks ago at the battle of Antietam bridge carrying off the wounded, fording the river and getting wet, then burying mortified corpse. Have had chill, fever, torments of my entire frame, without appetite and entirely prostrated."

Daniel died October 10, 1862. It is believed that his sister Sarah E. Donmill of Suffolk County, Long Island arranged for his burial somewhere on Long Island.

TIMOTHY N. TRAVER, Bro. Traver joined the Order in 1994 as a member-at-large. He is a member of the Civil War Society of Central New York and is a member of several reenactment groups including the 141st Pennsylvania Volunteer Infantry and the 126th New York Volunteer Infantry

Timothy N. Traver   *George A. Barnes*

Tim bases his right to membership on his great-great-grandfather, Pvt. George A. Barnes. Pvt. Barnes enlisted in Mansfield, PA March 28, 1864, in Co. F, 2nd Pennsylvania Veteran Volunteer Arty. He was discharged January 29, 1866. He died May 22, 1903. Tim also has four great-great-great uncles, the Gore brothers: Silas, killed July 2, 1863 at the Peach Orchard, Gettysburg; John, killed in South Carolina; Samuel, killed at Fredericksburg, VA and Hollis, the only surviving brother of the war.

Brother Traver lives in Vestal, NY with his wife Diane and sons Neil and Kevin.

BRUCE KEATS TROYER, is a charter member of Gen. Philip H. Sheridan Camp No. 2 Illinois and has been a member of the Sons of Union Veterans since 1992.

He bases his right to membership on Pvt. Montreville Hitchcock of Co. F, 3rd Regiment, Wisconsin Cavalry. He enlisted on February 1, 1862 and was discharged on February 17, 1865. He belonged to a GAR post in South Bend, IN. Pvt.

Bruce K. Troyer   *Montreville Hitchcock*

Hitchcock ran away from his Indiana home at age 19 to Wisconsin where he enlisted. He was stationed at Fort Scott, Kansas and later at Fort Insley, MO. He saw action guarding trains, skirmishing with the "bushwackers" and Quontrell's guerillas. He participated in the battles of Church in the Woods, Coon Creek, and Prairie Grove.

After the war he went back to live in South Bend, IN. He married Mary E. Drullinger on June 3, 1865. They had five children. Like many veterans, Montreville found it hard to adjust to a "normal way of life." He suffered a slight paralysis from a horse rolling over on him while in the cavalry. He died in March of 1921.

RICHARD VERLE UTT, lives in the Seattle, WA area and joined the SUVCW march 29, 1994 as a member-at-large. Rick's great-great-grandfather, Josephus Utt was a first lieutenant, Co. K, 14th Kansas Cav. Josephus saw action at the Battle of Poison Springs, AR in 1864. Josephus' nephew Levi H. Utt was a captain in the 7th Kansas Cav.

Richard V. Utt   *Josephus Utt*

Rick has two other great-great-grandfathers who fought for the Union. David Reese, private Co. B 57th New York Infantry and Phineas Bliss, private Co. C, 5th Minnesota Infantry

LYNFORD VOORHEIS, joined the Sons September 9, 1994, member-at-large in New York. Lynford's family was very active with GAR Post #241 and SOUV Camp #201, both of Friendship, NY. He lives in Friendship, NY. Edwin's two brothers, William and DeWitt were veterans serving in the 136th NYSV and 5th HNY Art. respectively.

His Civil War ancestor was father, Pvt. Edwin O. Voorheis, who served with Co. A, 5th NY Arty.

DAVID F. WALLACE, joined the SUVCW, Gov. Crapo Camp No. 145, Department of Michigan in November 1991.

He held offices as camp color bearer, camp organizer, camp commander, department junior vice commander, department senior vice commander, and is the current national secretary.

David F. Wallace

He bases his right to membership on his Civil War ancestor, Pvt. James Monroe Wallace (great-grandfather), of Co. I, 120th Ohio Volunteer Infantry. He enlisted on July 24, 1862, Shenandoah, OH and was discharged on October 5, 1865, Houston, TX.

He was a member of William D. Wilkins Post 91, Department of Michigan.

His great-grandfather's regiment was part of the original 13th Corps commanded by General Grant. He and his brother served in the Vicksburg Campaign in General Peter Osterhaus' 9th Div.

FLOYD E. WALLACE, joined the Sons, Gov. Crapo Camp No. 145, Department of Michigan, in December of 1991. He was a camp delegate to the Department Encampment.

His Civil War ancestor, was his grandfather, Pvt. James Monroe Wallace, Co. I, 120th Ohio Volunteer Infantry, who enlisted on July 24, 1862, in Shenandoah, OH. He was discharged on October 5, 1865, in Houston, TX.

Member of William D. Wilkins Post No. 91, Department of Michigan.

Floyd E. Wallace

His grandfather's regiment was ambushed at Snaggy Point on the transport *City Belle* in May 1864 during General Bank's Red River Campaign. Out of 750 officers and men, only 150 junior officers and men were able to make it to the opposite shore. Although his grandfather was fortunate enough to escape the ambush, his brother, Charles Wallace, spent the remainder of the war in the Confederate Prison Camp at Camp Ford in Tyler, TX.

PATRICK D. WALLACE, joined the SUVCW, Gov. Crapo Camp No. 145, Department of Michigan, in August 1994. He held offices as musician and camp color guard.

Civil War ancestor's name, James Monroe Wallace (second great-grandfather), private, Co. I, 120th Ohio Volunteer Infantry Enlisted July 24, 1862, Shenandoah, OH. Discharged October 5, 1865, Houston, TX.

Member of William D. Wilkins Post No. 91, Department of Michigan.

Patrick D. Wallace

Patrick is one of the first three Juniors elected and initiated into the Order. He received his obligation from Commander-in-Chief Keith G. Harrison. Patrick became a full member after his birthday in 1995.

JOE WALSH, joined the Sons, Abraham Lincoln #100, on December 3, 1994.

His Civil War ancestor, Cpl. John Reilly, 9th PA Cav., Co. D, served the entire war. Among the numerous battles he fought in were, Perryville, KY and Chattanooga/Chickamauga. He was hospitalized with malaria for four months. He was captured twice. The first time he was released on field parole. The second time, on October 12, 1864, he was captured while leading a charge into Lafayette, GA, and was sent to Andersonville Prison. He was released in April of 1865.

Joe Walsh

He returned to Wilkes Barre and was selected justice of the peace, and captain in Shields Guards. Reilly opened a grocery store and saloon. He married and fathered three daughters. On September 15, 1874, he was shot down and killed in the streets of Wilkes Barre at the age of 34, by a man who once was his friend. The man who murdered John Reilly was tried, convicted and hung.

ANDREW DIXON WARD, Bro. Ward joined the order in 1994, as a charter member of Lot Smith Camp #1, a camp-at-large in Salt Lake City, UT. He currently resides in Tempe, AZ.

Drew bases his membership on the service of his fourth great-uncle, George William Shiner, who was born on February 11, 1835 at Winchester, VA. Shiner enlisted as a private in Co. A, 14th Iowa Infantry, on January 1, 1864, and was discharged on August 8, 1865. After the war, he moved to Castle Dale, UT, where he died October 1, 1918. He was a member of Rousseau Post #2, Utah Department, GAR.

CHARLES PATRICK WARD, Bro. Ward became a junior in Lot Smith Camp #1, a camp-at-large in Salt Lake City, UT, in 1995. He resides in Salt Lake City.

Charles' membership is based on the service of his third great-uncle, William Morgan Posey, who was born in Indiana on December 27, 1839. Posey enlisted as a private in Co. G, 27th Illinois Infantry on August 20, 1861, and was discharged on June 12, 1862. After the war, he moved to Jerauld County, SD and died on March 1, 1904 at Mitchell, SD.

DUNCAN STEWART WARD, Bro. Ward was initiated into the Sons of Union Veterans in 1994, three days after his 14th birthday, as a charter member of Lot Smith Camp #1, a camp-at-large in Salt Lake City, UT. He currently resides in Tempe, AZ.

Duncan bases his membership on the service of his third great-uncle, Henry M. Posey, who was born in Indiana in 1843. Posey enlisted as a corporal in Co. B, 14th Iowa Infantry on October 1, 1861. His company was transferred to the 41st Iowa Infantry, and later redesignated Co. L, 7th Iowa Cav. He was discharged on October 31, 1864.

WILLIAM RAY WARD, CC, Bro. Ward affiliated with Lincoln-Cushing Camp #2, Department of Maryland, in 1991. In 1994, he organized Lot Smith Camp #1, a camp-at-large in Salt Lake City, UT, and was elected its first commander. During his term of office, an Auxiliary and a Sons of Veterans Reserve Company were also organized. He is company adjutant, holding the rank of corporal in the Sons of Veterans Reserve and is an associate member of the District of Columbia Commandery, Military Order of the Loyal Legion of the United States.

Bill's membership in SUVCW is based on the service of his third great-uncle, James Sloss, who was born at Colmonell, Ayrshire, Scotland on October 25, 1830, and emigrated to the United States in 1855. Sloss enlisted as a private in Capt. William Cogswell's Independent Btry., Illinois Light Arty. on March 1, 1862, and was discharged on June 5, 1865. After the war, he resided in Tama County, IA, where he operated a grain mill with his brother Allan.

Bro. Ward and his wife Jill are the parents of eight children, and reside in Salt Lake City, UT.

LEWIS D. WARNER, Bro. Warner joined the Order in 1993 as a member of the Col. George L. Willard Camp #154. He has held the positions of camp junior vice commander, press correspondent, and preservation chairman. On the state level he has served as New York Department Press Correspondent. Bro. Warner and his son, Christopher, also reenact the Civil War with the 125th New York Volunteer Infantry.

Lewis D. Warner   *Ezra Warner*

Ezra Warner, Lewis' great-great-grandfather, enlisted in Albany, NY on October 24, 1862 at the age of 16 in Co. A, 177th New York Volunteer Infantry During the siege of Port Hudson, LA, he was wounded while rushing Rebel breastworks. Pvt. Warner was discharged on September 10, 1863. On August 15, 1864, Ezra Warner re-enlisted and went into the 11th New York Independent Btry., where he served to the end of the war. He was mustered out on June 13, 1865. After the war Ezra served several terms as constable of Rotterdam, was a Schenectady deputy sheriff, and worked as a detective for the General Electric Company. He died in Schenectady, NY on April 17, 1913.

Bro. Warner and his son, Christopher, reside in Schenectady, NY.

ROBERT C. WARNER, joined the Lone Star Camp #1 on December 3, 1994.

He bases his right to membership on his father, Pvt. William Carter Warner of the 9th IN Cavalry, who enlisted on October 24, 1863 and was mustered out on July 12, 1865. He was a member of the James Shield GAR Post #208. He enlisted at the age of 15 and surrendered with his command at Sulpher Branch, Trestle, Alabama. He was released from Cahaba Prison Camp in April of 1865 and was a survivor of the Sultana Disaster on April 27, 1865. Pvt. Warner's two sons are still living: Robert C. lives in San Angelo, TX and William B. lives in Austin, TX.

WILLIAM B. WARNER, joined the Lone Star Camp #1 on December 3, 1994.

He bases his right to membership on his father, Pvt. William Carter Warner of the 9th IN Cavalry, who enlisted on October 24, 1863 and was mustered out on July 12, 1865. He was a member of the James Shield GAR Post #208. He enlisted at the age of 15 and surrendered with his command at Sulpher Branch, Trestle, Alabama. He was released from Cahaba Prison Camp in April of 1865 and was a survivor of the Sultana Disaster on April 27, 1865. Pvt. Warner's two sons are still living: Robert C. lives in San Angelo, TX and William B. lives in Austin, TX.

WILLIAM L. "BILL" WASHBURN, joined the Sons, Gov. Henry Crapo Camp No. 145 SUVCW Flint, MI on July 9, 1994. He held offices as camp guide 1995 Gov. Crapo Camp No. 145, Gov. Henry Crapo Award for 1994 for exhibiting dedication and service to the Gov. Crapo Camp and the Sons of Union Veterans of the Civil War, Michigan Department, SUVCW Color Guard, Sons of Veterans Reserve.

His Civil War ancestor, Pvt. Orson D. Bouck, Co. G, 6th MI Cav. He enlisted on December 1, 1862 at Vernon, MI, and was discharged on September 15, 1863 at Detroit, MI. He belonged to Capt. Henry F. Wallace GAR Post 160 Corunna, MI.

William L. Washburn   *Orson D. Bouck*

Orson D. Bouck, Bills great-great-grandfather was born March 10, 1819 at Genesee Falls, NY, now Rochester. He and his three brothers-in-law enlisted about the same time. Three of them in the 6th MI Cav. and one in the 10th MI Infantry. His oldest son also served in the 8th MI Cav. Orson fought at the Battle of Gettysburg July 1-3, 1863. He was discharged due to disability from exposure during that battle. He died February 6, 1907 at the age of 87. He was buried at Chalker Cemetery, Vernon Twp. Shiawassee County, MI in an unmarked grave until Memorial Day 1994 when his great-great-grandson Bill Washburn obtained a Civil War veterans headstone for the grave.

MYRON A. WATERMAN, Rochester, NY, joined Order as a member-at-large in 1995 and has four veteran ancestors: 1. Martin Boh, 34th New York Volunteers, 16th New York Heavy Arty. 2. John Waterman, 26th New York Volunteers (killed in action, Georgetown, MD). 3. Pvt. Horace Miller, Town of Annsville, NY, Co. F, 146th New York Volunteers, enlisted August 29, 1862 served to July 16, 1865. Involved in

Horace Miller   *Wesley Waterman*

battles of Bull Run, Five Forks, Petersburg, Fredericksburg and Gettysburg (Little Round Top). Member, Ballard Post No. 551 G.A.R. who provided a wreath upon his death, December 10, 1913. Married Mary Hanney, children; Elsworth, Fred, Ida, Harry, Elizabeth, Myron, Bertha. 4. Wesley Waterman, Annsville, Camden, NY, private, Co. H, 3rd Regt., New York Light Arty. Enlisted October 20, 1861 served to June 12, 1863. Methodist minister. Died September 11, 1919. Married Elizabeth Kibble, children: Lizzie, Charles, Rose, Wellington, Alice.

JOHN C. WEATHERELL, joined the Phil Sheridan Camp #4, California on November 19, 1994.

He bases his right to membership on his great-grandfather Pvt. James S. Weatherell of the 10th Cavalry NY, who enlisted in October of 1861 and was mustered out in November of 1864. He belonged to the G.D. Bayard Post #222 Olean, New York. James S. Weatherell, born in 1844, immigrated from Durham County, England. He enlisted into the 10th Cavalry at Elmira, New York. Enlistment records show him as a 21 year old, but the date of birth indicates he was 17 years old. He was captured twice, once in August of 1962 at Centerville, VA and again in May of 1964 at Haxhall, VA. He was paroled the first time. The second time, family recollections say, he escaped and was wounded. Official muster records do not indicate this and are incomplete.

BYRON E. WEED, joined the Curtenius Guard Camp #17, Michigan on November 30, 1993.

He bases his right to membership Sgt. Seth Henry Weed of the 1st New York Dragoons. Seth enlisted at the age of 29 as a sergeant in Co. I as the 1st NCO, on August 12, 1862 in Grove, NY. The regiment was originally the 130th NYVI. He was in the battles of Desert House, VA Suffolk, VA, Blackwater, VA, Manassas Plains, VA and was killed in the battle of Wilderness at Todd's Tavern, VA on May 7, 1864. He left behind a wife and a small son and daughter. GAR Post #296 Seth H. Weed in Canaseraga, NY was named in his honor.

Seth's brother, 1st Lt. Randolph Weed, fought with Co. A 104th NYVI. He was one of the first to enlist on September 30, 1861. He fought at Cedar Creek, Bull Run, South Mountain, Antietam, Sharpsburg, Fredericksburg, Chancellorsville, and Gettysburg. He was captured at Gettysburg. He was paroled and subsequently discharged on December 20, 1863 at Belle Plains, VA.

GEORGE JOSEPH WEINMANN, Bro. George was born in Greenpoint Brooklyn, NY, home of the Monitor. George joined the order in 1987 as a member-at-large and then joined the Oliver Tilden Camp 26 New York City, in 1991. George is the patriotic instructor, genealogist, co-editor of *Billy Yank* newsletter and color guardsman of the Tilden Camp. He is also a member of the Sons of the Revolution and other patriotic, historical and genealogical associations. He has ancestors dating back to the 1600s in America.

George J. Weinmann   Charles F. Weinmann

George bases his right to membership on his great-great-grandfather, Pvt. Charles Frederick Weinmann. Charles enlisted with his brother William Weinmann in New York City May 4, 1861, in Co. H, 9th Regt., New York Volunteer Infantry (Hawkins' Zouaves). He was discharged May 20, 1863. He was a member of the Hawkins Zouaves Minstrel and Theoretical group during and after the war. Charles was a cigar maker by trade, and he died April 3, 1879 in New York City.

JOHN VERNON WENDORPH, Bro. Wendorph joined the order in March of 1992. He is a member of the Col. George L. Willard Camp #154. He resides in Jacksonville, FL.

John V. Wendorph   John H. Wendorf

He claims his right of membership on his great-grandfather. Pvt. John Henry Wendorf enlisted in Albany, NY on January 19, 1862, in the 43rd Regt., Co. D, of the New York Volunteer Infantry He reenlisted as a veteran, January 28, 1864. He was captured at the battle of the Wilderness, in action on May 6, 1864. He suffered the horrors of prison in Andersonville, GA. He was eventually paroled, and following hospitalization in Charleston, SC, rejoined his company and was mustered out June 27, 1865. He died at West Sand Lake, NY, March 27, 1893. His remains rest in honored glory at Oakwood Cemetery, Troy, NY.

JOHN MARC WHEAT, was inducted into the Lincoln-Cushing Camp No. 2 on Memorial Day 1994 at Fort Myer, VA. Marc is a graduate of George Mason University School of Law and is married to the former Nancy Marie Gilliland, legislative director to Congressman Steve Largent. *See Who's Who in the East* (24th Ed) for further information.

Marc's great-great-grandfather Wilber Morehous Clymer was born August 22, 1838 in Burdette, Tompkins (now Schuyler), New York, the son of William S. and Clarissa L. (Morehous) Clymer. William was born in Pennsylvania and Clarissa in New Jersey. They moved to Jay County, IN about 1839.

According to Marc's grandfather, John Wilbur Wheat, his Grandpa Clymer would tell him "Sixty-one Stories" as a boy growing up in Arkansas. Grandpa Clymer stated that he enlisted in the Union Army twice, the first time under an assumed name. He was in a fight and hit a man in the head with an ear of corn. Thinking he had killed the man, he ran off and joined the Union Army, perhaps under the name of "Sam Brown" in a Darke County, OH regiment. During his first enlistment he fought at Lookout Mountain and served in the trenches at the Siege of Vicksburg.

John M. Wheat

At Vicksburg, under the cover of darkness, a shout from the Union lines of "Hey, Reb!" would reach the Confederate lines. A cry of "Hey, Yank" would reply, and under a ceasefire a little exchange would take place in no-man's land: a little coffee for sugar, and a little tobacco for salt. In the morning, volleys of gunfire would be traded.

While driving a caisson, a horse fell on him, injuring his leg and ribs. He left the service, and reenlisted under his own name after recuperating. His second enlistment was as a private in Co. I, 152nd Regt. of the Ohio National Guard.

He married his first wife Maria Elizabeth Ruble (July 1848-September 1912, both in Indiana, daughter of Jesse and Hannah (Aspy) Ruble on March 5, 1868 in Adams County, IN. She is buried in Crawford Cemetery, Wabash Township, Adams, IN.

After his wife's death, Grandpa Clymer moved near Waldo, Columbia, AR where he died on January 23, 1928. He is buried in Barlow Cemetery, Columbia, AR.

GEORGE THORNTON WHEELER, joined the SUVCW in 1995, on the one hundred-thirtieth anniversary of the end of the American Civil War. Born in Muskogee, OK in 1946, he is a sergeant of the Lawrence Kansas Police Department and a lifelong student of military history. His particular areas of expertise are the Civil War and World War II periods of conflict. With university degrees in Political Science and Police Science, he is a fellow of the company of military historians and the author of numerous articles and tracts on military history and police subjects.

George T. Wheeler

Wheeler's great-great-grandfather was Judge Amos Thornton of the Cherokee Nation. Judge Thornton was a private in Co. E, of the 2nd Regt. of Indian Home Guards, attached to the Kansas Infantry during the Civil War. Thornton served from November 11, 1862 until mustered out with a gunshot wound on July 6, 1863.

NORMAN F. WHEELER, a retired Coast Guard Chief Warrant Officer, lives in Bristol, RI and is a member of the A.A. Sherman Camp Number 18 of Uxbridge, MA. He joined the Sons in 1988 as a member-at-large. He is a past camp commander and holds the rank of sergeant major in the Sons of Veterans Reserve.

Norman F. Wheeler   William J. Wheeler

His Civil War ancestor is William Joseph Wheeler, a corporal in the 1st Massachusetts Light Btry. where he served with the 6th Corps from September 13, 1861 to September 14, 1864. Upon discharge he accepted a commission as second lieutenant of Co. K, 4th Massachusetts Heavy Arty. where he served until his resignation in February, 1865. He was a member of Stevenson Post 26, GAR, Roxbury, MA until his death in 1889 at the age of 51.

JERALD ALBERT WHITE, U.S. Army (Ret). Joined the Sons November 1993, Orlando A. Somers, Camp #1, Kokomo, IN.

Civil War ancestor, Charles Whelan Sherman, commissary sergeant, Co. K, 3rd Iowa Volunteers Cav. Regt. He enlisted August 20, 1861 and was discharged August 19, 1865.

He belonged to McConchie Post #35, GAR, Cass County, NE.

During the retreat from Brice's Crossroads he was caught in a gauntlet of gunfire by Forrest's Rebels, cut off from their command, Mr. Sherman and a comrade were forced to travel by darkness 125 miles to Memphis on foot. They lost their horses to gunfire and were tracked by bloodhounds for half a day. They shot the hounds in order to make their escape in sight of a Rebel camp.

MARK P. WHITNEY, joined the Sons in 1976, member-at-large.

He based his right to membership on his great-great-grandfather, Sgt. James W. Billings, of Co. B, 13th Michigan Infantry. He enlisted, at the age of 16, on December 10, 1861, transferred to U.S. Signal Corps October 23, 1863, and was honorably discharged on May 6, 1866. He was a member of the Clyde, KS GAR post. He was born near Fennville, Allegan Co., MI on October 31, 1845. He was in the battles of Shiloh, Perryville, Murfreesboro, Chickamauga, Chattanooga and the Atlanta Campaign. From company descriptive book, *James W. Billings, present on the field of battle September 19 and 20 at Chickamauga, conduct meritorious. Transferred to Signal Corps October 23/63 and final statements furnished by order Maj. Gen. Rosecrans."*

Mark P. Whitney   *James W. Billings*

He reenlisted as a veteran February 13, 1864. He was discharged at San Antonio, TX, age 20. He settled in Kansas in 1868 where he was married to Kate Anna Prince. Mr. Billings died May 12, 1903 at Clyde, KS.

JEREMY WICKERSHAM, is a charter member of Henry Casey Camp No. 92 which meets in Washington Court House, OH. He is the grandson of Raymond Morgan Grim, Jr. who serves as the camp secretary. Jeremy will graduate from high school in 1995. He is the son of Regina Grim and James Wickersham. He is also a member of Co. C, 20th Ohio Volunteer Infantry which is the Sons of Veterans Reserve Unit for the Henry Casey Camp.

He is the great-great-great-grandson of Pvt. William F. Grim, Co. K, 8th Ohio Volunteer Cav. and Pvt. Henry Ernest Schomburg, who served in Co. D, 5th Ohio Volunteer Cav. and Co. I, 140th Ohio Volunteer Infantry.

Jeremy Wickersham

He is the great-great-great-great-grandson of Pvt. John W. Rodgers who served in Co. G, 113th Ohio Volunteer Infantry He died at Camp Zanesville, OH on December 5, 1862 from the measles.

THOMAS ALAN WIGHTMAN, joined the U.S. Grant Camp #101 in 1991 and has served as Camp Commander.

He bases his right to membership on several Civil War ancestors, including: 2nd Lt. Levi Butts Wightman, who served from 1861-1865, in the 10th Illinois Volunteer Infantry and the 2nd Illinois Light Artillery at Vicksburg; Pvt. Daniel McIntyre who served from 1864-1865, in the 23rd Independent Battery of the New York Light Artillery and the 8th New York Heavy Artillery and took part in the Appomattox Campaign and the Grand Review in Washington, D.C.; Pvt. Hugh McLellan Beveridge who served from 1861-1862 with the 9th Illinois Cavalry; Pvt. Cyrus Jasper Vickery who served from 1861-1865 with the 11th Missouri Volunteer Infantry and was severely wounded in the jaw during the second assault on Vicksburg; and Pvt. Milton Hatridge who served from 1864-1865, in the 47th Missouri Volunteer Infantry, fighting at the battle of Pilot Knob, Missouri in September 1864.

BRIAN ALBERT WILHELM, joined Lyon Camp #10 New Jersey on July 28, 1995. Brian was the first junior member of Camp #10 SUV. He was involved with Open House at the Vineland Historical Society and he participated in the flagpole dedication at the Oak Hill Cemetery on July 9, 1995.

He bases his right to membership on Pvt. Nicholas B. Wilhelm of the 2nd Provisional Pennsylvania Heavy Artillery. He enlisted on February 25, 1864 and was mustered out on August 25, 1865. He belonged to Lyon Post #10 Vineland, NJ. He survived Cold Harbor and the Crater Battle at Petersburg.

Brian had additional Civil War ancestors including: Pvt. Elwood Fisher Co. G 3rd NJ Cavalry who enlisted on January 6, 1864 and was discharged on August 1, 1865; Pvt. Stacy Sloan Co. G 24th NJ Vol., who enlisted on September 2, 1862 and served until June 29, 1863; and Pvt. Samuel Shinn Cranmer, Co. H 29th Regt. NJ Inf. who enlisted on September 18, 1862 and served until June 30, 1863.

MATTHEW ROBERT WILHELM, joined Lyon Camp #10 New Jersey on February 5, 1994. Matthew Wilhelm is the color bearer for Camp #10. He was involved with Open House at the Vineland Historical Society and he participated in the flagpole dedication at the Oak Hill Cemetery on July 9, 1995.

He bases his right to membership on Pvt. Nicholas B. Wilhelm of the 2nd Provisional Pennsylvania Heavy Artillery. He enlisted on February 25, 1864 and was mustered out on August 25, 1865. He belonged to Lyon Post #10 Vineland, NJ. He survived Cold Harbor and the Crater Battle at Petersburg.

Matthew had additional Civil War ancestors including: Pvt. Elwood Fisher Co. G 3rd NJ Cavalry who enlisted on January 6, 1864 and was discharged on August 1, 1865; Pvt. Stacy Sloan Co. G 24th NJ Vol., who enlisted on September 2, 1862 and served until June 29, 1863; and Pvt. Samuel Shinn Cranmer, Co. H 29th Regt. NJ Inf. who enlisted on September 18, 1862 and served until June 30, 1863.

ROBERT JOHN WILHELM, joined Lyon Camp #10 NJ on August 23, 1987 and is the current Commander. He was involved in re-establishment of Baxter Camp #72 SUV. He help establish and organize the GAR room in the Vineland Historical Society and worked on the displays. He was involved with Open House at the Vineland Historical Society, the Camp research project to locate graves of Civil War veterans, Open House at the Millville Historical Society and with cataloging GAR articles. He participated in the flagpole dedication at the Oak Hill Cemetery on July 9, 1995.

He bases his right to membership on Pvt. Nicholas B. Wilhelm 2nd Provisional PA Heavy Artillery. He enlisted on February 25, 1864 and was mustered out on August 25, 1865. He survived Cold Harbor and the Crater Battle at Petersburg. He belonged to Lyon GAR Post #10 Vineland, NJ.

Another Civil War ancestor of Robert Wilhelm was, Pvt. Elwood Fisher Co. G 3rd NJ Cavalry who enlisted on January 6, 1864 and was discharged on August 1, 1865.

GEORGE WILKINSON, joined the James A. Garfield Camp #142 in August of 1994.

He bases his right to membership on Pvt. Henry C. Hart of the 17th OH Volunteers. He enlisted on April 27, 1661 and was mustered out on April 21, 1662. He became ill with measles and typhoid fever near Crab Orchard, KY in November, 1861. He remained in a house converted into a hospital for four months, and was near death several times. He received a disability discharge in April, 1862, and remained in poor health until his death in 1898 at the age of 55.

CRAIG KENNETH WILLARD, joined the Sons, Ellis Camp No. 9, Pennsylvania Department Germantown, Philadelphia, PA on September 18, 1966. Craig, who was born June 22, 1944, in Wilkes-Barre, PA, is single and resides in Narberth, PA.

He bases his right to membership on his Civil War ancestor, Pvt. John Isaac Willard (alias Wilyard), who served with Co. F, 11th NJ Vol. Infantry. He enlisted on September 1, 1864, Camden, NJ and was discharged on June 6, 1865 at camp near Washington, DC. He belonged to Captain James Taggert GAR Post #335, Sunbury, Northumberland County, PA.

Pvt. Willard participated in the following battles and skirmishes: Ft. Sedgwick, Poplar Springs, Boydton Plank Road, Ft. Morton (had three slight wounds and was not in the hospital), Hatchers Run, Armstrong House, Five Forks (was captured there and held about three hours, then was recaptured), capture of Petersburg, Amelia Springs, Farmville, and at Appomattox for Lees surrender. After an arduous service was honorably discharged June 6, 1865 at camp near Washington, DC, by reason of close of the war.

DAVID RAY WILLIAMS, became a member of the Orlando A. Somers Camp No. 1 of Kokomo, IN, on March 5, 1988. He is the son of Dr. Paul Williams and Patricia Ray Williams. A graduate of Indiana State University, Brother Williams is supervisor of design engineering at Delco Electronics. He is the son-in-law of Past Commander-in-Chief, Allen W. Moore and Barbara Tiley Moore. He is the great-grandson of Sgt. Wilber M. Williams.

Sgt. Wilber M. Williams enlisted on September 18, 1861, in Company D, 18th Ohio Volunteer Infantry and was discharged on November 9, 1864. He resided in Athens County, OH, where he was a farmer.

JAMES T. WILLIAMS, joined the Sons, Gilluly-Kingsley Camp #120, on May 25, 1994. He held office as camp senior vice commander.

James T. Williams

He bases his right to membership on his Civil War ancestor, Pvt. Eli Stull, who served with Co. F, 176 PA. He was drafted Militia Infantry. He enlisted on October 16, 1862 and was discharged August 17, 1863.

JOHN R. WILLIAMSON, joined the Sons on December 12, 1992 as a member-at-large.

He bases his right to membership on his great-grandfather, Pvt. George K. Williamson, who served with Co. B, 197th Pennsylvania Volunteer Infantry Regt. (100 Day Regt., 1864). He enlisted July 16, 1864 and was discharged November 11, 1864. He belonged to Post #63, Philadelphia, PA, and held the rank of post commander.

John R. Williamson   *George K. Williamson*

This regiment never saw combat. It was nicknamed "3rd Coal Exchange" and had only a Regimental Flag, no national colors were ever issued. The regiment served it's time at the Rock Island Barracks, Rock Island, IL, guarding Confederate prisoners of war.

JAMES EDWARD WILSON, joined General George Armstrong Custer Camp #1 in February of 1995.

He bases his right to membership on Pvt. William James Whitlock of Co. E 123rd Regt. New York Infantry. He enlisted on August 8, 1862 and was mustered out on June 8, 1865. He was an officer in the George Henry Thomas Post #5.

He and his younger brother, Arthur, enlisted on the same day and were in the same company and regiment. William James' brother-in-law died in the hospital in Savannah, GA.

PAUL PATTON WINKEL, JR., joined the Lincoln-Cushing Camp #2 of Washington D.C. in 1994. Mr. Winkel was with the 1st Cavalry Division in Vietnam.

He bases his right to membership on his great-grandfather Sgt. Charles L. Patton of the 8th Indiana Cavalry, who enlisted in 1861. He re-enlisted with good conduct and was promoted from Private to Sergeant. Patton was with Sherman all the way from Shiloh to The March to the Sea. He was captured in North Carolina and held for 26 days. He was mustered out at the close of the war in 1864.

ROBERT JOSEPH WOLZ, joined SUVCW August 16, 1963 into Philip Triem Camp 43 of Salem, OH. He is life member #61.

Served all camp offices Philip Triem Camp 43, Salem, OH. Enlisted Co. D, 19th Ohio Regt., SVR June 12, 1963. Promoted to corporal on February 12, 1964. Ohio Department Junior Vice Commander 1964-1966. Ohio Department Senior Vice Commander, 1966-1968. Ohio Department Commander 1968-1969 and 1972-1973, Ohio Department Historian 1965-1968, Ohio Department Counselor 1968-1982, Central Region Senior Vice Commander 1970-1971, Central Region Commander 1971-1972, Chairman, National Reconstruction of the Order Committee, 1968-1969, Chairman, National Education and Americanism Committee 1976-1977.

Robert J. Wolz

Promoted to second lieutenant, National Service Staff, National Chaplain, 1969-1970. Promoted to Quartermaster General SVR 1970 with rank of captain. National Patriotic Instructor 1970-1971. Promoted to position of the Adjutant General, SVR with rank of major. National GAR Highway Officer 1971-1972. National Junior Vice Commander in Chief 1972-1974. National Senior Vice Commander in Chief 1974-1976.

He derived his right to membership from both his great-grandfathers.

Edwin Donaldson, Pvt., Co. K 191 Pennsylvania Volunteer Infantry from February 14, 1965 to June 28, 1965. John Wolz, Pvt., Co. F, 87th Pennsylvania Volunteer Infantry from February 14, 1965 to June 29, 1965 and a great uncle, James McKean, lieutenant colonel, 139th Pennsylvania Volunteer Infantry April 10, 1963 to July 5, 1964 (died in service).

Edwin Donaldson belonged to the GAR Post in New Galilee, PA and later in East Palestine, OH.

John Wolz belonged to the GAR in Pittsburgh, PA.

DONALD H. WORKMAN, is a member of Wa-bu-no, Camp No. 53. He held offices as camp commander, Michigan Department Council and Junior Vice Commander.

His Civil War ancestor was his great-grandfather, Sgt. Joseph F. Workman, who served with Co. D, 80th Indiana Infantry. He enlisted on August 16, 1862 and was discharged on June 22, 1865. He belonged to Thomas J. Brooks Post #322 of Loogootee, IN.

Donald H. Workman   *Joseph F. Workman*

In the fall of 1863, Nancy E. Workman cut a lock of hair from the head of her newborn son, Donald's grandfather, Joseph Nathaniel, tied it neatly with a purple ribbon, mounted it on a small piece of paper and signed the baby's name. The child's father, Joseph F., carried the precious memento throughout the war in a wallet which he kept in the breast pocket of his uniform. During a battle, a rebel bullet struck the soldier on the chest, but did not pierce the wallet, thus saving his life. The blond lock of hair remains a treasured family heirloom to the present day.

RUSSELL J. WUNKER, joined the Sons based on his ancestor, Frederick Wilhelm Hillmann, who was born in Demmin Prussia on June 8, 1834. Emigrating to America in the early 1850s he first settled in Milwaukee, WI where he married Arna Frederike Wilhelmine Remmert on October 19, 1858.

Soon after they moved to Hamilton County, OH and eventually had nine children. Fred Hillmann responded to his nations call and first enlisted at Camp Clay, Pendelton, OH on May 10, 1861. The regiment, recruited by Maj. Burbank was designated the 1st Regt., Kentucky Volunteer Infantry and mustered in June 5. Hillmann was attached to Co. D, under Capt.

David Y. Jones. At the time he was listed as 5'-10' of light complexion with blue eyes. His occupation was listed as locksmith and blacksmith. Remaining in camp until July 10, the regiment was ordered to Ripley and then Charleston and attached to the Kanawha Brigade. Service included Gauley, Camp Piatt and Gauley Bridge. Sunday September 1 they skirmished at Boone Court House where the regiment broke up a confederate military encampment and routed the enemy.

Russell J. Wunker   *Frederick W. Hillmann*

On September 12 in a skirmish 20 miles south of Charleston, Fred Hillmann was Captured the records list him as "taken prisoner by the rebels in a fight on the bank of the Coal River three miles above Peytona, VA" (present day West Virginia).

He was confined in Richmond September 24 and sent to Columbia October 31. By December 3 he was back in Richmond and "sent home March 1, 1862 by General. Winder". His parole was signed in Salisbury, NC on May 28, 1862 and he reported to Camp Chase, OH July 18.

On July 29, 1862 he was "found incapable of performing duties" and discharged by a surgeons certificate and General Order #36.

It appears that he may have served in the defense of Cincinnati under General Lew Wallace in early September 1862 as part of the "Squirrel Hunter" Home Guards.

After the war he proudly marched in The Veterans Parade at the Carthage (Cincinnati) Fair wearing a ribbon which proclaimed him one of "The Boys of '61".

He resided in Hartwell, OH until his death on August 15, 1917 at age 83. Mrs. Hillmann received her Veteran's Widows Pension until her death September 6, 1919.

CHARLES C. YATES, joined the Sons, as a member of Memphis Camp No. 1 of Tennessee on May 5, 1990. He has held the office camp commander.

His Civil War ancestor, Cpl. William H. Bell, served in Co. G, 2nd West Tennessee Cav., Co. G, 7th Tennessee Volunteer Cav., U.S. Army. He enlisted August 5, 1862, and died as a prisoner of war on December 24, 1863.

Charles C. Yates

Charles' great-grandfather, Cpl. William H. Bell, was a 36 year old farmer living in Carroll County, TN with his wife and five children when he enlisted in the U.S. Army on August 5, 1862. He was promoted to corporal in the 2nd Regt., Co. G on September 28, 1862.

Unfortunately, he was captured on June 10, 1863 and transferred to the Confederate Military Prison in Richmond, VA known as Libby. Actually, he, along with most other non-commissioned officers, was confined on the infamous "Belle Island". He died on December 24, 1863, as a result of the inhuman treatment that he and other prisoners received. The cause of death listed as rheumatism and acute diarrhea.

PAUL THOMAS ZEIEN JR., joined the Sons, George Armstrong Custer, Camp One on September 12, 1991.

His Civil War ancestor, great-great-great-grandfather Pvt. John Batterson, served with Co. H, 7th Iowa Volunteer Infantry. He enlisted on August 25, 1862 and was discharged on May 31, 1864.

Paul also had another great-great-great-grandfather, William H. Houghland who served in the Civil War. He was a private in Co. B, 47th Regt., Iowa Vol. Infantry. He was mustered in on May 2, 1864 and mustered out on September 28, 1864.

DANIEL CHARLES ZWIENER, joined as a member-at-large on May 30, 1995.

He bases his right to membership on his great-great-grandfather Corporal Franz Zwiener of Co. E, 20th Wisconsin Vol. Infantry, who enlisted on August 12, 1862.

Franz emigrated from Prussia to America in 1857 with his son and wife and eventually moved to Milford, WI where he had three more sons. When the war broke out, Franz wanted to enlist, but feared that his son, Anton who was 16, would do the same, leaving no one to tend the family farm. After a time, Anton, having moved out, tried to enlist but found he was too young. He was told that his father had enlisted and Anton would be needed to help his mother on the farm.

Franz Zwiener   *Anton J. Zwiener*

Eventually, both Franz and Anton would fight in the war. Franz had enlisted into the Wisconsin Infantry on August 12, 1862, at the age of 35. He fought at Prairie Grove, Van Buren, Vicksburg, Mobile Bay, and Franklin Creek. He was injured at the Franklin which ended his army career and he was discharged on July 14, 1865.

Anton had served with General Banks and his failed campaign along the Red River in Texas. Anton and Franz met up around the time of Mobile Bay.

Franz and Anton returned to farming together after the war. Franz passed away at the age of 91 on March 28, 1918 and was buried next to his beloved wife Theresa in St. Columbanus Cemetery near Blooming Prairie, Minnesota.

Sons of Union Veterans of the Civil War Roster

A

Abell, Richard B.
Able, Donald E.
Abrahams Jr, John H.
Abrams, Jerry A.
Abshire, Jimmie Earl
Ackerman, David
Acton, Charles Henry
Acton, Kenny R.
Acton Jr, Charles Henry
Adams, Ellis C. L.
Adams, Herbert C.
Adams, Jeff
Adams, Joseph F.
Adams, Joseph T.
Adams, Ronald G.
Adams, Sidney R.
Adams, William C.
Adams Jr, Paul W.
Addison, Carl E.
Aeberli, David L.
Ahern, James
Ahlvin, Martin C.
Ainsworth, Rickey W.
Aisenbrey, William E.
Akers, Harold W.
Albaugh, James
Albert, Bruce S.
Albert, Donald L.
Albert, Ronald Lester
Albright, Arnold W.
Albright, John
Alcorn, Raymond E.
Alcorn, Roger A.
Alcorn, Roger C.
Alexander, Bob
Alff, Edward P.
Alger, William E.
Allen, Alfred L.
Allen, Charles G.
Allen, Earl E.
Allen, Federick J.
Allen, James Timothy
Allen, Michael F.
Allen, Thomas James
Allen, William J.
Allgyer, Roy R.
Allison, David L.
Allport, Tom
Allwein, James
Allwein, Paul J.
Allyn, David E.
Alminde, Paul
Altland, Forest
Alves, Arthur
Alvis, Edward A.
Amaducci, Edward C.
Ambacker, Robert
Amsler Jr, Robert J.
Anania, William C.
Anderson, Gerald W.
Anderson, Ernest J.
Anderson, Jeffrey
Anderson, John E.
Anderson, Mark E.
Anderson, Nathan M.
Anderson, Victor J.
Andrascik, Stephen
Angotta, Jim
Ankrom, Albert Daniel
Ankrom, Maurice E.
Anneley, Harry
Anneley, John E.
Anthony, Albert L.
Anthony, Merrill D.
Antill, John G.
Arango, Ruben D.
Archer, John
Armistead, Gene C.
Armistead, Starkey E.
Armstrong, Douglas R.
Armstrong, Kent L.
Armstrong, Michael
Armstrong, Thomas E.
Arndt, David
Arndt, Roan
Arner, Frederick B.
Arnold, Mark L.
Aronis, Ronald M.
Arrequin, Phillip
Arthur, Todd D.
Asher, Gilbert B.
Ashley, Keith D.
Astel, Stephen P.
Astleford Sr, Timothy
Athey Jr, Kenneth
Atkins Jr, Floyd D.
Atkinson, Elmer F.
Atkinson, Frank E.
Atkinson, J. Edward
Atkinson, James
Atkinson, John H.
Atkinson, Richard M.
Atwood, John E.
Auch, George D.
Austin, James T.
Austraw, Henry H.
Aves, Lavern
Aves, Layton
Ayer, Thomas G.
Ayers, Charles L.
Ayers, D. Jon
Ayers, Matthew R.
Ayers, Stanley
Aylesworth, Daniel J.
Aylesworth, Giles H.
Aylesworth, J. Norman
Aylesworth, Jim
Aylesworth, John M.
Aylesworth, Joshua W.
Aylesworth, William R.
Aylsworth, Michael
Ayres, R. W.

B

Babcock, Timothy H.
Babcock II, Gerald
Bachmann, Paul
Backauskas, Michael J.
Backensto, Eric Michael
Backus, Keith
Backus, Mark S.
Bagley, Gilbert B.
Bagnall, Gary A.
Bailey, David C.
Bailey, Merlyn C.
Baker, Charles
Baker, Jerry A.
Baker, John D.
Baker, Richard E.
Baker, Robert L.
Baker II, Harrison
Baldus, John C.
Baldwin, Willard
Ball, Thomas E.
Bandow, Gilbert C.
Baney, John P.
Bankert, Leon F.
Bannan, Robert A.
Bannon, John F.
Barber, Leonard
Barboza Jr, Manual A.
Bardarik, Bruce R.
Bardeen, Charles R.
Barker, Laurence F.
Barlow, D.. Brooks
Barlow, Henry F.
Barnes, Jeffrey L.
Barnes, Jeremy
Barnes, John F.
Barnes, John W.
Barnes, Mark A.
Barnes, Steve
Barnes, Teddy L.
Barnett, Alan
Barney, Warren E.
Barnhart, Jack
Barr, George H.
Barraclough, Bruce A.
Barrell, John B.
Barrett, Timothy W.
Barrett, Wayne J.
Barry, James F.
Barry, Michael T.
Bartel, Steven B.
Barth, David
Barth, James S.
Bartholf, Howard E.
Bartholf, Ryan E.
Bartholf, Scott V.
Bartholf, Stephen H.
Bartholomew, Robert E.
Bartlett, Michael C.
Barton, John
Bash Sr, Michael F.
Bass III, Kenneth C.
Bateman, Brandon S.
Bateman, John M.
Bateman, Richard W.
Bateman, Robert J.
Bateman III, Joseph F.
Bateman Jr, Joseph F.
Bateman Jr, Robert J.
Bauer, Stephen B.
Baughman, Harry
Bauman, Dale
Bauman, Kirby
Baxter, Gregory S.
Bayles Jr, Ronald L.
Beach, Richard
Beach, Thomas M.
Beals Jr, Raymond A.
Bean, Donald R.
Bearce, R. Michael
Beard, D. Michael
Beard, John H.
Beauchamp, Mark L.
Bechtold, Lewis Dean
Beck, Lynn H.
Beck, William E.
Becker, David C.
Becker, Dr Harry G.
Bedlyon Jr, Boyd F.
Bee, Robert
Beggs, Richard K.
Behringer, Samuel
Beitz, Phillip
Belcher, Gary
Belcher, Norbert
Belcher, Peter A.
Belcher, Stephen F.
Belding, Donald
Belert, Kevin J.
Bell, Donald
Bell, Lt Col Crittenden
Bell, Richard
Bellenger, Ronald
Bellerud, Otis Hal
Bellor, Joseph
Bellow, John J.
Bellyoung, Jerome
Belvin, Jerry
Benack, Richard A.
Benda Jr, Frederick R.
Bender, Thomas H.
Benell, Duane A.
Benjamin, Bart S.
Bennett, Alan
Bennett, Daniel V.
Bennett, Elmer J.
Bennett, Herb L.
Bennett, Paul V.
Bennett, Randy
Bennett, William R.
Bennett, Herbert D.
Bennett Jr, Charles W.
Bennetts, Marc R.
Benrud, Charles H.
Benton, David D.
Benton, Virgil L.
Berezovske, David J.
Bergelt, Patrick R.
Bergelt, Paul R.
Bergelt Jr, Philip R.
Bergelt Sr, Philip R.
Berger, James
Berger, Melvyn S.
Berger, Thomas
Bergquist, Brian C.
Berna, Edwin F.
Bernache, William J.
Bernish, Jeffrey
Bernner, David C.
Bernstorf, Philip W.
Bernton, Tashoff
Berridge, Ronald
Berridge, Ryan
Berry, Henry C.
Berry, Philip R.
Bertke, Joe P.
Beston, Laurence O.
Beston, Richard C.
Betterly, Richard D.
Bettinson, Robert M.
Betz, Philip J.
Beuth, Simon
Bezuyen, Glenn L.
Bicker, David G.
Bickford, Brian T.
Bickford, David W.
Biddle, Richard
Billings, Elden Eugene
Binning, G. R.
Birberick, John R.
Birmingham, John M.
Bish, James D.
Bish, James A.
Bishop, Harry W.
Bishop, Harry P.
Bishop, Robert M.
Bittinger, Craig
Bittinger, Donald
Black, Brian J.
Black, Douglas N.
Black, Herman T.
Blackburn, Harold L.
Blackett, Larry L.
Blair, Barton
Blair, Jack
Blair Jr, James J.
Blaisdell, Hal N.
Blake, Clifford F.
Blakeley, David S.
Blakeley, Harry R.
Blakeley, Jeffrey A.
Blakely, Robert G.
Blakeman, David M.
Blaker, Maj Gordon A.
Blanthorn, George A.
Blinebury, Lawrence J.
Blinebury Jr, Joseph
Blodgett Sr, Floyd
Blohm, Patrick H.
Bloom, Daniel J.
Blow, Harold
Blue, Steven E.
Blum, Richard H.
Bly, James L.
Bly, Lee
Bly, Robert J.
Boa Jr, Joseph M.
Boak, Donald R.
Boak II, Donald R.
Bodge, Willard C.
Boehm, Donald J.

Boeskool, Daniel L.
Boldt, William
Bolen, Daniel P.
Bolles, Dennis J.
Bollinger, Richard
Bolyard, Kent
Bond, John R.
Bond, Thomas J.
Booher, Del Victor
Booher, Ned P.
Boone, Gerald M.
Booth, Donald Wade
Booth III, William H.
Boppel, John W.
Bosely, John G.
Bosh, Alan
Bosley, Douglas K.
Bosley, Jan L.
Bosley, Ronald W.
Bosman, Walter M.
Botsford, Harris F.
Botteicher, Thomas E.
Bouvier, Francis
Bouvier, Kenneth
Bowden, Harry L.
Bowen, Rev Norman A.
Bowers, Carl W.
Bowers, Charles M.
Bowers, Harold E.
Bowers, Ronald
Bowers, Steve A.
Bowers, Steven E.
Bowers, Terry B.
Bowers, William H.
Bowersox, J. Richard
Bowham, William
Bowman, Leroy
Boyd, Don
Boyd, Duane
Bpnvouloir, Gerald
Bracken, Hon Frank A.
Brackman, Joseph
Bradbury Jr, Stephen H.
Bradbury Sr, Paul E.
Braden, John
Bradford, Kevin
Bradley, Melvin J.
Brady, Scott
Brady II, James
Brague, Norman
Branch, Ellis S.
Brand, Michael C.
Brandon, John T.
Branson, Duane C.
Brashear, David S.
Brass, David E.
Brasser, Dale J.
Braun, Mark
Braund, Richard
Bravy, George T.
Breakwell, David
Breakwell Sr, David T.
Breckner, Mark L.
Breiner, Charles M.
Brennan, Bill
Brennan, Mark
Brennan, Ronald W.
Brennan Jr, Philip M.
Bresee, Thomas B.
Bresneman, Thomas
Bretz Jr, Rev Donald W.
Brewer, Garry
Brewer, Mark E.
Brickner, Thomas W.
Bridgwater, Christian H.
Bridwell, Dennis J.
Briggs, Errol
Briggs, Jeff
Briggs, Robert A.
Brinkman, Robert H.
Brinkman, William Guy
Britton, Mark
Brobst, Richard
Brock, Michael R.
Brockway, John H.
Brodd, Thomas
Brodie, Edward Fulford
Brogle, James J.
Bromley, Robert
Bronson, Glenn C. S.
Bronson, John O.
Bronson, Wade H. S.
Brooks, Kenneth
Brookshire, Carl A.
Brower, Ronald L.
Brown, Arthur C.
Brown, Charles
Brown, Donald
Brown, Donald E.
Brown, Ellsworth W.
Brown, Francis C.
Brown, Gregory A.
Brown, Howard F.
Brown, Jeffrey P.
Brown, Jeremy B.
Brown, Jim
Brown, Norman D.
Brown, Odell
Brown, Richard
Brown, Richard C.
Brown, Robert G.
Brown, Robert A.
Brown, Robert
Brown, Ronald E.
Brown, Russell R.
Brown, Steven D.
Brown, Sylvester
Brown, Terry M.
Brown, William M.
Brown, William K.
Brown Sr, William
Browne, Robert
Brumfield, R. Carlyon
Bryan, David G.
Bryg, Gary
Bub, Michael
Bubb, Kirby
Buchanan, Martin
Buck, Edward C.
Buck, James R.
Budler, Michael
Buffamoyer, David S.
Buffamoyer, Mark E.
Buffington, Thomas E.
Bunnell, Daniel
Bunnell, William
Burbank, Mathew S.
Burbank, Robert E.
Burchard Jr, Henry C.
Burden, Jeffrey C.
Burg, Kevin
Burgess, George
Burgin, Phillip A.
Burk, Anthony P.
Burk, Jon
Burke, Thomas
Burns, Thomas F.
Burns, William John
Burns III, Robert W.
Burns Jr, James G.
Burridge, C. Wayne
Burroughs, Randall
Burt, Warren
Burton, Paul C.
Burton, Robert E.
Bury II, Gordon R.
Buschmann, John R.
Bush, Ralph
Bussawich, Stan
Butcher Jr, Robert
Butler, Dale H.
Butler, Dr Bruce B.
Butler, Milton Y.
Butler, Robert
Butler Jr, Lyle A.
Butler Sr, David A.
Butman, Gardner M.
Butterfield, Kenneth
Buxton, Robert
Byrne Jr, Paul J.

C

Caddy, Orwin W.
Cahoon, John G.
Cahoon, Stephen
Cahoon Jr, Donald B.
Cain III, Edward A.
Calabrese, Alex
Caldarelli, Richard
Calder, Dale F.
Caldwell, Drexell
Caldwell, William N.
Calhoon, George F.
Callahan, William J.
Cameron, Christopher D.
Cameron Esq, John C.
Camien, Ralph R.
Campbell, Richard T.
Campbell III, John
Cancelliere, Carmen A.
Cannon, Clyde
Cannon, Thomas A.
Canwell, Harold W.
Capwell, Benjamin F.
Carbaugh, Charles
Carlo, John W.
Carlson, David B.
Carlson, Dr Roger D.
Carlson, Jeffrey G.
Carlson, Merle
Carlson, Randall L.
Carlson, Rev Paul R.
Carmer, George
Carmer, Wm Franklin
Carmichael, Jack K.
Carmichael, Jack W.
Carmosino, Sal
Carney, John W.
Carney Jr, John A.
Carnprobst, John
Carpenter, Eugene
Carpenter, Horace Nye
Carpenter, Larry
Carpenter, Richard A.
Carpenter Jr, George D.
Carpenter Sr, Brian S.
Carr, William F.
Carrera, Salvatore
Carroll, Walter G.
Carroll, William V. N.
Carroon, Robert G.
Carson, Bruce G.
Carson Jr, Alexander G.
Carter, Joseph O.
Carver, James F.
Cary Jr, Robert H.
Casamer, Douglas M.
Case, Lynn M.
Casline, Jamie S.
Casline, Jeffrey L.
Cassio, Irvin
Castle, Sidney
Catlett, Kenneth R.
Cauldwell, Frederick S.
Cavalier, Philip A.
Cavanaugh, Rodney E.
Cavanaugh III, George M.
Cavender, William B.
Cavender, William K.
Cavender, William R.
Cavender Jr, William K.
Cecero, Glen A.
Celmer, Stanley
Chace III, George F.
Challahan, Daniel J.
Challahan, Timothy T.
Chambers, Charles E.
Chambers, Ken
Chapman, Ronald B.
Chapman, Wade
Chapman, William T.
Charland, Michael
Chassels, John L.
Chauvin, Daniel A.
Cheney, Donald
Chesnut, N. Robert
Chew III, A. Kendall
Chier, Donald A.
Chisholm, Douglas C.
Chramosta, Rick L.
Chriscaden Jr, Kenneth C.
Chrisman, Glenn L.
Chrispyn, Douglas W.
Christian, Charles L.
Christie, Richard
Christman, Roger
Church, James E.
Church, Steve
Church III, Coleman F.
Clancy, Thomas
Clanton, Robert
Clapsaddle, Dale H.
Clark, Alan
Clark, Barry P.
Clark, Charles
Clark, Hugh
Clark, James V.
Clark, James A.
Clark, Kenneth
Clark, Larry J.
Clark, Robert T.
Clark, Ronald E.
Clayborn III, William J.
Clement III, Roy L.
Clement Jr, Roy L.
Clements, James S.
Clifford, Philip J.
Clooney, Vincent
Coates, Douglas
Coates Jr, Louis B.
Coats, Jr, J. B.
Cobb, Richard
Coblentz, Jacob
Cochran, John C.
Cochran, Joshua W.
Codding, Layman Edward
Coddling Jr, Ernest M.
Codigan, Francis C.
Codigan, Kevin J.
Coffelt, Jerry A.
Coffman Jr, Dean F.
Cohan, Richard C.
Cohoon, Jerry
Cohoon, Leo
Coin, Ken
Colburn, Rolland D.
Cole, Ralph
Cole, Raymond
Cole, Thomas
Coleman, James B.
Coleman, Newton C.
Coleman, Clifford B.
Collar, Donald P.
Collar, Jeffrey Paul
Collar, Patrick Aaron
Collette, Clarence A.
Colley, Douglas F.
Colley, James
Collier, Dale
Collier, Gary A.
Collier, Shannon R.
Collins, Carroll J.
Collins, Dean J.
Collins, Harry G.
Collins, Paul Lee
Collins, William E.
Combs, Fred
Comee, Irving
Compston, Kevin B.
Conforti, Alfred F.
Conger, David A.
Conklin, David E.
Conklin, Robert
Conley, Edward T.
Conley, Timothy

Conley Jr, Edward F.
Conlow, Robert E.
Connard, George W.
Connell, James R.
Connell, Michael J.
Conrad, Donald
Conrad, Mark Blair
Conroy, Cyril J.
Conte Jr, George A.
Conwell, Gary
Cook, David L.
Cook, Dr Wayne B.
Cook, Francis J.
Cook, Gordon
Cook, Jonathan C.
Cook, Matthew
Cook, Michael
Cookenham Jr, Walter
Coomer Jr, Robert F.
Coon, Alan D.
Coon, John R.
Cooper, Charles R.
Cooper, Everett K.
Coppel, Lewis
Corbett, Lawrence
Corbett, Mark T.
Corbett, Walter
Corbett IV, Lawrence W.
Corbin, Vernon Gary
Corcoran, Thomas
Cordell, Robert R.
Corey, Eric A.
Corey, Fred
Corfman, Daniel
Corfman, Charles
Corley, Edward
Cornell, Craig R.
Corning, Edgar E.
Corson, Barry A.
Costello, John E.
Costello, William C.
Costigan, Arthur
Cothern, John William
Cottle, Robert
Cottrell, Mark
Cottrell, Steve
Cottrell, Weston F.
Couch, Carl G.
Couling, Alan L.
Coulson, James F.
Coulton, Peter M.
Counts, Charles
Couris, John G.
Coval, John J.
Covelens, Patrick
Covelens, Sean
Covelens Jr, James
Covell, Carlton E.
Covey, Leslie E.
Cox, Bradley
Cox, Christopher L.
Cox, Clifford
Cox, Donald J.
Cox, Gregory
Cox, Norman L.
Cox, Ronnie
Cox, Shawn

Cox Jr, Donald P.
Coyle, Charles
Craft, John
Craig, Colin
Crain, Richard W.
Cramp, Cliff
Crane, Gary
Crane Jr, James R.
Crawford, James D.
Crawford, McClenand B.
Crawford, Robert H.
Crawford, Samuel
Crawford, William
Crawford Jr, Thomas C.
Creek, Malcolm A.
Cregar, Charles
Creyer, Kenneth H.
Crilley, Charles M.
Crilley, Douglas M.
Crisp, Jay W.
Crispin, Guy
Crockatt, David William
Crockett Jr, Thomas H.
Croisant, Ray
Cromwell, Richard
Crorkin, Ken
Crump, J. Griffin
Cryder, Wayne F.
Cubberly, Richard
Cuckler, William T.
Culbertson, Robert Lee
Cullen, Edward
Cullen, F. Kevin
Cullinane, Henry
Culp, Michael
Cummings, Scott A.
Cummings, Terrence R.
Cunningham, John D.
Cunningham, Gary
Cunningham, James T.
Cunnion, Frank
Cupps, Robert
Cureton Jr, William
Curfman MD, David R.
Curtis, Clinton
Curtis, George H.
Curtis, Paul
Cushard, Edgar
Cusson, Robert H.
Cutchens, Jack O.
Cuyler, Brent L.
Cuyler, Louis E.
Cuyler, Richard
Cypert, James R.

D

Dahm, Richard
Daily Jr, Jerry
Daley, Norman G.
Daley, Tim
Dallery, Edgar L.
Dampier, Brian
Daniels, Anthony
Daniels, Kenneth J.
Daniels, Robert M.
Daniels, Thomas
Danielson, David

Dannecker, Russell
Darby, Donald E.
Darby, Ryan
Dark, James W.
Darling, Mikell C.
Darlington, E. Dillwyn
Darnell, Billy J.
Dartt Sr, William H.
Dates, Jason R.
Daubert, Frederick F.
Dauchy, Robert G.
Davidson, Kerry
Davis, Cameron P.
Davis, Charles E.
Davis, Charles A.
Davis, Clyde
Davis, Donald D.
Davis, Dr Lee W.
Davis, George
Davis, Harold
Davis, J. Brooks
Davis, James Herbert
Davis, Jeffrey S.
Davis, Mark
Davis, Michael
Davis, Robert
Davis, Steven W.
Davis, Warren R.
Davis, Wayne
Davis, William K.
Davis III, James R.
Davis Jr, John H.
Davis Jr, William A.
Davison, Robert
Dawson, Dan
Dawson, John C.
Daxby, Donald
Day, James
De Cook, Stephen K.
Dean, Homer
Deatrick Jr, David R.
Debo, Darrell
DeCastro, Allen
Deckenback, Ronald
Decker, Charles F.
Decker, David W.
DeCusati, Andrew
Dee, Anthony S.
Deeben, John P.
DeForest, Robert W.
DeHaan, Herman J.
Deible, Jerry M.
Delacy Jr, Anthony B.
Delaney, Harry A.
DeLaney, Robert E.
Delano, Andrew C.
Delano, Clinton T.
Delano, Hugh S.
Delano, Lance C.
Delbridge, Tim C.
Dellacato, David
Dellion, Michael
Delman, Richard D.
DeMoll, Octavius N.
Demond III, Ulysses Grant
DeMott, Joseph J.
Dempsey Jr, Raymond

Denbow, Carl Jon
Denison, Donald G.
Dennis, John D.
Dent, Ross S.
DePathy, Mark
DePeyster, Pierre J.
Derby, Daniel W.
Derby, Robert L.
Derby, Thomas D.
Dern Jr, Charles H.
DeRosa, Jeffrey A.
Derr II, Dennis Clark
Dershem, Paul E.
Desloover, Charles
DesRosiers, Joseph A.
Deutsch, William
DeVeau, Scott D.
Dever Jr, William J.
Devlin, Edward
Devlin, Robert William
DeVoe, Richard Paul
Devol, Jerry B.
DeVre, John
DeWert, Gordon H.
Diamond, James Walter
Dick, Stanton
Dickens, Keith T.
Dickens, Norris S.
Dickerson, Laurence E.
Dickey, Dale L.
Dickey, Gary Allen
Dickey, Kenneth M.
Dier-Zimmel, Kevin
Dietz Jr, David W.
DiFazio, John M.
Dile, Kenneth C.
Dilley, Thomas
Dillon, John A.
Dillon, Walter
DiLoretto, Daniel V.
Dingman, Justin L.
Dinstel, Edward R.
Dix, Walter G.
Dixon, Dodd D.
Dixon, Peter A.
Dluge, Robert L.
Doenges, Rev Richard
Dolan, John E.
Dollar, Nicholas J.
Dolph, Allen N.
Dolph, Dr Gary E.
Doman, Victor E.
Donahue, Malcolm M.
Donahue, Joseph R.
Donly, Joseph
Donly III, Joseph
Donohue, Robert J.
Donovan, Matthew H.
Dorney, James D.
Dorrington, Leo
Dostall, Roger J.
Doty Sr, Willard E.
Doud, Raymond Gary
Douglas, John
Douglas Jr, Harry E.
Douglass Jr, James B.
Dover, James

Dow, Gary
Dow, James E.
Dow, Randy
Dowd, Craig W.
Dowd, Edgar
Downey, Richard
Downing, David
Doyle, Daniel S.
Doyle, Merlin T.
Doyle, Timothy
Doyle, Warren A.
Doyle, William
Drake, Harold L.
Drake, Paul D.
Drake, Paul R.
Drake, Raymond
Drake, Robert
Drew, Michael
Drew Jr, Louis E.
Drew Sr, John A.
Drisscoll, John
Droege-Binsfeld, John
Drolsbaugh, Robert E.
Druckemiller, Robert M.
Druckemiller, Roger M.
Drzewiecki, Mike
Dudley, Michael D.
Duffel, Edward James
Duffy, George J.
Dugan, Goodling H.
Duke, Alan R.
Dumas, David W.
Dumond, Henry F.
Dunbrack, Melvin H.
Duncan, Herbert E.
Duncan, John
Duncan II, Clarence
Dunham, Lester R.
Dunham, Phillip
Dunkelberger, Karl
Dunkelman, Mark H.
Dunlap, George R.
Dunlop, Ross T.
Dunn, Craig L.
Dunn Jr, James
Dunn Jr, Walter K.
Durling, Fred A.
Durning Jr, Thomas F.
Durrell Jr, C. A.
Duryea, Cleon
Dusenberry, Kenneth A.
Dutcher, Desmond G. I.
Dutcher, Laurence I.
Dutcher III, Russell K.
Dutcher Jr, Russell K.
Dvorak, William C.
Dwyer, Douglas A.
Dyer Jr, Dr Robert

E

Eaby, Douglas B.
Eads, Fred
Earle, James S.
Early, Jack Jones
Early, Stephen B.
Earnshaw, George W.
Easterwood, Paul A.

Eastman, Albert R.
Eastman, Roland E.
Eaton, David
Eberhardt, John C.
Eberling, Bob
Eberly, Robert E.
Ebert, Robert D.
Echelberger, Randy
Eck, Dean
Eck, James E.
Eck, Robert J.
Eck, Robert T.
Eckert, Charles H.
Eckert, Thomas
Eckley, Harry W.
Eckley, Mark S.
Eddingfield, David Dean
Eddingfield, Edward R.
Eddingfield, Steven G.
Edmundson, James E.
Edmundson, James V.
Edwards, Charles G.
Edwards, Mark A.
Effle, Bill
Eichelman, Fred Dr R.
Eichhorn, Gary E.
Eichinger, Frederick
Eikenberry, Gayle A.
Eiklor Sr, Luther E.
Eisenberg, Robert
Eker, Darrell J.
Eker, Dennis L.
Eker, Donald B.
Ekstrand, Kenneth P.
El, Albert L.
Elberfeld, Michael R.
Elberfeld, Robert
Elder, Paul W.
Eldgr, Paul W.
Eldridge, Joseph P.
Eldridge, William W.
Elkins, Roger B.
Eller, Byron H.
Eller, Edwin
Elliott, Lyman
Elliott Jr, Ward J.
Elliott Sr, Ward J.
Ellis, Keith A.
Ellis, Thomas
Elmore, Steven
Elswick, William
Emerick, Benjamin P.
Emerick, David J.
Emerick, Jonathan D.
Emerick, Peter B.
Emerick, Thomas L.
Emerick, Thomas J.
Emerson, Randy
Emery, Steven Glen
Emett, Michael S.
Emmerich, Anthony
Enderle, Ross
Engel, John C.
England Jr, L. Stanford
Engler, Charles
English, Joseph

Eno, Frederic M.
Eno Jr, Stanley W.
Enright, Edmund
Ensley, Brian J.
Epley, John W.
Erb, Mike E.
Erffmeyer, Robert
Erickson, Mahgon
Erlick Jr, Ralph P.
Errington, Timothy A.
Erwin, Raymond Maurice
Eshelman, Edgar M.
Essenwein, Richard
Estep, Richard J.
Esterline, John D.
Estervig, Nathan
Estridge, Willard G.
Etter, Randy L.
Etter Jr, Thomas C.
Etters, James E.
Evans, Edward L.
Evans, Jeffery
Evans, Louis
Evans, Rodney
Evans Jr, Otis
Evans Sr, Otis
Evelien, Harry
Everett, Don W.
Everett, Herbert D.
Everhart, Donald R.
Ewald, Erich L.
Ewald Jr, Harold K.
Ewing, Clay
Ewing, James C.
Ewing, Thomas E.
Excell, William C.
Excell, William S.

F
Faatz, Edward A.
Fahey, Edward P.
Faig, Fred
Fairchild, Timothy G.
Falcetti, James
Falcetti, Steven
Falcetti, Victor
Faley Jr, Thomas E.
Faling, Douglas J.
Falkowski, John C.
Faller, Philip E.
Falzini, Mark W.
Farley, James A.
Farrar, Arlan
Farrell, John F.
Farrell, William
Farris, Kenneth
Fasnacht, Clair M.
Fasnacht, Scott M.
Faubion, Craig S.
Faulkner, David S.
Faust, Eugene
Feeney, Thomas
Feeny, Eric L.
Feist, Albert C.
Feist, Leonard
Felber, Robert A.

Feldmeyer, Karl F.
Felker, Barry L.
Felty, Robert
Fenton, Blondell T.
Fenton, Tom
Ferguson, Cecil Wayne
Fern, Thomas B.
Feron, David
Ferraro, Gerald L.
Ferraro, Julius G.
Ferrick, Raymond J.
Ferricks, Donald D.
Ferris, James Gary
Ferry, John W.
Fetrow, Earl E.
Fetterman, Charles
Fetters Jr, George F.
Fettinger, Mike
Fick, Ronald L.
Fickett Jr, George L.
Fields, W. Brooks
Finchenor Jr, George
Finchenor Sr, George A.
Findon, George
Finn, Richard W.
Finney, Thomas
Fish, Donald G.
Fisher, Reilley E.
Fisher, William R.
Fisk, Frederic M.
Fiske, Gregory
Fitzpatrick, Kelly D.
Fitzsimmons Jr, Clarence H.
Flagg, George E.
Flaherty, Robert T.
Flaherty, Thomas M.
Fleck, William J.
Fleck, William R.
Flegle, Larry
Fleming, Robert C.
Flesher, Robert Lee
Fletcher, Roland A.
Fletcher, William
Flora, James D.
Fluhart, Danny M.
Flynn, Eugene P.
Flynn, William
Flynn II, Ellis
Foersterling, Terry
Fogerson, Larry W.
Foight III, Frank A.
Foltz, George E.
Fontella, Jason J.
Foote, John
Ford, Larry
Ford, Raymond
Ford, Stephen O.
Forsyth, Michael J.
Forsythe, Roger W.
Foster, George
Foster, James
Foster, Milton L.
Foster, Paul E.
Foulks, Stuart J.
Fournier, Ronald F.
Foust, Arnold B.
Fout, Stanley L.

Fox, Arthur B.
Fox, Victor I.
Fox, William G.
Fraboni, James
Fradella, Gary
Frain, Michail S.
Frake, Timothy P.
Francis Jr, John
Frank, Eric M.
Frank, Richard L.
Frankenberg, Ernst
Frankenfield, William L.
Frantz, Karl J.
Frantz Jr, Ivan E.
Frantz Sr, Ivan E.
Fraser, Bert
Fraunfelter, Charles R.
Fraunfelter, Eric R.
Fraunfelter, Gregory R.
Fraunfelter, Jeffrey R.
Fraunfelter, Kevin R.
Fraunfelter, Ray K.
Frech, Philip
Freck, William
Frederick, Edward R.
Frederick, Francis R.
Frederick Jr, Robert W.
Freeman, Bryan E.
Freeman, Edward P.
French, William A.
Friday, Sgt James R.
Friedel, Michael G.
Friedline, James H.
Friend, Jerry S.
Fronkier, James T.
Frost, Howard T.
Fry, James E.
Fry, Michael J.
Frye, David A.
Frye, James
Fryer, Larry K.
Fudger, Allen L.
Fuehr, Elmer
Fuhrmann, Kenneth R.
Fuller, Charles R.
Fuller, Harold W.
Fuller, Larry R.
Fuller, Michael J.
Fuller, Perry G.
Fullerton, Donald M.
Fulmer, Tim K.
Fulton, Paul
Funck, Jeffrey A.
Funck III, Charles
Funk, Earl H.
Funk, John L.
Furman, Norman R.
Furney, Harmon
Furst, Paul

G
Gabehart, Richard
Gaboriault, Paul H.
Gabriel, James
Gaffin, Beau
Gaffin, Carl
Gage, David P.

Gage, Herbert R.
Gagne, Kevin D.
Galbraith, Charles Thomas
Gale, Gordon E.
Gallagher, David
Gallagher, Eugene W.
Gallagher, Jeff
Gallant, Kevin J.
Gallant, Roger M.
Galli, Anthony P.
Galvin, John J.
Gamble, Robert R.
Gamm, Charles R.
Gammache, Michael E.
Gammell, Charles V.
Gancas, Ronald
Gaouette, Mike
Gardner, Calvin
Gardner, John W.
Gardner, William H.
Garesche, Winston
Garey, Benjamin C.
Garland, Leroy
Garner, John
Garner, Steven C.
Gasper, Joseph L.
Gass, James B.
Gaughan, Thomas J.
Gauthier, Joseph L.
Geary, Francis J.
Gebhart, Victor H.
Geelan, Charles W.
Geer, Ronald
Geesey, Edwin P.
Gehrig, John A.
Geist, Jeffrey
Gelzhiser Jr, Wilbert
Gentz, Roy G.
Gentzel, Warren G.
Genzel, Ron
Genzel, Stanley G.
George, Daniel P.
Georgia, David C.
Gerald, Kenneth
Gerard, Thomas
Geris, Anthony
Gerke, Robert E.
Gerke, Theodore
Gerlander, Lee
Gerlander, Randal
Gerlander, Todd
Gerritsen, Francis
Getman, Clyde J.
Gettings, Duane
Getty, James A.
Geyer, John
Giampetruzzi, Robert F.
Gibble, Stephen R.
Gibson, Gary L.
Gibson, Hubert C.
Gibson, Mark
Gibson, Norman
Gibson Jr, Elwood Watson
Gidley, Warren
Gidley Jr, Russell M.
Giffey, Neil
Giffin, Terrance A.

Gifford, Aylmer H.
Gilbert, John
Gilbert, Lloyd T.
Gilbert, Michael T.
Gilbert, Ralph
Gilday, Brian P.
Gilday, Harry N.
Gill, Ron
Gilland, Leroy W.
Gillespie, Jerry L.
Gillette, Paul S.
Gillilan II, Richard L.
Gillis, Vern D.
Gillmor, Clarence
Gilman, Christopher W.
Gilmore, Michael C.
Gilson, Charles D.
Gilson, Michael L.
Gimber, Steve
Gittings, Floyd E.
Glass, Christopher D.
Glass, Richard A.
Gleason, Frederick B.
Gleason, Wayne
Glendinng, Peter
Glennon, P. Clarke
Glennon, Rogers
Gloeckner, David E.
Goddard Jr, William Carl
Godfrey, Edwin L.
Goethe, Maynard
Gogel, Richard J.
Goggin, William
Goldberg, Richard A.
Goldsberry, Drennan H.
Goldsberry, Randall L.
Goldsmith, Gaylen
Gooch, Rex Allen
Goodwin, Albert J.
Goold, Roy D.
Goolsby, Charles R.
Gorbet, Clay
Gordon, Jim
Gordon Jr, Henry A.
Gordon Jr, James H.
Gore, Edward R.
Gore, Thomas S.
Goret, Mark
Gorgane, Robert J.
Gorman, Terrance
Gosling, Brian H.
Gottschalk, Michael D.
Gottwald, Arthur P.
Gould, Federick E.
Gould, William W.
Gould IV, William B.
Gowen, Dana L.
Gowen II, Dana L.
Gowens, Olen R.
Grable, Daniel H.
Gradeless, Donald E.
Grady, Paul W.
Graham, Norbert
Graham, Robert M.
Graham, Thomas W.
Grant, Calvin Stewart
Grant, Malcom Allen

Grant, Norman W.
Graves, Daniel Vernon
Graves, Roger
Gray, Allen B.
Gray, Dennis B.
Gray, Robert G.
Gray, Rodney W.
Grayshaw, James R.
Greaves, James P.
Greeley, Donald
Green, Dewey
Green, Gerald
Green, Harold
Green, John J.
Green, John
Green, Robert E.
Green III, James E.
Green Jr, James E.
Green, Guy R.
Greene, Philip H.
Greene, Richard
Greenlee, Edward M.
Greenwalt, Richard L.
Greer, John A.
Gregory, Alfred
Gregory, John B.
Gregory, Jonathan M.
Gregory, Robert J.
Gregory, Russell C.
Grenshaw, Fred
Griffen, Robert
Griffin, Ernest
Griffith, Gary
Griffith, Neil
Griffiths, John G.
Grilley, Charles
Grim, Christopher
Grim, David
Grim, George
Grim, Harold
Grim, James
Grim, Max
Grim, Paul
Grim, Raymond M.
Grim, Robert Elroy
Grim, Rodney R.
Grim, Willard
Grimes, Johnie
Grimm, Webster H.
Grismer, James A.
Groce, Walter R.
Groft, Charles J.
Grosebeck, Geoffrey A.
Gross, Albert G.
Gross, Richard
Grothe, Jack G.
Grove, S. Allen
Grover, Robert L.
Groves, Duane A.
Groves, Steven A.
Grow, Albert J.
Grubb, F. Dale
Grumme, Franz A.
Grunska, Kip M.
Gruver, Carl E.
Guarinello, James
Gubbe, Dale K.

Guider, James J.
Guillotte, William J.
Guiot, Brian
Guldan Jr, Joseph A.
Gulick, Brad N.
Gumm, George J.
Gummere, David C.
Gumpf, David S.
Gunn MD, Albert E.
Gunvelsen, Krist D.

H
Hackel, Donald Lee
Hackney, W. Gery
Haecker, Rex
Hafer, Sebastin R.
Haffner, Craig A.
Hageman, Kevin W.
Hager, William R.
Haggerty, Walter
Hainer, Garrie
Haines, Christopher H.
Haire, Dan M.
Halbert, James W.
Halbert, Virgil A.
Hale, Daniel A.
Hale, David
Hale, Paul
Hales, Wayne A.
Hall, Dan G.
Hall, Herbert P.
Hall, Jason W.
Hall, Richard
Hall, Robert R.
Hall, Robert N.
Hall Jr, Malcolm S.
Hall Jr, Robert E.
Hallenbeck, Brian
Haller, Matthew F.
Halpin, William J.
Halsey, Richard L.
Halsey Jr, Hobert S.
Hamilton, Jimmy L.
Hamilton Sr, Charles
Hammer, James L.
Hammer, Lowell V.
Hammer, Theodore F.
Hammer Sr, Arthur W.
Hampton, Robert D.
Hanlon, Jeffrey C.
Hann, David
Hann, Herbert
Hann, Scott
Hannon, Barry T.
Hans, Daniel W.
Hanscom, Theodore R.
Hansley, Robert
Hanusik, William
Harbison, Bruce R.
Harbour, Michael
Hardenburg, Darrell Owen
Harding, Douglas M.
Harding, Steven E.
Hardy, Arnold
Hardy, Herbert
Hardy, Lester R.
Hare, William

Harkness, David W.
Harper, Douglas A.
Harper, Glenn
Harper, Wayne
Harrington, David P.
Harrington, Robert
Harris, Chris M.
Harris, David E.
Harris, Herbert C.
Harris, Jeffrey N.
Harris, Kenneth W.
Harris, Phillip Lee
Harris, Richard A.
Harris, Ronald Lee
Harris Jr, Jessie D.
Harrison, George
Harrison, John W.
Harrison, John
Harrison, Keith G.
Harrison, Nathan Lewis
Harrison, Richard
Hart, John M.
Hartford, John H.
Harthy, Charles O.
Hartley, Joseph G.
Hartman, Andrew T.
Harvey, Paul
Harvey, William B.
Haskins, Wyman
Hatch, William F.
Hatleberg, James L.
Hauff, Robert
Hauff, Thomas
Hawk, Randall
Hawk Jr, Russell W.
Hawkins, Charles S.
Hawkins, Elwood E.
Hawkins, Sean
Haws Jr, John F.
Hay, Gene R.
Hay, David L.
Hayes, Edward J.
Hayes, Edward
Hayes, Gerald J.
Hayes, Greg
Hayes, Oliver W.
Hayes, Thomas
Hayes Jr, Donald P.
Hayes Jr, G. Joseph
Hayner, Harold C.
Hayner Sr, Clyde H.
Hayward, James Bert
Hazel, Robert W.
Heagy, Charles J.
Heald, Robert W.
Healey, Paul
Healy, Robert
Heaton III, Hylon
Heberling, William G.
Heckman, Robert M.
Heenan, Charles
Heffner, Robert W.
Heidt, Michael P.
Heim, Jack
Heiman, Gerard G.
Heimbach, Paul J.
Heiple, Hon James D.

Heiple, Jeremy H.
Heiple, Jonathan J.
Heiple, Roger
Heisler, Charles E.
Held, Frederick G.
Heller, Charles E.
Heller, James B.
Heller, Robert V.
Helm, L. Dean
Helm, Terry
Hembel, Alan G.
Hemcher, George H.
Henderson, Raymond T.
Henderson, Richard
Hendrickson, Paul L.
Hendrickson, Terry L.
Hendrickson III, Samuel T.
Hendrickson Jr, Samuel T.
Henke, Cliff
Henne, Franklin S.
Hennessey, Paul
Hennessy, Paul R. L.
Henry, Robert
Henry Jr, Roy Lee
Hensler, William A.
Hensley, Robert M.
Hepler, Robert R.
Herlinger, Fred W.
Herlinger, James A.
Herman, Richard
Herrman, Douglas E.
Hershberger, Kenneth D.
Hervan, Joseph W.
Hess, Edward V.
Hewitt, Donald R.
Heydenrich, James G.
Heywood Jr, Robert P.
Hibbert, Robert G.
Hickerson, John W.
Hickey IV, Dennis J.
Hickrod, G. Alan
Hicks, Leroy W.
Hiestand, Richard
Higgins, Floyd
Higgins, John J.
Higgins, Stephen S.
Higley Jr, Wayne E.
Hile, Thomas W.
Hileman, Roger D.
Hilfiker, Gary
Hill, Dave
Hill, Karl F.
Hill, Richard A.
Hill, Richard J.
Hill, Stephen W.
Hill, Welcome E.
Hillard, Jeffrey
Hillery, Thomas H.
Hilligoss, Edward E.
Hilliker, Dale L.
Hilliker, David L.
Hills, Duane
Hills, John L.
Hillsgrove, Raymond A.
Hiltner, Michael
Hilton, James E.

Hilton, Tobias
Hilton Sr, John D.
Hilyer, Jack M.
Hines, Roger W.
Hinger, Harry
Hinkley, James C.
Hinkley, Willard
Hinner, Harold H.
Hinner, Wade H.
Hinton, Danny
Hinton, Neal J.
Hipfel, Steven J.
Hirschmann, Arthur K.
Hirschy Sr, Joseph A.
Hitchcock, Andrew
Hitchery, Joseph L.
Hittle, Gen J. Donald
Hively, Henry Lyman
Hoadley, Linn P.
Hoar, Jay S.
Hobart, Clifford
Hobbs, Michael
Hoch, Curtis P.
Hoch, Don E.
Hodgens, Stephen
Hodges, Harold H.
Hodges, Merle J.
Hodges, Paul
Hodgson, James R.
Hoffer, Donald L.
Hoffman, Howard A.
Hoffman, Philip E.
Hoffman III, R. Jacob
Hofmann, Joseph D.
Hogan, Brian
Hogan, Edward
Holbrook, Frederick
Holbrook, Thomas C.
Holbrook Jr, Samuel P.
Holcombe, Ronald M.
Holdgrieve, Irwin
Holgate, Wayne B.
Holien, Kim B.
Holmes, Everett J.
Holmes, Gary
Holmes, Scott W.
Holmes Sr, Clyde R.
Holser, William C.
Holt, Bruce
Holt, Charles
Holt, Craig
Holt, Dave
Holt, H. Barry
Holt, Mark
Holt Jr, F. Russell
Holter, Roy A.
Holton, Todd D.
Hooks, Matthew M.
Hooper, Paul W.
Hooper, Wallace
Hooper, William W.
Hoover, David A.
Hoover, William
Hopkins, Charles M.
Hopkins, Don R.
Hopkins, James
Hopkins Jr, Leroy T.

Horcher, Rudolph F.
Horgan Jr, Michael R.
Horn, William R.
Hornberger, Robert
Horr, Charles
Horvath, John D.
Hosier Jr, Scott F.
Hosler, Roderick A.
Hosmer, Roger
Hotaling, Kerry G.
Hotaling, E. Gage
Houchin, Joe
Houghtaling, Gary
Houghtaling, Gerald (Jack)
Houghtaling, Rick
Houghton, Allen N.
Houser, Jack K.
Houston, Jerry E.
Hovis Jr, Logan W.
Howard, Dennis
Howard, Melvin R.
Howard, Steven R.
Howe, Herbert F.
Howell, Keith M.
Howell, Kent Francis
Howell, Samson A.
Howey, Allen W.
Hoxie, Wilbar M.
Hoyt, George L.
Hoyt, Rodney
Hubbard, Charles T.
Hubbard, Joseph H.
Huber, Douglas M.
Hudkins, James
Hudson, Timothy R.
Huebner, Richard A.
Huebner, Ronald G.
Huff, Grover R.
Huff, Paul
Huffman, Philip D.
Huffman, Harry V.
Hughes, Ben F.
Hughes, Carroll L.
Hughes, Donald
Hughes, John
Hughes, John B.
Hughes, Sean O.
Hull, Harvey
Hull, Jeffrey Lee
Hull, LaVail
Hulshart, Carl M.
Hulshart, Rance
Humes, Alex B.
Hummer Jr, Wayne G.
Humphrey, Erwin
Humphrey, John T.
Humphrey, Richard H.
Humphreys, Storer
Hunsaker II, Robert M.
Hunt, Aaron
Hunt, David P.
Hunt, Geoffrey R.
Hunting, Roger B.
Hutchinson, James M.
Hutchinson, Paul J.
Hutchinson, Ray
Hutchinson, Thomas F.

Huth, Michael
Hutton, Kenneth
Hyland, Matthew

I
Ihrig, Bryan
Immel, Paul L.
Immel, Paul M.
Ingram, Jack E.
Ingram, James C.
Isaacs, Bertram

J
Jackson, Franklin R.
Jackson, Herbert W.
Jackson, Richard L.
Jackson, Robert J.
Jackson, Stephen T.
Jacobs Jr, Fritz F.
Jacobson, Nels A.
Jaeger, Steven D.
Jaegers, James C.
James, Bob
James, Earl
Jarvinen, Paul
Jarvis, Albert
Jarvis, Lawrence
Jayne, Bob E.
Jenkins, Douglas E.
Jenkins, John D.
Jenkins, Kirk C.
Jenkins, Raymond W.
Jenkins, Robert R.
Jennette, Harold G.
Jessop, Jim
Jewett, Edwin E.
Jindra, Robert
Johnson, Andrew M.
Johnson, Andrew L.
Johnson, Charles
Johnson, Clayton R.
Johnson, Dan G.
Johnson, David L.
Johnson, David B.
Johnson, Donald W.
Johnson, Flip
Johnson, Gary
Johnson, Glen B.
Johnson, Harold K.
Johnson, James P.
Johnson, Jay W.
Johnson, Jeffrey
Johnson, Jerry A.
Johnson, Leroy W.
Johnson, Michael
Johnson, Owen C.
Johnson, Philip C.
Johnson, Robert H.
Johnson, Theodore S.
Johnson, Thomas L. W.
Johnson, Thomas R.
Johnson, Walter
Johnson, Ward S.
Johnson, Charles O.
Johnson Jr, George D.
Johnson Jr, Thomas
Johnston, Christian R.

Johnston, David
Johnston, James
Johnston, James E.
Johnston, Keith A.
Johnston, Kevin Lee
Johnston, Peter L.
Johnston, Robert J.
Johnstone, Allen M.
Johnstone, Thomas S.
Jones, Barclay
Jones, Charles R.
Jones, Charles W.
Jones, John H.
Jones, Craig A.
Jones, David M.
Jones, David A.
Jones, Gerald G.
Jones, J. Kevin
Jones, Michael M.
Jones, Phillip C.
Jones, Ralph
Jones, Ralph A.
Jones, Richard E.
Jones, Ronnie C.
Jones, Russell W.
Jones, Hugh A.
Jones Jr, Myron E.
Jones Jr, Norman R.
Jordan, Pat
Jordan, William
Joyce, James M.
Joyce, John C.
Judge Jr, John F.
Judkins, Albert

Julian, Robert
Jumper, William

K
Kabli, John S.
Kaiser, M. Luther
Kaithern, John
Kalldin Jr, Charles A.
Kamman, Paul
Kammerer, George E.
Kanable, G. E.
Kane, Francis
Kane, George G.
Kane, Kevin M.
Kane, Michael T.
Kane, Patrick S.
Kane, Paul J.
Kane, Peter F.
Kane, Peter M.
Kane, Robert J.
Kane, Charle
Kannenberg, Burton
Kappes, Stephen A.
Kappler, Richard P.
Kardos, Danny P.
Karrick, Robert J.
Kasten, William A.
Katcher, Philip
Kater, Edward G.
Katz, Blaine K.
Kaub, John Russell
Kaufer, Louis
Kauff, John R.
Kaufman, Herb S.

Kaup, Daniel
Kaup, Harry J.
Kaup, Nicholas
Kaut, George
Kavanaugh, Patrick J.
Kazmarek, Russell
Kearney, Robert
Kearns, Christopher J.
Kedzierski, Brent
Keefer, Preston H.
Keegan, Thomas J.
Kegerise, Paul C.
Kegerise, Scott E.
Kegerreis, George D.
Keister, Wesley
Keith, Carter C.
Kelble, Williams
Kelleher, Robert J.
Kelleher, William K.
Kellerman, Charles W.
Kelley, John
Kelley, Patrick
Kellis, William A.
Kelly, Anthony J.
Kelly, David
Kelly, Dennis B.
Kelly, Dennis G.
Kelly, Donald L.
Kelly, Edward J.
Kelly, John Berry
Kelly, Joseph
Kelly, Patrick
Kelly, Patrick M.
Keltz, James
Keltz, Ray
Kenaga, Leland A.
Kendall, Sean F. C.
Kennard, Dwight C.
Kenneally Jr, George V.
Kennedy, Leo
Kennedy, Robert
Kennedy, Shawn
Kenney, Alton D.
Kenney, George
Kenny, James A.
Kenny, Lawrence
Kent, Robert
Kenworthy, Merrell T.
Kern, Craig A.
Kern, Lester A.
Kerr, Andrew M.
Kerr Jr, Elder M.
Kessler, Joseph R.
Kessler, Paul F.
Kettler, Mark A.
Keune, Bradford
Keuthan, Fred B.
Kidney, William
Kienast, Richard
Kierstead, John A.
Killen III, Harry E.
Killian, Stephen B.
Killough, Donald T.
Kimball, Bradley G.
Kimbrough, Albert C.
Kimbrough, Albert E. C.
Kimbrough, Jonathan R.

Kindred, John D.
Kindred, Sherwood L.
King, Benny
King, Billy Jo
King, Crawford A.
King, Lt Daniel G.
King, Orval
King, Thomas F.
Kingsley Jr, Arthur B.
Kinyon, John
Kinyon, Paul J.
Kirby, Daniel
Kirby, Richard
Kirchner, Lee M.
Kirchner Jr, Russell W.
Kirk, Charles M.
Kirmiss, Arthur P.
Kissel, Philip L.
Klaneski, James J.
Klaus, Gary
Klaus, Thomas
Klemiato, John
Klenk, Christopher R.
Kline, Mark I.
Kline, Mike
Kline, Robert J.
Klinepeter, David J.
Klipstein Sr, James R.
Kloth Jr, Maj Harold W.
Klubertanz, Harold
Klumb, Robert M.
Knapp, Gordon A.
Knaus, Ronald W.
Knell, George
Knepp, Lloyd P.
Knight, Christopher Grant
Knight, Douglass R.
Knight, George Samuel
Knight, Glenn B.
Knight, Glenn F.
Knight, John B.
Knight, Robert H.
Knize, Mike
Knowles, Robert D.
Knowles Jr, Robert G.
Knox, Roger M.
Knudsen, Jr., Lewis F.
Knuese, Paul
Koch, Noel C.
Koehr, James G.
Koehr, James E.
Koene, Wayne
Koentz, Bernard W.
Koentz, Bernard W.
Kopcak, Fred
Kopp, Curtis
Kosik, Dan W.
Kosta, Marvin
Kramer, Edwin K.
Kramer, Edwin C.
Kramer, Michael
Kramer Sr, Franklin J.
Kranich, Roger E.
Krasche, Robert
Kratt, James H.
Kratts, Stephen C.
Kraus, Robert

Krecota, Darrin
Krecota, Jason
Krecota, John S.
Kreisher, Ken
Kreps, Mark R.
Krichten, Jacob
Krieser, Curtis D.
Krieser, Edward J.
Krieser, Kenneth S.
Kroger, Donald J.
Krol, Steven D.
Kroll, C. Douglas
Kroninger, Karl
Krug, Maurice H.
Kucker, Richard C.
Kuepfer, Jack W.
Kuhlman, Jacob Paul
Kuhn, Charles
Kuhn, Paul
Kuhn, Thomas
Kummerow, William
Kunkler, Francis M.
Kuntz, Timothy J.
Kurtz, Don
Kurtz, Gary
Kurycz Jr, Walter
Kuzma, Kevin
Kwolek, Conrod

L

LaBanta, Thayne C.
Lackey, Allan M.
LaCount, Walter G.
Laine, Bruce C.
Laing, Clifford J.
Lalancette, Robert J.
Lambert, David A.
Lambert, J. Lester
Lambert, Richard Linn
Lamoureux, Louis
Lamphere, Carl Edward
Lamphere, Mark Douglas
Lamphere Jr, Lloyd Dean
Lamphere Sr, Lloyd Dean
Lancaster, Ivan D.
Lander, Richard H.
Lane, Donald B.
Lane, R. B.
Langston, Scott M.
Langworthy, Charles
LaPenta, James
LaPorte, William
Larkin, Charles W.
LaRosa, Brent
Larson, Donald P.
Larson, Richard
Larson, Terry
LaRue, Robert
Lassor, Leonard L.
Latham, Calder B.
Latham, Dale W.
Latham II, Carl
Latham III, Carl R.
Latham Sr, Larry Wayne
Latture, S. Gayden
Lauda, Billy G.
Lauderbaugh, George

Laughlin, David W.
Laughlin, Henry P.
Laughlin, V. William
Laux Esq, Russell F.
LaVertue, Theodore A.
Lavis, Jack C.
Lawler, Joseph P.
Lawrence, Daniel Willis
Lawton, Thomas
Lazzeri, John
Leach, Adam K.
Leas, Brian A.
Leasure, Joseph C.
Leathers, Richard
Leavens, Kenneth W.
Lebcowitz, Gary
Leber, Fred
Leber, Frederic R.
Leber, Ralph H.
Leberknight, Cecil K.
Lebert, Robert G.
LeBlanc, Brian
LeCompte Jr, Lester
Lee, James O.
Lee, Randy B.
Lee, Richard F.
Leech, Holman E.
Lefler, L. G.
LeForge, Thomas E.
Leggee, Richard Elmes
Lehman, James B.
Lehto Jr, Paul V.
Leibrandt, Jon
Leicht, Steve
Leistritz, Paul
Leman, Creel E.
Lemanski, Michael
Lemieux, Albert
Lenfest, Sibley H.
Lennon, Brian M.
Lent, Frederick
Lentz, William C.
Leonard, Louis F.
Leonard, Peter M.
Leone, Daniel R.
Leone, Gerard
Leonhardt Sr, Gary A.
Lerner, Richard J.
Lesselyoung, John
Letcher, David W.
Leveck, Richard C.
Levine, Lawrence A.
Lewis III, John M.
Lewis, James T.
Lewis, John C.
Lewis, Joseph
Lewis, Mark S.
Lewis, Robert P.
Lewis, Robin W.
Lewis, Stephen
Lewis, William V.
Lewis, William F.
Ley, Harry P.
Lianza, Peter F.
Libengood, Robert T.
Lieber, Raymond
Likens, Warren F.

Lincoln, Alfred T.
Lindberg, Kip A.
Lindberg, William G.
Linder, Carl
Lines, Harry K.
Lininger, Walter
Linnell, John N.
Linnell, Lloyd L.
Linnell, Nathan C.
Linnell, Robert W.
Linnell, Virgil E.
Linnell, William R.
Lintemuth, Gerald M.
Lipp, Francis
Lisarelli, Daniel F. B.
Listenberger, Eric D.
Listenberger, Richard L.
Little, Melvin W.
Little, William J.
Little, William E.
Loba, Dennis R.
Locke, Dr Bryan D.
Lockwood, Raleigh B.
Loeper, Raymond J.
Loewe, Thomas E.
Loftus Jr, John J.
Logan, Charles H.
Logan, Darin P.
Lohrstorfer, John
Loke, Edward M.
Loke, Edward N.
Loll, John L.
Lomas, George T.
London, Joseph C.
Long, Andrew J.
Long, David
Long, Eugene
Long, George W.
Long, Jack L.
Long, Richard Bradley
Long, Richard M.
Long, Robert
Long Jr, Joseph
Longstreth, W. Thatcher
Longuer, Clayton J.
Lonnberg, Charles M.
Lookwood, David J.
Lookwood, Raleigh B.
Loomis, Alan R.
Loomis, David
Loomis Jr, Richard R.
Loose, John W. W.
Lord, Laurance
Lord, Richard
Lord, Robert W.
Lord, Robert
Lowe, Bob
Lowe, Charles A.
Lowe, Charles
Lowe, Rudie Dean
Lowe, William H.
Lowery, Martin
Lowery, Robert Lee
Lowery Jr, Martin
Lowery Jr, Norman S.
Lucas, Martin L.
Lucashu, John

Luckenbill, John H. J.
Lufkin, Richard P.
Lund, Robert Matthew
Lundberg Jr, Raymond F.
Lupo, Hank
Lusk, Lawrence
Luth Jr, Frank W.
Lycore, Richard
Lyford, Herbert G.
Lyles, Donald B.
Lynady, Gerald J.
Lynch, John
Lynch, Joseph D.
Lynch, Thomas J.
Lynch, Charles C.
Lynds, Max Leigh
Lyon, Alton F.
Lyon, Robert
Lyon Jr, Frederick W.
Lyons, James T.
Lystash, John Chester

M
Mabie, Sylvester M.
MaCauley, Richard E.
MacDonald, Paul M.
MacDougall, Malcom P.
MacEachern, Donald F.
MacGregor, David C.
MacGunnigle, Bruce
MacIntyre, Stewart E.
Mack, Donald S.
Mack, John F.
MacNemar, Dunbar L.
MacPherson, Ronald G.
MaDan, Thomas E.
Madden Jr, Joseph T.
Madert III, John H.
Madert Jr, John H.
Magee, Lawrence P.
Maguire Jr, Edward
Maier, Albert
Maier, Eugene P.
Maillard, Michael D.
Makos, John
Mallory, Donald N.
Mallow Jr, Lewis P.
Malmberg, Robert
Malone, Todd
Maloney, Ronald
Mamminga, Kevin M.
Mamminga, Michael A.
Mangan III, Thomas Joseph
Manifold, Edward M.
Manley, Gary D.
Mann, Erik J.
Mann, John
Mann, Michael C.
Mann, Walter H.
Mann Jr, Lloyd B.
Mannigan, Michael M.
Mannin, Richard G.
Manning, Russel
Manser, Harry M.
Mansfield, Bernard
Mansi, Joseph A.
Mantel, Kenneth H.

Manville, Gary
Mapes, Harold R.
Marchand, Michael
Marcum, Donald
Maris, William C.
Markland, Arville G.
Markland, Christopher C.
Markley III, William A.
Marley, James G. D.
Marlin, Kenneth L.
Marlow, Larry
Marlowe, Christopher L.
Marsden, Joseph R.
Marshall, Frank I.
Marshall, Kevin G.
Marshall, Larry
Marston III, Charles S.
Martel, Patrick T.
Martin, Dr David G.
Martin, Jeff
Martin, John M.
Martin, Kenneth H.
Martin, Kenneth A.
Martin, Paul D.
Martin, Raymond
Martin, Ricky T.
Martin, William
Martins, Eric C.
Masemer, Maurice J.
Mason, Chris
Mason, George
Mason, Lawrence E.
Mason, Mark
Mason, Thomas
Mason, William F.
Mason Jr, Al
Matheny, James R.
Matika, Lawrence
Matos, David
Matt, Christopher
Matteau, Mark A.
Mattila, Richard
Mattix, Jeff
Matty Sr, Thomas A.
Matz, Virgil
Mauzey, Bill
Max, Edward
Maxfield, Herbert Scott
Maxwell, Randy L.
Maxwell Jr, Donald Power
May, John M.
May, Stephen
May, William V.
Mayhew Sr, Jonathan T.
Mazalewski, Michael
Mazzaccaro, Patrick J.
McAfoose, James
McAllister, Edward
McAllister, Gordon F.
McAneny, J. Frank
McAniff III, John Thomas
McBride, Mark
McBride, Ralph W.
McCabe, Michael
McCafferty, James A.
McCandles, Eric G.
McCann, Eugene

McCann, Robert L.
McCardell, W. Michael
McCarthy, Bernard
McCarthy, Francis X.
McCarthy, Joseph T.
McCarty, James A.
McCashion, Kevin A.
McCauslin, John R.
McChessney, Kenneth W.
McCloskey, Dennis C.
McClure, Donald K.
McClure, Mark S.
McComb Jr, William J.
McConnell, William A.
McCool, Geoffrey E.
McCormick, William J.
McCourt, James Francis
McCoy, John C.
McCoy, Richard A.
McCray, Kevin
McCrea, Dr Robert
McCreedy, Michael Joseph
McCullough, Clark D.
McCullough, Greg E.
McDaniel, James
McDaniel, Keith A.
McDaniel, Stephen K.
McDannald, Vernon A.
McDermott, Frederick T.
McDonald, John T.
McDonald, Ed
McDonald, Gerald
McDonald, Joseph W.
McDowell, Lee
McElfresh, Wayne
McElhinny, David G.
McElhinny, Irvin E.
McElroy, Jack R.
McElroy, Mark
McFadden, Michael
McFarland, Warren C.
McGarey, Gordon F.
McGarrigle, John A.
McGill, Thomas
McGinn, Robert C.
McGinnis, James C.
McGinnis, Monti I.
McGlynn, Edward
McGonigal, Ronald E.
McGowan, Bradley S.
McGowan, John J.
McGrath Sr, Robert D.
McGraw, Gary K.
McGraw, Lukas R.
McGraw, Rex G.
McGreevy, Brian A.
McGregor, Michael A.
McGregor, Ralph F.
McGuire, Dan
McGuire, Leo C.
McHall Jr, Rex R.
McInerny, Len E.
McIntire, Dennis P.
McIntyre, John F.
McKelvey, Glenn Wayne
McKenna, George A.
McKenna, Thomas P.

McKenzie, Basil
McKeon, Robert H.
McKibben, Paul W.
McKinch, Terrance Lee
McKinley, Robert L.
McKnight, Robert V.
McKown, Barrett L.
McKown, Justin
McLaughlin, Daniel F.
McLaughlin, Donald
McInturf, Robert C.
McMahon, Thomas
McMaster, James
McMaster, Thomas
McMaster, Fitzhugh
McMaster Jr, William
McMaster Sr, William J.
McMillan, Michael W.
McMullen, J. Clyde
McMullen, Lawrence J.
McMullin, Albert L.
McNally, Randy D.
McNeely, Lawrence
McPike, Warren E.
McQuade, Theodore
McQueney Jr, John R.
McRell, James E.
McVicker, Elwood
McWilliams, Douglas L.
Mead, Daniel J.
Meade, John
Medert, David V.
Medert, David M.
Medert, John
Medert, David R.
Mehaffey, Scott
Mehaffey, William M.
Mehl, Thomas W.
Meier, Tim
Meier, William
Meiers, David Calvin
Meisner, Jacob
Meissner, William
Melcher, Gayle E.
Mellen, Charles J.
Mellor, Clark W.
Mendoza, Richard F.
Mercer, Jerry M.
Mercer Jr, Charles
Meredith, Robert N.
Merithew, Paul A.
Merithew, Perley A.
Merrell, Herbert E.
Merrett, Arthur L.
Meserve, Frank
Mesker, James P.
Metcalf, Keith
Metcalf, Robert D.
Metz, John
Meyers, Jerry
Meyers, Randy
Meyhers, John C.
Michael, Eric G.
Michaels, Ralph J.
Michaels, Stephen A.
Michaels Jr, Harry D.
Michel, William B.

Michel, William P.
Middleton, Darrell N.
Mierka, Gregg A.
Mierka, Robert J.
Miers, Kerry
Miesen Jr, Wayne Gerald
Mikesell, Larry
Milam, Michael
Milberger, William A.
Miles, Gregory D.
Milhoan, Rhett A.
Miller, Adam
Miller, Bruce W.
Miller, Carl G.
Miller, Chancey P.
Miller, Daniel H.
Miller, George H.
Miller, Harold N.
Miller, Harold F.
Miller, James O.
Miller, James H.
Miller, Max D.
Miller, Norman R.
Miller, Walter L.
Miller, Wayne Dunbar
Miller, Woodrow W.
Miller Jr, George S.
Miller Jr, Ralph R.
Milligan, Edward S.
Milligan, John M.
Milligan, Joseph
Milligan, Michael E.
Mills, David R.
Mills, Jack
Mills, Joseph W.
Mills, Justin G.
Mills, Marc E.
Mills, Matthew A.
Mills, Richard L.
Mills, Robert S.
Mills, Sherman W.
Mills III, John A.
Mills Jr, Raymond
Mills Sr, Raymond
Milnes, Russell H.
Milton, Thomas C.
Milton, Thomas A.
Mingus, James
Miniaci, Mike
Minnich, Kenneth D.
Minor, Guy D.
Minor, Kenneth V.
Mitchell, Robert A.
Mitchell, Thomas
Mitchell Jr, Howard E.
Mix, Richard L.
Mixner, Lee C.
Moberly, Richard L.
Mockerman, Milton E.
Moeckel, J. Edward
Moesta, Roy D.
Moffatt, Richard D.
Moffitt Jr, Frank E.
Mohn, Thomas B.
Mohring, James A.
Molitor, Scott
Moll, Nathan E.

Monaghan, Neil R.
Mondschein, Karl
Mong, Kenneth
Mong II, Kenneth
Monroe, Charles H.
Monroe, Gerald P.
Monroe, Mark E.
Monroe, Richard L.
Montague, Carrington
Montelius, William C.
Montford, C. Edward
Mooers, Yale W.
Mook, Conrad P.
Moon, Oran B.
Moon, Robert R.
Moon Jr, John T.
Mooney, Ralph
Moore, Allen W.
Moore, Edward
Moore, Elmer L.
Moore, Jack Lee
Moore, Jason
Moore, Jerry
Moore, John D.
Moore, Mike
Moore, Paul Arlon
Moore, William J.
Moore, William O.
Moore, William
Moore IV, Harrison G.
Moquin, William D.
Moran, David S.
Moran, Gordon
Moran, Joseph F.
Morel, Rev Paul A.
Morey, Albert A.
Morey, Charles W.
Morgan, Gene W.
Morgan, Kirby R.
Morgan, Lee
Morgan MD, Vernon W.
Morganthaler II, Fred J.
Morganthaler I, Frederick J.
Moriarty, Gregory A.
Morlen, Kris
Moroz, John F.
Morran, Michael P.
Morran, Peter J.
Morris, Albert T.
Morris, James
Morris, John E.
Morris, Robert
Morris, William Roger
Morris, William E.
Morriseau, Harold
Morse, Owen H.
Morse, Ruel A.
Morse, Thomas E.
Mort, Thomas
Mortimore, Harold E.
Morton, Kim Allen
Mosier, Andrew T.
Moss, James J.
Moss, James H.
Mott, Clayton E.
Mottice, Lynn G.
Mourning, James G.
Moury, Dennis R.
Mueller, Mark
Mueting, James A.
Mueting, Wallace J.
Mulhall, Eugene F.
Mulholland Jr, William R.
Mullaly, Kenneth H.
Mullay, John J.
Mullay, Kevin
Mullen, Joseph A.
Mullen, Kevin J.
Mulligan, James
Mullin, Lawrence
Mullin, Raymond C.
Mumper, John M.
Muncert, Eric S.
Muncert Jr, Harry W.
Mund, Frederick Al
Munkenbeck Jr, George J.
Munroe, James W.
Murdock, Robert W.
Murphy, Charles C.
Murphy, Charles E.
Murphy, James
Murphy, John J.
Murphy, John Michael
Murphy, Philip J.
Murphy, Richard L.
Murphy, Robert C.
Murphy, Thomas D.
Murphy, Timothy M.
Murphy, Timothy
Murphy, William A.
Murray, David
Murray, Francis J.
Murray, Paul Joseph
Murray, Reid J.
Murray, Craig B.
Murray, William
Murrell, Thomas
Musbach, Jack Lester
Musser Jr, Brent E.
Myers, Harold L.
Myers, John P.
Myers, Mark David
Myers, Ronald
Myers, Thomas
Myers, Thomas Allen

N
Nadeau, Lester D.
Nagel, Eric
Nagle, John A.
Nagle, Thomas
Narehood, Ermin D.
Narsavage, Stephen P.
Nash, John F.
Nash, Wayne A.
Navorska, David A.
Nay, Ronald
Naylor, Ron
Neal, James
Neal, James W.
Neal, William B.
Neal III, James R.
Neal Sr, James Ralph
Nedela, James S.
Neely, James E.
Neely, John
Neely, Robert
Neiss, Shawn
Neiss Jr, R. David
Neiss Sr, Roland D.
Nelson, Allen M.
Nelson, David A.
Nelson, David
Nelson, Dean C.
Nelson, William C.
Nelson II, Charles
Nelson III, Charles
Nelson Sr, Charles A.
Neubauer, Duffy
Neuman, Robert
Neville, Edgar A.
Neville, Thomas E.
Newey, Richard C.
Newman, Deron S.
Newman, Dieter E.
Newman, George F.
Newton, George
Newton, Robert
Newton III, Francis C.
Newton Jr, Francis C.
Nicholas Jr, George B.
Nichols, Allen G.
Nichols, James L.
Nichols, Raymond
Niederhaus, Danny Dean
Niederwerfer, Frank
Nielsen, Paul C.
Niermeyer, Doug
Nimmo, Brent
Nix, Jeffery
Nogar, Daniel A.
Nogar, James Harvey
Nolan, Alan T.
Noone, Samuel H.
Norcutt, Edward J.
Norris, George E.
Norris Jr, Howard E.
North, David W.
Norton, Chauncey A.
Nosbaum, John
Nottage, George W.
Nourse, David L.
Nourse, Peter C.
Noyes, C. Lee
Noyes, Robert L.
Nunemaker, Howard
Nuoffer, George T.
Nuoffer, Robert
Nurnberger, Daniel
Nutt, Robert C.
Nye, Michael Earl
Nyulassie, Jack

O
O'Brien, John E.
O'Brien, Joseph
O'Brien, Kevin
O'Brien, Kevin G.
O'Brien, Thomas E. G.
O'Connell, Kent T.
O'Connell, Lenahan
O'Connor, Francis J.
O'Connor, James P.
O'Connor, Joseph E.
O'Dea, Thomas E.
O'Halloran, George W.
O'Halloran, John D.
O'Lague, John
O'Leary Jr, Francis H.
O'Neil Jr, Joseph B.
O'Neil Jr, Robert E.
O'Neil Sr, Robert E.
O'Neill, John Markos
O'Reilly, Michael G.
O'Rourke, John F.
O'Sullivan, Curtis H.
Oakley, Kenneth A.
Obermeyer, John
Ockerbloom, John
Ockerbloom, Nelson
Odell, Charles
Ogden, Don
Ogden, John P.
Ogletree, Gregory W.
Olds, David H.
Olds, John W.
Olds, Thurston W.
Oliver, Allen M.
Oliver, Jerry
Olsen, Jeffery L.
Olsen, Roger L.
Olson, Daniel A.
Ominski, George M.
Oneil, Max
Onstott, Charles A.
Opperman, Craig A.
Orcutt, Harry G.
Orebaugh, James L.
Orebaugh, L. H.
Orlebeke, W. Ronald
Ormerod, Douglas S.
Orr, Albert E.
Orr, Nathan L.
Orr, Richard D.
Orr, Robert J.
Orrell III, Reverdy L.
Orrell IV, Reverdy L.
Ortlip Jr, C. Warren
Orton, Jerome L.
Osborne, Elthea
Osborne, Jerry
Oswald Jr, George E.
Othmer, Richard T.
Otterstein, Robert M.
Ouhrabka, Jan M.
Ours, Randall D.
Overby, Andrew E.
Owen, Andrew M.
Owen, Harold M.
Owens, Calvin
Owens, Harry J.
Owens, Ronald J.
Oxenham, Thomas

P
Pace, Don C.
Pagani, Peter
Page, Arthur S.
Page, Dale
Page, Thomas L.
Page, Thomas O.
Pahl, James B.
Pair, George
Palazzolo, Joseph M.
Palazzolo, Salvatore
Palmer, Robert A.
Pangburn, Macklin
Pangburn, Mark L.
Paprocki, Robert
Paresi, Robert P.
Paris, Philip R.
Park, Alex
Park, B. Tim
Park, J. Douglas
Parker, Dean E.
Parker, Paul A.

Parker, Gerald W.
Parkinson, John N.
Parkinson, Marvin E.
Parks, John W.
Parks, Edward W.
Parks, Michael A.
Parks, William O.
Parks III, William O.
Parmenter, Richard
Parthemore, Don
Partington, Richard O.
Partridge, Brian Lee
Patch, Jack
Patenaude, Henry M.
Patrick, Jeffrey L.
Patterson, James O.
Patterson, D. Gene
Patz, Roger A.
Paul, Allen E.
Paulson, Joseph
Pavlosky Jr, Edward J.
Paxon, Jason
Payne, Norman L.
Pearce, John E.
Pearce, Walter B.
Pearce, William S.
Pearsall, Gerald H.
Pearson, Michael A.
Pearson, Robert
Pearsons, Michael
Peck, James L.
Peco, Michael E.
Peco, Michael G.
Pederson, Norman S.
Pedley, Steven A.
Peglow, Donald G.
Peglow, Steven C.
Peifer, Charles E.
Peiper, Clarance
Peiper, Ralph C.
Penhallow II, David P.
Penland, Thomas
Pennell, Donald J.
Penrod, David P.
Pereira, Joseph
Perkins, Donald R.
Perras, David
Perrott, Dale
Perry, Donald R.
Perry, Ronald
Perry Jr, George
Pershing, Arthur
Petaccio Jr, Joseph F.
Peters, Abie
Peters, Brian G.
Peters, John E.
Peters, Richard
Petersen, Shannon
Peterson, Alan E.
Peterson, Dana Andren
Peterson, David E.
Peterson, Kent A.
Peterson, Michael G.
Petrie, Kenneth G.
Petrovic, Robert M.
Pettinger, Donald P.
Pettit, Edward
Petz, Dr Weldon

Phelph, Richard J.
Phelps, Michael J.
Phibbs, Richard Miles
Phillips, Alan C.
Phillips, Donald K.
Phillips, John E.
Phillips, Paul Michael
Pickles III, William W.
Pickrell, Donald E.
Piela, Jack
Pierce, Dr Preston E.
Pierce, John H.
Pierce, Michael
Pierce, Myron
Pierson, Lawrence B.
Pierson, Robert E.
Pifer, Allen A.
Pikor, Joseph W.
Pinson, William A.
Pitts, Neal C.
Plante, Aram A.
Plante, Gerald T.
Plante, Joseph A.
Plaskett, Delbert
Pochiba, David J.
Poehler, Herman
Pohl Jr, Col Clifford
Pohlod, Leonard G.
Pollard Sr, John C.
Pomeroy, David J.
Pond, David
Ponticelli, Fred
Ponticelli, Ward
Pontious, William
Poole, Glenn A.
Poole, John R.
Poplar, Melvin
Portell, Robert
Porter, George C.
Porter, Harry L.
Porter, Richard E.
Post, David M.
Post, Douglas
Post, Pvt Jeffrey
Potts, Richard R.
Poulton Jr, William S.
Powderly, Charles F.
Powell, George L.
Powell, George J.
Powell, Gerald L.
Powell, Sean E.
Powell, Walter L.
Powell Sr, Ronald C.
Powers, John J.
Pownall, Kevin I. (Kip)
Prater, Stan
Pratt, Richard W.
Pratt II, Abner K.
Pray, Donald
Prebeck, Michael A.
Pregler, John T.
Presbrey Jr, Wendell B.
Presbrey Sr, Wendell B.
Presher, David L.
Preston, David L.
Previts, Federick S.
Previts, William H.
Price, Donald L.

Price, Donald
Price, Eric N.
Price, Michael L.
Price, Philip
Price, Robert
Priest, Bobby Wayne
Prince, Edgar
Prince, Ralph T.
Prince, Thomas R.
Prittie, Thomas J.
Proctor, Rob
Provencal, Armand G.
Pucciarelli, J. Peter
Pucciarelli, John Patrick
Pucciarelli, Joseph J.
Pugh III, Francis K.
Pugh Jr, Francis K.
Pulis, John L.
Pullen, John J.
Pulver, Fred H.
Purcell, David William
Putz, Fred E. W.
Pykare, James

Q
Quigley, Douglas
Quigley, Michael J.
Quinlin, Bradley J.
Quinn, Robert R.

R
Rabach, Clarence F.
Rabadan, David J.
Radabaugh, Jonathon
Radabaugh, William
Radeleff, Mark C.
Raese, David
Rakestraw, Todd E.
Ralls, Stephen A.
Ralston, Gary F.
Ralston, Sean F.
Ramsey, Guy
Randall, George H.
Rapple, Darlow W.
Rarick, Bradley A.
Rash, Bernard F.
Rath, Jeffery O.
Ratz, Floyd J.
Raudenbush, Miles
Rauscher, Randy
Rave, William J. M.
Ravinet, Ernest
Rawson, Vaughn J.
Ray, Leonard L.
Ray, Stephen E.
Rayborn, James
Raybourn, David
Raye, John
Rayer Sr, Frank R.
Raymond, Jeremy P.
Raymond III, Richard
Raymond IV, Richard
Rea, Kenneth W.
Ready, Duane
Ready, Vernon C.
Reardon III, Peter James
Rebillot, Todd J.

Reddin, Michael L.
Redding, Gary C.
Redding, Gordon L.
Redinger, Steve
Redumski, James L.
Reed, Carlyle M.
Reed, Daniel J.
Reed, David N.
Reed, Henry A.
Reed, Herbert
Reed, Jerry E.
Reed, John
Reed, Jon
Reed, Marvin W.
Reed, Neal L.
Reed, Randall D.
Reed, Richard P.
Reed, Rick L.
Reed Jr, William C.
Reese, Loran
Reese, Orla R.
Reese, Robert H.
Reeser, Arthur H.
Reeves, John
Regan, Jonathan M.
Regan, William
Rehkopf, David D.
Reid, Richard J.
Reid, Robert
Reilly, Peter
Reilly, Steven J.
Reily, Jon A.
Reimer, Thomas
Reinbargar, Richard S.
Reinewald, Rev Henry
Reinhard, Jeffery
Rementer III, Francis L. E.
Renkin, William M.
Resh, Brian E.
Reves, Craig Alan
Reynold Jr, Harold B.
Reynolds, David
Reynolds, Roland F.
Reynolds, William J.
Reynolds III, William T.
Reynolds Jr, Harold B.
Rhoads, Thomas L.
Rhode, William D.
Rhodes, Kenneth A.
Rhodes, Robert H.
Rhodes, Toby
Rice, Michael E.
Richards, S. Grant
Richards, Thomas H.
Richards, Timothy D.
Richards Jr, William A.
Richardson, Arthur J.
Richardson, Clarence
Richardson, Douglas J.
Richardson, John
Richardson, Richard
Richiusa, Joseph J.
Richmond, Robert N.
Richter, Mark A.
Ricker Jr, Joseph A.
Ricker Sr, Joseph A.
Ricks, Thomas M.
Riddell, James L.

Riddell, Marc P.
Riddle, William G.
Rideout, Carlton
Riegle, Charles W.
Rieske, Max
Riester, Delmar Frank
Riggins, Charles Tim
Rightmire, Clark B.
Rightmire, Dennis Taylor
Rightmyer, Thomas N.
Riley, David J.
Riley, Dr Joseph H.
Riley, Michael
Riley, Scott
Riley, Thomas
Riley Jr, John J.
Rinehart, Verne
Rion, Ira S.
Riordan, John
Ripkey, Douglas R.
Ripley, Robert
Rippey, Joseph S.
Risher, Gordon
Rising, George C.
Risk, David M.
Ritchie, William H.
Rittendyr, John
Ritter, David
Rittinger, Robert
Ritz, Thomas
Robbie III, Norman
Robbins, Allen
Robbins, Edwin G.
Robbins, Richard J.
Robbins, Ronald K.
Roberson, Keith L.
Roberts, David
Roberts, Donald L.
Roberts Jr, Richard R.
Roberts Sr, George F.
Robertson, William
Robinson, Frank
Robinson, Gerald C.
Robinson, Hamilton L.
Robinson, James E.
Robinson III, John Stark
Roche Jr, Gary D.
Rodio, William
Rodriguez, Sidney E.
Roe, Jerry D.
Rogers, Kirk M.
Rogers, Leon B.
Rogers, Philip W.
Rogers, Ronald D.
Rogers Jr, Charles A.
Rohrer, Craig L.
Rohrer, Dan E.
Rolfe, John
Rolfe, William
Rollins, Howard F.
Rollins, Robert E.
Ronaldson, Douglas W.
Roney, John C.
Rongitsch Jr, John D.
Ronk, John H.
Roof, Paul W.
Roome, Gary F.
Roosa, Bryan R.

Roschinsky Jr, Nicholas
Rose, Leland S.
Rose Jr, William F.
Rosenberg, Donald J.
Ross, Michael C.
Rossio, Steven A.
Rothermel, Ray W.
Rothrock, Roger Lee
Rounds Jr, Charles E.
Rountree, Glenn H.
Rouse, Clarence E.
Roux, George A.
Rowan, Steve
Rowe, Glenn A.
Rowe, Paul B.
Rowe Sr, James W.
Rowland, Joe
Roy, John
Royston, Perceal
Rubenfeld, Jack
Ruhl, Kent
Ruley, James
Runkle, Harry M.
Runner, Martin W.
Rush, Jonathan
Russell, Eugine E.
Russell, James
Russell, Jeremiah
Russell, Rickard D.
Rutherford, John
Ryan, Jeff
Ryan, John E.
Rychwalski, Joseph T.
Rydenski Jr, Jesse A.
Ryder, Wilton A.
Ryerson Jr, William
Ryerson Sr, William

S
Saffell, Hal
Sakelarides, Michael G.
Sallade, Gary A.
Saltz, Howard W.
Sampson, Eric T.
Sampson, Jeffrey S.
Sanborn, Ernest S.
Sander, Kay L.
Sanders, Brent
Sanders, Carl E.
Sanders, Larry
Sandherr, Michael E.
Sandstrom, Robert Carl
Sandwick, Charles W.
Sanford II, G. Eliot
Sargent, Arthur D.
Sargent, David
Sargent, Ronald B.
Sargenti, Anthony
Saunders, Hobart P.
Saur, Michael A.
Sautter, Bruce R.
Savko, Bernard
Sawyer, Clifton E.
Sawyer, Leon C.
Sayre, David B.
Saytier, Kim
Sayton, Frank

Scales, Joseph
Scalley, Brice F.
Scarlota Jr, Frank
Schaaf, Joseph R.
Schaefer, Andrew Louis
Schaeffer, Forest R.
Schaeffer, Karl
Schaffer, Clayton J.
Schaffer, Richard J. C.
Schaffer, Thomas G.
Schall, Donald
Schaller, Martin N.
Schaller, Rees F.
Schalles, Paul H.
Schanning, Joel G.
Schar, Warren A.
Scheib, Gerald P.
Schillaci, Salvatore V.
Schimming, Randy W.
Schlenker, David
Schlenker, Richard C.
Schlesier, Philip
Schmeltzle, Dale R.
Schmidt, Dennis J.
Schmidt, Elmer W.
Schmidt, George H.
Schmidt, William A.
Schmincke, Eric J.
Schnack, Robert W.
Schnack Jr, Robert W.
Schneider, David
Schneider, Fred
Schoenleber Jr, William
Schollmeyer, Jay
Schrader, David E.
Schroeder, Darrell C.
Schroeder, J. R.
Schroeder, Joseph
Schroeder, William C. M.
Schroeder Jr, John
Schulz, George A.
Schulz, Michael
Schulze, Kurt
Schurman, John J.
Schwartz, Veryl D.
Schwartz, William
Schweitzer, Robert M.
Schwemmin, Bruce R.
Schworm, Norman C.
Scinta Jr, Ralph
Scofield, Russell
Score, Donald G.
Scott, Dan D.
Scott, David R.
Scott, Donald E.
Scott, George F.
Scott, Jon W.
Scott, Raymond
Scott, Richard L.
Scott, Steven M.
Scott Jr, Gregory J.
Scruggs, James M.
Scruggs, Robert G.
Scull, Paul
Seagriff, Edward M.
Searles, Clarence E.
Searles, Jerry L.
Sears, Robert M.

Seaton, Leo
Seck Jr, Joseph G.
Seese, Donald J.
Seguin, Kenneth E.
Seibert, Chad
Seibert II, John Rix
Seibold III, A. Bingham
Seifert, Jack
Seifert, Scott
Seits, Laurence E.
Seitz, James R.
Sembach, Robert
Semple, Raymond E.
Senner, James C.
Sergenian, Haig H.
Sering, John Samuel
Seum, Rev Clark
Sexton Jr, Charles T.
Seymore, Marvin
Shadel, George
Shadel Jr, Ralph
Shadman, George
Shadyac, Joseph
Shafer, David F.
Shaffer, Joseph M.
Shaffer, Robert C.
Shaffer III, L. Blaine
Shank, Adin K.
Shanks, Bill
Shanks, James R.
Shannahan, Thomas
Shannon, Kenneth
Shannon, Roger F.
Sharp, Gerald T.
Sharp, Robert A.
Sharp, Robert W.
Sharp Sr, Robert L.
Sharrock II, Charles E.
Sharrock Sr, Charles E.
Shaughnessy, Edward
Shaw, Arthur
Shaw, Charles A.
Shaw, Eugene D.
Shaw, Henry M.
Shaw, James H.
Shaw, John E.
Shaw, Kim D.
Shaw, Mark M.
Shaw, Ned F.
Shaw, Robert C.
Shaw, Ronald E.
Shaw Jr, Elmer W.
Shay, Brian
Shay, Dale
Shay, Gordon
Shea, Jonathon
Shea, Timothy F.
Shearer, Dean H.
Shedenhelm, Tim
Sheeron, Martin J.
Sheffer Jr, Elmer E.
Sheftel, Robert B.
Shellhammer, Douglas L.
Shepard, Byrd
Shepard, Howard
Shepard, Valentine H.
Shepherd, Richard A.
Shepherd, Thomas

Sherlock, Richard D.
Sherman, John R.
Sherman, Nathan L.
Shew, Kenneth
Shibley, Richard
Shick, Clyde D.
Shick, Robert
Shields, James L.
Shields, James J.
Shields, Joseph J.
Shields, Stephen L.
Shindledecker, David P.
Shinn, Allan
Shinn, Ronald S.
Shoemaker, David L.
Shoemaker, Ralph
Shoemaker, William M.
Shoffner, John W.
Shook, Robert
Shores, James L.
Short, William
Shugars, Thomas U.
Shull, Michael A.
Shull, Richard B.
Shull, Ronald G.
Shultz, David
Shultz, Loring
Shumway, Brian J.
Shurtleff, Steven J.
Siegle, David K.
Siemsen, Stephen H.
Sierk, Randall L.
Sievertson, Jeffrey M.
Siglag, Howard
Sikorski, Wilfred J.
Silocka, Richard A.
Silvis, John
Sime, Gaert W.
Simmons, Clinton H.
Simmons, James A.
Simpson, Lee O.
Simpson, Robert J.
Sipes, Dale E.
Sipes, Gary L.
Sisler, Kurt
Sives, Kevin A.
Skinner, Jack Donald
Skinner, Ray
Skowronski, William E.
Skuce, Donald S.
Slade, Michael
Slanker, Frank M.
Slavens, Earl
Slifer, Paul H.
Slifer, Robert J.
Slingerland, Roland
Sloan, Daniel A.
Sloan, Michael J.
Sloat, Marshall
Small, Harold C.
Smallman, John A.
Smallwood Jr, Grahame T.
Smarsh, John D.
Smart, Jeffrey A.
Smith, Allen
Smith, Allen F.
Smith, Benjamin G.
Smith, Capt Mark A.

Smith, Clayton R.
Smith, Don P.
Smith, Donald James
Smith, Donald D.
Smith, Donald E.
Smith, Douglas C.
Smith, Douglas E.
Smith, Edward P.
Smith, Emerson P.
Smith, Ernest D.
Smith, Eugene
Smith, Fred
Smith, George
Smith, Gerard J.
Smith, Harold A.
Smith, James H.
Smith, James Y.
Smith, Joel P.
Smith, Kalmin D.
Smith, Kenneth K.
Smith, Kenneth E.
Smith, Kenneth W.
Smith, Kenrick K.
Smith, Laramie James
Smith, Larry Robert
Smith, Leland L.
Smith, Lloyd S.
Smith, Michael W.
Smith, Nicholas A.
Smith, Paul R. G.
Smith, Peter A.
Smith, Richard G.
Smith, Roy
Smith, Thomas M.
Smith, Thomas
Smith, Timothy
Smith, Timothy M.
Smith, Vincent P.
Smith, Wesley
Smith, William
Smith, William W.
Smith Jr, Arthur P.
Smith Jr, Harman S.
Smith Jr, Roy Stewart
Smith Sr, Jimmy
Smith Sr, Stanley S.
Smithcors, Clarence
Smock, David
Smyser, Robert M. F.
Smyser I, Richard H.
Smyser II, Richard H.
Snavely, Robert L.
Sneed, Dr Thomas
Snellbaker, Arthur
Snider, Ernest
Snover, Robert A.
Snow, Scott L.
Snyder, Barry
Snyder, Eugene R.
Snyder, Gardiner W.
Snyder, Herman T.
Snyder, Leroy R.
Solyan, James B.
Sommer, Raymond L.
Sommer, Raymond
Sorgi, William
Southwood, Donald G.

Southwood, Michael R.
Spangler, David S.
Sparks, Donald G.
Spatz, Karl W.
Spaulding, John
Spaulding, William
Speaks, Dean K.
Spears, James R. H.
Spears, John
Speck, Forrest Gregg
Spence, Mark
Spencer, George
Sperzel, Larry A.
Spiegel, George F.
Spiegel, Philip Charles
Spiegel, Theodore A.
Spiegel, Thomas J.
Spiegel Jr, Charles J.
Spirko, Joseph
Spohn, Julius J.
Spring, Dane A.
Spring, Patrick M.
Spring III, Walter S.
Spring Jr, Walter S.
Springer, Robert
Sproehnle, Harry
Spry, Lowell E.
Spurr, Jerome L.
Srodes, James L.
St. Germain, R. F.
Staats II, Charles J.
Stabo, Anthony
Stacy Jr, Michael M.
Stafford, James
Stafford, William L.
Stahl, James L.
Staiger, Ronald H.
Stanard, Edward E.
Stanhope, Glenn R.
Stanley, Mitchell F.
Stanton, Shelby L.
Stanton, Walter A.
Stapleton, William F.
Stark, Mike
States, Carl
Stebbins Jr, William R.
Stecher, Edward J.
Steele, Charles C.
Steele, Gayle H.
Steele, Scott P.
Steele II, Milton
Steele III, Milton
Stegall, Mathew
Steiger, Robert C.
Steih, Jason C.
Steih, Wilbur C.
Steindel, David
Steinmaker, Donald
Stenson, Kim
Stephens, Glenn W.
Stevens, Willard M.
Stevens, Peter
Stevens IV, Samuel S.
Stevenson, Craig Lee
Stevenson, Donald
Stevenson, Dylan O.
Stevenson, Gary L.
Stevenson, Jeffery L.

Stevenson, Jr, Ralph L.
Stewart, Cameron S. L.
Stewart, Charles
Stewart, David P.
Stewart, Thomas
Stewart, William J.
Stewart MD, Dale D.
Stice, Daniel R.
Stinson, Brandt
Stinson, Byron
Stinson, Manly
Stinson, Tom J.
Stites, Robert A.
Stivers, Kenneth L.
Stockham, Chad
Stockham, David E.
Stockham, David W.
Stockham, Eugene
Stockham, Glen
Stockham, Joseph
Stockham, Joseph L.
Stockham, Thomas
Stone, Grover
Stone, Lee David
Stone, Ronald D.
Stover III, Richard M.
Strack, Brian
Straiger, Ronald
Straight, Richard E.
Stratton, Dene B.
Strayer, Charles L.
Streeter, Glynn
Streeter, Howard
Streit, Alan M.
Strickland, Steven A.
Strickler, Kenneth J.
Stroad, Malcom D.
Strom, Raymond A.
Strong, Everett D.
Strong, Kendall
Strong Jr, Jarvis A.
Stroschine, Lee R.
Stroupnar, Charles L.
Struble, Michael T.
Stuckey, Scott W.
Stuewer, Frederick M.
Stultz, James R.
Sturgis, Robert L.
Stutzman, Harry S.
Stutzman, Mark A.
Sudell, William B.
Sullivan, Allan R.
Sullivan, Charles W.
Sullivan, Christopher
Sullivan, Donn H.
Sullivan, James M.
Sullivan, James V.
Sullivan, John S.
Sullivan, Paul MichaeL
Sullivan, Richard G.
Sullivan III, Daniel C.
Sullivan Jr, Robert E.
Sultzbaugh, John S.
Summerfield, Charles
Sutter, Gurney D.
Sutton, John M.
Suydam, Jonathan Ward

Swan, Steven R.
Swanson, Reubin Ted
Swart, Lee
Swearingen, David R.
Sweeney, Alan H.
Sweeney, Robert E.
Sweet, Robert T.
Sweetman, George
Swett, Russell J.
Swift, Allen
Swift, Richard
Swogger, Larry
Symborski, John J.
Synnamon, Brendan
Synnamon Jr, William
Synnamon Sr, William

T
Tackitt, Robert D.
Tagsold Jr, Parker
Tagsold Sr, Parker
Tait, Frank A.
Talbot, Michael L.
Talley, James C.
Tallman, Russell E.
Tallmudge, Thomas
Tamberelli, Alfred
Taplin, Theo G.
Tarburton, Ron
Tate III, James P.
Tatlock, Carleton B.
Tatlock, David C.
Tatro, Lawrence R.
Taylor, Allan D.
Taylor, Douglas
Taylor, Gene A.
Taylor, Thomas D.
Taylor, Stephen
Taylor, Thomas T.
Taylor III, Emmett P.
Teaford, Kevin D.
Teague, Douglas E.
Teague, Michael G.
Teague Sr, Charles H.
Teague Sr, Harold A.
Teal, Chester B.
Tedford, James
Teeling, Larry
Tegart, Robert T.
Tegethoff, Richard
Telless, Robert W.
Telless, Robert H.
Tellier, Keith D.
Templin, Jerry
TenBrink, Charles J.
Tenglund, Gerald M.
TerBurgh, Daniel R.
TerBurgh, David N.
Terry, Steven M.
Terry II, John Bascom
Tesch, Richard W.
Thalken, Michael
Thayer, Darryl
Thayer, John G.
Thiebaut, Thomas Yale
Thiebaut Jr, Jay Keith
Thiel, John C.

Thody, Stanley W.
Thomas, John E.
Thomas, Keith C.
Thomas, Lew M.
Thompson, Clyde
Thompson, Daniel P.
Thompson, Elmer C.
Thompson, Jake A.
Thompson, James T.
Thompson, James
Thompson, James G.
Thompson, John A.
Thompson, John
Thompson, Rob R.
Thompson, Robert E.
Thompson, William W.
Thompson, Woodrow W.
Thomson Jr, Kenneth C.
Thorpe, William S.
Thresher, Mark
Thurber, Wesley E.
Thurston Jr, James E.
Tice, H. Wayne
Tieman, Roger
Tiffany, Norman O.
Tilton, Bradley
Tinklepaugh Jr, Clyde L.
Tippett, Russell K.
Todd, George M.
Todd, Wayne G.
Tomkiell, Benjamin J.
Tooker, Randal
Tooley, Mark D.
Tope, Boyce M.
Torguson, Michael D.
Torpey, Richard T.
Toth, Joseph
Tovey, David C.
Towery, Jeff
Towne, Richard
Townsend, Franklin R.
Townsend, Raymond L.
Townsend, Robert E.
Tracy, Michael T.
Traver, Timothy
Trayer, Clyde
Trayer, John
Treat, Frank
Treat, Franklin
Tredinnick, Douglas L.
Trentham, Robert D.
Tribbie, M. K.
Tribbie, Robert
Trim, Richard
Trimble, Michael M.
Trimble, Richard W.
Trimble, Stanley
Trimm, Hugh B.
Trimmer, Robert W.
Trimmer Jr, John M.
Trofatter, Kirk C.
Tropio, Thomas J.
Trotter, Donald J.
Troudt, John L.
Troup, Richard E.
Trowbridge, Michael L.
Troyer, Bruce K.

Trudeau, N. Andre
Truex, Michael R.
Trulock, James A.
Tucker, Charles H.
Tucker, Charles E.
Tucker, Frank J.
Tucker, George E.
Tucker, Kevin
Tucker, Walter
Tucker II, Charles E.
Tuckey, Dale G.
Tuckey, Matthew M.
Tudor, Adrien Frank
Tull, William F.
Tumey Sr, Robert C.
Turbot, Steve
Turner, William L.
Turner Sr, James
Turo, Ron
Turpin, Charles A.
Turpin, David A.
Turton, Dr William J.
Tuttle, Douglas
Twietmeyer, Scott
Tyler, Edward H.

U
Uhlinger, Charles W.
Uhrie, David
Ulrich, Gary
Ulrich, Robert S.
Underwood, James D.
Ungart, James
Ungart, Jason
Upham Jr, William H.
Utt, Richard V.

V
Vail, Harold
Valentine, Steven Richards
Valentino, Rudolph J.
Vallone, Ronald T.
Valori, John P.
Van Crytzer, Marc
Van Nuys, Robert C.
Van Tassell, Kenneth W.
Van Wormer, David Lee
Vandegrift IV, Edward M.
VanDuser, Douglas
Varian, James A.
Varney, Harold
Verhoff, Andrew J.
Vermilya, John
Verney, Robert E.
Vest, Stephen M.
Vician, Royal B.
Vince, Tom
Vochatzer, Donald E.
Vogelman, Seth J.
Vogin, L. Scott
Von Allmen, Ray
Von Der Heydt, Vernon
Von Deylen, Keith R.
Vondersmith, Fletcher S.
Voorheis, Lynford
Vosburg, Brent L.
Vouk, Kurt J.

W

Wachob, James R.
Wade Jr, Harry E.
Waffler, Burdell E.
Wagers, David Lyman
Waggoner, Lonne
Waggoner, Mark L.
Wagner, C. W.
Wagner, Roy R.
Wagoner, Donald L.
Wain, Paul
Waite, Donald
Waitt Jr, Robert W.
Waldron, David L.
Walker, Clarence H.
Walker, Gregg T.
Walker, John
Walker, Joseph W.
Walker, Josh
Walker, Mathew H.
Walker, Richard
Walker, Steven R.
Wallace, David F.
Wallace, David Thomas
Wallace, Floyd E.
Wallace, John
Wallace, William N.
Walls, John
Waltenbaugh Jr, Harry
Waltenbaugh Sr, Harry
Walter, Edward M.
Walter, Gregory A.
Walton, John James
Walton Sr, M. Richard
Wang, Earl R.
Wang, Gary O.
Wang, Mark H.
Wang, Samuel D.
Ward, Charles D.
Ward, David A.
Ward, David H.
Ward, John
Ware Jr, Robert J.
Wareing IV, J. Charles
Warne, William
Warner, Ernest
Warner, Gary D.
Warner, Lewis D.
Warner, Robert C.
Warner Jr, John W.
Warren, Gordon
Warren, William
Warthen, Benjamin P. H.
Washam, Paul A.
Washburn, William L.
Washburn Jr, Charles E.
Wasilewski, John J.
Waskie, Anthony
Wassenar, Dale
Wassenar, Richard
Waterman, Myron A.
Waterous, Frank
Watson, Dr William E.
Watson, Duncan C.
Watson, Gary L.
Watson, John
Watson, Wesley
Watson, William J.
Watts, William A.
Way, Maurice
Weatherell, John G.
Weaver, Charles I.
Weaver, George
Weaver, Kenneth
Webb, Gary D.
Webb, Herbert
Webb, Michael J.
Webber, Charles Robert
Weber, Harold
Weber, Myron L.
Webster, Bernard
Webster IV, Charles D.
Weed, Byron Ellsworth
Weidensaul, Thomas H.
Weidlich, Ray V.
Weidmayer, Mark
Weigl, Steven A.
Weinmann, Frank
Weinmann, George J.
Weir, Dr Thomas E.
Weisman, Martin
Weiss, Robert K.
Welch, John C.
Welch, Lawrence M.
Welch, Robert H.
Welch, William F.
Welch III, Joel J.
Welcher, Fred Steven
Weld, Theodore
Weldon, Steve
Weldon Jr, Felix N.
Welke, Brian J.
Wells, Douglas J.
Wells, Edward J.
Wells, Robert
Wells Jr, Frederick
Wendorph, John V.
Wentzien, William T.
Werkheiser Sr, Sterling
Werner, Frank E.
Werner, Quinn E.
Wertz, Howard E.
West, Jeremiah
West, Lawrence H.
West II, Harold M.
Westlake, Steven
Weston, Craig
Weston, Eric
Weston, Gary F.
Weston, Homer F.
Weston, Mark
Wetzel Jr, Philip
Wheat, John Marc
Wheeler, Adrian R.
Wheeler, Cpl Danny J.
Wheeler, Danny L.
Wheeler, David K.
Wheeler, Donald E.
Wheeler, George Scott
Wheeler, George T.
Wheeler, Harry J.
Wheeler, Howard
Wheeler, James A.
Wheeler, Lloyd F.
Wheeler, Norman F.
Wheeler, Richard J.
Wheeler Jr, Kenneth
Wheeler Sr, Kenneth T.
Wheeler Sr, Roger A.
Whitacre, Ronald
White, Bruce E.
White, Douglas R.
White, J. Andrew
White, Jason
White, Jerald A.
White, Maurice L.
White, Phillip N.
White, Ralph A.
White, Richard L.
White Jr, Harry A.
White Jr, Robert E.
Whited, LTC R.. M.
Whitehead Jr, James H.
Whitehouse, Robert L.
Whitney, Mark P.
Whitted, Michael
Wick, James G.
Wickerham III, Howard L.
Wickersham, Jeremy
Wickline, Albert
Wiedenhaus, Jerry
Wiegand Jr, Arthur J.
Wiegold, Richard
Wiesian, Robert W.
Wight, George V.
Wightman, Thomas
Wilcock, Russell A.
Wilcox, Malcolm D.
Wilcox, Roderick L.
Wilde, Ralph C.
Wilder, Harold
Wilder Jr, Jack A.
Wildt, Jim
Wiley, Clifford J.
Wilhelm, Matthew
Wilhelm, Robert
Wilk, John
Wilke, Lynn H.
Wilkens Jr, Leon F.
Wilkeson, Charles A.
Wilkinson, Timothy E.
Wilkinson, Todd J.
Wilkinson Jr, A. Warren
Wilkinson Jr, George H.
Wilks, Dennis J.
Willard, Craig Kenneth
Willer, Robert
Willey, Donald
Willey, Mark J.
Willey, Robert E.
Willey, Robert J.
Williams, David
Williams, David P.
Williams, Gary
Williams, Getty W.
Williams, Herbert K.
Williams, James Thomas
Williams, Jamie G.
Williams, Jeffrey W.
Williams, Matt
Williams, Paul David
Williams, Reginald K. V.
Williams, Richard A.
Williams, Scott
Williams, Getty W.
Williams, Stanley
Williams, Theodore J.
Williams, Theodore
Williams, Thomas
Williams, Timothy R.
Williams, Wilfred A.
Williams, William E.
Williams Jr, Ryon P.
Williamson, John R.
Williamson, Michael J.
Willich, Richard R.
Willmering, Thomas R.
Willoughby, W. Jackson
Willshaw, Frederick A.
Wilson, Allen G.
Wilson, Arthur F.
Wilson, Douglas
Wilson, Fay P.
Wilson, Malcolm
Wilson, James E.
Wilson, Kirk R.
Wilson, Ned A.
Wilson, Phil
Wilson, Richard
Wilson, Robert
Wilson, Robert Walter
Wilson, Rolland A.
Wilson, Samuel
Winer, Dave
Wingett, David
Winkel Jr, Col Paul P.
Winkelhoff, Paul J.
Winn, Glenn L.
Winslow, Paul F.
Winter, Charles
Winter Jr, Charles
Wirtalla, Russell
Wirth, Reginald M.
Wise, Kenneth J.
Witmyer Jr, Robert A.
Witt, John A.
Wittnebent, Philip H.
Wolf, Daniel I.
Wolf, Elmer J.
Wolf, Grover C.
Wolfe, Howard
Wolfe, Jeffrey T.
Wolfe, Thomas
Wolford, Jerry L.
Wolz, Robert J.
Womack, W. Michael
Wong, William R.
Wood, Calvin E.
Wood, Eugene D.
Wood, Joseph H.
Wood, William G.
Wood IV, Robert G.
Wood Jr, Stacy B. C.
Woodbury, Richard L.
Woodin, Ronald R.
Woodman, Gary R.
Woodruff, Daniel
Woodruff, Gerald F.
Woodward, Francis
Woodward, Leeman E.
Woodward, John D.
Woodward, Timothy
Woolson, Donald F.
Woosley, Sr, Joe M.
Worcester, Dale M.
Workman, Donald H.
Workman, Scot Ralph
Workman, Sean Robert
Worth, H. Ray
Worthington, Lyle T.
Worthington, Steve
Wotring, Donald R.
Wren, Dennis R.
Wright, Earl M.
Wuytack, Claude
Wyman, Wayne P.
Wyszumiak, Ed P.

Y

Yagley, Christopher J.
Yahrling, Charles
Yaple, James Gale
Yarrington, Ronald M.
Yates, Brian E.
Yates, Charles C.
Yates, Timothy W.
Yax, John H.
Yax, Solon J.
Yeager, Charles L.
Yeager, William
Yeager Jr, Robert W.
Yensel, James M.
Yess, Edward C.
Young, Charles D.
Young, David A.
Young, J. Eugene
Young, Richard K.
Young, Robert
Young, Rodney O.
Young, Wayne J.
Young, William A.
Young III, George E.
Young Jr, Arthur F.
Young Jr, Richard

Z

Zabecki, Konrad J. T.
Zabecki, David T.
Zaidel, Peter A.
Zebiak, Paul M.
Zebrasky, Robert D.
Zeckman, Earl W.
Zeek, Raymond
Zeien Jr, Paul T.
Zerr, Carl
Ziegler, Louis E.
Zienko, Christoplia M.
Zimmerman, Frederick
Zimmerman, Gary Lee
Zimmerman, Raymond N.
Zimmerman, Roy
Zinn, Philip
Ziss, Robert C.
Zook Jr, George T.
Zorger Sr, Duane
Zwiener, Daniel C.

www.ingramcontent.com/pod-product-compliance
Lightning Source LLC
Chambersburg PA
CBHW081849170426
43199CB00018B/2857